The
Modern
West...
Experien...

The
Modern
Western
Experience

ROBERT ANCHOR

University of Southern California

PRENTICE-HALL, INC., *Englewood Cliffs, New Jersey 07632*

Library of Congress Cataloging in Publication Data

Anchor, Robert. (date)
    The modern Western experience.

    Includes bibliographies and index.
    1. Civilization, Modern—18th century.   2. Civili-
zation, Modern—19th century.   3. Civilization, Modern
—20th century.   4. Civilization, Occidental.
5. Europe—Civilization.   I. Title.
CB357.A55   940.2   77-16712
ISBN 0-13-599357-1

© *1978 by* Prentice-Hall, Inc., *Englewood Cliffs, N.J. 07632*

PRINTED IN THE UNITED STATES OF AMERICA

10 9 8 7 6 5 4 3 2 1

PRENTICE-HALL INTERNATIONAL, INC., *London*
PRENTICE-HALL OF AUSTRALIA PTY. LIMITED, *Sydney*
PRENTICE-HALL OF CANADA, LTD., *Toronto*
PRENTICE-HALL OF INDIA PRIVATE LIMITED, *New Delhi*
PRENTICE-HALL OF JAPAN, INC., *Tokyo*
PRENTICE-HALL OF SOUTHEAST ASIA PTE. LTD., *Singapore*
WHITEHALL BOOKS LIMITED, *Wellington, New Zealand*

To
my Mother,
and in memory of my Father and Lynne

CONTENTS

chapter three
FIN DE SIÈCLE:
1880–1914   *121*

chapter four
ERA OF TOTAL WAR:
1914–1945   *170*

chapter five
SINCE THE SECOND WORLD WAR:
The Contemporary Experience   *250*

PREFACE

This book attempts to acquaint the reader with the persons, events, movements, and ideas that have had the greatest influence on modern Western civilization. The emphasis is upon those topics—revolution, industrialization, secularization, and the problems, hopes, and fears that grew out of them—that have persisted throughout the modern period and have contributed most to our present ideas of and attitudes toward the modern world.

The book is divided into five broad chapters. The first part of each chapter deals with political, social, and economic developments; the second, with the intellectual and cultural life of the period under discussion. Each chapter revolves around a particular issue or set of issues and is meant to form a coherent whole, not simply a prelude to what follows. The unifying theme of the book is the ways in which modern Western civilization over the course of time has come to terms—or, in some cases, failed to come to terms—with its revolutionary origins.

My choice of subjects and my approach to them make this book somewhat different from other historical surveys. First, I have given more than usual coverage to intellectual and cultural developments. The creative achievements of a civilization are, after all, its finest achievements and the ones by which it is judged and remembered. Second, *The Modern Western Experience* is intended to be an instrument for active teaching and learning. It is designed to encourage independent thought and judgment on the part of the reader and to provide scope and flexibility for further exploration into particular problems, personalities, and issues according to the reader's interests. Finally, if this book stimulates readers to think intelligently about the meaning of the past for them and about their own individual roles in the history of their times, it will have served its purpose.

ROBERT ANCHOR
University of Southern California

The
Modern
Western
Experience

ORIGINS OF THE MODERN WEST: 1789–1848

A TRIPLE REVOLUTION

Modern Western civilization began to take shape in the late eighteenth century as the result of three concurrent upheavals so far-reaching in their effects as to justify calling them revolutionary. One was an economic and industrial upheaval centered in England, the so-called Industrial Revolution. The second, the French Revolution, was a political and social upheaval centered in France, but encompassing much of the Western world on both sides of the Atlantic. The third was an intellectual and cultural revolution centered in Germany, but also international in scope. The net effect of this triple revolution was so great as to render the predominantly agrarian, hierarchical, traditionalistic old order obsolete and to set in motion those forces that we have since come to associate with modernism: industrialization, urbanization, and the secularization of thought and culture.

This triple revolution did not merely mark the end of one era and the start of another; it also challenged some of Western man's oldest and most cherished beliefs, notably his dependence on nature, his faith in a divine being, and his reverence for the past. It launched him on an uncharted adventure that has not yet run its course and for which these age-old dependencies offered little guidance. All of this did not happen

1

overnight, of course. It was the work of more than half a century, from the 1790s to 1848, a watershed period during which the new forces contended with the old order for ultimate supremacy in the West and eventually in the world at large.

The French Revolution

At least three basic conditions seem to underlie any revolutionary situation. One is a deep and general discontent with the existing order. Second is a powerful vision of a better world. And third is the material means and determination necessary to translate that vision into reality. This combination of conditions, manifesting itself variously in different countries, incited a series a political uprisings in the second half of the eighteenth century throughout the Western world—in Switzerland, the Low Countries, Ireland and, of course, in the American colonies and France. Robert R. Palmer, in his *The Age of the Democratic Revolution*, has described the background of this political ferment as follows:

> By a revolutionary situation is here meant one in which confidence in the justice or reasonableness of existing authority is undermined; where old loyalties fade, obligations are felt as impositions, law seems arbitrary, and respect for superiors is felt as a form of humiliation; where existing sources of prestige seem undeserved, hitherto accepted forms of wealth and income seem ill-gained, and government is sensed as distant, apart from the governed and not really 'representing' them. In such a situation the sense of community is lost, and the bond between social classes turns to jealousy and frustration. People of a kind formerly integrated begin to feel as outsiders, or those who have never been integrated begin to feel left out.... No community can flourish if such negative attitudes are widespread or long-lasting. The crisis is a crisis of community itself, political, economic, sociological, personal, psychological, and moral at the same time. Actual revolution need not follow, but it is in such situations that actual revolution does arise. Something must happen, if continuing deterioration is to be avoided; some new kind or basis of community must be formed.[1]

Of all the political disturbances that occurred in the late eighteenth century, the French Revolution was by far the most significant. France was then the most powerful, prestigious, and advanced country on the European continent and was geographically central to the Western world. Also the "crisis of community" was more acute and chronic in France than elsewhere. Mounting social conflict, political discontent, in-

---

[1]Robert R. Palmer, *THE AGE OF THE DEMOCRATIC REVOLUTION: A Political History of Europe and America, 1760–1800*, Vol. I *THE CHALLENGE*. Copyright © 1959 by Princeton University Press; Princeton Paperback, 1969: p. 21. Reprinted by permission of Princeton University Press.

tellectual dissent, and the growing inability of the government to rule had torn at the fabric of French society ever since the death of King Louis XIV in 1715. The French Revolution was also more prolonged and violent than the others. Beginning as a civil war over the issue of internal reform, it soon spilled over the national boundaries of France into Europe at large and beyond, transforming Western political life forever. Finally, the French Revolution, in contrast to the others, was not fought for the particular rights of a particular people, but for supposedly universally valid human rights, as encapsulated in the revolutionary slogan: liberty, equality, fraternity! For these reasons, the French Revolution succeeded in firing the imagination of Western mankind more than any other political event in modern history until the Russian Revolution in the twentieth century.

The great ideals of the French Revolution were proclaimed in the *Declaration of the Rights of Man and of the Citizen,* presented to the National Assembly in August 1789 by representatives of the angry and unfairly treated Third Estate, which included the whole population except the powerful and privileged clergy and nobility (the First and Second Estates). The *Declaration* asserted that liberty, property, security, and resistance to oppresion are "the natural, inalienable, and sacred Rights of Man." Popular sovereignty, the self-determination of peoples, the legal equality of all citizens, and the separations of powers in government were also written into the *Declaration,* which was modeled in large part on the American Constitution adopted across the Atlantic a year earlier. But, whereas in America there were no kings or powerful nobles and clergy to resist the proclamation and implementation of such novel rights, in France and throughout Europe the *Declaration* amounted to nothing less than a sweeping repudiation of a deeply entrenched feudal hierarchy that had existed since the Middle Ages.

According to the *Declaration,* the king could no longer rule by fiat, but only by the consent of the governed. In one stroke, it abolished the special privileges of the nobility and clergy—notably exemption from taxation and their monopoly of high offices—and proclaimed the equality of all citizens before the law: equality of opportunity, equitable taxation, and the drastic reform of civil and ecclesiastical institutions. It asserted that the nation was a community of free men sharing equally in rights and responsibilities, not a social pyramid existing for the sake of a privileged minority at the top, which defended its position by appeal to tradition rather than to justice.

In regard to property, however, the authors of the *Declaration,* themselves property owners and political moderates like their American counterparts, resisted radical democratic and egalitarian demands and held that property also is a sacred and inalienable "natural" right. The

Declaration, therefore, went so far as to repudiate the existing traditionalistic semifeudal order, but not so far as to proclaim social democracy based on economic equality. Instead, it favored a constitutional
monarchy based on a propertied elite expressing itself through a representative assembly. In this respect, the great manifesto of the French
Revolution was as much an assertion of specific bourgeois interests as of
universal human interests. It thereby provided for the eventual rise of a
new form of social and economic elitism—that of the liberal middle
classes, which in the eighteenth century formed only one, although the
most active and articulate, element of the Third Estate.

It was one thing to pronounce the existing political order null and
void, but quite another to bring a new one into being. Many questions
still remained to be answered. What form should the new government
take? What would be the role of those displaced from power? How were
the rights proclaimed by the *Declaration* to be guaranteed? What type of
constitution should be written? And, perhaps the most immediately
pressing question of all: who should deal with these matters and how?
Even as the National Assembly met at the Royal Palace in Versailles, the
peasants, faced with bad harvests and crushing taxes, were rioting in the
countryside. And on July 14, 1789, a crowd of Parisians, alarmed by
the concentration of troops around Versailles and the king's apparent
intention to disband the Assembly, stormed the Bastille, an almost empty
old prison regarded as the symbol of oppression. Such turbulence naturally fueled political passions, threatened to broaden peaceful reform
into violent revolution, and intensified the bitter factional disputes that
divided the Assembly as it began the actual planning of the new government.

The leaders of the first phase of the Revolution, from 1789 to 1791,
were moderates; some even were enlightened aristocrats like Mirabeau
and Lafayette, who wished to transform France peacefully from an absolute monarchy into a constitutional monarchy on the English model.
During these years, the Assembly completed its work of writing a new
constitution, which became effective in 1791, and provided for a systematic and thorough reorganization of French political, economic, and
institutional life. It abolished the old ineffective ministries, the autocratic
form of government, the inequitable system of taxation, the exclusionist
gilds, the old venal titles of nobility, the self-seeking regional parliaments, and the hundreds of antiquated local systems of law and
municipal administration. In their place the new constitution divided the
country into eighty-three equal "departments" and introduced a uniform system of municipal administration with elected officials at every
level. National sovereignty was to be exercised by a one-chamber Legislative Assembly, and the executive power of the king was to be sharply

curtailed. Torture was forbidden, and new legal procedures were drawn up. Equality of rights was extended to Protestants and Jews.

Not so democratic was the constitution's distinction, based on wealth, between "active" and "passive" citizens. All citizens were to enjoy the same civil rights, but only those paying a specified amount of taxes had the right to vote and to act as "electors" of department officials and representatives to the Legislative Assembly—an ingenious distinction which obviously favored the comparatively affluent middle classes. Barriers to the free movement of goods within the country and to free contractual arrangements between individuals were abolished, thus paving the way for a more vigorous economy to supersede the stagnant system of gilds, privileged companies, and other economic monopolies. Church lands were confiscated and sold to raise revenue, to reduce the power and autonomy of the Church, and to make more land available to land-hungry peasants who could afford to buy it.

One of the most far-reaching but self-defeating acts of the Assembly was the Civil Constitution of the Clergy, passed in 1790. It was intended to subordinate the Catholic clergy to the state by requiring that parish priests and bishops, like other public officials, be elected by the general voting public, including non-Catholics, and be paid by the state and further requiring that they take an oath to uphold the Civil Constitution. The effect of the Civil Constitution, which was denounced by the Vatican, was to split the French clergy, to divide the political and religious loyalties of many Frenchmen, and to mobilize public opinion abroad against the Revolution as a whole.

Even as the constitution was being written, the revolutionary tide was rising. The Civil Constitution hardened the lines between those who supported and those who opposed the Revolution. Counterrevolutionary aristocrats, dispossessed Catholic clergymen, and moderate reformers, all fearful that the Revolution had already gone too far, began to emigrate and agitate abroad against the Revolution. In June 1791 the weak and vacillating King Louis XVI himself attempted to flee France and seek help abroad. He and his family were captured near the border and returned to Paris virtual prisoners; Louis was forced to accept the status of constitutional monarch. This episode served only to increase distrust of the king and heighten revolutionary feeling. Also, the new freedoms of press and assembly enabled the more radical revolutionaries, notably the Jacobins, to organize themselves into effective political clubs, to publicize their views, and to win wide popular support, especially among the lower classes of Paris and other large towns.

The second phase of the Revolution began when the new regime went into effect in 1791. The moderates in the newly created Legislative Assembly were greatly outnumbered by the more extremist Girondins, a branch of the Jacobin society supported mainly in the provinces, whose leaders, Brissot, Condorcet, and Mme. Roland, wished to spread the Revolution abroad in a "war of peoples against kings".

Even before general war broke out in 1792, the Revolution was having a great impact abroad. The doctrines of the Revolution gained wide acceptance abroad because they proclaimed the rights of all men, regardless of time or place, race or religion, nation or social class. As early as 1789, the brilliant young romantic poet, William Wordsworth, hailed the Revolution in his famous lines: "Bliss was it in that dawn to be alive, But to be young was very heaven!" The great voice of conservatism, Edmund Burke, denounced the Revolution for its disregard of history and its immoderateness in his widely read *Reflections of the Revolution in France* (1790). He was answered by the radical, Thomas Paine, who defended the Revolution in his *Rights of Man* (1791).

The Revolution also aroused enthusiasm among cosmopolitan German thinkers, including Goethe, Kant, and Hegel. Nationalists in Po-

Fall of the Bastille, July 14, 1789; Insurgents storm prison that was the symbol of the Old Regime's oppression.

land, Hungary, Ireland, and Spanish America seized upon the Revolution as a means to liberate their countries from foreign rule. In North America, Alexander Hamilton branded the party of Thomas Jefferson as pro-Jacobin. To the lower classes everywhere the Revolution held out the promise of liberation from social and economic oppression. Opposed to it were the monarchs and aristocracies of Europe, the Vatican, and the politically aroused émigrés. In short, pro- and antirevolutionary feeling was running strong throughout Europe and the Western world by 1791. Not since the Reformation had a movement stirred so many people in so many places to such a pitch of excitement and anticipation.

In 1792, Austria and Prussia formed an alliance to put down the Revolution by force. Thus began a series of wars between France and various coalitions that would last, with short reprieves, for more than twenty years. The wars engulfed all of Europe, but, generally, the states that opposed France, singly or in combination, were Austria, Prussia, England, and Russia. Initially, the first coalition met with some military success on the French borders. But the threat from abroad and the war cries of the Girondins and other even more radical Jacobin leaders aroused French national feeling to a feverish pitch. Recruits from all parts of France streamed into Paris, and those from Marseilles brought with them the *Marseillaise,* the first modern national anthem, which called upon "the children of France" to defend their homeland against foreign tyrants. In the making was a new type of political loyalty and patriotism that identified the individual with the nation as a whole, not with a particular region, social class, or religious group. The French army recruited in 1792 was the first modern national army in the sense that only talent and dedication to the nation and its ideals determined an individual's rank. Henceforth, the army would become the very epitome of the national will and the spearhead of the Revolution. War fever, peasant unrest, food shortages, and the dissatisfaction of the Parisian lower classes with the early results of the Revolution led to new explosions. In August 1792 the working-class quarter of Paris rose in revolt, seized and imprisoned the king and royal family, and set up a new revolutionary municipal government in Paris. This insurrection launched the third and most extreme phase of the Revolution, the Jacobin phase and the Reign of Terror.

A new National Convention convened on September 20, 1792, and power fell to the more radical Jacobin faction called the "Mountain," which was supported by the Paris insurgents and led by Marat, Danton, Saint-Just, and the most famous and controversial of all the revolutionaries, Maximilien Robespierre. On this same day the French armies won their first victory at Valmy, and on the following day the Convention abolished the monarchy and declared France a republic.

Under pressure from the Mountain, the Convention put Louis XVI on trial, found him guilty by a one-vote majority, and executed him early in 1793. The 361 deputies who voted for his execution were now regicides who no longer could turn back to a more moderate course or consider a restoration of the Bourbon monarchy in France. The program of the new Convention was to repress anarchy, civil strife, and counterrevolution at home and to win the war against France's enemies abroad. To achieve these goals, in April of 1793 the Convention chose twelve of its members, including Robespierre, to form a Committee of Public Safety and granted it almost dictatorial powers.

Thus began the Reign of Terror. The Committee struck in every direction at those it suspected of opposing or obstructing the Revolution. Its victims ranged from the highest to the lowest on the social scale. It hounded down the more moderate Girondin political leaders and eventually even members of the Mountain itself. It is estimated that between the spring of 1793 and the summer of 1794, some thirty thousand people were executed and another ten thousand died in prison. Although mild by twentieth-century standards, the often inhuman and atrocious way in which the Terror went about its bloody work aroused fear and revulsion in every quarter, left a wake of bitterness and hostility to revolution of any sort, and even presaged some of the ghastly methods, all too familiar in the twentieth century, of liquidating real and imagined political opponents.

In June 1793, the Committee drafted and the Convention adopted a new republican constitution, which, although suspended indefinitely because of the emergency situation, revealed some of the intentions of its authors. It provided for universal male suffrage, but it provided for no separation of powers, no limit on the power of the state, and no guarantees of individual liberties. It favored a democratic dictatorship based on the popular will, but with power delegated to a small leadership. Compared with the earlier constitution, the Jacobin constitution was more democratic, more egalitarian, and more genuinely concerned with the common man. But it had less regard for legal procedures, individual rights, and political pluralism.

In still other ways the Committee sought to legislate on behalf of the lower classes. It called for price controls and other economic regulations. It eased the financial obligations of the peasants and made it easier for them to buy land confiscated from the Church, from émigré nobles, and from enemies of the Revolution. It provided social services and planned to introduce universal elementary education. It abolished slavery in the French colonies. But by the summer of 1794, the consolidation of the Revolution at home, the military success abroad, and the increasing bloodiness of the Terror aroused Robespierre's many enemies. Robespierre himself was not a power-hungry monster, as some of his enemies depicted him. On the contrary, he personally detested violence and was famous for his incorruptibility and love of virtue—that is, his absolute dedication to the Revolution. But the very qualities which enabled him to rise to power in a crisis situation—fanaticism, inflexibility, and insensitivity to suffering—were responsible in large part for his downfall. In July 1794 he and many of his close associates were executed, and the Terror came to an end.

During the next several months, Jacobins sympathethic to Robespierre were hunted down and the Committee of Public Safety was disbanded. In 1795, a moderate, middle-class constitutional republic, known as the Directory, was formed; it lasted for the next four years. The government of the Directory sought to return to the aims of the Girondin era. But it was plagued from the right by royalists who agitated for the restoration of the Bourbon successor, Louis XVIII, and from the left by radical remnants of the working-class insurgency of 1793 headed by the first modern revolutionary socialists: François "Gracchus" Babeuf and Filippo Buonarotti. The government succeeded in suppressing the movement from the left by executing and deporting its leaders. But the royalist danger was much greater, and to help quell it the government called upon a brilliant young Corsican general, Napoleon Bonaparte (1769-1821).

Napoleon had defeated the Austrians in Italy when he was called upon to save the government in 1797, and with the help of his army, the royalists were suppressed. But the weak and divided government was now more dependent than ever on the army, which was rapidly becoming the prime force in French and European politics. Napoleon's star now began to rise. Later that year on his own initiative, he concluded the treaty of Campo Formio, by which Austria recognized the French-dominated Cisalpine Republic in Italy and the French annexation of Belgium and the German left bank of the Rhine. Smaller revolutionary republics under French auspices already existed in the Netherlands and Switzerland. In May 1798 Napoleon landed a force in Egypt in a bold move to strike at British power in the eastern Mediterranean. But his army was disasterously defeated when the British fleet, under the command of Admiral Nelson, cut off its supplies. Meanwhile, the government of the Directory continued to falter. In 1799, with affairs going badly both at home and abroad, Napoleon, encouraged by a political faction fearful of the government's collapse, abandoned his army in Egypt, rushed back to Paris, and overthrew the government in a quick, bloodless coup, proclaiming a new republic called the Consulate and headed by himself.

Napoleon's career after 1799 was spectacular. He had already directed a brilliant campaign in Italy, demonstrated his diplomatic skills at Campo Formio, and turned his military misadventure in Egypt into political gain. In the years that followed, he won stunning victories at

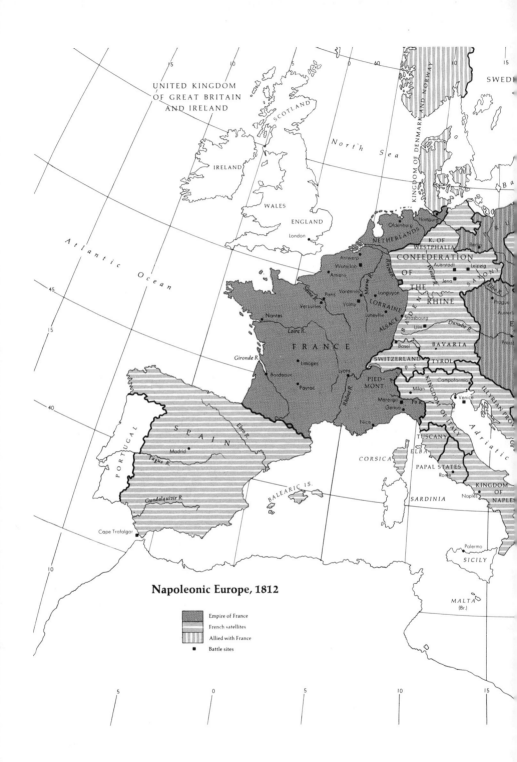

Napoleonic Europe, 1812

Empire of France
French satellites
Allied with France
■ Battle sites

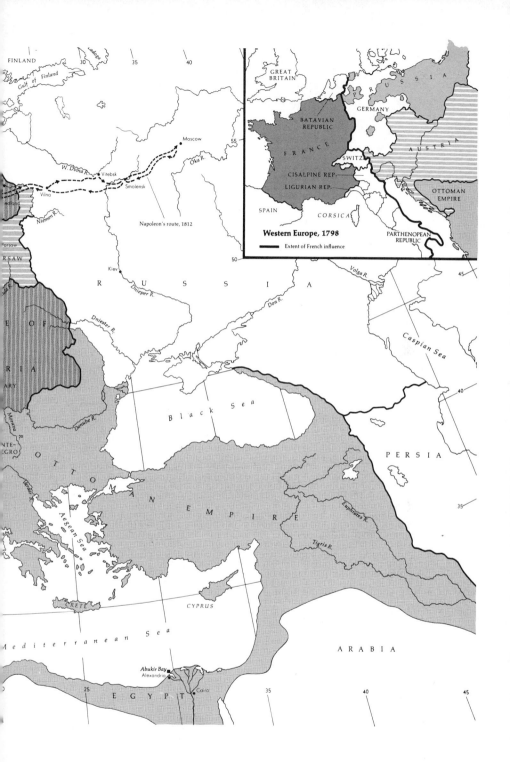

FINLAND

Gulf of Finland

Moscow

W. Dvina R. Vitebsk

Smolensk

Vilna

Niemen R.

Napoleon's route, 1812

Oka R.

RSAW

Kiev

R U S S I A

Dnieper R.

Dniester R.

E OF

R I A

ARY

Danube R.

NTE-
GRO

Don R.

Volga R.

Caspian Sea

B l a c k   S e a

O T T O M A N   E M P I R E

P E R S I A

Euphrates R.

Tigris R.

A e g e a n   S e a

CRETE

CYPRUS

M e d i t e r r a n e a n   S e a

ARABIA

Abukir Bay
Alexandria

E G Y P T

Cairo

Western Europe, 1798

GREAT
BRITAIN

BATAVIAN
REPUBLIC

GERMANY

P R U S S I A

F R A N C E

SWITZ.

CISALPINE REP.

LIGURIAN REP.

A U S T R I A

OTTOMAN
EMPIRE

SPAIN

CORSICA

PARTHENOPEAN
REPUBLIC

Extent of French influence

Marengo, Austerlitz, and Jena; his inspired armies, under the command of brilliant marshals, marched into most of the capitals of Europe, spreading the ideals of the Revolution and the legend of their leader as they went. Napoleon's victories abroad formed the basis of his popularity at home, although in the end they proved to be his and France's undoing. In 1804, he dropped the title of first consul, declared himself emperor, and proceeded to establish his brothers as kings in Italy, Germany, Holland, and Spain. In 1806, he imposed his continental blockade of English goods, which was designed to weaken his long-time enemy and chief obstacle to a unified Napoleonic Europe. In 1812, faced with rising nationalistic resistance to his conquests and increasingly imperious rule in Spain, the German states, and Russia, Napoleon amassed an army of some seven hundred thousand soldiers, the largest ever yet assembled in Europe, and began the invasion of Russia in an episode later immortalized by Tolstoy in his epic novel, *War and Peace.*

After more than a decade of almost uninterrupted success on the battlefield, Napoleon had finally overextended himself. Having reached Moscow, Napoleon was forced into a disastrous retreat by the Russian army, under the command of Prince Kutuzov. There followed a series of defeats that destroyed the once Grand Army. In 1814, the allies forced Napoleon to abdicate and exiled him to the island of Elba. A year later, he escaped and returned to France, where he tried to recapture power from the newly restored and unpopular Bourbon king in a last-ditch effort known as the Hundred Days. However, on June 18, 1815, he was defeated at Waterloo by allied forces under the command of the Duke of Wellington. Napoleon surrendered and was exiled to the island of St. Helena, where he died in 1821.

Napoleon, the Man

Napoleon ruled in the manner of an enlightened despot. His policy was to consolidate the Revolution at home and extend its benefit abroad, even if by dictatorial means. He realized that, to achieve stability, the government would have to unite the whole nation behind it: peasants, landowners, the urban poor, the educated classes, royalists, and revolutionaries. This lack of unity had been a chronic failing of the many governments in France since 1789. To gain the support of the whole nation, Napoleon guaranteed the revolutionary achievements of the Girondin and Jacobin eras, including the civil and legal rights contained in the *Declaration of the Rights of Man and of the Citizen:* equality of opportunity, religious toleration, educational opportunity, and the full employment made possible by an ever-expanding army and its needs. To the peasants, he guaranteed the land they had already acquired and the end of feudal dues. To the middle classes, he offered financial stability and opportunity, orderly administration, equitable taxation, and career advancement through talent—a policy which had enabled Napoleon himself and many of his marshals to rise from lowly origins to the height of power. To appease the Church, he concluded a Concordat in 1801 with Pope Pius VII that restored to the papacy some authority over the French clergy in exchange for papal recognition of the French Republic. To appease the aristocracies of Europe, he took the title of emperor, played the demigod, recreated a new nobility loyal to himself, divorced his childless first wife (the commoner Josephine) and, in 1810, married Marie Louise, daughter of the Habsburg emperor and niece of the former French queen Marie Antoinette, whom the revolutionaries had executed [soon after] her husband in 1793. And to all the French, Napoleon promised not only national security, but also territorial expansion, military glory, and a united Napoleonic Europe modeled on and headed by France.

Napoleon set down his system of administration in a series of codes concerned with civil, criminal, and commercial procedures that later came to be called the Napoleonic Code. These codes laid down clear and precise rules for administrators, judges, and the business classes. The codes, which were to be uniformly applied and efficiently administered, provided for legal guarantees of civil equality, protection of the family and property from the government, efficient and impartial procedures in the courts, civil marriage and divorce, and laws regarding business dealings favorable to an economy of private enterprise. But the codes left women and workers in a socially and politically inferior position and failed to provide strong guarantees for the freedoms of speech, press, and assembly. When applied to countries outside France, the codes replaced the old feudal systems of law and administration and brought about drastic changes in the social structure. When introduced into Italy in 1806, they struck down the remaining feudal rights, abolished the judicial rights of the Church, confirmed civil marriage, and reinforced the principles of civil and legal equality. The introduction of the codes into parts of Germany in 1807 established equality before the law and religious liberty, abolished serfdom and feudal rights, put an end to the traditional privileges of the nobility, and established a system of equitable taxation. Long after Napoleon's military exploits evaporated into glorious memories, his codes remained to testify to his historical greatness.

Napoleon so dominated his time as to arouse the most violent feelings for and against him. Goethe praised him as the destroyer of an old, moribund order and the architect of a new and better one. Beethoven originally dedicated his Eroica symphony to Napoleon, and Hegel hailed

Napoleon portrait by David.

(British Museum.)

him as a "world-historical individual" in a class with Alexander the Great and Caesar. Peasants and workers, liberal bourgeois and oppressed national groups, revolutionary intellectuals and would-be reformers—all who had suffered under the old order and had benefited from the Revolution—hailed Napoleon as a hero and liberator. Even some of his enemies, enlightened aristocrats and the autocratic rulers of Prussia and Austria, recognized the superiority of many of Napoleon's military and administrative innovations and adopted them. But the monarchs and old aristocracies of Europe scorned him as a dangerous and vulgar upstart; the Church distrusted him; conservatives denounced him as a disruptor of the time-tested historical order of things; and antirevolutionary nationalists in Spain, the German states, England, and Russia pictured him as a foreign conqueror bent on transforming Europe into a French empire. What is certain is that Napoleon was a man of extraordinary

Napoleon on H.M.S. Northumberland.

(British Museum.)

talent, energy, and vision, who opportunity and circumstances enabled
to reshape Western and even world history. Under his leadership, the
Revolution, which had been largely an episode in the national history of
France until his arrival, flamed into an epoch-making chapter in history
the impact of which continued to be felt for fully a century after his
departure.

THE INDUSTRIAL REVOLUTION

The Industrial Revolution, though less dramatic than the French Revolution, was no less significant. No precise dates can be stated for the
Industrial Revolution because the scientific and technological advances
and the social and economic conditions out of which it grew began centuries earlier and because industrialization is still going on, faster now
than when it began. Nevertheless, by the 1780s, the shift from hand tools
to power machinery was far enough along to justify taking that decade as
the starting point of man's permanent liberation from and mastery over
nature by the machine. By the 1840s, with the construction of the rail-

roads and implementation of a factory system of production in Britain and the start of industrialization in Western Europe and North America, the Industrial Revolution was an accomplished fact.

The Industrial Revolution began in Britain because only there did all the conditions exist at the time for its development. Britain possessed good harbors on every coast—Glasgow, Liverpool, Bristol, Southhampton, London, Newcastle, and others. Distances were short; natural barriers were negligible; the building of canals was relatively easy where rivers were inadequate for inland transportation. Britain also possessed the rich and easily accessible deposits of coal and iron ore necessary to industrialization. And the streams of the Pennine range provided easily harnessed water power.

Economically, Britain possessed the largest merchant marine in the world and engaged in regular trade not only with her own colonies but also with the Baltic states, the Turkish empire, the Spanish and Portuguese colonies, and West Africa. This flourishing trade had produced a wealthy merchant class with a surplus of capital, which exceeded the investment opportunities available in commerce itself by the late eighteenth century. Napoleon's blockade of British goods to the continent, far from weakening Britain's economy as intended, accelerated her development of markets beyond Europe. The prosperous landowning class had also grown rich by converting agriculture from a system of predominantly subsistence farming to an advanced capitalist system that was geared to profit-making through the sale of agricultural products in a nationwide market. This conversion was accomplished by the introduction of improved agricultural methods, including a more scientific system of crop rotation, more efficient tools, a greater use of fertilizers, and the "enclosure" of open fields and common pasture; all of these increased and improved productivity while reducing its cost. The "enclosure acts" in particular, which continued throughout the eighteenth century and culminated during the Napoleonic wars, concentrated the ownership of land in the hands of relatively few wealthy landowners and dispossessed many small landowners, who, in desperate straits, were forced to migrate to the towns and become factory laborers. The excess capital of both the merchant and the wealthy landowning classes was made available for new investment opportunities by an efficient banking system, with its cornerstone the Bank of England, founded in 1694, and several private banks such as Barclay's and Martin's.

Finally, Britain had enjoyed a high degree of political stability since the constitutional struggles of the seventeenth century and the ascent of Parliament over the king. Although it did not represent the nation as a whole, Parliament did rule effectively on behalf of the vigorous and prosperous upper classes which dominated it. Success in foreign wars, culminating in the Napoleonic wars, also increased British power and prestige and solidified national pride and unity. All of these conditions—good physical resources, worldwide markets, an abundance of food, the availability of a large labor force, the accumulation and concentration of surplus capital, and a high degree of political stability and national unity—enabled Britain to initiate the Industrial Revolution.

The Industrial Revolution began with the mechanization of the textile industry and the construction of textile factories, or mills as the British called them, in and around the Midlands town of Manchester. A large and growing world market for cotton goods already existed, and if means could be found to increase production and reduce cost, huge profits could be made. The means were provided by a series of relatively simple and inexpensive inventions that greatly accelerated the process of spinning and weaving. In 1733 a weaver named John Kay invented the fly shuttle, which increased the output of the loom and enabled one worker instead of two to operate it. In 1764 another weaver, James Hargreaves, invented the spinning jenny, which combined several spindles in a single spinning machine that could be operated by one worker. In 1769 Richard Arkwright patented the water frame, a device that applied water power to spinning. A few years later, he discovered a process whereby carding and spinning could be combined in one operation and performed in one factory. In the 1780s, he replaced water power in the operation of his spinning machinery with the steam engine.

The steam engine, perfected by James Watt a few years earlier, was probably the most important and scientifically complex multi-purpose invention of the century. Arkwright also possessed considerable business acumen. In the 1780s he built the first spinning mill in Manchester, then went on to become a rich industrialist whose factories became the model for the whole textile industry. In 1784 Edmund Cartwright built the first power loom, which had about ten times the capacity of a handloom. The production of raw cotton was greatly increased by the cotton gin, invented in 1793 by the American, Eli Whitney.

The number of cotton mills in Manchester increased from one in the 1780s to fifty-two by 1802. Between 1790 and 1820, the cotton industry rose from ninth place to first among British industries and accounted for almost half of all British exports. The cotton industry was the first to meet the basic criterion of a modern industrial revolution—by producing such vast quantities at such a rapidly declining cost, it was able to break free of dependence on existing demand and to create its own market. In showing how the investment of surplus capital in industry could be made profitable and how cheap and readily available labor, resources, and inventions could be used, the cotton industry stimulated heavy investment in more expensive, riskier, and technologically more complex forms of industrialization.

The next step to industrialization was the mechanization of transportation and related industries. A whole network of canals, financed by both public and private investment, was built to transport coal quickly and economically to the new industrial centers and to link them with each other and with their ports. The steam engine was at first so cumbersome that its application was limited to Arkwright's spinning machines and to the coal fields, which provided the fuel to drive them. Soon after 1800, however, the steam engine was sufficiently perfected to be used to propel river boats, as Robert Fulton showed in the voyage of his paddle-steamer up the Hudson River in 1807. In the 1820s steam engines, already used in coal fields to drive wagons mounted on metal rails, were experimented with to propel larger vehicles of the same sort over longer distances. In 1829 George Stephenson, an engineer at the Tyneside mines, perfected a locomotive called the *Rocket* and demonstrated that it could travel at twenty-nine miles per hour pulling a thirteen-ton load. The perfection of the steam locomotive made possible the flurry of railroad building that transformed not only the transportation industry, but also the whole natural and social environment of the industrially

Soho Engineering Works at Birmingham, England. Where James Watt and Matthew Boulton manufactured steam engines, 1775–1800.

(The Granger Collection.)

advanced Western societies. So great was the railroad's demand for coal and iron during the 1830s and 1840s that these natural resources soon replaced cotton as king and initiated a whole new phase of industrialization.

Manchester was the first and foremost of the many factory towns, or Coketowns as they came to be called, that sprang up within a generation in the Midlands and the north of Britain where the coal and iron lay. They were drab and dirty places, blackened with factory smoke and the soot of the coal mines, overcrowded and unsanitary. The workers lived in hastily built and closely packed tenements all alike in appearance, often housing whole families in a single room. Because low wages usually made it necessary for women and children as well as men to work long hours in the factories and mines, the workers' health, family life, and morals deteriorated. The concentration of industry also ravaged the natural environment. The coal mines permanently scarred the landscape; the grime from coal used for power poisoned the air; mountains of slag grew up around the mines; rivers were polluted by chemical dyes used to color the textiles and by every other kind of waste; the railroads slashed through countryside and city center alike; the noise from the mills, steam engines, and trains reverberated constantly throughout the city.

Manchester and the other Coketowns grew so rapidly and haphazardly, and industrialization was such a new experience, that the cities were unprepared to deal with the problems rapid growth posed, such as adequate sanitation, urban planning, police protection, and other essential social services. Manchester, which grew in population from about twenty-five thousand in 1772 to four hundred fifty-five thousand in 1851, had no municipal government and no representation at all in Parliament until the 1830s. And until 1835 Britain had no regular procedure for incorporating cities. Consequently, the new factory towns lacked the officials, the facilities, and the tax-raising and law-making powers necessary to deal with their problems. No form of zoning or even of sanitary controls was exerted by the national government over the early builders; therefore, expansion was largely dictated by the quest for quick profits. Moreover, not until passage of the first Factory Act of 1819 was there any regulation of working conditions, and unionization by the workers was forbidden by law.

Social Implications

Morally and intellectually the people of the early industrial era, entrepreneurs and workers alike, were unprepared to cope with the new environment they were creating. Their religion, culture, and political institutions had been formed long before the advent of industrialization and without reference to it. The inhabitant of Coketown continued to believe in a religion conceived by and for a pastoral society, but while toiling in the mines and mills he was losing all touch with nature. He continued to believe in an almighty God, but it was difficult to find evidence of His mercy and justice in an atmosphere of greed, selfishness, and indifference to suffering. He continued to believe in the dignity of the individual, but rarely had the common man been so degraded and left so helpless and destitute by his living and working conditions. He continued to believe that man is responsible to and for his fellowmen, but now life for the laboring poor was at all times consumed by the struggle to survive, and life for the prosperous was governed by ruthless competition and the ceaseless drive to acquire ever greater wealth. He continued to believe in the family, although never before had family life been so sorely tried. He continued to believe that government should serve the people, but the government scarcely recognized his existence. In sum, he began to realize only slowly that the education, customs, beliefs, social groups, and political views he had known in the past were archaic and out of place amidst "the dark Satanic mills" of Coketown.

The new industrialists subscribed to the ideas of the emerging science of "political economy"—the ideas of Adam Smith, Jeremy Bentham, Thomas Malthus, and David Ricardo, all forerunners of the so-called Manchester school of economics. Smith, writing at the dawn of the industrial age, had argued, in his classic *Wealth of Nations* (1776), for laissez faire capitalism in its purest form. This was the theory that the economic order functions best when each individual is allowed to pursue his self-interest without interference from the government or any other noneconomic institution. The only regulation on economic activity should be the "natural" law of supply and demand, which produces a harmony of interests among competing individuals seeking to buy in the cheapest market and to sell in the dearest. Such a system is best, Smith had claimed, because it is the most productive and hence in the interest of all, even the lowliest laborers, who would benefit from the general rise in the standard of living.

Bentham fathered the utilitarian view that society should strive for the greatest happiness of the greatest number, happiness understood as the enjoyment of pleasure and the avoidance of pain. In his *Introduction to the Principles of Morals and Legislation* (1789), he drew up a detailed table of types of pleasure and pain and how they can be measured quantitatively. Bentham agreed with Smith that each person knows what is best for himself and that, given the opportunity, he will pursue it and thus contribute to the general welfare of all. Going beyond Smith, however, Bentham called for the reform of any institution that failed to meet the criterion of utility or to promote the unity of individual and social interests. Utilitarianism did not preclude moral and social benevolence. Some industrialists, notably Robert Owen, did in fact undertake various social reforms on behalf of the working classes. According to Bentham's theory, however, such benevolence was not a peculiarly moral or social duty, but simply another way of bringing happiness to the person who practiced it.

Malthus and Ricardo held to the views of Smith and Bentham, but their optimism was tempered by the widespread misery of the early industrial age. In his *Essay on the Principle of Population* (1798), Malthus presented the depressing theory that population tends to outstrip food supply and that, unless mankind voluntarily limited the growth of population, war and famine would continue to limit it as it had in the past. Malthus hoped, but did not really expect that mankind in general and the prolific lower classes in particular would exercise the sexual self-restraint necessary to achieve the only humane balance between population and food supply. But unless this happened, Malthus warned, the misery of the working classes would continue, because only by reducing the supply of labor would its value increase.

Malthus' application of the lw of supply and demand to population formed the basis of Ricardo's famous "iron law of wages," solemnly set forth in his *Principles of Political Economy* (1817). Ricardo contended that the price of labor always tends toward the subsistence level because, as soon as workers receive more than the base minimum to keep them alive, they breed more children who in turn consume the excess and thereby reduce the working class once again to the subsistence level. Little wonder that political economy acquired the reputation of being the "dismal science"! In general, however, political economy taught the industrialists that laissez faire capitalism is the most productive economy and operates in the interest of all, and that the good society is a body of independent individuals who freely enter into contractual relations for mutual benefit. It stated that the social good is nothing more or less than the arithmetical sum of individual pleasures, that it results automatically and inevitably from private self-seeking, and that no matter how much suffering such a system entails, it is still the best, or at any rate, the least evil system possible.

Laborers of the Revolution

The laboring poor saw things quite differently, of course. Most were perfectly aware that they were victims of a system blatantly biased in favor of the wealthy middle classes. Most held the view, expressed by the eighteenth-century poet Oliver Goldsmith that "laws grind the poor, and rich men rule the law." Most also realized that they had the choice of either being ground down or rebelling. At first, groups of desperate workers called Luddites, mostly former artisans and skilled craftsmen, reacted to the new system by smashing the machines they blamed for their troubles. In 1816 workers rioted in London against the newly enacted Corn Law, a tariff that preserved the high price of grain. Again, in 1819 a huge gathering of discontented workers in Manchester demanded universal male suffrage, annual elections, and repeal of the Corn Laws; it was put down by force in what was dubbed the Peterloo Massacre. On the continent, silk workers in Lyons rose in rebellion in 1831 and again in 1834, and Silesian weavers revolted in 1844.

Between 1815 and 1848, workers throughout Europe made their first efforts to create unions, workingmen's associations, and educational and cultural programs for workers. They also began to channel their discontents into the emerging movements of radicalism, republicanism, socialism, and Chartism. Nothing that the workers did before 1848 seriously threatened the social order or substantially improved their conditions. But without the attempts they made, both peaceful and violent, to gain social justice and a stake in industrial society, there would have been no Reform Act of 1832, no repeal of the Corn Laws in 1846, no factory legislation throughout the 1840s, and no social revolutions that would sweep over continental Europe in 1848.

Industrialization on the Continent

Industrialization was delayed on the European continent by the French Revolution and the Napoleonic wars and by the absence of the physical and historical conditions that enabled Britain to set the pace. But after 1815 and on an even larger scale after 1830, the Industrial Revolution reached and began transforming large parts of Europe, including Belgium, the French provinces of Alsace and Lorraine, the province of Saxony, and the Ruhr and Saar valleys in Germany, northern Italy, Bohemia, and the region around Vienna. The restoration of peace, the more effective system of administration introduced by Napoleon, the abolition of some customs barriers, the determination of governments to stimulate their economics, and the growth of population and its migration from the countryside to the cities—all served to foster industrialization on the continent.

Following the British example, the major Western European states, slowly at first but rapidly after 1830, began constructing roads, canals, and railroads. At first, the continent relied heavily on British machines, money, business acumen, and skilled labor, much to the profit of Britain. British businessmen and engineers built the railroad from Paris to Rouen, opened the Hibernia coal mines in the Ruhr, modernized the cotton industry of Normandy, and founded the world's largest engineering firm in Belgium. Soon Europeans were improving upon British technology and making their own innovations. Friedrich Krupp of Essen improved upon the existing technique for producing iron. The Borsig company of Berlin developed an improved locomotive in the 1830s. The Hamburg-Amerika steamship line was founded in 1847. The Wendels of Lorraine made progress in integrating the various stages of iron production. By the middle of the century, Britain was still far ahead of the rest of the world in industrial development, but the gap was closing and the advanced parts of Western Europe were beginning to face the same social problems and discontents that Britain had known since the 1790s.

THE SPIRITUAL REVOLUTION: ROMANTICISM AND IDEALISM

The third thrust of the triple revolution came to fruition in romanticism and idealism. Although international in scope, these movements achieved their fullest development in Germany. While the French Revolution was ushering in a new political order and the Industrial Revolution a new economic order, romanticism and idealism were at work reshaping Western thought and culture. Romanticism began as a protest against the artistic standards of eighteenth-century classicism, and idealism, as a protest against the philosophical empiricism and rationalism of the Enlightenment. But the often esoteric doctrines advanced by a growing number of brilliant and restless artists and intellectuals soon gave rise to broad movements that expressed the very consciousness of a world in revolution and voiced its hopes and fears, its expectations and disillusionments. Romanticism and idealism were more than intellectual movements in the usual sense. They were the first distinctively modern spiritual movements; they permeated and permanently transformed every sphere of creative life in the Western world.

ROMANTICISM

Romanticism, the first of the two movements to develop into a significant historical force, was such an extremely complex, diverse, and sometimes self-contradictory phenomenon as to defy any precise or easy definition. Part of the difficulty in defining romanticism lies in the fact that the romantics themselves scorned all traditional rules of art and deliberately nurtured a cult of individuality, iconoclasm, and eccentricity. Typically, the romantics were intensely subjective and often expressed themselves in obscure and mystical language. They delighted in multiple meaning, partial expression, illusion, and irony. And they were drawn to the ephemeral and exotic, the unusual and unpopular, the imaginative and unreal in their choice of subject matter. Romanticism gave rise not only to a new, anarchic style of art, but also to a new, anarchic type of personality—the bohemian, the dandy, the outsider, and the vagabond. All of these were deliberately cultivated techniques by which the romantic declared his independence from the obsolete classicist cultural standards and demeaning system of patronage of the prerevolutionary era.

But if the romantics rebelled against the old semifeudal order that was now in decline, they soon became disillusioned with the emerging new bourgeois order as well. The romantics were inspired by the ideals of the revolutionary era, but were appalled by its realities. Most of them detested the ugliness and social havoc caused by industrialization, the indignities, economic suffering, and dehumanizing work habits fostered by capitalism, and the spiritual and psychological shock produced by the sudden and violent destruction of age-old traditions, values, and institutions in the course of the French Revolution. Above all, the romantics detested the vulgar materialism and philistinism of the ascending bourgeois: their reduction of art to but another pleasure and their reduction of the artist to but another producer forced to sell himself and his commodity in a competitive market to survive.

What the romantic saw in the emerging new order was only a new form of social tyranny, injustice, and indifference to the humanizing effects of culture. It was only natural, therefore, that he should feel alone in an alien and hostile world and that he should view art no longer as just another vocation, but as a whole way of life different from and superior to any other. For the romantic, culture could no longer be the reflection or servant of society; rather, it became the repository of pure ideals in an imperfect world and the romantic, their inspired personification and prophet. "Poets are the unacknowledged legislators of the world," Shelley proclaimed in the famous last line of *A Defence of Poetry* (1822).

A precise definition of romanticism is also difficult because of its variations from one country to another and from one phase of its development to the next. English romanticism began as a conservative reaction to the devastating impact of industrialization on the social and aesthetic environment. The early English romantics—Blake, Wordsworth, Coleridge, and Southey—reacted to industrialization by invoking the ideal of a nature unspoiled by man, the simplicity and humanity of life before the advent of the "dark Satanic mills," the spontaneity and innocence of childhood, and Blake's mystical vision of a New Jerusalem.

French romanticism began as a conservative reaction to the political and psychological dislocations caused by the French Revolution. The early French romantics—Chateaubriand, Madame de Staël, Constant, and Senancour—were aristocratic by background and temperament. In the France of Napoleon, they were dissidents and outsiders, aware that history was going against them. They reacted by sentimentalizing the medieval past and turning inward to contemplate the workings of their complex, restless, troubled souls.

Romanticism in Germany served principally as a spiritual escape from a stagnant and degrading social order that the declassed artist, contemptuous of both the oppressive nobility and the subservient middle classes, could not hope to influence. Romanticism flourished in Germany partly because so few opportunities existed for the expression of personal, social, and political discontent, other than flight from the world by way of the artistic imagination. There, romanticism grew into a full-blown worldview, governed by the idea that life on earth is, by its very nature, painful and imperfect and also by a ceaseless longing (*Sehnsucht*) for an ideal, a harmonious state of mind, and being not of this world. This German version of romanticism was exemplified by Novalis, who believed that art should make "the world become a dream, and the dream become the world;" by Kleist, who prophecied that "only when men eat of the tree of knowledge once more will they return to a state of innocence;" and by E. T. A. Hoffmann, for whom the world always remained "an eternal, inexplicable misunderstanding."

In general, early romanticism was critical of the French and Industrial Revolutions and their effects. But the advent of the Restoration in 1815, the last desperate effort to undo the results of the age of revolution (including freedom of speech and expression) spurred many romantics of the second generation, notably Shelley and Byron, Hugo and Heine, to campaign against oppression and reaction. Another shift occurred in the 1830s when the permanent consolidation of the bourgeoisie and its drift to the Right plunged romantics of this period into bitter despair, defeatism, and fierce denunciation of the bourgeois betrayal of revolutionary ideals. This shift is evident in the novels of Stendhal, in the dramas of Victor Hugo and George Büchner, and in the poetry and polemical writings of Heinrich Heine during this time. Romanticism was now on the wane, giving way to the social realism of Balzac and the early Victorian novelists, on the one hand, and to the "art-for-art's-sake" aestheticism of Theophile Gautier and his circle on the other.

However, despite its nebulous character and many permutations, romanticism did manifest a consistent set of traits throughout its development. First and foremost, the romantic was obsessed with the age-old biblical theme of the fall of man from an original state of innocence and harmony with himself and nature into a state of discord and knowledge of evil. Second, the romantic was infatuated with the abnormal—

criminals and madmen, tragic heroes and saints, fools and underdogs, dreams and fantasies, the sickly and ugly—all telling testimony to man's fallen state and to the romantic's own sense of being homeless and alone in the world. Third, the romantic yearned to recall and keep alive the memory of man's original state, frantically seeking to rediscover and resurrect lofty notions about religion, nature, primitive societies, the spirit of the people, and especially the Middle Ages. But the last and most precious vestige of man's original state the romantic discovered in imaginative intuition, which finds its supreme expression in art. For that reason, romanticism held, art is superior to real life. Always the romantic was tormented by what he believed was an intolerable and insoluble tension between unattainable ideals and unacceptable realities.

Two of the major inspirations for these views were the life and writings of Jean-Jacques Rousseau (1712–1778) and the philosophy of Immanuel Kant (1724–1804). Rousseau was the very prototype of the romantic personality: sensitive and sentimental, eccentric and iconoclastic. He had based his whole sweeping critique of Western civilization on the hypothesis that artificial and civilized acquisitions—property and government, culture and morals—had in the course of history triumphed over and suppressed man's original and natural traits: freedom, simplicity, and organic wholeness. Inspired by Rousseau, Kant had also taught that the dilemma of society is due to a basic conflict between the natural and civilized elements in the human makeup.

Neither philosopher had believed that a return to nature was possible any longer; the moral corruption of mankind had gone too far for that. But both Rousseau and Kant had believed that the problem of civilization could be solved by the creation of a political order, a perfect republic, in which freedom and law would coexist. The republic they had envisaged would more than compensate man for his history of strife and suffering by restoring to him the freedom and human wholeness he had enjoyed in the state of nature, and by providing him at the same time with the security and amenities of civilization that would enable him to realize his highest human potential.

The romantics accepted the diagnosis but rejected the cure, especially as Rousseau and Kant themselves had explicitly rejected revolution as a means to achieve their perfect republic (although Kant did not oppose the Revolution when it broke out in France). The romantic rejection of a political solution to the problem of restoring harmony to human life was fortified by Kant's teaching that the mind can know reality as it appears to the senses, but not as it exists in itself—that is, as unconditioned by space and time and the other operations by which the mind structures reality. If reality in its pure state cannot be known, if the mind is inescapably shackled to the transitory world of appearance, reasoned the romantic interpreters of Kant, how can man be held morally and politically responsible for himself or for anyone else? One of those interpreters, Heinrich Kleist, who committed suicide at the age of thirty-four, voiced the despairing romantic response to Kant, by asking: "When human reason does not suffice to comprehend itself, the soul, life, and the things around it, when after millennia we still question the existence of right—can God demand responsibility from such creatures? . . . What can it really mean to do evil, as far as the effects are concerned? What is evil? Absolute evil?" Many other great thinkers throughout the century would wrestle with these questions: Baudelaire and Kierkegaard, Dostoevsky and Nietzsche, to mention but a few.

The only consolation that Kant's philosophy afforded the romantic was the theory that artistic genius transcends the limits of reason. Knowledge has its rules, and so does morality: the rules of reason. But artistic genius works in mysterious ways. It does not imitate, and cannot be imitated. It creates beauty, but without knowing how. It is not the expression of the intellect or will, but it is an original, spontaneous activity of the imagination. Therefore, there can be no science of beauty, but only a critique of beauty. The distinctive and uplifting feature of great art is that it harmonizes the natural and civilized elements in man. For that reason, Kant believed, the conflict between the two, which he thought was inherent in human history, could be resolved only when "art will be strong and perfect enough to become a second nature. This indeed is the ultimate moral end of the human species."

All of this gave expression to some fundamental changes in attitude toward the role of the arts and the artist in Western society. One was the emergence of an adversary relationship of the artist to society, the idea that the artist should be society's critic and conscience, not its entertainer, teacher, or reflection. Another was that art is a superior reality, a preferable alternative to a world degraded by bourgeois vulgarity, and that the artist is a superior specimen of humanity. The view that the artist is born and not made, that he is mysteriously inspired, that he is a genius—these inventions provided the romantic artist of the revolutionary period and after with a justification for existence in a world in which he found himself deprived of any other. The corollary of this inflated view was the idea that the artist is a tragic and alienated being, unable to function in the everyday world because of his peculiar talents and hostility toward society. Finally, romanticism gave birth to the view that inspiration does not originate in the artist's perception of or experience with the world, but rather in his private imagination or ego; and therefore, he should not seek to reproduce reality, but rather give free and unfettered expression to his soul. Not surprisingly, the favorite romantic art was music, the most purely inward of the arts and the one

Liberty Leading the People. Painting by Eugene Delacroix, 1830.
(The Granger Collection.)

least dependent on stimuli from the external world. The favorite romantic literary forms were lyrical poetry, the fairy tale, and the tragedy of
fate—the least space- and time-bound literary forms. The romantic
painter favored extravagant light and color effects, rather than clear form
and composition. In short, the romantic strove more for an emotional
impact than for an intellectual or moral experience.

The romantic movement, and its dream of the spiritual rebirth of man
through art, came to an end with the revolutions of 1848. To posterity
romanticism bequeathed an extraordinary legacy that included the
music of Beethoven, Chopin, and Berlioz; the paintings of Géricault,
Delacroix, -and Goya; and, in addition to the literary figures already
mentioned, the writings of Keats and Scott, Vigny and Musset, Friedrich
and August Schlegel, Manzoni and Leopardi, to mention only a few of a
very long list. The romantic legacy was so rich and suggestive that every
new development in Western culture since—social realism and naturalism, impressionism and the many varieties of post-impressionism, twentieth century cinematic realism, and existentialism—has retained something
of romanticism's original spirit. Along with the French and Industrial

The Dream of Reason Produces Monsters, By Francisco Goya, c. 1810–1815.
(The Philadelphia Museum of Art).

Revolutions, romanticism transformed the very foundations of life in the modern Western world.

IDEALISM

Idealism was a more strictly philosophical movement than romanticism, and it flourished in Germany better than elsewhere. It was a philosophy conceived mainly by and for university professors and was neither intended nor suited for mass public consumption, especially since one of its basic tenets was that the reform of society can be achieved only by a reform of the spirit, not by direct political or social action. Despite its academic origins and appeal, however, idealism came to exercise an extraordinary influence on the educated classes during the first half of the nineteenth century, and like romanticism, it has continued to be a powerful intellectual force ever since. Coleridge and Madame de Staël introduced the new variety of German thought into England and France respectively at a time when other nationalities still generally regarded Germany as a backward country and the German language as barbarous. Whole generations of German university students learned of the new philosophy, first from Kant in Königsberg, then from Schiller and Fichte in Jena, and later from Hegel and Schelling in Berlin. During the Wars of Liberation against Napoleon, many German bureaucrats and army officers—including the great Prussian reformers Stein, Hardenberg, Scharnhorst and Gneisenau—found support for their patriotism in Kant's equation of duty with moral freedom. The first wave of German nationalists and student political organizations, known as *Burschenschaften,* found inspiration in Fichte's bold *Addresses to the German Nation* (1808), which called for patriotism and pride in German culture. Romantics were inspired by Schiller's *Aesthetic Education of Man* (1795), and by Schelling's mystical conception of nature. Hegel's theories virtually dominated German intellectual life during the 1830s and 1840s and gave rise to the Young Hegelian movement, which included such distinguished future intellectual leaders as Bruno Bauer, Ludwig Feuerbach, Arnold Ruge, Max Stirner, Moses Hess, and for a time, Marx and Engels. In 1848, high-minded but politically inexperienced professors, students, and professional men fought unsuccessfully against the forces of reaction in the streets of Berlin and Vienna in the name of Hegelian freedom. Idealism touched the transcendentalist movement in America and became a major influence on the Russian intelligentsia during the third quarter of the nineteenth century. Even some of the great critics of idealism—Schopenhauer and Kierkegaard, Feuerbach and Marx— preoccupied themselves at length with Hegel's system and made it the point of departure of their own philosophies. Disillusionment with the results of the revolutions of that year sent idealism, like romanticism, into sharp decline after 1848. But toward the end of the century it was revived in Germany by the neo-Kantian and neo-Hegelian movements as a protest against positivism. In the twentieth century interest in Hegel was aroused in Italy by Bendetto Croce, in France by Jean Wahl and Alexandre Kojève, and in the United States by refugee intellectuals from Hitler's Germany, notably Herbert Marcuse. In short, idealism, in one form or another, has remained an important branch of Western philosophy from its origins to the present.

The strength of idealism, like romanticism, lay in its critical approach to human affairs and its assertion of ideals superior to real life. Before idealism, Western philosophy had been primarily concerned with the nature of ultimate reality and how it can be known. Idealism shifted the emphasis to the relationship between man and the world and how he acts upon it. English empiricism and French rationalism had held that appearance and reality are one and the same and that the laws governing the mind are reducible to those that govern matter. The proof offered was that all knowledge derives from experience and everything in experience can be known. Whatever is not given in experience cannot be known and, therefore, cannot be said to exist. (The existence of God, for example, is an article of faith or probability, but not of knowledge.) Therefore, our impressions and ideas of things are adequate to the things themselves; a sort of preestablished harmony exists between the two. From this it followed that the chief task of philosophy was to establish the scientific criteria that could explain fully and precisely the facts of everyday experience.

By contrast, idealism held that the mind contains concepts like causality, possibility, relationship, and others that apply to experience but do not derive from it (a priori concepts). Accordingly, the laws that govern the mind cannot be reduced to those that govern matter. On the contrary, the mind imposes on matter its own concepts, logical, mathematical, scientific, and philosophical. And since such concepts derive from a source other than experience—either from a realm beyond experience (objective idealism) or from within the mind itself (subjective idealism)—we must distinguish between appearance, from which we receive only impressions, and the realm the idealists called reality, from which we receive our ideas; that is, the concepts by which we order our impressions. There is no preestablished harmony between mind and matter; the mind is superior to the things it comprehends and produces a harmony according to its own laws. For idealism, therefore, the task of philosophy was not to explain the facts of existence, which is the province of science, but rather to investigate how the mind structures the world and acts upon it. This line of thought was initiated by Kant, whose philosophy was the starting point of idealism as well as of German romanticism.

Idealism began with Kant's distinction between reality as it appears to our senses (the phenomenal world) and reality as it exists in itself, unconditioned by our perception of it (the noumenal world). This epistemological question was the subject of the first of Kant's three great philosophical critiques, the *Critique of Pure Reason* (1781). The basis of Kant's distinction between the phenomenal and noumenal was his discovery that in the very act of perceiving the world, the mind structures it. This it does by means of space and time—not properties of things but forms of conception contained in the mind—and by a priori concepts—again, categories of the mind, not learned from experience but necessarily presupposed by it. This process of structuring or synthesizing ap-

pearances occurs in three stages: sensations are transformed into perceptions within the forms of space and time (which are not given in
sensation); perceptions are transformed into experience by means of a
priori concepts (e.g., cause, substance, reality, possibility, necessity, and
others that are not given in perception); experience is transformed into
systematic (synthetic a priori) knowledge by means of general principles,
which Kant called Pure Ideas (e.g., the soul, the world, and God, which
are not given in experience).

This process of structuring enables us to know things as they *appear*,
but not as they *are* in themselves—that is, as unstructured by these operations of the mind. Although we cannot know *what* things are in themselves, we can, and logically must, assume *that* they have such an existence. Reason cannot know ultimate reality; but within its own proper
sphere, the realm of phenomena, reason is sovereign, the master of
experience and not its subject. Knowledge is possible not because things
are rational, but because the mind is. The mind makes sense out of
experience, which otherwise would remain senseless. This is what Kant
meant when he called his system a "Copernican revolution" in philosophy.

Kant's successors were intrigued by this philosophy that proclaimed
the autonomy and creativity of the mind. They were impressed also by
Kant's moral teachings, which stressed individual freedom and responsibility. Like romanticism, Kant's philosophy flourished in Germany because discontent with the old order could find expression only in systems
of thought that asserted the superiority of mind over matter and that
predicated the reform of politics and society on a reform of the spirit.
But many of the intellectuals inspired by this conception of philosophy
found difficulty with Kant's distinction between appearance and ultimate reality. Chief among them was Johann Gottlieb Fichte (1762–
1814), who claimed that it was a contradiction to assert the existence of
something about which nothing by definition can be known. Fichte began, therefore, by refuting Kant's conception of ultimate reality as unknowable. And he concluded that, if the "thing-in-itself" exists neither
within nor beyond the world of appearance, it must originate, along with
all other concepts, within the mind itself. On this view, reality does not
exist apart from the mind which posits it. Consciousness, or the ego, as
Fichte called it, is the ground of both appearance and reality; they are
but two manifestations of consciousness. From this standpoint, the world
is nothing more or less than the sum of mankind's total activity, the
product of its collective ego. To educate the will to reason and to correct
the conditions, social, political, and institutional, in accordance with general human needs as defined by the collective ego: that, Fichte believed,
was the proper task of philosophy. And he showed the way by devoting
himself to projects for the educational and political reform of Germany.

Fichte's bold revision of Kant's philosophy, which conceived the world as the creation of the collective ego directed toward practical ends, was the original form of subjective idealism. Fichte's assertion of consciousness as the ground of all being endorsed romanticism and pointed in the direction of existentialism. His conception of philosophy as essentially practical foreshadowed Marx's famous dictum that the point of philosophy is not merely to interpret the world but to change it.

Idealism culminated in the philosophy of Georg Wilhelm Friedrich Hegel (1770–1831), who attempted to synthesize the objective idealism of Kant and the subjective idealism of Fichte. Hegel agreed with Fichte and the other critics of Kant that ultimate reality cannot be so sharply separated from appearance as to be unknowable. But he could not agree with Fichte that appearance is nothing more than a creation of the subjective ego. In fact, Hegel began by rejecting the whole notion of a categorical distinction between appearance and reality. Existence, he believed, cannot be neatly divided into two separate spheres and explained in terms of one or the other. Appearance and reality, although not identical, are inextricably interrelated. To the extent that they are two different things, philosophy must consider this discrepancy itself as an essential part of existence. The key to understanding the world in its totality, Hegel argued, is precisely its contradictory character, which only a logic of contradiction, dialectical logic, is able to explain. To emphasize this point, Hegel called his version of idealism phenomenology, which literally means the logic of appearance, a logic which recognizes the inherently contradictory nature of existence and seeks to explain it.

Hegel attributed the contradictory character of existence to the fact that the world is in a constant state of flux. The world is not a static thing but a dynamic process of ceaseless becoming, an as yet unfinished product that is more like a growing, evolving organism than a machine. Nothing can be understood except in relation to the whole it is a part of, a whole that has not yet run its course. Consequently, no system of knowledge can claim to be valid for all time, but each system is valid at a particular stage of the world's development. New developments engender new knowldge that negates the old, which is negated in turn by further new developments, and so on. But each new stage of development marks an advance over the preceding stage in that both the world and the systems of knowledge which man creates to comprehend it are progressing toward a final, lasting resolution of all contradictions, toward a perfect unity of appearance and reality and of thought and being. That is why Hegel was the first major modern philosopher to put history at the center of his system. For history, he believed, is nothing less than the process by which the world comes to understand itself; philosophy is nothing more than the reflection of the world's self-understanding at any given time. In the last analysis, history and philosophy are but two aspects of the same thing: existence in its totality, or what Hegel called the Absolute.

Thus, Hegel conceived history not merely as the record of mankind's development, but as the life-process of reason itself. This self-realization of reason in time proceeds dialectically, through the production and resolution of contradictions, until such time as a perfect and lasting synthesis of all essential aspects of the world will have been achieved. This is what Hegel meant by his well-known and controversial statement that what is rational is real and what is real is rational. He did not mean that everything that exists is rational or that everything rational exists. He only meant to convey the view that reason is immanent in history (not purely transcendent, as Kant had believed, nor purely subjective, as Fichte had believed). Hegel also believed that reason is the only force that gives continuity and direction to history (because it is universal and identical with itself at all times). And he believed that the impact of reason on history is what makes it comprehensible to the historian (for whom history otherwise would remain a lot of sound and fury, signifying nothing). Reason is free—"thought determining itself in absolute freedom," as Hegel defined it—and, being free, reason aims at the actualization of freedom "as the final purpose of the world."

Hegel's idealistic conception of history did much to inspire serious and widespread interest in historical studies throughout the nineteenth century. It implied that history, despite the abundance of catastrophes and setbacks, the injustices and the irrationality it entails, is ultimately, even if not always obviously, on the side of right. History, like a living organism, is a single, indivisible unity that will reveal its full meaning and that of its various phases only at the end. Thus, no matter how insignificant or terrible events may seem at any given time, the future remains open-ended and destined to redeem all that has gone before. Hegel's philosophy, and especially his philosophy of history, marked the high point of idealism. Idealism had progressed from Kant, who had liberated reason from dependence on the external world, to Fichte, who had mobilized reason against the world, to Hegel, who now proclaimed the sovereignty of reason over the world. Idealism differed from romanticism by denying that the contradictory nature of reality is forever insurmountable. But it was as a method of criticizing the existing order of things in the name of a superior ideal of life on earth that idealism, like romanticism, entered the mainstream of Western thought.

THE RISE OF IDEOLOGIES

The triple revolution permanently destroyed the old equilibrium but failed to produce a new one. Instead, it unleashed the forces that would divide Europe and the West throughout the nineteenth century. The basic division was between those who accepted the revolutions and their results and those who did not. The basic issue was whether the West would build on its revolutionary foundations or seek to revert to the old prerevolutionary order. This polarization manifested itself in all spheres of life, especially in the rapid proliferation of ideologies and ideological movements that took place during the Restoration. It is significant that liberalism, conservatism, radicalism, socialism, nationalism, and a host of other "isms" all came into being and crystallized at approximately the same time, during the first postrevolutionary generation. Although liberalism eventually emerged triumphant in the West, it never went unchallenged and never succeeded in holding absolute sway anywhere, not even in England, the homeland of liberalism. The very fact that the triple revolution gave rise to so many competing ideologies all at once was itself one of its most significant effects. For it guaranteed that the revolutionary temper would continue and that disequilibrium would remain a constant feature of life in the Western world. Ideologies are, after all, competitive and combative doctrines, not disinterested systems of thought or belief. Ideologies are interpretations of the world from a particular viewpoint, and they are inextricably linked to particular material, social, or political interests. They are or imply programs of action, not enlightenment for its own sake nor truths that their advocates expect everyone to accept. Ideology thrives, therefore, where belief in general standards and norms has broken down. The romantic poet, Alfred de Musset, aptly described the mood of disorientation of the dawning age of ideology in the following passage from his widely read *Confessions of a Child of the Century* (1836):

> Three elements entered into the life which offered itself to these children: behind them a past forever destroyed, still quivering on its ruins with all the fossils of centuries of absolutism; before them the aurora of an immense horizen, the first gleams of the future; and between these two worlds—like the ocean which separates the Old World from the New— something vague and floating, a troubled sea filled with wreckage, traversed from time to time by some distant sail as some ship trailing thick clouds of smoke; the present, in a word, which separates the past from the future, which is neither the one nor the other, which resembles both, and where one cannot know whether, at each step, one treads on living matter or on dead refuse.

The Restoration

The purpose of the Congress of Vienna that convened in 1814 was to restore order after twenty-five years of upheaval. To the congress, however, order meant a restoration of the old, prerevolutionary status quo and therefore suppression, or at least containment, of the new forces unleashed by the triple revolution. This illustrious gathering of representatives of the governments that had defeated Napoleon—the architect of the Restoration, Prince Klemens von Metternich of Austria, British Foreign Secretary Castlereagh, the Russian Tsar Alexander I, the Prussian minister Hardenberg, the wily French delegate Talleyrand, plus the host of lesser dignitaries—were deeply conservative men steeped in the Old Regime. Despite their political realism, far-sightedness, and diplomatic skillfulness, they were incredibly blind to the significance of the events they had lived through. Of no one was this more true than Metternich himself, a gifted but pompous egoist rigidly opposed to change or innovation of any kind throughout his long career. His whole policy was the negative one of preserving the status quo for as long as possible. The congress was a splendid, sumptuous affair, a constant round of parties, balls, concerts, and parades set against the colorful background of the magnificent Habsburg capital and skillfully orchestrated by Metternich to produce the illusion that the previous twenty-five years had been little more than an unfortunate but ephemeral interlude. In reality, this lavish aristocratic festival was the last brilliant afterglow, the danse macabre of a dying order.

The congress agreed on three points: (1) that the great powers should work together to suppress any future revolution in Europe and to achieve a stable balance of power, (2) that a number of buffer states should be established around France to prevent any future French aggression, and (3) that "legitimate" rulers who had been ousted during the Revolution, including Louis XVIII of France, Ferdinand VII of Spain, and Ferdinand IV of southern Italy, should be restored to power. To guarantee these agreements, Austria, Russia, Prussia, and Britain formed a Quadruple Alliance, by which they pledged "to employ all their means to prevent the general tranquility (the object of the wishes of mankind and the constant end of their efforts) from being again disturbed." Alexander I went a step further and proposed a Holy Alliance, a union of "throne and altar," which he persuaded the jittery Austrian emperor and Prussian king to sign. These agreements formed the basis of what came to be known as the "Metternich system," an alliance its chief author sought to uphold by every means available—military force, police spies, censorship, and diplomatic maneuvering—for the next thirty-three years. Metternich's system made no concessions to the new industrial classes, to liberalism or nationalism, or to social and political reform of any kind. The strength of the system lay in its ability to unite the forces of the Right: monarchs, aristocracies, and churches. Its weakness lay in its rigid opposition to the forces of the future.

Two dangers above all threatened the Alliance. One was the ever-present prospect of social revolution by the peasantry, regardless of nationality, against the great landlords and against the newly restored "legitimate" rulers, whose power rested on the aristocracy and church. The other was nationalist revolution, likely to be fomented by middle-class liberals and republicans in Western Europe and by the economically depressed lower nobility or an aroused peasantry in Eastern Europe. The first big test of the Alliance came in 1820, when revolution in Spain and Italy prompted Metternich to call a meeting of the great powers at Troppau to authorize armed intervention to suppress it. Great Britain, now under Tory government, and France, now headed by the restored Bourbon king, opposed intervention; the three Eastern autocracies, Austria, Prussia, and Russia, supported it. Metternich proceeded to suppress the Italian rebels, but British and French opposition undermined his policy of collective security.

A year earlier, the assassination of a petty Russian agent in Germany by Karl Sand, a fanatical member of one of the extremist German student groups, had enabled Metternich to strengthen his hand there. Adamantly opposed to the unification of Italy and Germany, both bordering Austria, he forced through the German Diet in 1819 the infamous Carlsbad Decrees, which imposed severe restrictions on the German universities and press and established a spy system to uncover subversive activities. The outbreak of the Greek revolt against Turkish rule in 1821 forced Metternich to call another conference of the great powers the following year at Verona; now his strongest argument for collective security was the contagion of revolution. The British again opposed intervention, but France agreed to put down revolution in Spain.

The revolutions of 1830 dealt an even more severe blow to Metternich's system. The July Revolution in France that year, launched by moderate liberals and radical workers, deposed the "legitimate" Bourbon king, Charles X, and installed Louis Philippe, the "bourgeois monarch," who ruled on behalf of the wealthy middle classes until 1848 when both he and Metternich were driven from power. Once again, Paris was the center of revolution, which quickly spread to Italy, Germany, and elsewhere. In 1830 the Belgians revolted against their union with the Dutch and gained independence. Polish nationalists revolted, although unsuccessfully, against their Russian overlords; Metternich faced a new wave of uprisings in northern Italy and Germany, which he managed to suppress once more. The same year a Whig ministry, led by George Canning and Robert Peel, replaced the Tory government in Great Britain and broke with the Metternich system altogether. The events of 1830 permanently broke the hold of the Restoration in Western Europe. But Metternich, ever dedicated to "propping up mouldering buildings," as he himself put it, managed to stay in command in Central and Eastern Europe for another eighteen years.

To summarize, neither the forces of revolution nor those of reaction were able to maintain the upper hand between 1789 and 1848. Liberalism and nationalism, socialism and democracy were on the march, but the forces of conservatism and reaction were still strong enough to contain them. During this time, Europe fell increasingly into two hostile camps: the liberal, middle-class West, which favored constitutional government, individual liberties, and industrial progress; and the autocratic East, which resisted all of these forces in the name of the prerevolutionary social and political order. Unless one or the other camp could win out decisively, more revolution lay in store. The result would be the final revolutionary wave of 1848.

Liberalism

During the early postrevolutionary years, it was by no means certain that liberalism would eventually gain the upper hand over its ideological competitors. Industrialism was still confined mainly to a small corner of northwestern Europe and would forge ahead rapidly on the continent only after 1830. Even in England, only a small fraction of the workers were employed in factories as late as the 1830s. Therefore, despite industrial progress and the emergence of a powerful class of industrialists, the traditional agrarian features of Western economic life remained preeminent. Moreover, liberals faced powerful opposition from all sides: from the aristocratic landowning classes determined to resist further setbacks; from the conservative governments bent on resurrecting the prerevolutionary political and social order; from the churches disturbed by liberal free-thinking and materialism; from artisans and skilled craftsmen threatened with extinction by machine production; from rebellious factory workers crushed by exploitation; and from disillusioned artists and intellectuals. Finally, no one except liberals themselves believed any longer in the moral superiority of the liberal cause. Whereas before the triple revolution liberals had identified their cause with the universal rights of man, afterwards they began to identify it increasingly with the interests of the now economically dominant middle classes.

Nevertheless, conditions favorable to success were on the side of liberalism. First and foremost, liberalism was the ideology of the dominant social class and the one class at the time that stood unequivocally for progress. The nouveaux riches middle classes of the early nineteenth century may have been callous, vulgar, exploitative, hypocritical, and the like. But they were also the best educated, the most energetic and ambitious, the most enterprising and self-confident. It was the middle classes that had provided most of the leadership of the triple revolution and had gained the most from it. Throughout the Restoration, the middle classes could rightly claim that they and they alone were reshaping the world. They could *act;* the other classes could only *react.* The revolutions had left the conservative classes confused, demoralized, and on the defensive. The factory proletariat was not yet large and well-organized enough to pose any serious threat to middle-class dominance. Even such bitter critics of liberal society as Balzac and Marx stood in awe of the bourgeois triumph. The bourgeoisie, Marx wrote in the *Communist Manifesto,* "compels all nations, on pain of extinction, to adopt the bourgeois mode of production; it compels them to introduce what it calls civilization into their midst, that is, to become bourgeois themselves. In a word, it creates a world after its own image."

Another factor in favor of liberalism was that it flourished in Britain, which emerged from the Napoleonic wars well on its way to becoming the most powerful nation on earth and an inspiration to liberals everywhere. The roots of liberalism were deeper in Great Britain than anywhere else, going back to the Glorious Revolution of 1688, the triumph of the Whigs, and the political philosophy of John Locke. Thereafter, Great Britain followed the liberal course of constitutional and representative government, guarantees of individual rights, and a free market economy. British liberalism gained impetus in the eighteenth century from the French Enlightenment and from the writings of David Hume, Adam Smith, and the utilitarians. As British industrialism was the work of liberals, they naturally interpreted the profits they derived from it as a sign of the superiority of their ideas. In France also, liberalism became the dominant ideology in the wake of the Enlightenment, the French Revolution, and the reforms of Napoleon favorable to middle-class interests, especially his policy of opening careers to talent, which all future rulers of France retained. From these two revolutionary bases, liberal ideas infiltrated the rest of Europe, even remote Russia, where they inspired the Decembrist revolt of 1825, which marked the first step in Russia's own course toward revolution.

A third factor in favor of liberalism was that it proved to be the most vital, comprehensive, and mature of the new ideologies. Liberal theory had already been in the making for more than a century and had won the assent of the most advanced philosophers and reformers, from Spinoza and Locke to Voltaire and Bentham. It had been the single most powerful impetus to the triple revolution, which in turn educated a whole new generation of liberal leaders and further consolidated the liberal movement. Thus, liberalism in 1815 was a body of ideas that had withstood the test of time, critical examination, and historical crisis; liberal leaders were for the most part men of experience, intelligence, and action. Early or classical liberalism, as expounded by the eighteenth century *philosophes* and utilitarians, had been as doctrinaire as any ideology. Once in power, however, and forced to make concessions to growing opposition from the Left and Right during the nineteenth century, liberals learned to adopt a more pragmatic and practical stance, thus turning the necessities of compromise and adaptation into the virtues of moderation and flexibility. These virtues helped liberalism prevail where it was already the dominant ideology, as in England, France, and the United States, and to at least survive where it was not the dominant ideology, as in Germany, Austria, and Italy. From the early nineteenth century to the mid-twentieth century, liberalism underwent so many transformations and assumed so many different forms that it is difficult to discern any common denominators underlying its development. But at least two interrelated ideas persisted, the two basic ideas of liberalism everywhere and at all times: individualism and self-determination.

These ideas may now seem familiar and unexciting. But when they were first applied on a large scale, they were as novel and revolutionary as the revolutionary events which vaulted them to preeminence. Liberalism was the first major theory in the history of Western thought, and has remained the *only* one from its inception to the present, to hold that the individual is a self-sufficient, self-contained being whose freedom and well-being are the sole reasons for the existence of society. Ancient Greek and Roman thought had typically conceived the individual as subordinate to the community. Medieval theory had, of course, regarded the individual as subordinate to God and the Church. Liberalism's chief adversaries, conservatism and socialism, also viewed, although from opposite standpoints, the interest of society as distinct from and superior to the interest of the individual. But, whether liberals favored very limited government, as in the early nineteenth century, or very extensive government and social legislation, as in the twentieth, the basic guideline of genuine liberalism has always been to maximize the freedom and well-being of the individual. The idea that government should serve the people, nothing more or less, was an innovative and distinctively liberal conception of the function of government, regardless of its size or power. Although liberal societies themselves have failed, often and badly, to live up to this simple but noble ideal, no society before the revolutionary era (except the British) even acknowledged it; no nonliberal society since then has even remotely approached it.

By freedom, the liberals meant freedom from restraint, choice, and self-determination, insofar as this autonomy of the individual did not infringe on the right of others to the same autonomy. It did not include social democracy or economic equality, although these principles were not necessarily incompatible with liberal views. Freedom conceived in this way, liberals held, leads to progress in terms of greater knowledge, higher living standards, increased maturity, and more complex and efficient social institutions and relationships. Freedom and progress were inseparably linked in liberal thought; freedom is sacred because it serves progress, and progress is the fruit of freedom.

Liberals believed that self-determination is possible and necessary because the individual is the best judge of his own interest; and each individual possesses all the necessary resources, primarily reason, to work out his own destiny. Since man is a rational being, he has the right and duty to act on his own initiative. Regardless of external circumstances, he is never merely a pawn without a mind and will of his own. Hence, the liberal emphasized education as an indispensable prerequisite to individual responsibility and self-government. He conceived education as a practical means to prepare the individual for responsible involvement in the world, not as a means to enforce conformity through indoctrination nor as an end in itself. He also emphasized the importance of the here and now. Therefore, the liberal, with his overriding concern with the individual, concentrated on the present, on what is possible now. By contrast, the conservative looked to the past as normative, and the radical concerned himself with the present only insofar as it contained the seeds of the future.

Liberals conceived the good society as one that enhances individual freedom. They believed that good government is self-government, that it works through representative institutions, parliamentary procedure, the separation of governmental powers, and rule by laws expressing the will of the citizens and applying equally to all. They believed that such a political system would ensure rational debate and legislation, responsible ministeries, and impartial administration. As a further guarantee of good government, liberals demanded freedom of the press and of assembly to assure full publicity of all governmental actions. Liberals believed in private property because it gives the individual a stake in society and, therefore, makes him more responsible, and also because they believed that success in private life is the best guarantee of success in public life. They advocated economic individualism (i.e., laissez faire capitalism) because, in keeping with the views of the political economists, they regarded it as the most productive type of economy and the one that allows for the greatest measure of individual choice. Economic inequality is admissible, liberals held, because it does not detract from the individual's moral dignity, nor does it conflict with equality of opportunity and equality before the law.

In the international sphere, liberals believed in the balance-of-power system, designed to give each nation the maximum opportunity to determine its own course of action. And liberals advocated free trade because they believed that the elimination of tariffs would increase international trade by making it easier to exchange goods at a lower cost, and by enabling each country to produce what it was best suited for, thereby increasing the wealth of all nations. Liberals believed in tolerance and open-mindedness because a liberal society is pluralistic, embracing a wide range of interests and opinions. But liberals tended to oppose in practice anything that stood in the way of progress, especially the established churches and landed aristocracies. They also distrusted and feared the unpropertied, and therefore supposedly irresponsible, lower classes. And liberals generally opposed war and revolutionary change because they disrupt progress, enlarge the powers of government, and involve great expense.

These were, of course, general principles and attitudes, which varied considerably from time to time and from country to country. French liberals, for example, tended to stress social harmony and cooperation with antiliberal forces more than the British. And the German economist, Friedrich List, although a liberal, disputed laissez faire economic theory and free trade on the grounds that they profited only the already industrially advanced countries like England and would impoverish those on the threshold of industrialization, like Germany and the United States. Moreover, liberals everywhere increasingly adapted their position to the interests of the middle classes, who were liberalism's chief supporters and beneficiaries. Nevertheless, these general principles and attitudes guided and galvanized the liberal movement, whose leaders in the early nineteenth century in Great Britain were the political economists, the utilitarians, and such distinguished intellectual political figures as Thomas Babington Macaulay and John Stuart Mill; in France, Benjamin Constant, Victor Cousin, Jean Baptiste Say, Destutt de Tracy, and Alexis de Tocqueville; and in Germany, Wilhelm von Humboldt, Friedrich List, Karl von Rotteck, and Karl Theodor Welcker. Their's were the ideas by which liberals would be held accountable to themselves and to their critics.

Conservatism

Conservatism arose in reaction to liberalism and proved more effective as a critique of liberalism than as a movement with a feasible program of its own. Early conservatism found its main political strength in the Restoration governments of Metternich of Austria, Tsar Alexander I of Russia, the restored Bourbon king of France, Charles X, and the Tory party, which held power in England from 1815 to 1830. The social classes that supported conservatism were the still-powerful landed aristocrats and the peasants, who still formed the majority of the population. These classes had nothing to gain from the emerging new order and much to gain by a restoration of the old. Intellectual support for conservatism came from Edmund Burke, who had set forth the basic ideas of conservatism in his *Reflections on the Revolution in France* (1790), the

French émigré aristocrats, Joseph de Maistre and Louis de Bonald, Metternich's personal secretary, Friedrich Gentz, the historical school of jurisprudence in Germany led by Friedrich K. Savigny, and most of the early romantics.

Typically, the conservative viewed history as a great, indivisible continuum, not something that can be neatly divided into past, present, and future. Whereas the liberal typically viewed the past as but a prelude to the present, the conservative thought of history as a living presence, as the foundation of all subsequent experience. Just as the individual's past never ceases to act on him as a formative influence throughout his life, so too, each society's past is constantly at work shaping its development throughout its existence. And just as each individual is born into a ready-made social order, from which he receives all that makes him one of its members—language, culture, moral codes, and political institutions—so too, each new generation inherits from the preceding one a legacy of traditions and historical experience necessary to preserve social continuity.

Conservatives distrusted written constitutions and attempts to reorder society along rational lines on the grounds that these were artificial means to force history into a preconceived direction, and this could only lead to disorder, anarchy, or worst of all, revolution. As representatives of the unchanging rural and agrarian pattern of life of the premodern social classes, conservatives held that the good society is organic, not contractual. Its model is the family, whose members are bound together under the watchful eye of a patriarchal father by ties of blood and loyalty, common experience, and mutual interests. Society, conservatives believed, should not be a rationally conceived system of contracts, obligations, and mutual rights and responsibilities freely agreed upon by independent and equal parties. As against this liberal position, conservatives argued that society is not a mechanism but an organism, whose parts work to serve the whole. Society takes precedence over the individual as the whole organism takes precedence over any of its parts. The marks of a good society are stability and longevity, not progress and change. As Burke eloquently stated it, society is:

> A partnership not only between those who are living, but between those who are living, those who are dead, and those who are yet to be born. Each contract of each particular state is but a clause in the great primeval contract of eternal society, linking the lower with the higher natures, connecting the visible and invisible world, according to a fixed compact sanctioned by the inviolable oath which holds all physical and moral natures, each in their appointed place.

Conservatives made a fetish of history, but their intransigent opposition to progress prevented them from seeing where history was actually heading. Blindness to progress made it difficult for conservatives to explain what had gone wrong with history, what had caused revolution. So they tended to blame reason, or more specifically the rationalist Enlightenment, which had dared to meddle in matters too complex for human understanding, matters better left to take their own course. Consequently, conservatives typically denounced the emerging new order as a terrible mistake and sought desperately to restore the prerevolutionary order. "It were better," Burke wrote, "to forget, once for all, the *encyclopédie* and the whole body of economists, and to revert to those old rules and principles which have hitherto made princes great and nations happy."

In vain did conservatives try to follow Burke's advice, by inventing such incongruous doctrines as "Tory democracy" and "feudal socialism." In vain did landowning Tory "radicals" in England, France, and Germany take the side of the working classes against the liberal capitalists on questions of social reform, as if their common hostility to the ascending industrialists were sufficient to unite these two otherwise very disparate social interests. In fact, conservatism, although acutely sensitive to history, was able to assert itself effectively as an independent force only for a short time under the aegis of the Restoration. Thereafter, it would make an impact only by joining with other antiliberal forces: namely, the various churches; the autocratic (but not necessarily conservative) regimes of Napoleon III and Bismarck; the army and antirepublican forces in France and elsewhere toward the end of the nineteenth century; and, in the twentieth century, with a whole array of right-wing totalitarian political movements.

Conservative conceptions of the good society were unrealistic and thus came to little. Conservatives were more effective as critics of liberal middle-class society and its failings. The efficacy of their criticism lay in its moral and historical sensitivity. They argued that the overriding individualism of liberal theory ignores man as a social being and undermines the very concept of community, which mankind had always regarded as essential to life. The fanatical pursuit of self-interest does not lead to social harmony, they observed, but rather to social conflict, irresponsibility, and antisocial attitudes.

Conservatives argued that the measurement of happiness and progress solely in terms of material gain ignores man as a spiritual being. Far from leading to the greatest happiness of the greatest number, the pursuit of wealth as an end in itself impoverishes life and encourages selfishness and mediocrity. Conservatives also argued that liberalism, with its exaggerated emphasis on reason and intellect, ignores man as an emotional being and underestimated the complexity of human nature. Mankind, they claimed, had lived in contentment by instinct, tradition, and religious faith long before achieving a high intellectual level. Moreover, intellect itself is largely a product of society, and the development of intellect and the opportunities to exercise it depend on social and historical circumstances.

Conservatives also ridiculed the social contract theory of the origins of society and government as an unhistorical invention of liberal thought, designed to sanction popular sovereignty and representative political institutions. Contract cannot make authority legitimate, De Maistre insisted. "The essence of a fundamental law is that no one has the right to abolish it. For how could it stand above *all men*, if *some men* had made it? Popular agreement is not possible. And even if it were, an agreement is still not a *law* at all and obligates no one unless a higher power guarantees its enforcement." Conservatives, then, denounced liberal society as egoistic, antisocial, morally degrading, and intellectually unsound. Ignoring its positive and promising features, they observed only that liberal society destroys the community by atomizing it; that it leaves man rootless, restless, godless, without a sense of belonging, and thus susceptible to political and economic exploitation. One-sided though they were, these criticisms contained much justification and suggested that liberalism was less a body of supposedly universal truths than a partisan ideology which betokened a new tyranny, the tyranny of the aggressive, acquisitive middle classes.

Socialism

Another significant new ideology was socialism, which opposed liberalism from the left. As early socialism and conservatism both arose in opposition to liberalism, it is not surprising that they had much in common. Both viewed liberal theory as little more than the ideological mask of an upstart middle-class tyranny. Both held that liberalism in practice fostered injustice, anarchy, class conflict, and antisocial attitudes. Both denounced industrial capitalism as aimless, chaotic, exploitative, and grossly inequitable. Both flatly rejected the ideas of laissez faire and economic competition and agreed that society must be ordered and organized. Both agreed that man is by nature a social being; for whom society is not merely a necessary evil for the purpose of safeguarding strictly individual freedoms, but is rather a positive good, the human environment necessary to man's happiness and self-fulfillment. Both also agreed that at some time in the past, whether in prehistory, classical antiquity, or the Middle Ages, men had lived in a harmonious state that provided a model for the ideal community of the future.

Beyond this common opposition to liberalism, however, conservatives and socialists parted ways. For one thing, the socialists looked to the future and not to the past. All varieties of socialism, even the most unrealistic and utopian, held to the Enlightenment credo of reason, science, and progress. Socialists also accepted the French and Industrial Revolutions unreservedly. But they insisted that industry should serve the interests of all members of society and not just those who own the means of production, and that political participation should be open to all equally and not just to the propertied elite. Marx would later expand socialist theory to include certain elements of the German intellectual revolution, notably Hegel's historical dialectical approach to social development. Socialists also differed from conservatives in that they did not simply reject liberal society out of hand, but concentrated instead on the apparent inconsistencies between liberal ideals and practices. The poineers of socialism—Claude de Saint-Simon, Charles Fourier, and Étienne Cabet in France; William Godwin, Robert Owen, and Thomas Hodgskin in England; and Willhelm Weitling, Johann Karl Rodbertus, and Moses Hess in Germany—all accepted the Benthamite goal of the greatest happiness of the greatest number. But it was obvious to them that the large majority, the laboring poor, were denied happiness, and selfish individualism was incompatible with happiness. Owen spoke for all the early socialists when he wrote: "The primary and necessary object of all existence is to be happy, but happiness cannot be obtained individually; it is useless to expect isolated happiness; all must partake of it or the few will never enjoy it."

Socialists also agreed with the labor theory of value, as expounded by the great liberal thinkers from Locke to Ricardo. But if labor determined the value of a product, they asked, why did the majority of producers live on the brink of destitution? Their answer was that the capitalists appropriated as profit a part of the value the worker puts into the product, thus robbing him of his proportionate share of compensation. Their remedy was to eliminate the capitalists and thereby abolish exploitation. Liberals claimed that capitalism was the most productive and efficient economic system possible, that it worked in the interest of all, even if it allowed for great economic inequality. But how could it be the best system, countered the socialists, when the distribution of national incomes was growing increasingly uneven, when the rich were getting richer and the poor poorer? Such criticism, arising from the internal contradictions of liberalism, were persuasive not only on moral grounds, but also because during the formative phase of socialism, between the publication of Owen's *New View of Society* (1814) and Marx's *Communist Manifesto* (1848), depression, falling wages, technological unemployment, and uncertainty about the economic future grew all too conspicuous. Not only was liberal society immoral, argued the socialists, but it worked badly and resulted in the opposite of what its advocates intended.

The early socialists were spurred on by the sense of an unfinished revolution and were determined to carry liberal arguments to their logical conclusion. They agreed with liberals that the good society was a free and happy society, but they denied that liberty was possible without equality and fraternity. So convinced were the socialists that this view was a self-evident truth, consistent with reason, science, and progress, that they thought it had only to be proclaimed and illustrated in practice to be accepted instantly by the educated classes (the working classes, they thought, were as yet too backward and ignorant to act on their own behalf). Therefore, the early socialists devoted their efforts mainly to vigorous propaganda campaigns and to the creation of experimental socialist communities intended to serve as models for the future good society.

Robert Owen, the successful industrialist, founded such a community at New Lanarck in Scotland and another at New Harmony in Indiana. These were communities designed to show that a factory could be constructed attractively, that workers could be given decent housing and education, that wages could be higher than the subsistence level without loss of profit, and that a gradual increase of such communities could lead to a new and better industrial society. Étienne Cabet and Charles Fourier planned similar communities, a number of which were founded in America, including Brook Farm, which became best known for the outstanding literary figures it attracted. Most of these schemes failed within a few years because they were too narrowly based and paternalistic, too far removed from the centers of power and action, and too out of touch with the broad problems of early nineteenth-century Western society as a whole. But they did represent the first faltering attempts to work out a viable socialist alternative to liberal society.

THE SAINT-SIMONIANS   More important in the early history of socialism was Count Claude de Saint-Simon (1760-1825) and the movement that crystallized around his teachings and flourished during the 1830s and 1840s. The Saint-Simonians were less given to communal experiments and more concerned with persuading established governments to carry out their proposals for a planned industrial society. They were not, and did not call themselves, socialists, although they popularized the term. Saint-Simon preferred enlightened despotism to any other political system, because he believed that it was the only form of government able to unite and satisfy the various conflicting social interests of Restoration society. Eventually, his followers would find a powerful political leader sympathetic to their views in the person of Napoleon III, who became emperor of France in 1852.

Saint-Simon also called for a new aristocracy of scientists and technocrats to replace the defunct old aristocracy of priests and landed nobility.

He advocated public ownership of industrial and financial resources under the control of an elite made up of social engineers and "captains of industry," as he called them, whose job it would be to promote and direct such vast undertakings as railway and canal building and in general to coordinate and harness the labor and material resources of society to productive ends. He believed that the economy should serve the interests of all social classes, but he did not believe in equality. Instead, he favored a hierarchy with "spiritual power in the hands of the scientists, temporal power in the hands of the property owners, and the power to nominate those who should perform the functions of the leaders of humanity in the hands of all."

Such ideas were as compatible with the interests of the liberal middle classes as they were with those of the industrial proletariat. Most of Saint-Simon's followers were in fact bankers, businessmen, industrialists, and middle-class social reformers. Moreover, Saint-Simon did not believe that the conflict between capitalists and workers was inevitable or insoluble without revolution. Nor was he an economic determinist in his interpretation of history and society. But he was the first major social reformer to perceive that Europe had entered the industrial age, and that it was a new epoch in need of wholly new methods of government and social organization. He was also the first to explain history in terms of the rise and fall of social classes according to material changes in society, and the first to attempt a comprehensive science of society based on prediction. These were the Saint-Simonian ideas that paved the way for Marx.

THE RADICAL FRENCH SOCIALISTS   The most radical form of socialism before Marx appeared during the 1840s in France, where the memory of the French Revolution was still very much alive among the oppressed and exploited. Its leading representatives, Pierre Joseph Proudhon (1809–1865), Louis Auguste Blanqui (1805–1881), and Louis Blanc (1811–1882), were men inspired by the Jacobin phase of the Revolution and the revolutionary socialist ideas of François "Gracchus" Babeuf. Proudhon, the only major early socialist thinker of lower-class origins, denounced property as theft in his best known work, *What Is Property?* (1841), where he proclaimed the necessity of class warfare and the ultimate overthrow of the bourgeoisie by the proletariat. Opposed to the state and contemptuous of legal political processes, Proudhon proposed a strongly anarchist and populist or grass roots form of socialism. The only cure to economic injustice, he declared, was to abolish property, turn over the means of production to the workers, and reorganize society into self-governing federations of producers, which eventually would supersede the state. Marx later ridiculed Proudhon for his crude and unsystematic thinking, his sentimental attitude toward the worker, and his failure to see beyond the immediate interests of the working class to the future classless society. Nevertheless, Proudhon's revolutionary fervor, his burning sense of social justice, and his persuasive rhetoric made him the best known of the radical socialist leaders during the 1840s and 1850s.

Blanqui was the most militantly revolutionary of the three. Hardened by many years of imprisonment for his conspiratorial political activities, Blanqui called for the seizure of power by a highly disciplined revolutionary elite, which would remain in power as a dictatorship of the proletariat during the period of transition to full-fledged communism.

More influential at the time was Louis Blanc, editor of the *Revue de Progrès* and author of the *Organization of Work* (1840), who advocated a form of socialism more democratic than Saint-Simon's and less revolutionary than that of Proudhon and Blanqui. Blanc argued that the worker had the right to work and that the state had the duty to enforce that right. Accordingly, he proposed that the state establish and sponsor a system of self-governing "social workshops," or manufacturing centers, in which the workers would produce by and for themselves without interference or competition from private capitalists. The workshops would provide good wages and working conditions and thereby attract workers away from private industry. Gradually, this system would supplant private industry altogether, as private industry would no longer be able to compete with the workshops. Thus, socialism would come about democratically and peacefully.

A diluted version of Blanc's proposal was actually tried for a brief time by the provisional French government during the 1848 revolution. But conservatives, liberals, and nonsocialist democrats joined forces to oppose the workshops, and the government quickly dissolved them. It was in this atmosphere of ideological ferment in the 1840s that a small group of German revolutionaries in exile in Paris began to synthesize German philosophy with French left-wing political doctrines to form their own version of socialism. Among them were Karl Marx and Friedrich Engels.

Socialism before Marx made itself felt largely on such nonsocialist reform movements as Chartism in England, republicanism and political radicalism in France, and the Young Hegelian philosophical circle in Germany—groups which demanded more democracy, social justice, and economic security. But socialism did not become a major historical force until after the 1848 revolutions, when industrialization and the ranks of the factory proletariat expanded rapidly and most socialists gave up hope of achieving their goals peacefully within the existing framework of Western society. The early socialists prepared the way for Marx and the later anarchist and syndicalist modifications of Marxism. But they merely argued that socialism was desirable, rational, and humane, whereas Marx and the later socialists proclaimed that it was inevitable and scientifically verifiable. The division of society into classes, the succession of class-divided societies from ancient oriental despotism to modern bourgeois capitalism, the "internal contradictions," which eventually bring societies down and generate the forces of the next historical development, the primacy of the social and economic "substructure" on which all else depends, the coming proletarian revolution and the classless society—all of this was inevitable and scientifically verifiable, according to Marx, and these were the ideas that set him apart from his predecessors. But more of Marx in the next chapter, since his teachings did not come to the fore until after 1848.

Nationalism

Of all the new ideologies, nationalism was the most pervasive and broadly based. Patriotism and a sense of belonging to a unique community with a common language, a common culture, and a common past were nothing new in Western history. But until the revolutionary period, these loyalties had always been compatible with and overshadowed by the stronger traditional loyalties to church, dynastic state, and region. Only when these older loyalties began to break down under the impact of the triple revolution did nationalism begin to emerge in force—in opposition to these older loyalties and in conjunction with the growing demand for popular sovereignty. At this point nationalism became a liberal cause, the cultural and political expression of the will to collective self-determination and individuality. At the start of the French Revolution, the *Declaration of the Rights of Man* stated: "The source of all sovereignty resides essentially in the nation. No body, no individual, can exercise authority that does not expressly emanate from it." France then proceeded, during the revolutionary and Napoleonic years, to set the example of how nationalism could be used to unite a society and inspire it to great deeds.

Nationalism began as a liberal cause, but it was quickly taken up by all other social and ideological groups. The French Revolution, the political spearhead of liberal ideas, aroused national sentiment both among those who supported it and among those who opposed it. Napoleon made use of nationalism to conquer Europe; his enemies, now mindful of its powerful effects, used it to combat him. Resistance to French domination awakened national pride and solidarity in such nonliberal states as Spain, Prussia, and Russia. The defeat of Napoleon in 1815 and Metternich's relentless effort to suppress nationalism served only to inflame it further. Metternich correctly judged that nationalism was the gravest single danger to his attempt to reimpose on Europe the supranational order of the past. For nationalism was no longer confined only to the liberal middle classes. In addition, Prussian and Polish aristocrats, Spanish and Russian peasants, British Tories and workers, and everywhere in Europe conservatives and radicals, students and intellectuals of all social and political backgrounds found nationalism irresistible and proclaimed it the wave of the future. Throughout the nineteenth century, one people after another won independence from foreign rule and formed new nations: Greece and several Latin American countries in the 1820s, Belgium in the 1830s, Italy, Rumania, and Hungary partially in the 1850s and 1860s, and Germany in 1871. Those who failed—the Poles, Czechs, Slovaks, Irish, and others—did not cease to press their claim to statehood. In the old established state of Great Britain, nationalism took the form of renewed pride in the stability and soundness of British institutions; in France itself nationalism found strength in the memory of the glorious achievements of the revolutionary and Napoleonic years.

Nationalism acted as a unifying force, and therein lay its broad appeal and lasting strength. Not only did it fill the void left by the collapse of the supranational loyalties and political structures of the past. But also, in contrast to the other new ideologies of the time, nationalism asserted (often in hazy and emotional language) the cultural solidarity and political sovereignty, whether real or imagined, of the *whole* people.

Early nineteenth-century nationalist leaders—most of them young and politically inexperienced intellectuals—adopted the ideas of the eighteenth-century German philosopher-historian Johann Gottfried Herder (1744–1803), who has been called the father of modern nationalism. In his *Ideas on the Philosophy of the History of Mankind* (1784–90), Herder had taught that every people is unique and possesses a distinct national character, or *Volksgeist,* which has evolved very slowly over many centuries in the mysterious manner of a plantlike growth. A healthy society, he claimed, is one in which all of its institutions and culture arise out of its native character. An unhealthy society is one in which the *Volksgeist* cannot develop and express itself freely, either because it has been suppressed by foreign rule or because it has been corrupted by the intrusion of foreign cultural elements. No one people or culture is superior to any other, Herder believed, but all are and should be different. Together they form a concert of nations, each playing a different part but collectively producing a rich and magnificent polyphony. Herder himself was a product of the cosmopolitan eighteenth century. He was not a racist, and he explicitly denounced racism. But his mystical conception of the *Volksgeist* as something the members of a national community imbibe, as if by osmosis, suggested that national identity is a *natural* attribute, as inescapable as one's physical features, rather than a voluntary association that can be formed, dissolved, or changed at will. Such views did not necessarily imply racism. But under the right conditions, they could, and eventually did, lead to the conclusion that healthy nations are racially pure and racially pure nations are superior.

It was not the suggestion of racism in Herder's teachings so much as his doctrine of an indestructible *Volksgeist* and his paeans to the uniqueness of nations and the excellence of diversity that appealed to the early nationalists. Their claim that every people has a language, a culture, and a history of its own and that it is entitled to preserve and perpetuate this heritage formed the basis of their claim that every nation has the right to become a sovereign state encompassing all members of the same nationality. But since most Western states contained people of many different nationalities, and few states contained all the members of any one nationality, nationalism, carried to its logical conclusion, implied the overthrow of almost every existing government.

Because of its inherently revolutionary implications, nationalism was suppressed by the established authorities and its leaders were driven underground. They responded by forming secret societies, such as the Carbonari in Italy, and worked within Masonic lodges, student organizations, and the like to propagate their views that often assumed a conservative, liberal, or socialist complexion. Many of these societies, with their elaborate rites of initiation and secrecy to protect their members, deliberately cultivated a conspiratorial temperament. By the 1830s and 1840s, as nationalism grew stronger and more vociferous, it surfaced in the form of broad movements such as Young Italy, Young Germany, Young Poland, and similar movements in other countries.

One of the most influential of the early nineteenth-century nationalists was the Italian Giuseppe Mazzini (1805-1872), founder of the Young Italy movement in 1831 and spiritual leader of the *risorgimento* or resurgence, which led to Italian unification in 1870. Mazzini began as a member of the secret organization known as the Carbonari. He was imprisoned in 1830 for his revolutionary activities, then popularized the cause of Italian unification abroad while in political exile in Paris and London. For him, the liberation of Italy from foreign and papal rule and its unification under a republican government was a holy cause, to which he dedicated his life and talents as a publicist, moral philosopher, and political organizer. Mazzini sympathized with the social-democratic views of Louis Blanc. But he distrusted both liberals and socialists because they put class interests above national solidarity. Throughout his life, Mazzini preached that duty to the state is intermediate between duty to family and duty to God. Nationalism was popularized in France by Felicité de Lamennais, Edgar Quinet, and by the great French historian of the time, Jules Michelet (1798-1874), who made the French people the hero of his widely read *History of France* (1833–1867).

Nationalism was especially strong in Germany, where it interacted with romanticism and idealism. Political reformers and army officers who had fought against Napoleon, students and professors, poets and philosophers—all joined in calling for a unified Germany, some in the form of a loose confederation of constitutional states, others under the leadership of the strongest German state, which at that time was Prussia. Since German nationalism was largely an outgrowth of anti-French feeling and found its base in autocratic Prussia, it tended to be conservative and often reactionary. This was true of such outspoken agitators as Ernst Moritz Arndt, Achim von Arnim, and Friedrich "Father" Jahn, who preached a crude *völkisch* nationalism, replete with patriotic songs, duelling, drinking, muscle-building exercises, linguistic purism, a cult of ancient German customs, and anti-Semitism. An intellectually superior and somewhat more liberal form of nationalism was advanced by the philosophers Fichte, Hegel, and Humboldt, and by the most eminent German historian of the century, Leopold von Ranke (1795–1886).

In Eastern Europe, nationalism took the form of opposition to foreign rule and manifested itself in a host of cultural revivals: Slavic, Magyar, Greek, Rumanian, and others. In general, conservative nationalists, who predominated in rural Central and Eastern Europe, stressed the value of their own distinctive customs and folkways, culture, and historical development. By contrast, liberal and democratic nationalists, predominant in urban Western Europe, demanded more self-determination, more participation in government, more representative institutions, and more individual rights and freedoms. Before the 1848 revolutions, nationalism served chiefly as a weapon against autocratic governments in the name of the people. After 1848, nationalists, fearful of the ascending democratic and socialist movements, began to look to the state as a bulwark against revolution and as a force working for internal order and national glory.

THE 1848 REVOLUTIONS

The deadlock between the forces born of the triple revolution and those opposed to it resulted in a new wave of revolutions in 1848 that extended from Scandinavia to Southern Italy and from France to Central Europe, sparing only Great Britain and Russia. Most of the issues were substantially the same as they had been in 1789: the demand for constitutional and representative government, civil liberties, the political unification of national groups, the abolition of aristocratic and ecclesiastical privilege,

The Revolution of 1848 in Paris. Storming of the Royal Palace

(The Bettmann Archive)

and an end to serfdom where it still existed. What was new in 1848 was that these demands were far more widespread and irrepressible than ever before. Moreover, the revolutionaries of 1848, unlike those of the past, demanded not only freedom from oppression, but also full inclusion in society. This was no longer the goal of relatively small groups of political and social reformers and intellectuals only. Whole classes and nations now demanded to be fully included in society—not as a privilege but as a right. They insisted that their rights, interests, and dignity be acknowledged and institutionalized, and it was this aim that predominated in 1848. Class consciousness and ideological passions reached a new high that year. The middle classes were now wealthier and more assertive than ever before; the rapidly growing working classes were better educated, organized, and more independent; and the nationalities and peasantries of Central and Eastern Europe were aroused against foreign rule and aristocratic oppression. This massive tide of discontent, aggravated by a rapid growth in population, social disruption caused by industrialization and urbanization, and serious crop failures in 1846 and 1847, could no longer be contained.

The year of revolution began with an uprising in January in Palermo, Sicily, against Emperor Ferdinand II. It was followed by similar revolts in most of the larger Italian cities. In France, Parisian republicans and radicals revolted against King Louis Philippe on February 22. Two days later, he abdicated and his chief minister, François Guizot, who had almost without exception opposed republican and socialist demands throughout the eighteen-year July Monarchy, resigned, and France became a republic once more. Events in France encouraged the Chartist movement in England, and its radical faction prepared itself to use force to back up Chartist demands for universal male suffrage, vote by ballot, equal electoral districts, payment of members of Parliament, and abolition of property qualifications for political candidates. The government rejected a Chartist petition containing millions of signatures, and clashes between Chartists and police occurred in Liverpool and elsewhere. Insurrection was barely averted when a plot to overthrow the government was revealed by a government spy. The menace of revolution passed in England, and complacent satisfaction with the stability of British institutions set in. But tens of thousands of discouraged Chartists emigrated to America, and the Chartist editor of *Red Revolution* wrote: "Who does not see and feel that he belongs to an enslaved and degraded class is a *fool*."

Inspired by the February uprising in Paris, workers and students rose in rebellion in mid-March in Vienna and Berlin. To Europe's amazement, Metternich resigned and fled to England, and the king of Prussia promised a constitution and liberal reform. Revolution quickly spread to other German states, and a parliament assembled in Frankfurt to draw up a federal constitution for the whole of Germany. Early in March, the Hungarian Diet, aroused by the popular nationalist leader, Louis Kossuth, demanded Hungary's independence from Vienna and drew up a new constitution, which the harassed and bewildered Emperor Ferdinand granted. He made similar concessions to the Czechs in April, following a revolt in Prague.

Centers of Revolution

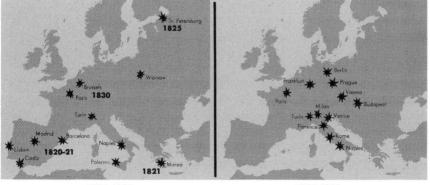

1820-1830   1848-1849

By the spring of 1848, some fifty separate insurrections had taken place, almost all in large towns where the new social classes with their discontents and ideologies were concentrated. Everywhere established governments had fallen with incredible swiftness. The French and Vienna governments had collapsed within a few days, Germany was in upheaval, and war raged in Italy. By May, new constitutions had been or were being prepared in France, Prussia and many other German states, Austria, Hungary, Bohemia, and several Italian states. Everywhere revolutionaries were busy planning republican governments, drawing up constitutions, preparing for national unification, and demanding an extension of the vote and guaranteed civil rights. And serfdom, where it still existed outside Russia—in Galicia, Bohemia, and Hungary—was abolished and the peasants were freed from legal control by their aristocratic landlords.

The tide began to turn in June. Conflict had arisen between the moderate and extremist revolutionaries; the old governments, stunned by events thus far, began to reassert themselves; and the peasants, once emancipated, turned against the city-centered revolutions and supported the governments in their decision to crush them by force. The moderate liberal government of wealthy bourgeois that had taken over in France in February turned against the radical and socialist rebels. It ordered the suppression of the national workshops originally proposed by Louis Blanc and implemented by the government to provide jobs for the mounting number of unemployed workers. Bitter class warfare raged in Paris between June 24 and 26. During these "Bloody June Days," some ten thousand persons were killed and eleven thousand insurgents taken prisoner. The ultimate victor in this political struggle was Napoleon's nephew, Louis Napoleon Bonaparte. He was elected president of the Second Republic in December 1848 because a large majority of voters, mostly peasants and bourgeois, revered his famous name and believed his promise to restore order. He did so, but only by assuming dictatorial powers and declaring himself emperor three years later.

The first victory of the counterrevolutionary old Vienna government also came in June of 1848 when Emperor Ferdinand ordered his ruthless but capable General Windischgrätz to bombard Prague where a Slav congress was in session to decide the future of Bohemia. The Austrian commander in Italy, Radetsky, then defeated the king of Sardinia at Custozza on July 25 and restored Lombardy and Venetia to Austria. In Hungary, where the Magyar majority led by Kossuth was repressing its own national minorities, the Croatians rose against the Budapest government in September under their leader, Jellachich, who appealed to Vienna for military aid. Thjis development precipitated a second insurrection in Vienna, which Windischgrätz managed to put down by the end of October after severe fighting. The counterrevolutionary Austrian army, Catholic clergy, and landowning aristocracy then forced Emperor Ferdinand to abdicate. He was succeeded in December by the eighteen-year-old Francis Joseph, who would rule until the dissolution of the Habsburg Empire sixty-eight years later.

During the early months of 1849, revolution flared up again in Germany and northern Italy. In Rome, a republic was proclaimed under three triumvirs; one of these was Mazzini, who had rushed back to Italy from England to take part in the republican uprising. But by March, the counterrevolution was in control. Radetsky defeated the king of Sardinia a second time at Novara on March 23; the new Habsburg emperor allowed Russian troops to crush the tenacious Magyars under Kossuth; Mazzini and his republicans were driven from Rome by a French army dispatched by Louis Napoleon.

Heartened by the success of counterrevolution elsewhere, King Frederick William IV of Prussia recalled his troops to Berlin in November 1848 and rescinded his promise to grant Prussia a constitution. The following March he spurned the Frankfurt Parliament's request that he become emperor of a unified Germany. The Frankfurt Parliament, an assembly of distinguished but politically inexperienced professional men and intellectuals, had, despite many difficulties, managed to write a constitution it hoped the Prussian king would accept and enforce as emperor. But the assembly had no military force or political authority of its own. Moreover, the majority of moderate liberal representatives refused to sanction popular insurrection or to yield to the democratic demands of radicals and thus deprived the assembly of the support and force of the lower classes. The assembly was also torn between those who wished to include Austria and other predominantly German areas of Eastern Europe in a unified Germany and those who wished to exclude Austria and settle for a more realistic smaller Germany under Prussian leadership. This issue aroused the apprehensions of the Slav assembly, meeting in the spring of 1848 in Prague. Its members feared German expansionism in Eastern Europe and the Czech members refused an invitation to attend the Frankfurt Parliament, further weakening the forces of revolution.

When the Prussian king rejected the assembly's offer to head a unified and constitutional Germany, the humiliated Frankfurt Parliament simply dispersed with nothing to show for its efforts. The few extremists who stayed on and tried to uphold the constitution by appeal to popular action were driven from Frankfurt in June by Prussian troops, who then proceeded to stamp out the remaining strongholds of insurrection in Saxony, Bavaria, and Baden. During the months and years that followed, thousands of disappointed German liberals emigrated to

America, enriching their new homeland with a wealth of skills and talents. But America's gain represented a further loss to the liberal cause in Germany; it had never been very bold or resolute in the first place, and now it had to knuckle under a new wave of reaction.

By the end of 1849, the last flames of revolution had been snuffed out. Judged by their own objectives, the 1848 revolutions had failed. The new social classes and ideologies had not won out over conservatism and reaction. On the contrary, the distrust between liberals and socialists, and among the various national groups in Central Europe, had only weakened the revolutionary cause and sown the seeds of bitter future conflicts. And none of these originally urban movements had very much to offer the peasants after their emancipation. The outcome of the revolutions also discredited the Jacobin, romantic, and Hegelian ideals which had inspired them. In a few small states—Denmark, Holland, Belgium, Switzerland, and Sardinia—constitutional government was more firmly entrenched than before 1848. But Italy and Germany remained divided, the Habsburg empire was still intact, Russia continued to be a fortress of reaction, and France lapsed into a new form of autocracy. Great Britain had made great progress toward political and social reform during the 1830s and 1840s, but not enough to satisfy the discontented workers and lower middle classes.

One thing the revolutions did accomplish, however, was to sweep from power the archaic Restoration governments and all they stood for and to pave the way for a whole new political, social, and spiritual reorganization of Western society. The 1848 revolutions themselves did not signify a new beginning. But they did climax more than a half century of upheaval, during which the foundations of the modern Western world were laid.

BIBLIOGRAPHY

General Works for the Modern Period

COATES, WILLSON H. and WHITE, HAYDEN V. *An Intellectual History of Western Europe.* vol. 2: *Since the French Revolution.* New York: McGraw-Hill Book Co., 1970.

DOBB, MAURICE. *Studies in the Development of Modern Capitalism.* Rev. ed. London: Routledge & Kegan Paul, 1963.

FRIEDELL, EGON A. A *Cultural History of the Modern Age.* Translated by C. F. Atkinson, vol. 3. New York: Alfred A. Knopf, 1933.

GOMBRICH, ERNST H. *The Story of Art.* Rev. ed. London: Phaidon, 1966.

HALLOWELL, JOHN H. *Main Currents in Modern Political Thought.* New York: Holt & Co., 1950.

HAUSER, ARNOLD. *The Social History of Art.* Translated by S. Godman. New York: Alfred A. Knopf, 1951.

HEER, FRIEDRICH. *Europe, Mother of Revolutions.* Translated by C. Kessler and J. Adcock. London: Weidenfeld & Nicolson, 1972.

HÖFFDING, HARALD. *A History of Modern Philosophy.* 2 vols. Translated by B. E. Meyer. London: Macmillan & Co., 1924.

MASON, STEPHEN F. *A History of the Sciences.* Rev. ed. New York: Collier, 1962.

MOSSE, GEORGE L. *The Culture of Western Europe: The Nineteenth and Twentieth Centuries.* Chicago: Rand, McNally, 1961.

MUMFORD, LEWIS. *Technics and Civilization.* New York: Harcourt, Brace & Co., 1934.

NEF, JOHN U. *Western Civilization Since the Renaissance: Peace, War, Industry and the Arts.* New York: Harper & Row, 1963.

ROLL, ERIC. *A History of Economic Thought.* Rev. ed. London: Faber & Faber, 1961.

SABINE, GEORGE H. *A History of Political Theory.* 3d ed. New York: Holt, Rinehart & Winston, 1961.

STROMBERG, ROLAND N. *An Intellectual History of Modern Europe.* New York: Appleton-Century-Crofts, 1966.

WILLIS, FRANK R. *Western Civilization, An Urban Perspective,* vol. 2: *From the Seventeenth Century to the Contemporary Age.* Lexington, Mass.: D. C. Heath & Co., 1973.

General Works for the Revolutionary Period

BREUNIG, CHARLES. *The Age of Revolution and Reaction, 1789-1850.* New York: W. W. Norton & Co., 1970.

HOBSBAWM, ERIC J. *The Age of Revolution, 1789-1848.* London: Weidenfeld & Nicolson, 1962.

LESLIE, R. F. *The Age of Transformation, 1789-1871.* London: Blandford Press, 1964.

TALMON, JACOB L. *Romanticism and Revolt, Europe 1815-1848.* London: Thames & Hudson, 1967.

The following four books in The Rise of Modern Europe series, edited by William L. Langer:

ARTZ, FREDERICK B. *Reaction and Revolution, 1814-1832.* New York: Harper & Brothers, 1934.

BRINTON, CRANE. *A Decade of Revolution, 1789-1799.* New York: Harper & Brothers, 1934.

BRUUN, GEOFFREY. *Europe and the French Imperium.* New York: Harper & Brothers, 1938.

LANGER, WILLIAM L. *Politics and Social Upheaval, 1832-1852.* New York: Harper & Brothers, 1969.

The following two books in The Fontana History of Europe series, edited by J. H. Plumb:

DROZ, JACQUES. *Europe between Revolutions, 1815-1848,* trans. by R. Baldick. London: Collins, 1967.

RUDÉ, GEORGE. *Revolutionary Europe, 1783-1815.* London: Collins, 1964.

The French Revolution and Napoleonic Europe

GERSHOY, LEO. *The French Revolution and Napoleon.* New York: Crofts, 1933.

GEYL, PIETER. *Napoleon: For and Against.* Translated by O. Renier. New Haven: Yale University Press, 1949.

GODECHOT, JACQUES L. *France and the Atlantic Revolution of the Eighteenth Century, 1770-1799.* Translated by H. Rowen. New York: Free Press, 1965.

HAMPSON, NORMAN. *The First European Revolution, 1776-1815.* London: Thames & Hudson, 1969.

KAFKER, FRANK A. and LAUX, JAMES M. eds. *The French Revolution: Conflicting Interpretations.* New York: Random House, 1968.

LEFEBVRE, GEORGES. *The Coming of the French Revolution.* Translated by R. R. Palmer. Princeton, N. J.: Princeton University Press, 1947.

———. *The French Revolution.* 2 vols. Translated by E. M. Evansons. New York: Columbia University Press, 1962.

———. *Napoleon.* Translated by H. F. Stockhold. London: Routledge & Kegan Paul, 1969.

MARKHAM, FELIX M. H. *Napoleon and the Awakening of Europe.* London: English Universities Press, 1954.

MATHIEZ, ALBERT. *The French Revolution.* Translated by C. A. Phillips. New York: Alfred A. Knopf, 1928.

PALMER, ROBERT R. *The Age of the Democratic Revolution.* 2 vols. Princeton, N. J.: Princeton University Press, 1959.

The Industrial Revolution

ASHTON, THOMAS S. *The Industrial Revolution, 1760-1830.* London: Oxford University Press, 1958.

Cambridge Economic History of Europe, vol. 6: *The Industrial Revolution and After.* Cambridge: The University Press, 1965.

CAMERON, RONDO E. *France and the Economic Development of Europe, 1800-1914.* Princeton, N. J.: Princeton University Press, 1966.

CLAPHAM, JOHN H. *The Economic Development of France and Germany, 1815-1914.* 4th ed. Cambridge: The University Press, 1961.

CLARK, GEORGE N. *The Idea of the Industrial Revolution.* Glasgow: Jackson, 1953.

FORBES, ROBERT J. and DIJKSTERHUIS, EDUARD J. *A History of Science and Technology.* Baltimore: Penguin Books, 1963.

GRAMPP, WILLIAM D. *The Manchester School of Economics.* Stanford, Calif.: Stanford University Press, 1960.

HAMEROW, THEODORE S. *Restoration, Revolution, Reaction: Economics and Politics in Germany, 1815-1871.* Princeton, N.J.: Princeton University Press, 1966.

HEILBRONER, ROBERT. *The Worldly Philosophers.* New York: Simon and Schuster, 1953.

HENDERSON, WILLIAM O. *The Industrialization of Europe, 1780-1914.* London: Thames & Hudson, 1969.

HOBSBAWM, ERIC J. *Industry and Empire: An Economic History of Britain since 1750.* London: Weidenfeld & Nicolson, 1968.

KUZNETS, SIMON S. *Modern Economic Growth: Rate, Structure, and Spread.* New Haven: Yale University Press, 1966.

LANDES, DAVID S. *The Unbound Prometheus: Technological Change and Industrial Development in Western Europe from 1750 to the Present.* London: Cambridge University Press, 1969.

MCMANNERS, JOHN. *Lectures on European History; Men, Machines and Freedom, 1789-1914.* Oxford: Blackwell, 1966.

POLANYI, KARL. *The Great Transformation: The Political and Economic Origins of our Time.* New York: Farrar & Rinehart, 1944.

ROSTOW, WALTER W. *The Stages of Economic Growth: A Non-Communist Manifesto.* Cambridge: The University Press, 1960.

THOMPSON, EDWARD F. *The Making of the English Working Class.* London: Gollancz, 1963.

WARD, JOHN T. *The Factory Movement, 1830-1855.* New York: St. Martin's Press, 1962.

The Spiritual Revolution: Romanticism and Idealism

ANCHOR, ROBERT. *Germany Confronts Modernization: German Culture and Society, 1790-1890.* Lexington, Mass.: D. C. Heath & Co., 1972.

ARIS, REINHOLD. *History of Political Thought in Germany from 1789 to 1815.* London: Allen & Unwin, 1936.

BARZUN, JACQUES. *Romanticism and the Modern Ego.* Boston: Little, Brown & Co., 1943.

———. *Berlioz and the Romantic Century.* Boston: Little, Brown & Co., 1950.

BATE, WALTER J. *From Classic to Romantic.* Cambridge, Mass.: Harvard University Press, 1946.

BOWRA, MAURICE. *The Romantic Imagination.* Cambridge, Mass.: Harvard University Press, 1957.

BRINTON, CRANE. *The Political Ideas of the English Romantics.* London: Oxford University Press 1926.

BRION, MARCEL. *Art of the Romantic Era.* Translated by D. Carroll. London: Thames & Hudson, 1966.

CLIVE, GEOFFREY. *The Romantic Enlightenment.* New York: Meridian Books, 1960.

EVANS, DAVID O. *Social Romanticism in France, 1830-1848.* Oxford: Clarendon Press, 1951.

FRIEDLAENDER, WALTER. *David to Delacroix.* Translated by R. Goldwater. Cambridge, Mass.: Harvard University Press, 1952.

FRYE, NORTHROP, ed. *Romanticism Reconsidered.* New York: Columbia University Press, 1963.

GLECKNER, ROBERT F. and ENSCO, GERALD E., eds. *Romanticism: Point of View.* Englewood Cliffs, N. J.: Prentice-Hall, 1962.

HARRIS, RONALD W. *Romanticism and the Social Order, 1780–1830.* London: Blandford, 1969.

HOOK, SYDNEY. *From Hegel to Marx.* New York: Reynal & Hitchcock, 1936.

HUGO, HOWARD, ed. *The Portable Romantic Reader.* New York: Viking Press, 1957.

KELLY, GEORGE A. *Idealism, Politics and History: Sources of Hegelian Thought.* Cambridge: The University Press, 1969.

LOVEJOY, ARTHUR O. *Essays in the History of Ideas.* Baltimore: Johns Hopkins Press, 1948.

LUKÁCS, GEORG. *Goethe and his Age.* Translated by R. Anchor. London: Merlin, 1968.

MacINTYRE, ALASDAIR ed. Hegel: *A Collection of Critical Essays.* Garden City, N.Y.: Anchor Books, 1972.

MARCUSE, HERBERT. *Reason and Revolution: Hegel and the Rise of Social Theory.* London and New York: Oxford University Press, 1941.

McLELLAN, DAVID. *The Young Hegelians and Karl Marx.* London: Macmillan Co., 1969.

PECKHAM, MORSE. *Beyond the Tragic Vision: The Quest for Identity in the Nineteenth Century.* New York: Brazilier, 1962.

PRAZ, MARIO. *The Romantic Agony.* Translated by A. Davidson. New York: Meridian Books, 1956.

REISS, HANS, ed. *Political Thought of the German Romantics, 1763–1815.* Oxford: Blackwell, 1955.

TALMON, JACOB L. *Political Messianism: The Romantic Phase.* New York: Praeger, 1960.

WOLFF, ROBERT P., ed. *Kant: A Collection of Critical Essays.* Garden City, N. Y.: Anchor Books, 1967.

The Restoration

BERTIER DE SAUVIGNY, GUILLAUME DE. *Metternich and his Times.* Translated by P. Ryde. London: Longmans, Green, 1962.

FERRERO, GUGLIELMO. *The Restoration of Europe: Talleyrand and the Congress of Vienna, 1814–1815.* Translated by T. R. Jaechel. New York: G. P. Putnam's Sons, 1941.

GRUNWALD, CONSTANTIN D. *Metternich.* Translated by D. Todd. London: Falcon, 1953.

KISSINGER, HENRY A. *A World Restored.* Boston, Houghton Mifflin Co., 1957.

NICOLSON, HAROLD G. *The Congress of Vienna.* New York: Harcourt, Brace & Co., 1946.

SCHENK, HANS G. *The Aftermath of the Napoleonic Wars: The Concept of Europe—An Experiment.* London: Kegan Paul, Trench, Trubner, 1947.

Liberalism

BULLOCK, ALAN and SHOCK, MAURICE, eds. *The Liberal Tradition: From Fox to Keynes.* London: Black, 1956.

HALÉVY, ELIE. *The Growth of Philosophical Radicalism.* Translated by M. Morris. London: Faber & Gweyer, 1928.

KRIEGER, LEONARD. *The German Idea of Freedom.* Boston: Beacon Press, 1957.

LASKIE, HAROLD. *The Rise of Liberalism.* London: Allen & Unwin, 1936.

LETWIN, SHIRLEY R. *The Pursuit of Certainty.* Cambridge: The University Press, 1965.

MANUEL, FRANK E. *The Prophets of Paris.* Cambridge, Mass.: Harvard University Press, 1962.

ROHR, DONALD G. *The Origins of Social Liberalism in Germany.* Chicago: University of Chicago Press, 1963.

RUGGIERO, GUIDO DE. *History of European Liberalism.* Translated by R. G. Collingwood. Oxford: The University Press, 1927.

SCHAPIRO, JACOB S. *Liberalism and the Challenge of Fascism: Social Forces in England and France, 1815–1870.* New York: McGraw-Hill, 1949.

SIMON, WALTER M., ed. *French Liberalism, 1789–1848.* New York: John Wiley & Sons, 1972.

THOMAS, RICHARD H. *Liberalism, Nationalism, and the German Intellectuals, 1822–1847.* Cambridge: Heffer, 1951.

Conservatism

EPSTEIN, KLAUS. *The Genesis of German Conservatism, 1770–1806.* Princeton, N.J.: Princeton University Press, 1966.

KIRK, RUSSELL. *The Conservative Mind: Burke to Santayana.* Chicago: Henry Regnery Co., 1953.

MELLON, STANLEY. *The Political Uses of History: A Study of Historians in the French Restoration.* Stanford, Calif.: Stanford University Press, 1958.

RÉMOND, RÉNE. *The Right Wing in France: From 1815 to De Gaulle.* Translated by J. M. Laux. Philadelphia: University of Pennsylvania Press, 1966.

VIERECK, PETER R. *Conservatism Revisited.* New York: Charles Scribner's Sons, 1949.

WOODWARD, ERNEST L. *Three Studies in European Conservatism.* London: Constable, 1929.

Socialism

CARR, EDWARD H. *Studies in Revolution.* London: Macmillan & Co., 1950.

CAUTE, DAVID. *The Left in Europe since 1789.* New York: McGraw-Hill, 1966.

COLE, GEORGE D. H. *A History of Socialist Thought.* 4 vols. London: Macmillan & Co., 1953–58.

EGBERT, DONALD D. *Social Radicalism in the Arts.* New York: Alfred A. Knopf, 1970.

GRAY, ALEXANDER. *The Socialist Tradition: From Moses to Lenin.* London: Longmans, Green, 1946.

LANDAUER, CARL. *European Socialism: A History of Ideas and Movements from the Industrial Revolution to Hitler's Seizure of Power.* 2 vols. Berkeley: University of California Press, 1960.

LICHTHEIM, GEORGE. *A Short History of Socialism.* New York: Praeger, 1970.

MANUEL, FRANK E. *The New World of Henri Saint-Simon.* Cambridge, Mass.: Harvard University Press, 1956.

PLAMENATZ, JOHN. *The Revolutionary Movement in France, 1815–1871.* London: Longmans, Green, 1952.

WILSON, EDMUND. *To the Finland Station.* New York: Harcourt, Brace & Co., 1940.

Nationalism

BARNARD, FREDERICK M. *Herder's Social and Political Thought: From Enlightenment to Nationalism.* Oxford: Clarendon Press, 1965.

KEDOURI, ELIE. *Nationalism.* Rev. ed. New York: Praeger, 1961.

KOHN, HANS. *Prophets and Peoples: Studies in Nineteenth-Century Nationalism.* New York: Macmillan Co., 1946.

MINOGUE, KENNETH R. *Nationalism.* New York: Basic Books, 1967.

SHAFER, BOYD C. *Nationalism: Myth and Reality.* New York: Harcourt, Brace & Co., 1955.

SNYDER, LOUIS L. *The Meaning of Nationalism.* New Brunswick, N. J.: Rutgers University Press, 1954.

The 1848 Revolutions

DUVEAU, GEORGES. *1848: The Making of a Revolution.* Translated by A. Carter. New York: Vintage Books, 1968.

FEJTÖ, FRANCOIS, ed. *The Opening of an Era, 1848.* London: Wingate, 1948.

HAMMEN, OSCAR J. *The Red '48ers: Karl Marx and Friedrich Engels.* New York: Charles Scribner's Sons, 1969.

LOUGEE, ROBERT W. *Midcentury Revolution, 1848: Society and Revolution in France and Germany.* Lexington, Mass.: D. C. Heath & Co., 1972.

NAMIER, LEWIS B. *The Revolution of the Intellectuals.* Oxford: The University Press, 1946.

WHITRIDGE, ARNOLD. *Men in Crisis: The Revolutions of 1848.* New York: Charles Scribner's Sons, 1949.

AGE OF MATERIALISM: 1848–1880

AFTERMATH OF REVOLUTION

The 1848 revolutions failed to achieve the victory of liberalism, democracy, and social justice. But they did succeed in sweeping away the tottering structure of the Restoration. Gone was the high-minded romantic and idealistic utopianism that had come in the wake of the triple revolution. But gone, too, was the die-hard conservatism of Metternich, which had been based on a hopelessly obsolete alliance between throne and altar and a policy of containment of the newly emerging forces of modernization. A new mood now settled over Europe and the West: a blend of disillusionment with the old and fascination with the new; a distrust of intellectual speculation and infatuation with hard facts; an indifference toward the past and a boldly optimistic attitude toward the future.

This new mood manifested itself in the advent of *Realpolitik,* politics based on power rather than on ideals, whose leading practitioners were Napoleon III, emperor of France from 1852 to 1870, and Count Camillo Benso di Cavour and Otto von Bismarck, the architects of Italian and German national unification during this same period. The new mood manifested itself also in Karl Marx's tough-minded revolutionary theories, which claimed to be more realistic than the "utopian" socialism of the first half of the century, which Marx scorned. Liberals themselves, originally dedicated to the ideals of liberty, equality, and fraternity, now concerned themselves more with material well-being and with strengthening the political and social position of the middle classes. The new mood pervaded Victorian England, proud, prosperous, and practical. It was evident in the triumph of positivist philosophy, Darwinian science, and in the enthusiastic acceptance of industrial civilization, symbolized by the Great Exhibition held in London in 1851, the first international exhibition of its kind. Improved technology, notably the railroad and steamship, transformed the great capitals of London, Paris, and Berlin into world cities, bustling hubs of global commercial and industrial networks. To the well-off, the world city represented opportunity, fashion, and taste, epitomized by the *gaieté parisienne*. To the poor, it was a place of uncertain employment and hunger, overcrowding and disease, symbolized by London's East End. The new mood also found expression in the rise of the social novel and the school of naturalism, both of which emphasized the impact of the environment on human character and action.

Materialism, then, came to pervade all spheres of life in the Western world during the third quarter of the nineteenth century. It was more of a *Zeitgeist* than an ideology in the strict sense, since no one particular social class monopolized it. True, the liberal middle classes were materialism's principal advocates and beneficiaries. But this was more because they were now the dominant economic and social stratum than because there was any special affinity between liberal and materialistic values. Charles Dickens and Matthew Arnold, John Stuart Mill and Alexis de Tocqueville, all good liberals, were stern critics of the adverse effects of excessive materialism on the quality of human life. By the same token, reactionaries and radicals could be every bit as materialistic as the liberal middle classes. Napoleon III and Bismarck fully appreciated the value of science and technology, power and prosperity in sustaining essentially reactionary regimes. So too did the French count Joseph Arthur de Bogineau, founder of "scientific" racism, and the Prussian historian Heinrich von Treitschke, in formulating reactionary ideology. Radical Marxists in turn prided themselves on the discovery and demonstration that material conditions govern the historical process as a whole.

Materialism triumphed after mid-century because *all* preindustrial intellectual, moral, and social models, whether conservative, liberal, or radical, were now obsolete. In order to survive at all, these movements had to adapt to the new urban and industrial setting, to the now indisputable dominance of the middle classes and growing importance of the factory proletariat, and to the reality of emerging mass society. Even the critics of materialism, to be effective, had to learn to speak its language and appreciate its importance. What occurred during the age of materialism, and under its aegis, was the transition of those Western countries where tradition was most eroded from preindustrial to industrial societies. This transition in turn marked the completion of the secularization of Western culture and laid the foundations of contemporary history.

INDUSTRIALISM ON THE MARCH

During the first half of the nineteenth century, industrialization had been confined mainly to England and a tiny corner of northwestern Europe. By mid-century, it had spread to parts of France and Germany, to northern Italy and western Hungary, and to Bohemia and the environs of Vienna. During the third quarter of the century, the United States, Russia, and Japan also began to industrialize. All of these countries began to enjoy real and unprecedented prosperity in the Victorian age. Its basis was expansion of the heavy industries related to coal, iron, and steel. In 1856, Henry Bessemer perfected the technique of converting pig iron into steel. The Siemens-Martin process, developed during the sixties, made possible the refinement of low-grade ores and scrap

Factory in Tewkesbury, England, around 1860.

(The Granger Collection).

iron. And in 1878, the introduction of the Thomas-Gilchrist process for removing phosphorous from ore made large, but hitherto unsuitable, deposits available for steel production. These advances in turn acted as a spur to the mining industry, which began to scar the landscape of the English Midlands, Belgium, French Lorraine, and the Saar and Ruhr valleys in Germany. By the end of the century, steel had become the main metal in industrial construction.

Change was also rapid in the fields of transportation and communication. Most of Europe's railroads were constructed during the third quarter of the century. The Union Pacific Line, completed in 1865, linked the East and West coasts of the United States and capped America's westward expansion. Russia, also eager to push to the Pacific, began railroad construction inthe seventies. The first refrigerator car was used on railroads in 1851, thereby facilitating the transportation of perishable products over long distances. By 1900, railroad lines stretched across Europe to Constantinople and Vladivostok and across the United States from New York to San Francisco. In 1857, the *Great Eastern,* a ship built entirely of steel and equipped with a screw propeller, was launched, and from it the first transatlantic cable was laid in 1866. Other submarine cables were laid during the seventies, linking Europe with the Far East. By 1870, steel had replaced wood in the construction of ships, and soon after the steamship, equipped with a coal-fuelled compound engine and driven by a screw propeller, supplanted the wind-driven sailing vessel for water transport. During the seventies, the electric streetcar made its first appearance and soon replaced horse-drawn vehicles as the chief means of urban public transport. The electric telegraph was invented in 1844 and the telephone in 1876. Thomas A. Edison inaugurated a whole new era of artificial lighting with his perfection of the incandescent bulb in 1878. The typewriter, high-speed printing presses, and the inexpensive production of paper also made their appearance during the seventies, as did the Universal Postal Union, which was established to regulate international mail service.

Technological advance occurred also in the agricultural and chemical industries. The mechanization of farm equipment made possible the cultivation of vast new acreages in the Americas, Australia, and Asian Russia. The new food supply reduced the threat of famine and stimulated population growth. The chemical industry contributed artificial fertilizers, improved seed strains, and new breeds of domestic animals. It also developed alkalies, soaps and bleaches, animal and vegetable oils, drugs, and synthetic dyes. In 1867, Alfred Nobel discovered a safe method for making dynamite from nitroglycerin, and twenty years later he developed an improved variety of gunpowder that would revolutionize the armaments industry. In the field of hygiene, Joseph Lister,

Robert Koch, and Louis Pasteur evolved the germ theory of disease, which created a whole new attitude toward sanitation and public health and led to the development of vaccines and other measures of disease prevention.

The pace of industrial expansion was quickened by the formation of joint stock companies, stock exchanges, trusts, and investment banks, all of which made possible the large-scale and more efficient production of goods. The small business was still the bedrock of Western economic life; but the large new financial institutions, which raised money by selling stocks and bonds to a public tempted by the prospect of huge profits, were the chief impetus to industrial expansion. Eventually, they would supersede the small business as the dominant economic unit. Moreover, governments, quick to see that such institutions could add to national strength and prosperity, not only relaxed economic restrictions, but actively aided big business through state-sponsored banks, subsidies, tariffs, and tax concessions. Governments also adopted the practice of selling stocks and bonds to the public, thus freeing themselves from dependence on loans from private banks. Consequently, the new financial institutions, headed by shrewd and ambitious men and sanctioned by both government and the investing public, quickly became hallowed symbols of Western society. True, the economies of the industrially advanced countries went through periodic cycles of prosperity and depression. But the depressions were never so severe nor so prolonged as to shake the public's faith in the blessings of industrial capitalism.

Social Impact of Industrialization

Such drastic changes were bound to have far-reaching effects. The new increase in food supply and manufactured goods resulted in a population increase that swelled the labor force and created the consumer demand necessary to industrial expansion. Although many jobs in old industries were eliminated, factory production created many more new ones and succeeded in absorbing much of the increase in the labor force. The new mode of large-scale factory production, improved transportation, and the abolition of serfdom in Russia and all Western European countries and of slavery in the United States by the early 1860's—all combined to stimulate massive migrations to the cities, migrations which have continued to the present day. Bad as conditions were for the laboring poor in the burgeoning new industrial centers, conditions were worse, generally speaking, for the rural poor, despite many attempts throughout the century to romanticize rural life. In quest of a better life elsewhere, some seventy percent of Europe's population migrated to the cities, causing so great an increase in their size and number as to trans-

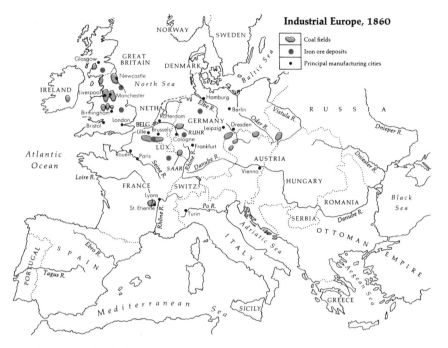

Industrial Europe, 1860

form Europe within but a generation or two from a predominantly rural to a predominantly urban society.

This transformation signified more than a mere redistribution and reorganization of population. It thrust to the fore new social types, generated new attitudes and aspirations, and created new problems and possibilities. Money and securities displaced land as the chief form of wealth. The new business classes, shrewd, ambitious, and greedy, displaced the wealthy landed classes, motivated by honor, tradition, and good breeding, as leaders of the new society. The urban proletariat, liberated from the land only to be enslaved by the factory and the "iron law" of wages, displaced the peasantry as the principal exploited class.

The new industrial society consisted of "two nations," as Benjamin Disraeli, British prime minister from 1874 to 1880, put it: those in command of things and those who were things to be commanded. The one inhabited London's opulent West End, the other its impoverished East End. The one occupied fashionable town houses, the other slum tenements. The one grew rich from labor, the other groaned under it. During the early part of the century, most industrial workers had acquiesced to middle-class political leadership. After the failure of the 1848 revolutions, however, workers became increasingly aware of the divergence between their interests and those of the middle classes, and they began to form economic and political organizations, such as trade unions and socialist parties, designed to promote their interests. But both classes were products of industrialization and depended upon it for their very existence. Despite the hypocrisy and inequities, the ruthlessness and miseries it engendered, industrialization was too far along by the Victorian age for either class to seriously consider turning back.

Preindustrial patterns of thought and behavior were not compatible with the impersonal and anonymous ethos of the new urban order. Those who migrated to the cities were forced to seek new ties and attachments, new moral and intellectual standards. Occupational and political affiliations began to supplant traditional local, family, and religious ties. The population concentrated in the cities, uprooted, diverse, and restless, was much more susceptible to the influence of new ideological trends than the more stable and integrated population scattered throughout the countryside. Cities were becoming the centers of mass political and social movements, breeding grounds of radical doctrines and revolutionary organizations, of reform movements and religious sects, of professional societies and discontented intelligentsias. Newspapers and periodicals shaped public opinion, and public opinion became a force that decision-makers had to reckon with. Men in the cities were changing the world, but they were being changed in turn by the world they were making.

Another significant effect of industrialism was the sharp increase in the functions and powers of the state. Government supervision was necessary to carry out such major reforms as the abolition of serfdom, the enforcement of labor legislation, and the management of urban growth. Public transportation, provision for sanitary facilities, and the maintenance and equipment of standing armies and navies—all had to be administered, regulated, and paid for. Governments were called upon to stimulate the economy, to help build and maintain railroads, to construct highways and harbors, and to operate postal and telegraph systems. The growing demands on the state required the recruitment of ever larger numbers of civil servants, resulting in an enormous expansion of government bureaucracy. The cost of enlarged government could be met only by an elaborate, efficiently administered system of taxation made possible by increased productivity and the availability of more money.

Governments, however, were by no means disinterested servants of the people. Increased bureaucratic authority, compulsory military service, public education, official censorship, and the mass media all enabled governments to control and manipulate their populations more effectively than ever before. The expansion of governmental powers, although indispensable to industrial society, at the same time posed the threat of a new political tyranny. The twentieth-century totalitarian goal of a completely controlled society still lay far in the future, but one of the seeds of its growth lay in the rapid enlargement of state power during the Victorian age.

The principal political ideologies of the past had all distrusted big government. Once it came into being, however, they had to learn to cope with it—through propaganda and ideological indoctrination, by forming mass political parties and training professional political leaders, and by mobilizing public opinion. During the third quarter of the century, most people were still too preoccupied with material progress to be overly concerned with the dangers of big government. But it was gradually becoming apparent, especially to the oppressed, the disenfranchised, and the exploited, that regardless of what governments professed, they constituted powerful vested interests in their own right, which, like any other vested interest, sought to augment themselves. Precisely because the state now monopolized unprecedented power, political issues became more urgent and consequential than ever before.

Critics of Industrialization

Protests against industrialization are as old as the Industrial Revolution itself. The Luddites and machine-breakers, whom the machine threw out of work, were among the first to oppose it. Farmers complained that the iron horse poisoned the air and frightened the animals. As early as 1829, the great Scottish moralist, Thomas Carlyle, warned against the evils of mechanization in his essay, "Signs of the Times." In 1835, Alexis de Tocqueville, on a visit to England, described the city of Manchester as a "foul drain, a filthy sewer. . . . Here humanity attains its most complete development and its most brutish; here civilization works its miracles and civilized man is turned almost into a savage." And, in 1845, Friedrich Engels published his almost classic study of industrial exploitation, *Condition of the Working Classes in England in 1844.*

During the Victorian age, the voices of criticism mounted. Some of England's greatest novelists, notably Charles Dickens, produced unforgettable literary descriptions of London's teeming poor. Gustave Doré and George Cruickshank depicted their sufferings visually in paintings, book illustrations, and engravings. John Ruskin and William Morris criticized industrialization as being destructive of the aesthetic and social environment. To these could be added the apprehensions of a host of lesser commentators and whole volumes of official reports on the problems and damaging effects of industry on the physical and human environment. More recently, Lewis Mumford has called nineteenth-century industrial production the "paleotechnic phase" of technology, a phase in which it ceased to utilize and began to exploit and interfere with

Over London by Rail. engraving of working-class slum by Gustave Doré, 1872.
(The Granger Collection)

natural processes. He described it as a phase in which an abrupt shift of emphasis from human to strictly monetary values occurred, one in which labor ceased to be a means to an end and became an all-consuming end in itself, never-ending drudgery for the exploited and exploiter alike. Jacques Ellul, in *The Technological Society* (1954), went so far as to claim that technology tends to assume a life of its own and to usurp and exorcise all competing systems of values; that it must ultimately enslave all mankind to its dehumanizing processes and effects.

Yet, to this day the critics of industrialization, although numerous, persistent, and persuasive in their argumentation, have had curiously little effect on the actual course of events. One reason is that they have never represented a large and powerful constituency; even less have they represented the industrialists and industrial working classes, from whose ranks few of the critics sprang. If anything, trade unions, socialist parties, and underdeveloped countries usually have called for more, not less, industrial development. Moreover, critics have rarely suggested a realistic alternative to industrialism other than a return to a vaguely defined, supposedly superior preindustrial past. Many men have admired Thoreau, but few have imitated him. Finally, the critics have done little to explain why industrialization, despite its many serious drawbacks, has swept and continues to sweep all before it. What powerful motives, what expectations, what attitudes toward nature, man, and the future drive mankind, and especially Western mankind, in search of more elaborate, expensive, and potentially dangerous technology? These questions have yet to be satisfactorily answered.

To the Victorians, certainly, industrialism meant liberation from the age-old Damocles' sword of scarcity and famine. It meant the possibility of a longer, healthier, more secure life. It meant social opportunity and the prospect of untold profits and power. It meant everything that went into the making of the wonderful myth that so captivated the Victorian imagination: Progress. The problems posed by advanced industrialization—exhaustion of natural resources, pollution of the environment, and enslavement of man to the machine—did not yet seem beyond solution and in any case were outweighed by the advantages. As quaint and cocksure as the Victorian age may seem from the vantage point of the late twentieth century, it produced and adjusted to an industrial environment that survived the age itself and has since gained momentum throughout the West and the world.

REALPOLITIK AND NATIONALISM

Politics is always concerned, to a greater or lesser extent, with power. But rarely do politicians openly proclaim that power is the only, or primary, guideline of their actions, as Bismarck did in his famous statement: "The great questions of the day will not be decided by speeches and resolutions of majorities, but by blood and iron." Several factors favored the upsurge of *Realpolitik*. One was widespread disillusionment with the political idealism that had failed in the 1848 revolutions. Another was the rapid expansion of governmental functions discussed above. A third was the economic and technological developments that enabled governments to function more effectively: improved business and accounting methods, improved transportation and communications, and improved armaments and military procedures. Finally, there was the growing enthusiasm for materialistic values, which politicians could not appeal to without fear of offending or alienating public opinion.

Realpolitik was autocratic politics. It fared best among peoples deeply divided internally and lacking a strong sense of national identity and broad, unifying, representative institutions. Even in England, however, widely admired for her national unity and time-tested political institutions, paternalism and arrogance were marked features of Queen Victoria's long reign from 1837 to 1901. Even the dignified, tradition-bound Francis Joseph I, Habsburg emperor from 1848 to 1916, resorted increasingly during his long reign to the methods of *Realpolitik* to cope with the rising tide of nationalism among his multinational subjects—a tide that finally ruined his empire. But the classic lands of *Realpolitik* were France, Italy, and Germany. And its classic practitioners were Napoleon III (1808-1873), Count Camillo Benso di Cavour (1810-1861), and Otto von Bismarck (1815-1898).

These statesmen were definitely not power-crazed fanatics. On the contrary, they were cool and calculating Machiavellians, who pursued well-defined ends. Napoleon III's goal was to restore to France the greatness and hegemony in world affairs that it had enjoyed under his famous uncle, Napoleon Bonaparte. Cavour and Bismarck aimed to bring about the long overdue national unification of their respective countries and to raise them to the status of great powers. All three leaders subscribed to the view that politicians must seek what is attainable, not necessarily what is desirable; the latter approach, they thought, had been the fatal flaw of their predecessors. It was their methods, not their goals, that were new. None was a conservative, liberal, or radical in the then accepted sense of these terms. They made use of any ideology when and as it served their purposes. Nor did they side with any one particular social class. For although they were all men of aristocratic background, they did not allow their personal conservative leanings to interfere with their expedient dealings with all social classes, aristocratic, bourgeois, and proletarian, according to their own conception of the national interest. These practitioners of *Realpolitik* were shrewd opportunists who firmly believed that, although power may not prescribe what a politician ought to do, it defines the scope of what he can do. Bismarck, especially, thought in terms of a "revolution from above," by which he meant the modernization of Germany under the aegis of autocratic government.

Napoleon III and the Second Empire

France had been deeply divided socially and ideologically since the French Revolution. The shaky Second Republic, founded in 1848 by an uneasy coalition of discontented workers, bourgeois, and intellectuals, was overthrown by Louis Napoleon in a coup d'état, and France succumbed to autocracy in 1851. A year later Louis Napoleon took the title Napoleon III and established the Second Empire, which lasted until France's disastrous defeat by the Prussians at Sedan in 1870. Influenced by the social teachings of Saint-Simon, Napoleon III instituted a program of state socialism, dictated from above but designed to benefit and unite all members of society. On the one hand, he suppressed political opposition, censored the press, reduced the legislature to a puppet body, and established an extensive police system. On the other, he expanded credit and made money available on easy terms to entrepreneurs of every sort—farmers, industrialists, builders, and shippers. He completed France's railway lines and developed the harbors of Marseilles, Brest, and Le Havre into centers of world shipping. He financed housing for workers, hospitals, orphanages, and extensive public works programs. After 1859, the high point of his career, he relaxed some restrictions on political opposition, granted amnesties, and advanced the cause of compulsory education. The Suez Canal, a project of French origin, was built between 1859 and 1869.

The new emperor's most glorious achievement was his transformation of Paris from a picturesque medieval city of narrow, winding streets into a modern city with broad, straight boulevards and avenues, spacious plazas and parks, and splendid architectural vistas. Under the direction of his able appointee to this task, Baron Georges Eugène Haussmann (1809–1891), Paris was provided with an adequate and safe water supply, an underground sewage system, and gas lighting. That the new city plan made the movement of troops and artillery through the streets easier and made revolts and the erection of barricades in workers' quarters more difficult did not detract from its splendor. Under Napoleon III, Paris became the showplace of the Western world. French and foreign intellectuals and artists congregated there and challenged the world with their advanced ideas and techniques. Parisians and visitors from everywhere could enjoy the Latin Quarter and sidewalk cafes, the then new department stores and numerous art exhibitions. They could be entertained also by the daring cancan, the cabaret shows, and the urbane music of Jacques Offenbach. During the Second Empire, Paris emerged as a sophisticated and cosmopolitan center that inspired admiration throughout the civilized world.

But there was another side to the Second Empire. The government's easy credit policy invited shady speculation and corruption in government. Louis Napoleon failed to win the allegiance of the working classes and intellectuals. In foreign affairs, he was no match for his famous uncle. He did succeed in establishing closer relations with England and in gaining some military prestige during the Crimean War with Russia (1854–1856). However, he became inextricably embroiled in Italian affairs, antagonized Austria, and suffered a severe setback in his imperial venture into Mexico in the 1860s. The final disaster was his crushing defeat by Prussia in a war that could have been avoided, a war that in 1870 brought the Second Empire to an end and a new German empire into being.

As a result of the Franco-Prussian War, France lost two of her northern provinces, Alsace and Lorraine, most of her iron deposits, and large tracts of valuable forest and farm land. Over 1.5 million of her citizens were transferred to the newly created German empire. Not least, French national pride had been dealt a severe blow, and the victorious Prussians exploited this humiliation to the full, laying the foundation for a future war between the two countries. In 1871, workers and radicals in Paris revolted against the new French government, headed by Adolphe Thiers, and plunged France into a civil war that lasted three months and ended in the defeat and mass execution of the rebels. Amid such bitterness and division, a new republic, the so-called Third Republic, was barely voted into power in the elections of 1875 and managed to survive constant crises until the outbreak of the Second World War. Napoleon III left France a mixed legacy: a modern economy and thriving culture on the one hand, but a record of defeat, cynicism, wounded national pride, and social conflict on the other. Both sides were the fruit of his *Realpolitik*.

Cavour and Italian Unification

The piecemeal unification of Italy between 1859 and 1870 was largely the work of Cavour. When he became prime minister of the Kingdom of Sardinia in 1852, Italy was still divided, as it had been for centuries, into about a half-dozen large states and several smaller ones, mostly under foreign rule. Cavour, like most of his countrymen, deplored this state of affairs and dreamed of a strong, united Italy. But he did not believe that unification could be achieved by the conspiratorial and revolutionary methods practiced by other prominent leaders of the nationalist movement, notably Mazzini and Garibaldi. Such methods, he had learned from the events of 1848, succeeded only in alienating the papacy and other powerful Italian interests. Cavour himself was a moderate liberal, a constitutional monarchist, and a wealthy landowner who had little sympathy for popular uprisings or republican sentiments. But he was also a "realistic" politician, willing to do whatever proved necessary to achieve his ultimate goal of unification. Thus, although he disapproved of republicans and radicals, he was willing to cooperate with them when necessary. Although he disliked war, he was willing to wage war to advance national interests. And although he distrusted foreign governments, he realized that, without their help, unification would be impossible.

Cavour, like Napoleon III, was an apostle of modernization. His first step as prime minister of Sardinia, the only native Italian dynasty, was to make it a model of progress, efficiency, and fair government that other Italians would admire. He supported the building of railroads and docks, the improvement of agriculture, and the development of trade. He worked hard to promote constitutional and parliamentary practices in government and to reduce the political and economic power of the Church in his state. In 1854, he brought Sardinia into the Crimean War on the side of England and France in the hope of gaining support for Italian unification at the peace negotiations. Four years later, he succeeded in manipulating Napoleon III into an alliance against Austria. Although Cavour gained less than he expected when France concluded a hasty peace with Austria in 1859, the war gave Sardinia control of most of northern and central Italy. By 1860, there existed a north Italian kingdom, the papal states in the center of Italy, and the Kingdom of the Two Sicilies in the south.

Giuseppe Garibaldi (1807–1882), a colorful and romantic popular leader, the opposite of Cavour both politically and temperamentally, made the next move by invading Sicily in 1860 with a band of volunteers known as "Garibaldi's Thousand." This expedition, supported only reluctantly by Cavour, was successful. By autumn, the south was freed from Bourbon rule and joined with Sardinia, and Garibaldi was moving north toward Rome. When Cavour died in 1861, all Italy except Rome, which was still under papal rule, and the northern province of Venetia, which was still in Austrian hands, was united under the leadership of Sardinia. A parliament representing all of Italy except those two territories officially proclaimed the Kingdom of Italy with the Sardinian ruler, Victor Emmanuel II, as king. Venetia was added in 1866, as a reward for Italian aid to Prussia in her war with Austria; Rome was annexed in 1870 after French troops, stationed there since 1849 to protect the pope against republican forces, were forced to withdraw to face the Prussians in the north.

Italy was at last a unified nation, the realization of a centuries-long dream of an Italian *Risorgimento,* or resurgence. But, in contrast to the other Western nation-states, the new Italy was not the political expression of a popular national will, nor the product of a long, gradual process of historical evolution. If anything, the passage of time had reinforced the strong regional differences within Italy and the role of the papacy and foreign powers in Italian affairs. Unification was imposed in the form of a "revolution from above;" it owed more to Cavour's political genius and the circumstances of international relations than to anything else.

Consequently, the new Italian state posed as many problems as it solved. Extreme nationalists were dissatisfied with the territorial limits of the new state because regions with large Italian populations, such as Nice and Savoy, had been ceded to France by Cavour in exchange for the alliance against Austria. Other regions, such as the Tyrol, were still in

Austrian possession. The pope and his successors, deprived of Rome and all other papal lands except the papacy itself, remained unreconciled to the new state until 1929. This policy created a conflict for the Italian between his Catholic and his patriotic loyalties, widening the rift between church and state. In addition, southern Italy was too steeped in premodern ways of life to adapt to industrialization and absorption into a highly centralized modern state. Finally, the political base of the new Italy was too narrow. Only about six hundred thousand out of a population of twenty million had the vote before 1913, when suffrage was significantly broadened. Most Italians were excluded from participation in political life during the critical formative decades of the new state. The government, which was neither truly representative nor subject to public scrutiny, could not respond effectively to public opinion or remain free from corruption. Like France, therefore, the new Italy reflected both the strengths and the weaknesses of *Realpolitik*.

BISMARCK AND THE SECOND GERMAN EMPIRE   Bismarck personified *Realpolitik* in its purest form. Almost single-handedly, he transformed Germany from a loose congeries of large and small states into a single unified state that, based on Prussian military might, would become the most powerful country in Europe after 1870. This was Bismarck's goal from the time he entered politics in 1862 to the end of his career in 1890 as chancellor of the newly created Second German Empire. He achieved it by a combination of aggression abroad and the exercise of autocratic authority at home. In the Danish War of 1864, the first of three well-planned and executed wars, he established Prussia as the center of German national sentiment. In the second, the Austro-Prussian War of 1866, he eliminated Austria from competition for leadership in German affairs and united all of northern Germany behind Prussia. In the third, the Franco-Prussian War of 1870, Prussia crushed France and swept the remaining German states, except Austria, into a new political structure officially proclaimed the Second German Empire in 1871. The rest of his career Bismarck devoted to consolidating his creation and constructing a protective alliance system with Russia, Austria, and Italy.

The unification of Germany was even less a product of the will and consent of the people than was Italian unification. It was a Prussian, not a German, achievement: the result of a Prussian military victory over a foreign country in a struggle abroad. Princes, aristocrats, and bourgeois; conservatives, liberals, and nationalists; democrats, socialists, and religious groups—they all had little to do with the unification of Germany. Bismarck, although personally partial to the interests of the ultraconservative Junker class he was born into, spoke for no particular social class but skillfully manipulated all of them to his own ends. All actions and policies that shaped the new German state during the first twenty years

Kaiser Wilhelm I's Proclamation of the German Empire at Versailles, January 18, 1871. Painting by Anton von Werner.

(Culver Pictures, Inc).

of its existence originated with him: the persecution of the Catholics in the 1870s and of the socialists in the 1880s; the amalgamation of the wealthier of the new industrial class with the old landed Junkers; the complicated system of foreign alliances formed to protect the new state and guarantee its hegemony on the continent; the social welfare programs enacted to undercut liberal and socialist programs; and his own personal role as peacemaker in Europe. Bismarck's legacy to Germany was impressive. It included a viable state, an alliance system to protect it, a federal constitution, a burgeoning economy, an advanced social welfare system, and even the beginnings of a colonial empire. But Bismarck achieved all this by undermining representative institutions and practices, weakening the political party system, encouraging social and religious divisiveness, and discouraging the spirit of self-determination.

Nation-building Throughout the Western World

Nation-building during the Victorian era, while advanced by *Realpolitik,* was not confined to countries in which it prevailed. Prussia's defeat of Austria in 1866 prompted the weakened Vienna government to conclude an agreement, known as the *Ausgleich* or Compromise, with Hungary in 1867. The *Ausgleich* satisfied the national aspirations of the Hungarians by giving them a large measure of autonomy within the Danubian empire, known officially thereafter as the Dual Monarchy of Austria-Hungary. Gladstone met with less success in dealing with the Irish question, which continued to plague British politics. Nationhood was saved in America after a bitterly fought Civil War that almost tore the young country apart. The Dominion of Canada was constitutionally established by the British North America Act of 1867. In the same year Mexico rid itself of an unwanted French emperor who had succeeded only in arousing national hostility to foreign rule.

Everywhere governments and national movements that had been staunchly opposed to each other before 1848 began to fuse. From the 1848 revolutions, governments had learned that they could no longer rule effectively without granting at least some concessions to growing national sentiment; national movements in turn had learned that they could not realize their aspirations unless they effectively influenced or cooperated with government. This new working relationship enabled the large countries to consolidate politically by 1870. But where national feeling failed to find effective political expression, as in Ireland, the Rhineland after the Franco-Prussian War, and Central and Eastern Europe—there political ferment and instability prevailed and would finally jeopardize almost a century of relative peace. If the Western world during the third quarter of the nineteenth century was dramatically transformed economically and socially by industrialization, it was also transformed politically by the consolidation of large nation-states, a move that would determine the course of world history for almost a century to come.

IDEOLOGICAL REORIENTATIONS

The major ideological movements—conservatism, liberalism, and radicalism—all of which had their roots in the preindustrial era, found it necessary to adapt to the changing material order. Conservatism was hardest hit. The traditionally conservative classes—aristocrats and peasants—found themselves either being absorbed into the new middle-class industrial order or being left behind by it.

Conservatism in Retreat

Conservative faith in tradition and in the past as normative for the present—a faith eloquently professed earlier by Edmund Burke, Joseph de Maistre, and Friedrich Gentz—no longer commanded wide respect. Nor was the idea feasible any longer that the good society was one based on an alliance between throne and altar, as the architects of the Holy Alliance had held. Religious faith generally was in decline and kings were beginning to recede to the level of mere figureheads. Real power lay with cabinet ministers, chancellors, and professional politicians. Moreover, romanticism and philosophical idealism, which had done so much to propagate conservative values in the first half of the century, suffered a sharp setback after 1848. Thus, deprived of constituents, power, and intellectual support, conservatism found itself in retreat. Unwilling and unable to offer a realistic program of its own, conservative ideology functioned mainly as a critique of Victorian society and its materialistic values, and as a refuge for those whom this new society dispossessed or disregarded.

Conservatism found its chief institutional strength in the Roman Catholic Church. Pius IX, pope from 1846 to 1878, actually sympathized with the new secular tendencies during his first two years in office to gain support for the Church among the ascending industrial classes. But with the outbreak of revolution in 1848 and its threat to the influence and material possessions of the Church, he reversed himself dramatically. He refused to support the Italian national cause against Austria (also Catholic), and hence was denounced as a traitor and forced into exile. He returned to Rome in 1850, convinced that secular materialistic values and Roman Catholic spiritual values were fundamentally incompatible. Thereafter, Pius IX became an uncompromising foe of secularism in any form and a stalwart defender of Catholic authoritarianism and dogma.

During the years of political reaction following the 1848 revolutions, Pius IX concluded advantageous treaties with several secular governments, which now regarded the Church as an ally against revolution. Having lost most of its territories four years earlier, the Vatican issued in 1864 the *Syllabus of Errors,* which condemned the leading secular movements of the time: liberalism, socialism, communism, natural science, secular education, and the separation of church and state. It was declared an error to believe "that the Roman Pontiff can and ought to reconcile himself to and agree with progress, liberalism and contemporary civilization."

In 1869, Pius IX convened the first ecumenical council since the Council of Trent in the sixteenth century; his purpose was to bolster papal authority in spiritual matters. A year later, as Italian troops occupied Rome itself and declared it the capital of the newly united Italy, the council proclaimed the infallibility of the pope when speaking officially (*ex cathedra*) on matters of faith and morality, since at such times he is supposed to be endowed with divine authority. This assertion of absolute papal authority in spiritual affairs took place even as the Church was loosing its last vestiges of secular power. At the same time, the concentration of Church authority in the papacy followed and paralleled the concentration of power in the centralized secular governments.

The new position of the Church alarmed many liberal Catholics, such as the distinguished intellectuals Lord John Acton and Johann von Döllinger, and those within the Church hierarchy who wished to limit papal authority. But papal absolutism served the Church well, enabling its leaders to act forcefully and in unison. The vast majority of Catholics remained faithful to the Church, even if doing so put them at odds with their secular environment, and they came to constitute bulwarks of conservatism within their respective countries. In still largely preindustrial areas with predominantly Catholic populations, such as southwestern Europe, Poland, Ireland, and Latin America, the Church met little opposition to its support of reactionary regimes and its resistance to modernism in any form. Even in the advanced countries, however, the Church held its own very well.

In Italy, where the Church clashed constantly with the secular government, Catholic loyalties remained firm. Napoleon III and Bismarck, one the head of a Catholic state and the other head of a state with a large Catholic minority, were both hostile to the Church but had to grant it extensive powers to gain support for their regimes. The only successful opposition to Bismarck came from the otherwise staunchly conservative Catholic Center Party, subsequently to become one of the strongest and most stable forces in German political life. The Church also played an indispensable role in sustaining the ultraconservative Habsburg regime.

The Church fared even better under Pius IX's successor, Leo XIII, pope from 1878 to 1903. He adhered to his predecessor's position on papal authority but sought to ease the conflict between the Church and the secular world. He relaxed the Church's opposition to science and argued that Catholicism was as compatible with democracy as with more authoritarian types of government. He encouraged the formation of political parties, which would operate within the framework of representative government, and believed that the Church should address itself to the urgent social issues of the day. In his encyclical, *Rerum Novarum* (1891), the pope endorsed the best of both capitalism and socialism and denounced the evils of each. All of this enabled the Church to play a vital role in world affairs, despite—or possibly because of—the loss of its territorial possessions.

Nevertheless, papal claims of absolute spiritual authority and such dogmas as the Immaculate Conception of Mary guaranteed that the Church would remain an essentially conservatiye institution. Non-Catholic nationalists, liberals, socialists, scientists, educators, and most intellectuals could scarcely subscribe to such views. And only the most conservative Catholics could accept them wholeheartedly. Consequently, although not always intentionally, the Church became a rallying point for conservative secular causes, such as the opposition in France to the Third Republic and to Alfred Dreyfus, a Jewish officer in the French army wrongfully accused and convicted of treason in 1895. Moreover, the Church's influence remained strongest where secularism had made least headway, in conservative and reactionary states.

Conservatism also gained strength from a scattered handful of intellectuals who fiercely denounced liberalism and democracy, materialism and progress and called for the restoration of spiritual and political elites. One was Thomas Carlyle (1795–1881), the great voice of conservatism in England, who carried on his defense (begun long before 1848) of these causes. Throughout his long and productive career, he campaigned vigorously against laissez faire capitalism and utilitarian philosophy, representative government and parliamentary procedure, all of which, he claimed, only degrade man and encourage mediocrity. History, he claimed, shows that society can save itself from these evils and realize its highest potentialities only by submitting to the leadership of heroes: men endowed with superior talent, wisdom, and moral integrity. This theory Carlyle tried to demonstrate in *On Heroes and Hero-worship and the Heroic in History* (1841) and in his tribute to Prussia's most formidable king, *History of Friedrich II of Prussia, Called Frederick the Great* (1858–1865).

In these and other writings, Carlyle depicted society as divided between the passive, slothful masses on the one hand, and heroic elites on the other. Society needs its heroes as children need their parents—a point not lost on an era that still held the family in pious esteem. It is true that Carlyle characterized his heroes as men of merit rather than privilege. But when it came to national and racial differences, he was not above asserting that the Teutonic peoples were superior to Latins, Jews, and Negroes because of their supposedly exceptional strength, virility, and virtue. This attitude did not offend Victorian Englishmen, who regarded themselves as the very incarnation of these allegedly Teutonic qualities and, therefore, entitled to rule over their inferiors at home and abroad. Carlyle frankly advocated a hierarchical order that reflected the values of the preindustrial landed gentry, and he opposed everything that stood in the way of its resurrection.

But Carlyle had more to offer the conservative cause than just his views. He attempted to embody in his own life the heroic values he praised in his writings. He was a forceful personality, a man of enormous energy and learning, and an independent thinker utterly dedicated to the truth as he saw it. He was a master of rhetoric and presented his case in the sharply moral terms that so appealed to Victorian readers. He had a quick eye for hypocrisy and was not afraid to criticize people in high places. He was one of the first to call attention to the dehumanizing effects of industrialism and excessive materialism. Above all, he understood the Victorian mentality as well as its most vigorous apologists; even as he criticized that mentality, he helped shape it. He inspired without seriously offending, because the virtues he praised, upper-class Victorians still respected, in theory if not in practice. Carlyle criticized the liberal order of his day, but in such a way as to leave it intact, and possibly even more self-assured than before, since his was a criticism society could tolerate.

If Carlyle hearkened back to the values of the pre-industrial gentry, the French count, Joseph Arthur de Gobineau (1816–1882), appealed to racism to explain the decline of the aristocracy, and with it, the decline of civilization itself. He purported to show, in his *Essay on the Inequality of the Races* (1853–1855), that the white race alone had created civilization, but in the course of time had been weakened by the infusion of inferior, non-Aryan blood. The aristocracy represented the white race at its best because its blood was purest, and this aristocracy of blood still existed among the Germans, from whom, Gobineau believed, the French aristocracy had originally descended. Such a view naturally flattered the Germans and was warmly welcomed by such rabid racists as the great German composer, Ricahrd Wagner, and his son-in-law, Houston Stewart Chamberlain, and by later imperialist and totalitarian apologists. But Gobineau's purpose was not so much to flatter a country in which the aristocracy had more power and prestige than it had in France, as to show that civilization was unalterably doomed. The failure of his own class, he claimed, was not its fault; it had been betrayed by liberals, socialists, and other internationalists and egalitarians who, however well-meaning, had invited the mongrelization of the white race. Gobineau's theory shifted the blame for the fall of civilization onto the enemies of his class and thereby implied that, if the aristocracy could not survive, no one would.

Conservative thought flourished more in Central and Eastern Europe, where modernism was just beginning to forge ahead during the Victorian age, than it did in the West. The two giants of Russian literature, Fyodor Dostoevsky (1821–1881) and Count Leo Tolstoy (1828–1910), both advanced conservative views, although from very different standpoints. Tolstoy, an aristocratic landowner, resembled Carlyle in his strongly paternal, moral, and mystical defense of the values of his class; while Dostoevsky, the son of a lowly army surgeon, renounced the radicalism of his youth and embraced a mystical, reactionary stance that found exporession in extreme anti-Western and anti-intellectual outbursts.

The conservatism of the widely influential German philosopher, Arthur Schopenhauer (1788–1860) took the form of a bitterly pessimistic assertion of the futility of man's efforts to transcend his insatiable irrational drives and to improve himself and the world around him. The best that a disciplined few can hope for, he believed, is the attainment of a Nirvana-like state of spiritual quiescence, which renders them oblivious to the world and its endless disappointments. Richard Wagner (1813–1883) denounced liberalism and the vulgar materialism of Bismarckian Germany by extolling in his many successful operas ancient pagan myths and the heroic virtues he ascribed to the precivilized Germanic spirit.

The great Swiss historian, Jakob Burckhardt (1818–1897), conceived history not as the story of the steady progress of mankind, but rather as a ceaseless struggle between the purely creative forces of culture, represented by the gifted few in every age, and the philistine majority. Burckhardt's famous disciple, Friedrich Nietzsche (discussed in the next chapter in relation to the rise of irrationalist philosophy) made Burckhardt's view of history the point of departure for his own sweeping conservative indictment of the whole of modern Western civilization. Russian conservatism culminated in pan-Slavism and German conservatism in pan-Germanism, movements which sang the praises of a vaguely defined, mystical folk soul supposedly impervious to change.

Liberalism in Transition

By mid-century, liberalism had established itself as the dominant ideology in the Western world. In England, the homeland of liberal ideas since the seventeenth century, it faced almost no serious opposition. Liberalism led England, and England led the world. There it seemed that history itself was on the side of the liberal cause. On the continent, liberalism did not prevail as completely, but the liberal class was now the single most powerful force in France and Germany. In eastern Europe, liberals were still a minority; in Russia, scarcely more than a small but growing intelligentsia. Where liberalism was strongest, its chief problem was to respond to the rising democratic and egalitarian demands of an advanced industrial society. Where liberalism was weakest, its chief problem was to gain political power. But everywhere classical liberalism, a product of the preindustrial age, faced new challenges not foreseen in the formative phase of its development: the social and human problems posed by industrial capitalism; the growing radical and conservative opposition to liberal values; governments capable of both protecting and threatening liberal interests.

The thinker most representative of the transition of liberal thought in mid-Victorian England was John Stuart Mill (1806–1873). Throughout his life and writings, Mill remained faithful to the liberal principles taught to him by his father, James Mill, himself a prominent liberal leader of the previous generation. But in his book, *Autobiography*, published in 1873, shortly after his death, the son confessed that in early manhood he had experienced a period of deep doubts about these principles, at least in the strictly utilitarian form in which he had learned them from his father. He continued to adhere to the characteristic liberal goal of the greatest happiness of the greatest number. "I never, indeed, wavered in the conviction that happiness is the test of all rules of conduct, and the end of life." But he now defined happiness as something more than the narrowly egoistic and mathematically calculable table of pleasures and pains conceived by Bentham and taught by his father.

Mill recovered from his personal crisis when he came to the realization, mentioned in his autobiography, that: "Those only are happy who have their minds fixed on some object other than their own happiness; on the happiness of others, on the improvement of mankind, even on some art or pursuit, followed not as a means, but as an ideal end. Aiming thus at something else, they find happiness by the way.... Ask yourself whether you are happy, and you cease to be so. The only chance is to treat, not happiness, but some end external to it, as the purpose of life."

Two influences led Mill to this conclusion. One was the romantic literature of Wordsworth, Coleridge, and Carlyle, who asserted the superiority of the emotions over reason and pure intellect. The other was the social teachings of the French reformers, Saint-Simon and the founder on the philosophy of positivism, Auguste Comte, Saint-Simon, gave new dimension to Mill's concept of happiness; Comte provided the external purpose necessary to achieve it. The result was a significant modification, but not an abandonment, of the liberal concept of individualism.

Mill continued to hold, in the tradition of Locke and the eighteenth-century *philosophes* and utilitarians, that the individual is the basic unit of society and his well-being and self-fulfillment the ends for which society exists. Although he grew in later life to sympathize with much in socialism, he always rejected it on the grounds that, no matter how noble in theory or benevolent in practice, socialism always subsumes the individual to the supposedly higher interest of society. In his famous essay, "On Liberty" (1859), one of the great contributions to liberal literature and the writing that Mill considered his best, he vigorously defended maximum individual freedom against the double danger of governmental incursions and the rising tide of mass conformity that betokened an eventual "tyranny of the majority." "If all mankind minus one were of one opinion, mankind would be no more justified in silencing that one person than he, if he had the power, would be justified in silencing mankind." Elsewhere in this essay, he wrote: "That so few now dare to be eccentric marks the chief danger of the time."

On the other hand, Mill redefined individuality so that it necessarily encompassed a social dimension—active participation in public affairs and positive fellowship in addition to mere freedom from external restraint. In *Autobiography,* he compared "the frank sociability and amiability of French personal intercourse, and the English mode of existence in which everybody acts as if everybody else (with few or no exceptions) was either an enemy or a bore." Mill held that true self-interest and the interest of society, far from being separable or mutually exclusive, are inseparably interrelated. The individual can fulfill himself only if he is an active member of society, and society can thrive only to the extent that it extends the right of participation to all its members. Mill's ideal human personality was not one who lives by and for himself; his ideal was neither a self-contained Robinson Crusoe nor any of a number of scoundrels who in Dickens' novels represented human qualities dear to his father's generation of liberals. (Scrooge was, after all, a good Victorian liberal, even if a caricature.) "Interest in the common good is at present so weak a motive in the generality, not because it can never be otherwise, but because the mind is not accustomed to dwell on it as it dwells from morning till night on things which tend only to personal advantage." Mill's ideal human personality was one who can find fulfillment only in a civilized community, and the purpose of the community is to enable him to do so. Consequently, he defended the liberal principle of laissez faire only to the extent that it maximizes individual liberty, and he advocated democracy and government regulation only to the extent that they maximize participation.

Mill's public life reflected his views. He consistently championed free speech and denounced censorship in any form. He was an outspoken advocate of equal rights for women, including the right to vote, and of state-supported compulsory education for all. He campaigned vigorously for the Reform Bill, passed in 1867, which provided a wide extension of the franchise for Parliamentary elections and marked a major step in the democratization of England. He also defended the right of workers to organize trade unions and looked forward to a time when society would "unite the greatest individual liberty of action, with a common ownership in the raw material of the globe, and an equal participation of all in the benefits of combined labour." In short, Mill endowed a liberalism with a heart and a social conscience, which made it more responsive to the needs of modern society. Only the individual was sacred to him, not dogmas, not even such favorite classical liberal dogmas as laissez faire capitalism and distrust of the state. It was this more open-minded, flexible, and comprehensive interpretation that sustained subsequent generations of liberals long after the dangers that Mill anticipated, and many he did not, became harsh realities.

The other major mid-century liberal thinker was the French aristocrat

Alexis de Tocqueville (1805–1859), whose writings Mill knew and admired. Many of the hopes and fears concerning democracy expressed by Mill in "On Liberty" first appeared in Tocqueville's classic work, *Democracy in America* (1835), which Mill reviewed favorably in the *Westminster Review*. Tocqueville had been the most intellectually distinguished of the many Europeans who, during the 1830s and 1840s, visited and observed America as a laboratory of democracy. He found much to praise in American life: the informality of relationships, the absence of hard and fast class divisions and aristocratic pretensions, a cheerful optimism, and a hardworking spirit. But there was also much about America that aroused his apprehension: garrulous patriotism, vulgar materialism, a dangerous concentration of power in the central government, a tendency to conformity, and a low level of civic-mindedness and general culture. On balance, however, Tocqueville was favorably impressed by American democracy, and he concluded *Democracy in America* with the statement:

> I am of the opinion that if we do not succeed in gradually introducing democratic institutions into our country, if we despair of imparting to all the citizens those ideas and sentiments which first prepare them for freedom and afterward allow them to enjoy it, there will be no independence at all, either for the middle class or for the nobility, for the poor or for the rich, but an equal tyranny over all.

Nevertheless, Tocqueville remained deeply attached to his aristocratic background and tastes. If he declared himself in favor of democracy, he did so more from resignation to its inevitability than from enthusiasm. Moreover, the 1848 revolutions, the collapse of the short-lived Second Republic, and the birth of the Second Empire (which seemed to Tocqueville to embody democracy's defects but not its virtues)—all served to diminish his faith in the ability of Europe, and especially France, to make a satisfactory transition to democracy. Tocqueville did not expect nor wish to see the European aristocracies restored to power. On the contrary, he argued in his second and last great work, *The Old Regime and the French Revolution* (1856), that the outbreak of the French Revolution was due in large part to the failure of the aristocracy to rule effectively and responsibly. In abusing its power thus, the aristocracy had forfeited its right to rule and had unleashed the democratic forces that ultimately would overthrow it. The aristocracy, therefore, had only itself to blame for its decline.

Still, Tocqueville regretted the passing of the aristocracy because, he believed, it could have served in Europe as a useful corrective to the defects of democracy. It could have acted as a brake on despotism by resisting the concentration of all political power in a central government. It could have reduced the possibility of a tyranny of the majority by curbing the democratic tendency toward social uniformity and con-formity. And because the aristocracy had always represented a civilizing force in Europe, Tocqueville believed that it could have counteracted the vulgar materialism and mediocrity to which democracy is prone, and could have set an example of cultural and intellectual excellence. In its aristocracy, Tocqueville believed, Europe had once possessed a valuable asset that even America lacked. Tocqueville was as dedicated as Mill to the liberal principle of maximum freedom for the individual and the right of all to seek happiness and self-fulfillment, with government regu-lation if necessary. He also shared Mill's belief that democracy is the logical extension of liberal principles and the political system most favor-able to their realization. But, unlike Mill, Tocqueville believed that the aristocracy, although a conservative force, could have served as an im-portant guarantee of the survival of liberal principles within a democ-racy. "When I entered life," he wrote in later years, "aristocracy was dead and democracy was yet unborn." Tocqueville's cause was tragic in the sense that he believed it desirable but no longer possible to combine the best features of both of these worlds.

A TOEHOLD IN GERMANY   If Tocqueville regarded democracy as inevi-table, German liberals in the third quarter of the century thought it more an impossible and not necessarily desirable dream. Even before 1848, German liberals had been more timid and circumspect than their Western counterparts. Subservience to the state was deeply rooted in German government, and German liberals had always been reluctant to assert unequivocally the sovereignty of the people and the right of revo-lution. They damaged their cause further in 1848 when their represen-tatives to the Frankfurt Assembly opposed revolution and an alliance with radical elements of the working class as means to achieve their goals of a unified, self-governing Germany (*Einheit und Freiheit*). The dissolu-tion of the Assembly by Prussian troops a year later left German liberals more demoralized than before and more inclined to capitulate, or at any rate to acquiesce, to autocratic government thereafter.

One consolation to German liberals was the constitution issued in 1850 by the Prussian king, Frederick William IV. It would remain in effect in Prussia until the end of the monarchy in 1918 and serve as a model for Germany's constitution after unification in 1871. The constitution was a farce, however, in that it gave preponderant power to the upper classes, exempted the army and cabinet ministers from constitutional regulation, making them responsible only to the king, and retained the medieval notion of the divine right of kings, long since discredited in the West. Still, some constitution was better than none; and this one, shabby though it was and although conceded by a king who had referred to the "forty-eighters" as "democratic filth," did provide for parliamentary consent to legislation and for certain restrictions on the executive branch of government. And these powers, though meager, enabled the liberals to influence German political life to some extent, even if only as a thorn in the side of autocracy.

The implications of the situation became evident during the constitutional crisis of the sixties, which brought Bismarck to the fore of German politics. In 1862, the king appointed this high-handed Junker, as contemptuous of representative government as the king himself, to try to browbeat the Prussian Diet into voting new taxes to support an army over which it had no control. Failing in this, he simply ignored the constitution and for the next four years illegally collected the new taxes, which nobody refused to pay. Prussia's stunning victory over Austria in 1866 satisfied the liberals' nationalism and enabled Bismarck to persuade the Diet to pass a bill of indemnity that, although acknowledging the government's wrongdoing during the previous four years, legalized its actions retroactively. The majority of liberals, who had resisted Bismarck until the Prussian victory, now flocked to his support. The liberal cause gained ground rapidly in Germany after unification, but only under the aegis of authoritarianism. By now, German liberalism was so compromised that it no longer posed a serious threat to an enemy that it had failed time and again throughout its existence to crush.

Under the circumstances, it is not surprising that German liberalism failed to produce a thinker of the stature of Mill or Tocqueville. Thousands of liberals, including such distinguished men as Carl Schurz and Joseph Weydemeyer, emigrated from Germany after 1848, thus depriving the liberal movement of valuable talent. Other gifted men, such as Richard Wagner and Heinrich von Treitschke, renounced their early liberal views and joined the reactionary camp. The best that liberals could do during the middle decades of the century was to cling to the meager powers granted by the constitution and try to achieve by legal means the goals they had failed to achieve by direct political action: civil equality, the subordination of government to due process of law, participation of the people in political decision-making, and individual rights. This is what they meant by the term *Rechtsstaat*—a liberal state achieved by legal rather than by political means. The whole idea was illusory, as the constitutional crisis of the 1860s demonstrated. It was a concept that only the politically inexperienced could have taken seriously. For in an age that acknowledged only power as the final arbiter of political affairs, the idea of a *Rechtsstaat* was clearly an anachronism. Nevertheless, this peculiarly German conception sustained, and was possibly the only theory that could have sustained, the liberal cause in Germany during the difficult Bismarck era and after.

Liberalism in Russia during the middle decades of the nineteenth century was confined to a small group of intellectuals who looked to the West as a model for the future development of their own still autocratic and economically backward country. Most found themselves strangers in their own land—far removed from the peasant masses, fearful of government oppression, vilified by conservative Slavophiles, and convinced of the need for sweeping political, economic, and social reform. Many emigrated to Western Europe, including the influential writers, Alexander Herzen (1812–1870) and Ivan Turgenev (1818–1883). Once there, many of these same expatriates, notably Herzen, became disillusioned with the West, renounced their former liberal views, and called upon Russian intellectuals to return to the peasant masses and form a populist movement that would serve as the basis of Russia's regeneration. Others, like the distinguished novelist Turgenev, resisted this temptation. In a well-known controversy of the 1860s that ended his friendship with Herzen, Turgenev remarked: "God forbid that we should fall into a blind veneration for everything Russian simply because it is Russian. God save us from narrow-minded and, to be honest, ungrateful attacks on the West. . . . The surest sign of strength is to know one's weaknesses and imperfections." Although sobered by the seamier side of life in the West—social injustice, crass materialism, industrial ugliness, and the degeneration of liberal ideas into bourgeois ideology—Turgenev nonetheless retained his faith that Russia's best hope for liberation from political oppression, poverty, and ignorance lay in her adoption of Western liberal ideas and institutions.

The plight of Russia, and of the Russian intellectuals in particular, was the subject of a flurry of writings that appeared during the reign of Alexander II, tsar from 1855 to 1881. Among them were Herzen's *My Life and Thoughts* (1852–1855); N. G. Chernyshevsky's novel, *What Is to Be Done?* (1863); Tolstoy's masterpiece, *War and Peace* (1866); and several of Dostoevsky's novels. An incisive treatment of this theme from a liberal standpoint was Turgenev's best known novel, *Fathers and Sons* (1862). The abrasive hero, Bazarov, is a "nihilist" and champion of things Western ("English washstands spell progress"), who finds himself completely out of place in his Russian surroundings. He cannot communicate with the peasants; he dismisses the older generation contemptuously as "romantic," and he alienates his only friend and the woman he loves. On the threshold of a brilliant scientific career, Bazarov contracts typhus and dies embittered, unfulfilled, and unloved. Although he had momentarily disrupted the lethargic, self-satisfied lives of all those around him, he is quickly forgotten and life resumes its usual course. The novel's message was that Bazarov, although arrogant and even slightly ridiculous, represented Russia's best hope—progress along Western liberal lines—but that what he stood for was doomed to failure from the start in the backward Russia of his time. Turgenev wrote to a friend of his country in relation to the West: "Russia is no Venus de Milo, kept in misery and bondage by a wicked stepmother. She is in fact the same kind of young woman as her elder sisters—except, I suppose, that she is a bit broader in the beam."

Liberal views began to bear fruit in the reforms of Alexander II. Although not a liberal himself, Alexander reluctantly acknowledged the need for change after Russia's defeat in the Crimean War and because of the growing power and prestige of the West throughout the world. He began in 1861 by abolishing serfdom, in effect making available the huge labor force necessary to industrialization. Three years later, he created a system of provincial and district councils, called *zemstvos,* which assumed the responsibilities of local self-government. A similar system was extended to cities and towns in 1870. Alexander also reformed the army and the judicial system along Western lines. All of these measures were designed to gain liberal support for his regime. But a Polish uprising in 1863 against Russian rule made the tsar more cautious, and he refused to take the next logical step, urged by liberals, of creating a national *zemstvo* or parliament.

The failure of the liberals to prevail on this all-important issue weakened their position and strengthened that of such radical groups as the nihilists and anarchists, who called for the complete overthrow of autocracy by violence and terror. After several unsuccessful attempts on his life, Alexander was assassinated by a member of a terrorist group on March 13, 1881, the same day he had signed an act providing for a significant enlargement of representative government at the national level. Alexander III, tsar from 1881 to 1894, abruptly abandoned his father's program of liberal reform and reverted to the harsh authoritarianism of earlier times. But he did retain the basic reforms effected by his father: peasant emancipation, judicial reform, and the *zemstvos.* In this way, Western liberal ideas were able to penetrate for a brief time a society increasingly torn between reaction and revolution.

Radicalism Turns Militant: Karl Marx

Socialism began in the early nineteenth century as a moral and emotional reaction to the dehumanizing effects of industrial capitalism. The factory proletariat was then still in its infancy, and socialism was the work of a few philanthropic reformers such as Robert Owen, Charles Fourier, and Claude de Saint-Simon. Although by 1848 socialism was gathering force under the leadership of such militant radicals as Louis Blanc, Pierre Joseph Proudhon, Wilhelm Weitling, and Moses Hess; it was still the cause of a discontented minority. It was not until the Victorian age that socialism evolved into a significant historical force, no longer merely a protest movement, but one which offered an alternative to the existing social and economic order. This was largely the work of Karl Marx (1818–1883) and his life-long friend and collaborator, Friedrich Engels (1820–1895), who provided socialism with a theory of history, a materialistic philosophy, an economic explanation of the evils of capitalism, a vision of a new society, and a theory of revolution designed to translate that vision into reality. It was their version of socialism, reinterpreted by their disciples from time to time to fit changing circumstances, that has since come to command the allegiance of hundreds of millions throughout the world.

In the early years of their collaboration, from their first meeting in Paris in 1844 to the publication of the *Communist Manifesto* in 1848, Marx and Engels were scarcely known, even to other socialists. Marx was then an obscure German intellectual in exile, whose writings, notably *The Economic and Philosophic Manuscripts* (1844), *The Holy Family* (1845), and *The German Ideology* (1846), analyzed and criticized capitalism and current German philosophy. Engels managed his father's textile factory in Manchester and came to Marx's attention through his study of the conditions of the English working classes, which Engels was in a position to observe first hand. The fruit of their labors of the 1840s was the *Communist Manifesto,* which contained in embryo their basic program of the future. It proclaimed that all history thus far has been the history of class conflict, that history so conceived is a dialectical process in which one class supplants another by virtue of a superior system of production, that the current struggle between the declining bourgeoisie and the ascendant proletariat can only be resolved by revolution, and that this revolution, the final class conflict, will be followed by an unprecedented and lasting "classless" society. It assigned to the Communist party the role of "midwife" of the workers' revolution, demanded the abolition of private property, and called upon the workers of the world to unite and overthrow their capitalist oppressors.

The *Communist Manifesto* had little effect on the events of 1848. It came too late to have any significant impact on the industrially advanced countries of Western Europe with socialist movements and leadership of their own and too early to influence central and eastern Europe, where a proletariat in the Marxist sense scarcely existed as yet. Nevertheless, the *Communist Manifesto* marked a significant turning point in Marx's development and in the history of socialist thought in general. It was at this point that Marx ceased to be merely a critic of the existing capitalist order and began to offer a program of his own, with features that differentiated it from other varieties of socialism, contemptuously dismissed by Marx as "utopian." In contrast to the more pragmatic and practical character of socialism in western Europe, Marx's program was intellectually bolder and more rigorous, more prophetic and dogmatic. It claimed to be more scientific than the others and more in keeping with the basic realities of history. Its denunciation of capitalism and demand for social revolution was fiercer. Marxism represented a unique blend of the scientific, the historical, the metaphysical, and the apocalyptic. If mid-nineteenth-century conservatism derived strength from the reverie of a supposedly simpler and more humanly satisfying past, rapidly being swept away by modernization, and if liberalism thrived on the seemingly inexhaustible achievements and prospects of the present, then Marxism, the radical extreme, aroused hope in a beatific future such as few secular doctrines before or since have succeeded in doing.

What enabled Marx's teachings to arouse such hope among the oppressed and exploited of the industrial age? One reason was his exalted conception of the proletariat as the liberator of all mankind, once and for all, from the travail and corruption of a history plagued by class conflict. The proletariat is the one class "which can invoke no *historical* but only its *human* title," a class which epitomizes "the *complete loss* of man, and hence can win itself only through a *complete re-winning* of man." Another reason was Marx's exalted conception of the liberation itself, a process Engels described as "the ascent of man from the kingdom of necessity to the kingdom of freedom." A third was Marx's belief in the necessarily revolutionary character of the proletariat. "Of all the classes that stand face to face with the bourgeoisie today," the *Communist Manifesto* says, "the proletariat alone is a really revolutionary class. The other classes decay and finally disappear in the face of modern industry; the proletariat is its special and essential product."

Marx's intense faith in the inevitability of the proletarian victory also enhanced his teachings. "What the bourgeoisie produces, above all, are its own gravediggers. Its fall and the victory of the proletariat are equally inevitable." Marx also emphasized to his advantage the imminence of the final revolution; for the bourgeois epoch, he claimed, is "the closing chapter of the prehistorical stage of human society." Men, even the most humble, have the power and the duty to alter the course of events. "The philosophers have only *interpreted* the world in various ways, the point is to *change* it."

As for capitalism, Marx effectively reduced it to but a transitory phase in the overall course of human development in his sweeping economic critique, *Das Kapital*, the first volume of which appeared in 1867. His theory of surplus value, whereby the worker under capitalism receives in wages only a fraction of the value of the commodity he produces, amounted to a scathing indictment of capitalism as blatantly criminal and exploitative. Not least, Marx effectively invoked the intriguing philosophical term, alienation, first used in the modern sense by Schiller and Hegel and especially appealing to nonproletarian intellectuals and moralists, to describe the spiritual plight of the worker under capitalism. "The *alienation* of the worker in his product means not only that his labor becomes an object, assumes an *external* existence, but that it exists independently, *outside himself,* and alien to him, and that it stands opposed to him as an autonomous power. The life which he has given to the object sets itself against him as an alien and hostile force."

As the ranks and discontents of the workers grew during the fifties and sixties, so also did the prestige of Marx's ideas. His was the dominant voice at the first meeting of the International Working Men's Association held in London in 1864, commonly known as the First International. His influence was especially great on the German socialist movement, which grew rapidly during the third quarter of the century and assumed leadership of the European socialist movement as a whole by the seventies. One feature that enabled Marxism to win out finally over its competition was that, despite its militant hostility toward bourgeois civilization, it actually appealed to some of the most pious beliefs of the Victorian age: an almost religious faith in science and progress, a materialistic conception of the human condition, and a lively sense of social justice. At the same time, contrary to Marx's own hopes and expectations, communism has always been least successful in the already industrially advanced countries. Historically, it has thrived in countries, like Germany in the middle decades of the nineteenth century and Russia toward the end, where Western influences were weak or nonexistent: countries in transition from an agrarian to an industrial economy but still lacking strong working-class movements with socialist aims.

THE VICTORIAN MOOD

The Victorians were proud of their new industrial prowess and the prosperity that resulted from it. Queen Victoria, whose name became synonymous with the age, herself epitomized the human qualities on which the age prided itself: industriousness, a sense of duty, moral self-righteousness, and patriotism. The Great Exhibition of 1851 symbolized the end of decades of political and economic discontent and the full reassertion of Britain's self-esteem. It was conceived by Victoria's husband, Prince Albert, who wished "to give us a true test and living picture of the point of development at which the whole of mankind has arrived in this great task of applied science and a new starting point from which all nations will be able to direct their further exertions."

The Crystal Palace, which housed the exhibition, was the creation of

Corridor of the Crystal Palace, 1851.

(The New York Public Library).

Joseph Paxton, a self-made man of many talents and personification of Victorian ideals. The completed building, constructed of mass-produced and standardized parts, housed 13,000 exhibitions in the categories of raw materials, machines, manufactured goods, and fine arts, fascinating the six million visitors from all over the world who came to see the exhibition. To Victoria, it was "the most *beautiful* and *imposing* and *touching* spectacle ever seen." To England's poet laureate Alfred, Lord Tennyson, it contained "All of beauty, all of use, That one fair planet can produce."

The virtues of hard work, thrift, and duty, celebrated by the Great Exhibition, were also propagated by a whole host of popular homiletic writings, notably Samuel Smiles' *Self-Help* (1859), which sold twenty thousand copies the first year and another one hundred thirty thousand during the next thirty years. The secret of the success of these collections of smug lay sermons on the virtues of industry and honesty was that they always linked the practice of such virtue with the reward of material prosperity. This ingenuous combination of moral striving and material selfishness went to the very heart of the Victorian mood.

One of the most prominent features of Victorian life was regard for respectability. The Victorians did not invent respectability, but they held it in higher esteem than any other Western people before or since. At worst, respectability meant little more than adherence to "good form" and publicly sanctioned standards of behavior; it became a code by which the now dominant middle classes claimed moral superiority over the crude lower classes on the one hand and over the libertine aristocracy on the other. At best, it represented a sincere desire for moral, social, and economic self-improvement. In both respects, as affectation and as sensitivity, Victorian respectability was a protest against the evils that came in the wake of modernization. Slums, unhealthy living and working conditions, exploitation of child labor, drunkenness, and prostitution were nothing new. However, these evils now existed on such a large scale, and were brought to public attention so readily by means of improved communications, as to arouse widespread public concern. It is against this background of social evils too overwhelming as yet to be dealt with effectively that the Victorian protest against sexual license, promiscuity, and proneness to preach the virtues of home and family must be seen. It is this background also which explains why the evangelical movement, with its emphasis on individual moral responsibility, suddenly swept the land during the early decades of Victoria's reign.

The Beginnings of Feminism

It is true that the theory and practice of Victorian morality often were inconsistent with each other and with the facts of life. This discrepancy was especially evident in relations between the sexes. In theory, the Victorian age considered both sexes as equal, although not the same. In fact, one law applied to the man and another to the woman, a double standard based on biological differences and on the almost total economic dependence and social inferiority of the woman. Typically, the Victorian woman's place was in the home, and she had to find whatever satisfaction and fulfillment she could in domesticity and motherhood. If she received any education, it was one that served little useful purpose, such as embroidery, singing, learning to walk gracefully, and the like. In contrast to the man, who could take up with prostitutes and mistresses, providing he did so discreetly, the woman was strictly forbidden any premarital or extramarital sexual relations.

Few escapes from such a restricted existence were available except through the lowly professions of governess, nurse, missionary worker, and seamstress. Actresses were looked upon as little better than prostitutes, and female participation in public life was almost unheard of. Children also were subject to the same fatherly authoritarianism as the women. Sons were taught to address their fathers as "sir," and caning and bullying were not uncommon, even at such distinguished educational institutions as Eton and Winchester.

However, the current opinion of Victorian morality as unrelieved hypocrisy and repression is a great exaggeration. And the image of Victorian family life as dull, sanctimonious, and reduced to abject acquiescence by a domineering father is largely a product of the late Victorian literary imagination, as found, for example, in Samuel Butler's novel, *The Way of All Flesh* (1903). In reality, the moral standard of respectability and the institutions of home and family served as effective protective barriers against the dangers and temptations of a harsh, exploitative, impersonal, and rapidly changing society. They inspired much allegiance, provided much satisfaction, and as a rule were not lightly transgressed. If Victorian women fell far short of equality with men, this injustice was due less to a deliberate male conspiracy than to the unthinking retention of older attitudes prejudicial to women, and to the fact that industrial society, still heavily dependent on physical strength and stamina, had not yet reached the point where female participation on a significant scale seemed possible or advantageous. Although these circumstances do not excuse the hypocrisy of an age that after all did pay lip service to the equality of the sexes, they do help to explain it.

Victorian women did make important strides toward improving their condition. Mary Wollstonecraft's *Vindication of the Rights of Women* (1792), an early landmark in the feminist cause, began to exert an influence on the great Victorian novelists' conception of the woman. Thackery's Becky Sharp, Charlotte Brontë's Jane Eyre, and many female characters in Trollope's novels, although not beautiful, appear as interesting and intelligent, able and ambitious human beings—a sign that the tide was starting to turn against the traditional male notion of women as adorable but brainless dolls. Philanthropic work enabled middle-class women to broaden their limited horizons, compensate for useless educations, and gain a measure of economic independence. Gradually, schools were founded to train women to work in hospitals, schools, and reformatories, and such work began to acquire respectability. Octavia Hill, Harriet Martineau, and the famous Florence Nightingale distinguished themselves for their charitable work and missions of mercy.

A significant step forward was the admission of women, starting in

1857, to the Social Science Association. The Association for the Promotion of the Employment of Women, founded the same year, also served to further women's interests. Queen's College for Women was founded in 1848 and Bedford College in 1849. By the 1860s, the influence of unmarried women on society was growing and moral questions were being discussed more openly and frankly. These developments, although little enough, suffice to show that the situation of women was neither static and rigid, nor uniformly bleak. As for the disciplinarian methods used in raising and educating Victorian children, they may seem appalling from the standpoint of permissive, post-Freudian standards. But a more blanced view is that they produced a type of young man "of utter integrity and courage, complacent, a little priggish, kind but insensitive and inexpressive" (Marion Lockhead, *Young Victorians*, 1959, p. 25). If the Victorians laid themselves open to the charge of excessive hypocrisy and sternness, it is less because this description fit them perfectly than because of their excessive zeal to be and appear at all times respectable and beyond reproach in all things.

Numerically, the respectable were not the largest segment of society, but they were the most zealous, articulate, and hence, the most influential force on public opinion. It was the respectable who formed the reading public and the respectable to whom the great novelists, the crown of Victorian culture, addressed themselves. In contrast to the major contemporary novelists on the continent, such as Flaubert, Turgenev, and Dostoevsky, the early Victorian novelists—Dickens, Thackeray, Charlotte and Emily Brontë, and George Eliot—were remarkably at one with their public. They accepted the society in which they lived without question. They shared its assumptions and voiced its hopes and fears. When they criticized it, they did so as many of their readers did. They were keenly aware of the social problems and evils of the day: the chaos caused by industrialization, mass poverty, and class conflict. But in the midst of mounting wealth, technological progress, and a general rise in the standard of living, the early Victorian novelists tended to believe, as did their public, that the problems and evils surrounding them were temporary and surmountable. There were dissenting voices: Carlyle, Ruskin, Newman, and later, Matthew Arnold. But even they called only for reform, not for sweeping change, and they spoke the moralistic language that the respectable loved to hear.

The later Victorian novelists, George Meridith, Thomas Hardy, and Samuel Butler, were more critical of their age, and their relationship to their public was closer to that of the twentieth-century novelist than to that of the early Victorians. Meridith, although highly reputable, was never a big seller; Hardy outraged public opinion of his day; Butler was regarded during his lifetime as eccentric. However, if respectable

Victorians were overly indifferent to and intolerant of serious dissent, the richness, diversity, and high level of critical awareness of the literature that did satisfy them attests to the scope and complexity of their mentality.

The Victorians, although proud of their materialistic civilization, were not altogether at ease with it. The much vaunted Crystal Palace was a step in the direction of a functional aesthetic consistent with an industrialized society. But the exhibitions it housed represented a profusion of styles, Baroque, Rococo, and Gothic, all jumbled together. Victorian taste in fact reveled in eclecticism and refused to develop a severely functional and uniform aesthetic appropriate to the new technology and materials.

Period revivals were the foundation of Victorian styles in art and architecture. Rococo and classicism were followed by a Greek and then a Gothic revival. The Germans had popularized the neo-Greek architectural style in the 1820s and then had experimented with neo-Renaissance palaces and high Gothic cathedrals. The French revived their own Renaissance and Baroque styles to replace the Roman style favored earlier by Napoleon Bonaparte. The English borrowed from both the French and Germans and continued to ransack their own past for something precious to reconstruct; they found it in the Elizabethan and Jacobean styles. Every period but their own seemed to interest the Victorians and especially the industrialists, who sought to remove themselves as far as possible from their tedious and grimy surroundings by the archaic design and stuffy interiors of their houses and the art objects within them.

By 1851, London could boast of squares and parks inspired by Romanticism, Gothic towers along the Thames, the British Museum inspired by Greece, and banks and clubs for the wealthy built in imitation of Florentine palaces. The city was a hodgepodge of period revivals, yet a surprisingly charming hodgepodge in some of the affluent districts. In 1851, Gothic was the most popular of the competing styles. The architect Augustus Welby Pugin, designer of the medieval court at the Crystal Palace, and John Ruskin in his *Seven Lamps of Architecture* (1849) praised the spiritual values of the Middle Ages as reflected in their art. Thomas Carlyle aroused historical interest in the heroic men and deeds of the medieval past, and Sir Walter Scott thrilled the readers of his novels with panoramic descriptions of the great battles and crusading kings of that period.

In 1848, a group of painters, led by Dante Gabriell Rossetti, founded the Pre-Raphaelite Brotherhood, which set the style of painting throughout the 1850s. Their re-creation in bright colors of scenes from medieval chronicles and innocent tableaux of religious and rural life were affectedly pious, sometimes ridiculous, and often smacked more of the erotic than the spiritual. Such painting was scarcely comparable in quality to the original and socially significant work of the contemporary French painters, Jean François Millet, Gustave Courbet, and Honoré Daumier.

Victorian taste was dominated by an insatiable fascination and infatuation with history. More often than not this preoccupation with the past was motivated by escapism, nostalgia for what was rapidly disappearing, an urge to be fashionable, or aimless antiquarianism. But if Victorian eclecticism was indiscriminate and sterile, it also signified a genuine effort to find value and a sense of spiritual and social identity in a shapeless, divided society undergoing rapid change.

The Darwinian Controversy

Two intellectual developments in particular captured the Victorian imagination. One was the theory of evolution of Charles Darwin (1809–1882), and the other was the philosophy of positivism, conceived by the French philosopher, Auguste Comte (1798–1857). The idea of evolution did not originate with Darwin. Since the eighteenth century scientists and philosophers had speculated, contrary to religious teachings, that the various species of plant and animal life were not immutable and fixed once and for all. Rather, they were the product of a process of constant change and had come into existence successively over very long periods of time, far longer than the four thousand years or so that churchmen estimated to be the earth's age.

Geologists in particular, notably James Hutton and Charles Lyell, had amassed a great deal of evidence from their studies of fossil remains to show that the strata of the earth's crust had been formed during successive geological epochs lasting millions of years and that the strata could be identified by the fossils they contained. The French naturalist Jean Baptiste de Lamarck had gone so far as to conclude from his classification of plants and invertebrates at the botanical gardens in Paris that species change because of their need to adapt to their environment and that they transmit these acquired characteristics to their offspring. Darwin and later biologists rejected Lamarck on both counts. But he did take the penultimate step of suggesting that species do not merely succeed but actually evolve from each other by the transmission of biological characteristics.

It was Charles Darwin, however, in his famous and controversial *On the Origin of Species by Natural Selection* (1859), who first presented a scientifically verifiable theory in support of the hypothesis that living organisms evolve. He was also the first to explain evolutionary change by natural selection: the (originally Malthusian) idea that, because population increases faster than food supply, a struggle for survival takes place in which the less fit species fail to reproduce themselves and die out, while the better fit survive and thrive. On this theory, nature acts as a sort of breeding mechanism, working (though not consciously or by design) to preserve those species, and those organisms within each species, best suited biologically to survive in a particular environment. Giraffes do not grow long necks in order to survive, as Lamarck had held; rather, giraffes survive because they already have long necks, giving them the advantage over their competitors for the available food supply. Should the environment change so as to render their long necks useless or disadvantageous in the struggle for survival, giraffes will not adapt to the change; they will die out, as did the saber-toothed tiger and all other extinct species. In the *Origin of Species,* Darwin explained natural selection as "the preservation of favorable individual differences and variations, and the destruction of those that are injurious." His theory of evolution was, then, simply the mechanically adjusted result of survival value as determined by biological inheritance.

In an age that prided itself on its scientific achievements and enlightenment, how could Darwin's theory arouse such controversy? Evolution and natural selection were not new ideas, nor had they been especially controversial prior to Darwin's work, when they still belonged to the realm of speculation. Thomas Malthus, author of the theory of natural selection, had himself been a clergyman; he used the idea to exhort mankind, especially the "morally lax" lower classes, to practice sexual restraint and Christian virtue. Darwin also respected the religious and moral codes of his day and was himself a model of Victorian respectability. But, in fusing evolution and natural selection into a unified, comprehensive, verifiable account of the biological record, supported by a mass of evidence meticulously gathered over a period of more than twenty years, Darwin produced a theory that struck at the very foundations of accepted belief. It challenged three basic religious beliefs of the time: that God had created the species immutable, that men had always been the highest form of creation, and that biological change occurred by design, specifically by providential design. Moreover, Darwin's theory collided headlong with a religious revival just reaching its peak under the leadership of such forceful personalities as John Henry Newman, Charles Booth, Thomas Arnold, and the popular novelist Charles Kingsley. The driving force of this religious revival was a search for social justice in a heartless industrial age; what Darwin seemed to preach was "survival of the fittest," a nature "red in tooth and claw," and a universe governed by chance and luck.

Darwin's theory challenged not only religious beliefs but also science itself, notably the Newtonian conception of a rationally ordered and harmonious universe, which hitherto had been an important component of enlightened Western thought. Against Newton's view that the universe functions like a clockwork, Darwin held that all living creatures are engaged in a constant struggle for existence and that the "survival of the fittest" is a law governing all aspects of life. Such a view obviously implied that strife is the law of the social world of man as well as the law of the animal realm. Although Darwin himself was reluctant to apply his findings to human society, both his critics and advocates were quick to recognize their social implications. Darwinian explanations of social phenomena were bleak, but nonetheless seemed to accord with reality. They found fertile soil in an era increasingly distressed by the problems of poverty, inequality, and social tensions. Under such conditions, who could claim to represent the interests of society as a whole? Who could believe that cutthroat economic competition and unbridled egoism would result in social cooperation and equilibrium? Where was the voice of reason in human affairs?

To these and related questions "social Darwinism" offered convincing answers. The poor were poor because they lacked intelligence and ambition. The rich were rich because natural selection favored them in the struggle for survival. Nationalists, imperialists, and racists could point to the privileged position of the dominant nations, social classes, and racial groups as evidence of their natural superiority and right to rule. Weaker groups either would have to resign themselves to eventual extinction, or else find consolation in the thought that, since evolution is a constant but haphazard and violent process, their turn might yet come. As conflict is the law of life, no individual, no political or social program, no ideology could claim, or even be required to claim, to represent the interests of society as a whole. Nor was it possible any longer to believe that a fundamental harmony underlies or results from social discord, as implied by the Newtonian model of nature.

As for the role of reason in human affairs, it was at best but a tool for survival, a rationalization of actions born of the blind and amoral but irrepressible instinct to survive. Man was merely an animal, the most complex to be sure, but an animal all the same. Darwin's shocking disclosure that man himself had evolved from a lower order of life, his argument in *The Descent of Man* (1871), effectively denied any qualitative differences, physical, mental, or moral, between the human species and the lower orders of life and thereby authorized the study of man by the same means and concepts that science applied to the rest of nature. Therefore, not only did Darwin's teachings challenge the specifically religious explanation of man's origin, but also they questioned the age-old humanistic view of man as a unique being in creation.

In short, what Darwin's followers found in his teachings was not simply an original and fruitful addition to scientific theory, but rather a wholly new model of nature that served both to explain and sanction the political, social, and ideological order. It enabled the powerful to justify their position on no other grounds than self-interest; at that time no other grounds would have been convincing anyway. It enabled the oppressed and deprived in turn to view their condition as fortuitous rather than warrented or inevitable and their interests as no less legitimate than those of the powerful. As Matthew Arnold noted, Darwin's theories resembled those of the new star of German philosophy, Arthur Schopenhauer, in that both conceived the universe as governed solely by accident and blind will or, if by gods, "gods careless of our doom." Each in his own way—Darwin reluctantly and inadvertently, Schopenhauer deliberately and enthusiastically—helped to open a Pandora's box of irrationalist doctrines (to be dealt with in the next chapter) that would flourish before the century's end.

In a famous debate at Oxford in 1860, Bishop Wilberforce, speaking for the anti-Darwinians, disclaimed his descent from an ape; to this Thomas Huxley, "Darwin's bulldog," retorted that he preferred an honest ape for an ancestor to a fool. However, not all those opposed to Darwin were religious, nor were all of his advocates as fiercely anticlerical as Huxley. Many clergymen quickly discovered that evolution was not necessarily incompatible with religion. On the other hand, some scientists, Adam Sedgwick, professor of geology at Cambridge, and Ernst von Baer, professor of physiology at Königsberg, for example, declared that Darwin's theory degraded mankind. The enlightened George Bernard Shaw later wrote that "if it could be proved that the whole universe had been produced by such selection [Darwin's 'survival of the fittest'], only fools and rascals could bear to live." The controversy continued unabated in England and abroad throughout the century. Scarcely any major thinker in the Western world escaped its effects or failed to take a position on Darwin's theory.

By 1900, the theory of evolution had largely carried the day; however, it was not yet a dead issue and would erupt again in 1925 at the famous Scopes trial in Tennessee. Regardless of how those involved in the debate viewed Darwin, his theory tore the mask of hypocrisy from the face of Victorian society and forced men to choose between believing what they wished and following science wherever it might lead, no matter how unexpected or distasteful the consequences. The authority and applicability of science, especially in regard to human affairs—that was the real issue of the Darwinian controversy.

Positivist Philosophy and Culture

The system of thought that Auguste Comte named positivism also vaulted to the fore in the third quarter of the century, and for much the same reasons as Darwin's theory. It flew in the face of religious orthodoxy, subsumed man to nature, and proclaimed the absolute authority of science. A disciple of Saint-Simon in his early maturity, Comte held that the spiritual and intellectual leadership of mankind must in time pass from the hands of ignorant priests and misguided political revolutionaries to those of a scientific elite, for only scientists possess the knowledge and selfless dedication to society that is capable of guaranteeing lasting stability and orderly progress. Moreover, because scientists are moral and intellectual leaders, not political revolutionaries, society has nothing to fear from them and can safely entrust such nonpolitical people with moral and intellectual authority, in much the same way that it had once entrusted the Roman Catholic clergy. Indeed, Comte conceived his elite of scientists or positivists (the mediators between science and society) as the only worthy successor to the priesthood that would respect, as the Church had not, the distinction between spiritual and temporal power and that would confine itself to the former.

The superiority of his system to all other programs of social reform, Comte asserted, was that positivists "substitute moral agencies for political. Thus we come again to our leading principle of separating spiritual from temporal power; a principle which, disregarded as it has hitherto been in the system of modern renovators, will be found in every one of the important problems of our time to be the sole possible issue." In short, Comte sought to fuse the characteristically conservative demand for the restoration of a social and spiritual hierarchy with liberal and radical demands for social and material progress. The idea of a priesthood of scientists possessing moral but not political power posed no threat to a materialistic age disillusioned with preindustrial intellectual traditions and in search of new and more appropriate sanctions. And it found fertile soil in the enlightened but autocratic and strife-ridden regimes of Napoleon III and Bismarck.

In support of his views, Comte elaborated the originally Saint-Simonian division of history into three stages based on the dominant mode of thought typical of each. Mankind had progressed, Comte believed, from an infantile theological stage to an adolescent metaphysical stage and stood in his time on the threshold of its final positive stage, when strict empiricism and respect for observed facts—those and only those—would come to prevail over all forms of unverifiable intellectual speculation. On Comte's view, history was not, as earlier philosophers had conceived it, the record of human development with all its foibles and inconsistencies, nor was it the story of man's progress toward freedom, nor was it a field of experiences serving to enrich man's spiritual life and capacity to make judgments. Rather, Comte conceived history as the story of the ultimate and inevitable triumph of scientific thought, culminating in the creation of a science of society itself: a sociology capable of analyzing, organizing, and answering to the needs of society with the same certainty and precision as scientists grasp and master the natural order. Such sweeping and one-sided interpretations of history were not uncommon in the nineteenth century. But what differentiated Comte's interpretation from those of Hegel and Marx was its thoroughly naturalistic character. Whereas Hegel and Marx visualized the end of history as man's liberation from nature, Comte conceived it as the fulfillment of human nature and man's perfect integration with the processes of the larger natural order. What Comte envisaged was the advent of a scientific utopia, endorsed by history, with himself as its prophet.

Comte was indeed the first great prophet of a technocratic social order and in this respect showed more predictive insight than either Hegel or Marx, whose intellectual inferior he was in other respects. His call for a science of society, based on verifiable facts and scientific techniques, accorded well with the realities and aspirations of the dawning age of materialism in which he lived, and it paved the way for the rapid development of the social sciences. The disciples of positivism were many and included some of the most distinguished and influential minds of the time. Among them were the French historians Hippolyte Taine and Ernest Renan; the English historians Henry Thomas Buckle and Walter Bagehot; the dean of German historians in the second half of the century, Leopold von Ranke; and the century's most ardent apostle of science and progress, Herbert Spencer.

Wide-ranging though their approaches to man's social existence were, the positivists all aimed to achieve a maximum of objectivity and scientific rigor in their studies, making use of firsthand accounts of events wherever possible and applying statistics, psychology, and environmental and ethnographic concepts to explain human behavior. Such "scientific" history broke new ground, but it was predicated on the assumption that all human behavior, past and present, individual and collective, is governed by the same or comparable laws as those that govern the rest of nature. Only on this assumption was it possible to propose a predictive science of society.

Positivism also pervaded the arts. It gave impetus in France to the "art-for-art's sake" movement, which aimed to purify art of extraneous sentiment and ideas and thereby free the artist to explore and represent reality as it is. Its leading literary advocates, Gustave Flaubert and Charles Baudelaire, thought of themselves more as careful observers of human behavior and skilled literary craftsmen than as champions of a social, moral, or political cause. Bourgeois society disgusted them, but they reacted to it either by dwelling on its seamier side, as Flaubert did in *Madame Bovary* (1857), or else by withdrawing into an aesthetic ivory tower, as Baudelaire did in his *Les Fleurs du Mal* (1857). Unlike the previous literary generation, these writers did not directly protest,

Monet working in his boat. Painting by Edouard Manet, 1874. Munich, Neue Inakothek.

criticize, or seek to offer a better alternative to the world around them. Instead, they acquiesced to it, even if reluctantly and bitterly, by remaining aloof but careful observers of the passing scene. In the visual arts also, the impressionists, among whom the cult of scientific aestheticism reached its peak, conceived painting as a purely perceptual experience, devoid of any conceptual or emotional content.

This union of science and the arts also gave rise to naturalism, which shared with positivism the assumption that the physical side of human existence—the senses, appetites, psychology, and instinct to survive—are more basic and significant than human social existence, which is but a superficial veneer. Like the aesthete, the naturalist artist was more concerned with understanding and portraying reality faithfully than with protesting or changing it. Also like the aesthete, the naturalist artist turned his back on the heroic and fantastic subjects of the previous literary generation and concentrated on ordinary people and commonplace events. The naturalist painters, Gustave Courbet, François Millet, and Honoré Daumier, like the impressionists, Edward Manet,

The Boulevard Montmartre. Painting by Camille Pissarro, 1897. Examples of impressionist painting.

(Washington, D. C., National Gallery of Art).

Claude Monet, and Edgar Degas, abandoned their studios and went out into the countryside and city streets the better to observe life directly and to work in natural instead of artificial surroundings.

The naturalist, however, was not as politically neutral as the aesthete. The sympathies of the leading naturalist writers—the Goncourt brothers, George Eliot, Turgenev, Dostoevsky, and later Guy de Maupassant, Emile Zola, and August Strindberg—were definitely with the lower classes, with society's victims and outcasts, and with unpopular causes. Their art offended public opinion not only because it seemed vulgar and seamy, but also because it suggested the potentially dangerous idea that bourgeois society restricted and suppressed, and perhaps ultimately would prove unable to contain, a revolutionary eruption of man's physical drives. In fact, naturalism posed no serious threat to the social order, because it held the pessimistic view that human physical nature is so unalterable and so incompatible with social existence as to preclude the possibility of any significant amelioration of the human condition no matter what the social order. Due to this basic impotence, naturalism in time lost its sting. And the bourgeois public eventually could even accept some of its socially harmless teachings, such as more relaxed sexual standards and the theory of psychological determinism put forth by the psychoanalytic movement, which was a late flowering of naturalism.

Positivism also had its critics. Comte and his disciples, because they conceived positivism as a moral but not a political force, depended upon an authoritarian social and political order to enforce its teachings. John Stuart Mill subscribed to Comte's idea of a harmonious society achieved under the leadership of a disinterested intellectual elite. But, as a staunch defender of individual rights and liberties, Mill denounced Comte's program as "the completest system of spiritual and temporal despotism which ever yet emanated from a human brain, unless possibly that of Ignatius Loyola." By the end of the century, a whole new generation of intellectuals and artists, alarmed by the mechanization of society, became disillusioned with the positivist faith in progress and the reduction of human behavior to crudely materialistic and deterministic terms. The idea of a scientific utopia did not die, but, viewed as a universal panacea to all human problems, it no longer went unchallenged. In the twentieth century, it has become increasingly evident that scientific achievements pose as many social and ethical problems as they solve and that the scientist is not an infallible demigod.

Waning of the Victorian Mood

The 1850s and 1860s were decades of prosperity and optimism. But events of the seventies, most importantly the Franco-Prussian War of 1870 and the financial crash of 1873, dealt the spirit of the two decades ushered in by the Great Exhibition a blow it never fully recovered from. The war plunged France into a severe and prolonged political crisis; it brought about the unification of a Germany now intoxicated with power and bent upon achieving great power status; and it planted the seeds of a future war between France and Germany to decide which would ultimately be supreme in Europe. The unification of Germany and Italy at about the same time, the recovery of the United States from its own Civil War and the intensification of its industrial expansion, and the entry of a rapidly developing Japan into world affairs—all put a new strain on the international balance of power hitherto dominated mainly by only two states: England and France.

England also entered a period of new challenges and difficulties. Her world monopoly of cheap manufactured goods was no longer secure against competition from Germany and the United States. The British working classes began to organize through trade unions and to demand a larger share of the national wealth and greater political participation. The extension of the vote to the working classes by the Reform Bill of 1867, the adoption of the secret ballot in 1872, and the extension of the vote to rural workers in 1884 served to sharpen class conflict in England and to arouse anxiety among the wealthy and powerful. The movement for home rule in Ireland, which became increasingly violent toward the end of the century, also added to political tension.

The financial crisis of 1873 sent the European economies into a slump that they did not fully recover from for twenty years. Prices and wages declined; European farmers, large and small, demanded tariff protection against cheap grains imported from the United States and Russia, and industrialists quickly followed suit. As early as the 1860s, the United States adopted tariffs to protect its infant industries from foreign competition. Germany enacted tariff legislation in 1879 and France in 1892. Only England, the chief beneficiary of a free-trade policy, resisted the trend. This revival of tariffs, recalling governmental policies of the seventeenth and eighteenth centuries, meant the decline of free trade and the rise of economic nationalism. The new industrial nations enacted tariffs to improve their position in world affairs, but tariffs meant economic rivalry between whole states, an enlargement of governmental control over domestic affairs, and indifference to the economic well-being of other countries. Economic anxiety also spurred the formation of trade unions and the spread of socialism, and it encouraged business interests to merge into corporations, cartels, and other forms of financial monopoly. All these developments marked a sharp setback for liberal economic theory and threatened individual freedoms. The highly centralized and regulated welfare state was still a long way off, but the older liberal doctrines of laissez faire economics, limited government, and individualism were rapidly disappearing.

Many of the intellectual developments discussed earlier also served to erode the optimism of the fifties and sixties. By 1870 the emergence of socialism in force and the growing influence of revolutionary Marxist teachings increased ideological tension, as did the shift of the Roman Catholic Church to an ultraconservative stance against modernism in any form. Liberals themselves, notably Tocqueville and Mill, were beginning to have doubts about whether liberalism in its original eighteenth-century form could survive and meet the needs of an expanding industrial order. Cynicism, irrationalism, and anti-intellectualism raised their heads in the racist speculations of Gobineau, in the tendentious philosophies of Schopenhauer and Nietzsche, and in the art of Richard Wagner.

Science—Darwin's theory and positivist doctrines in particular—by subsuming man to an amoral nature undermined traditional religious and humanistic moral views and provided sanctions for social inequality and conflict, authoritarian government, and imperialist expansion. Serious artists, disillusioned and disgusted with the vulgar matarialism and bourgeois degradation of those they saw around them and without confidence in their ability to influence affairs, either emphasized the seamier side of their social surroundings, recorded events passively, or withdrew into an ivory-tower aestheticism. This hardening of attitudes on all fronts was grounded, of course, in the deterioration of political and economic conditions during the seventies. By then, it was a matter of record that some of the great issues of the time had been resolved mainly by force: the outcome of the 1848 revolutions, the national question in Italy, Germany, and the United States, and the ruthless suppression of the Paris Commune in 1871. All the major Western states now maintained large standing armies, even in peacetime. Social and economic inequality and uncertainty also were undeniably on the increase. The mood of optimism and self-satisfaction of the previous two decades was by no means dead, but it no longer reigned supreme.

ORIGINS OF MODERN IMPERIALISM

In this atmosphere of political, economic, and ideological tension modern imperialism originated. No one particular factor caused it. Imperialism was the product of many forces at work during the seventies: economic instability, industrial expansion, social conflict, national assertiveness, political rivalry between the great powers, pride in Western civilization, religious philanthropy, scientific curiosity, and the supremacy of materialistic values. The acquisition of empire captured the Western imagination because it seemed to offer solutions to problems at home and new opportunities and advantages abroad. It was thought that territorial expansion would provide highly lucrative investment opportunities for surplus capital, captive markets for industrial production, new supplies of natural resources, strategic military ports and outposts, an outlet for surplus population, and an excellent opportunity to extend the blessings of science and Christianity and to demonstrate the superiority of Western civilization. Imperialism represented a new wave of Western expansionism on all fronts and, in its early phase, reflected the typical Victorian tendency to join the practice of high-minded virtue with economic opportunism and political arrogance.

England, in order to retain her hegemony in world affairs in the face of growing foreign competition, was the first to embark upon overseas expansion. The British already possessed a colonial empire, but it was made up mostly of territories settled by Englishmen with strong ties to their former homeland. With the exception of the United States, which had gained independence by force in the eighteenth century, the other territories began to acquire peacefully the right to self-government in the middle decades of the nineteenth century. New Zealand gained independence in 1854, four Australian colonies in 1861, Canada in 1867, and the Cape Colony in South Africa in 1872. Together with England, these former colonies formed the British Commonwealth, an arrangement that proved mutually satisfactory and profitable.

But the new imperialism differed significantly from older colonialism. The early colonies had been settled and developed by Europeans themselves and were modeled on the home countries from which the colonists had come. In their commercial dealings with native populations, Europeans generally had been content to purchase what those populations produced by their own preindustrial methods. By comparison, the new imperialism was characterized by the economic penetration, transformation, and exploitation of already-settled regions as well as by the political domination and subjugation of their populations. The success of Britain's imperial policy in India and Egypt demonstrated that the colonization of countries alien in race, religion, and culture and unsuitable for European settlement could, nevertheless, be highly profitable and politically advantageous, if military and administrative control was firmly maintained. By the 1880s, one-fifth of Britain's overseas investments were in India and almost one-fifth of her exports were sold there. Control of India also gave Britain a commanding position in the affairs of all East Asia. The architect of British imperialism was the exotic and venturesome Benjamin Disraeli, who proclaimed his expansionist views in a famous speech delivered at the Crystal Palace in 1872, two years before he became prime minister. In 1875, he borrowed four million pounds from the Rothschild family and bought the controlling interest in the Suez Canal to safeguard the route to India. A year later, he persuaded Parliament to name Queen Victoria empress of India, whereupon she emerged from mourning for the first time since the death of her husband in 1861. England was now launched on a course whose rewards could hardly have been foreseen by even the most ambitious of the early Victorians.

Missionaries and scientific expeditions paved the way for Britain's drive into Africa. The most famous of hundreds of missionaries who went there to convert the natives to Christianity was Dr. David Livingstone, who penetrated the interior of the Dark Continent in the 1840s and publicized the sufferings of the natives at the hands of Arab slavers. British boats were sent to patrol the African coasts to intercept slave traders. And one of the primary goals of the Gold Coast Colony, established in 1874, was to eradicate slavery in the surrounding regions. Beginning with the search for the sources of the Nile by Burton and Speke in 1866, scientific societies sponsored one expedition after another into the African interior to bring back information about the unknown continent.

Following the missionaries and explorers came the adventurers and businessmen; the most famous was Cecil Rhodes. With the discovery of gold, diamonds, other natural resources, and a cheap labor supply, the scramble for Africa was on. To maintain control over the Suez Canal, the British established a protectorate over Egypt in 1882 and soon extended their rule southward to the Sudan. From the Cape Colony in South Africa, taken from the Dutch in 1806, the British pushed northward. Bechuanaland was taken in 1885, Rhodesia in 1889, and Nyasaland in 1893. The Boer War (1899–1902) was caused by the British effort to force the independent states of the Transvaal and the Orange Free State, both inhabited by descendants of the original Dutch settlers of South Africa, to join in a Union of South Africa. The British also established themselves in East Africa and Uganda. Cecil Rhodes' dream of British control of Africa from the Cape to Cairo seemed close to realization.

Envious and shocked by the ease with which Britain was subjugating a whole continent, other European states soon joined in. The French became masters of most of North and Central Africa; the Italians took Libya, a piece of Somaliland, and established a protectorate over Ethiopia. The mineral-rich Congo fell to Belgium, and Portugal claimed the colonies of Angola and Mozambique. The Germans, eager to thwart the British, established themselves in East Africa and in the arid wastes of Southwest Africa. By 1900, only one-tenth of Africa had not been annexed by the Europeans, whereas twenty-five years earlier only one-tenth was in European possession.

In the Far East, the imperialists divided their attention between the South Pacific and China. The British annexed the Fiji Islands in 1874 and shared in the division of New Guinea with the Germans and Dutch in 1885. By the end of the century, Germany was in control of the Marianas and the Caroline Islands. France had extended its control from Tahiti to include the whole of the Society Islands and the Marquesas. The United States, after its victory in the Spanish-American War of 1898, annexed Puerto Rico in the Caribbean and acquired the Philippine Islands. In China, Britain had taken possession of Hong Kong in 1842 and had forced open a number of Chinese ports to Western trade. The French completed their conquest of Indochina in the 1880s, and the Japanese, victorious in a war with China in 1895, annexed Korea and Formosa. By 1900, imperialism had become a worldwide movement.

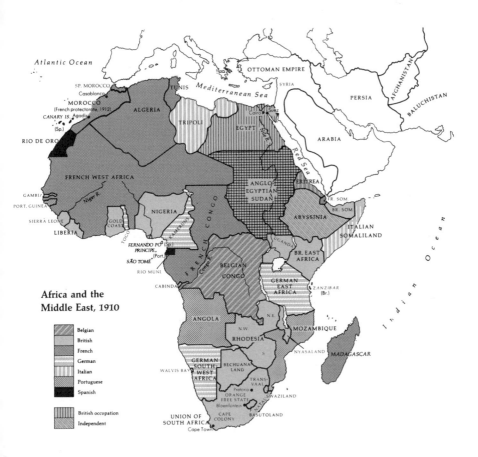

Africa and the
Middle East, 1910

Belgian
British
French
German
Italian
Portuguese
Spanish

British occupation
Independent

Britain, the biggest gainer, had acquired over four million square miles of new territory with a population of sixty-six million people.

Socialists attributed imperialism primarily to the accumulation and investment abroad of "surplus capital" and to the search for markets outside the country to absorb production above the demands of the home market. This was the thesis of the English socialist, John A. Hobson, in his pioneering analysis, *Imperialism* (1902), and later of Lenin in his tract, *Imperialism, The Highest Stage of Capitalism* (1916). According to them, if there had been a more even distribution of national income, there would have been no accumulation of surplus capital and consequently no real need for territorial expansion. Also, because the workers would have had more purchasing power, they would have been able to absorb the increase in production at home. The socialist interpretation was right as far as it went; economic self-interest was, of course, the prime impulse to imperialism, and huge amounts of capital were invested abroad. During the third quarter of the century, most of the capital exported by Europeans went to build up the white man's world: Europe, North and South America, and Australia. By 1900, most of the capital was going to the nonwhite, backward colonies, and the amount was much larger. In 1914, about one-eighth of Britain's total wealth was invested in her colonies.

Nevertheless, most of the colonies turned out to be far less profitable than originally anticipated. They accounted for little of the increase in world trade between 1870 and 1914. But the failure of the imperialists to realize the profits they expected from their colonies did not diminish their search for empire, for the political motive behind imperialism was as strong as the economic and inseparable from it. Profit was pursued in the name of national power and glory and took on the character of a crusade. The British spoke of the white man's burden, the French of their *mission civilisatrice*, and the Germans of their superior *Kultur*. The German colonies, for example, were of little economic value, but this did not discourage German expansionism. And the French, to gain an ally against Germany, had pumped more money into Russia by 1914 than into all their colonies combined. Nor was the imperialism of such economically lagging countries as Italy and Russia caused by pressure for investment opportunities and markets abroad. In both cases, the political motive was stronger than the economic.

Moreover, the working classes of the Western powers were themselves beneficiaries of the prosperity generated by imperialism. In this respect, imperialism performed a useful social function. The new prosperity the workers enjoyed served to mitigate their discontents, dampen their revolutionary ardor, and appease even the socialists among them, who officially condemned imperialism as a capitalist crime. The plain fact was that, by the end of the century, the possession of colonies, whether profitable or not, had become an accepted criterion of greatness, the indispensable sign of a Great Power. Britain and France had for centuries possessed colonies that had helped them to achieve greatness. It was only natural, therefore, that the new powers that came into being in the third quarter of the century—Germany, Italy, Japan, and the United States—should think that they must also have colonies.

In 1897, at the height of the imperial age, Britain celebrated Victoria's fiftieth anniversary as queen with a magnificent Diamond Jubilee. It was a very different event from the Great Exhibition of 1851, which had extolled British ingenuity and industriousness. The Diamond Jubilee was a glamorous affair in praise of the benefits and rewards of empire. It put on display princes from India, gold prospectors from Australia, Chinese police from Hong Kong, Dyak headhunters, Sudanese cavalry,

British and Indian Princes in the Jubilee Parade, 1897.
(Illustrated London News, June 26, 1897).

Fijian princesses, and prime ministers of the self-governing colonies. The squadron of Indian Lancers, manned by bearded Sikhs and Pathans and diamond-clad rajas with their wives dressed in golden cloth, thrilled the crowd watching the Jubilee procession make its way to Saint Paul's Cathedral behind a band playing "Three Cheers for India." The spectacle conjured up the image of brave young Englishmen quitting the comforts of home to spend long and lonely years in remote and inhospitable regions, dedicated to the dangerous task of bringing law and progress beyond the far reaches of civilization to their "new-caught sullen peoples, half devil and half child"—an image that the Indian-born Englishman, Rudyard Kipling, did more than any other writer to popularize in his many tales and descriptions of English and native life in India. The spirit of the Great Exhibition was still very much alive in England and throughout the Western world in 1897. But it now shared the field with forces from which a new world would emerge.

BIBLIOGRAPHY

General Works

BINKLEY, ROBERT C. *Realism and Nationalism, 1852–1871.* New York: Harper & Row, 1935.

BURY, J. P. T., ed. *The New Cambridge Modern History.* Vol. X: *The Zenith of European Power, 1830–1870.* Cambridge: University Press, 1962.

RICH, NORMAN. *The Age of Nationalism and Reform, 1850–1890.* New York: Norton, 1970.

Politics and Society

ADAMS, ARTHUR E., ed. *Imperial Russia after 1861: Peaceful Modernization or Revolution?* Boston: D. C. Heath Co., 1965.

ASHWORTH, WILLIAM. *A Short History of the International Economy, 1850–1950.* London: Longmans, Green, 1952.

BRIGGS, ASA. *Victorian People.* Chicago: University of Chicago Press, 1955.

———. *The Age of Improvement.* New York: Longmans, Green, 1959.

CAUTE, DAVID. *The Left in Europe Since 1789.* London: Weidenfeld & Nicolson, 1966.

CLARK, KITSON G. *The Making of Victorian England.* Cambridge, Mass.: Harvard University Press, 1962.

COBBAN, ALFRED. *A History of Modern France.* Vol. 2, *1799–1871.* London: Penguin Books, 1961.

FIELDHOUSE, DAVID K. *The Colonial Empires.* London: Weidenfeld & Nicolson, 1966.

HAMEROW, THEODORE S. *Restoration, Revolution, Reaction: Economics and Politics in Germany, 1815–1871.* Princeton, N.J.: Princeton University Press, 1958.

HOLBORN, HAJO. *A History of Modern Germany.* Vol. 3. New York: Alfred A. Knopf, 1969.

HOWARD, MICHAEL. *The Franco-Prussian War.* New York: Collier-Macmillan, 1961.

JACKSON, JOHN H. *Marx, Proudhon and European Socialism.* New York: Macmillan Co., 1958.

JÁSZI, OSCAR. *The Dissolution of the Habsburg Monarchy.* Chicago: University of Chicago Press, 1929.

KUCZYNSKI, JÜRGEN. *The Rise of the Working Classes.* Translated by C. T. A. Ray. London: Weidenfeld & Nicolson, 1967.

LAVER, JAMES. *Manners and Morals in the Age of Optimism, 1848–1914.* New York: Harper & Row, 1966.

LEVY, HERMANN. *The New Industrial System: A Study of the Origins, Forms, Finance, and Prospects of Concentration in Industry.* London: Routledge, 1936.

LONGFORD, ELIZABETH. *Queen Victoria: Born to Succeed.* New York: Harper & Row, 1965.

MOLLER, HERBERT, ed. *Population Movements in Modern European History.* New York: Collier-Macmillan, 1964.

MOOREHEAD, ALAN. *The White Nile.* London: Hamilton, 1960.

MORAZÉ, CHARLES. *The Triumph of the Middle Classes.* Translated by P. Wait and B. Ferryan. London: Weidenfeld & Nicolson, 1966.

MORRIS, JAMES. *Pax Britannica: The Climax of an Empire.* New York: Harcourt, Brace & World, 1968.

PFLANZE, OTTO. *Bismarck and the Development of Germany: The Period of Unification, 1815-1871.* Princeton, N. J.: Princeton University Press, 1963.

ROVER, CONSTANCE. *Women's Suffrage and Party Politics in Britain, 1866-1914.* London: Routledge & Kegan Paul, 1967.

SETON-WATSON, HUGH. *The Decline of Imperial Russia, 1855-1914.* New York: Praeger, 1952.

SMITH, DENIS M. *Cavour and Garibaldi, 1860: A Study in Political Conflict.* Cambridge: University Press, 1954.

SONTAG, RAYMOND J. *Germany and England: Background of Conflict, 1848-1894.* New York: Appleton-Century, 1938.

THOMPSON, JAMES M. *Louis Napoleon and the Second Empire.* Oxford: Blackwell, 1954.

THOMSON, DAVID. *England in the Nineteenth Century.* London: Penguin Books, 1950.

WHYTE, ARTHUR J. *The Evolution of Modern Italy.* New York: W. W. Norton & Co., 1959.

WILLIAMS, ROGER L. *The World of Napoleon III, 1851-1870.* New York: Collier-Macmillan, 1962.

———. *The French Revolution of 1870-1871.* New York: W. W. Norton & Co., 1969.

WRIGLEY, EDWARD A. *Industrial Growth and Population Change.* Cambridge: University Press, 1961.

Intellectual and Cultural Trends

ALLEN, WALTER. *The English Novel.* London: Penguin Books, 1954.

AVINERI, SHLOMO. *The Social and Political Thought of Karl Marx.* Cambridge: University Press, 1970.

BARZUN, JACQUES. *Darwin, Marx, Wagner: Critique of a Heritage.* New York: Little, Brown & Co., 1941.

BOWLE, JOHN. *Politics and Opinion in the Nineteenth Century.* London: Cape, 1954.

BURROW, JOHN W. *Evolution and Society: A Study in Victorian Social Theory.* London: Cambridge University Press, 1966.

CARR, EDWARD H. *The Romantic Exiles.* London: Gollancz, 1933.

———. *Studies in Revolution.* London: Macmillan & Co., 1950.

COWLING, MAURICE. *Mill and Liberalism.* Cambridge: University Press, 1963.

HIMMELFARB, GERTRUDE. *Darwin and the Darwinian Revolution.* New York: W. W. Norton & Co., 1959.

HOUGHTON, WALTER E. *The Victorian Frame of Mind, 1830-1870.* New Haven: Yale University Press, 1957.

HYMAN, STANLEY E. *The Tangled Bank: Darwin, Marx, Fraser and Freud as Imaginative Writers.* New York, Atheneum, 1962.

IRVINE, WILLIAM. *Apes, Angels, and Victorians: The Story of Darwin, Huxley, and Evolution.* New York: McGraw-Hill, 1955.

LEFEBVRE, HENRI. *The Sociology of Marx.* Translated by N. Guterman. New York: Random House, 1968.

LICHTHEIM, GEORGE. *Marxism: A Historical and Critical Study.* New York: Praeger, 1961.

LÖWITH, KARL. *From Hegel to Nietzsche: The Revolution in Nineteenth-Century Thought.* Translated by D. E. Green. London: Constable, 1965.

MARCUSE, HERBERT. *Reason and Revolution: Hegel and the Rise of Social Theory.* London and New York: Oxford University Press, 1941.

MAYER, J. P. *Political Thought in France from the Revolution to the Fifth Republic.* 3rd ed. London: Routledge & Kegan Paul, 1961.

MÉTRAUX, GUY S. and FRANÇOIS CROUZET, eds. *The Nineteenth-Century World.* New York: Mentor Books, 1963.

NOVOTNY, FRITZ. *Painting and Sculpture in Europe, 1780-1880.* Baltimore: Penguin Books, 1960.

PANKHURST, RICHARD K. P. *The Saint-Simonians: Mill and Carlyle: A Preface to Modern Thought.* London: Sidgwick & Jackson, 1957.

PRAZ, MARIO. *The Hero in Eclipse.* Translated by A. Davidson. London and New York: Oxford University Press, 1956.

ROSENBERG, JOHN D. *The Darkening Glass: A Portrait of Ruskin's Genius.* New York: Columbia University Press, 1961.

SHAFER, BOYD C. *Nationalism: Interpreters and Interpretations.* Washington, D.C.: Service Center for Teachers of History, 1959.

SIMON, WALTER M. *European Positivism in the Nineteenth Century.* Ithaca, N. Y.: Cornell University Press, 1963.

SNYDER, LOUIS L. *Race, a History of Modern Ethnic Theories.* New York and Toronto: Longmans, Green, 1939.

ST. AUBYN, GILES. *A Victorian Eminence: The Life and Works of Henry Thomas Buckle.* London: Barrie, 1958.

TRILLING, LIONEL. *Matthew Arnold.* 2nd ed. New York: Columbia University Press, 1949.

TUCKER, ROBERT. *Philosophy and Myth in Karl Marx.* Cambridge: University Press, 1964.

WATKINS, FREDERICK M. *The Political Tradition of the West: A Study in the Development of Modern Liberalism.* Cambridge, Mass.: Harvard University Press, 1948.

WIGHTMAN, WILLIAM P. D. *The Growth of Scientific Ideas.* New Haven: Yale University Press, 1951.

WILLEY, BASIL. *Nineteenth-Century Studies.* New York: Columbia University Press, 1949.

WILSON, EDMUND. *To the Finland Station: A Study in the Writing and Acting of History.* New York: Harcourt, Brace & Co., 1940.

FIN DE SIÈCLE: 1880–1914

SOCIETY IN TRANSITION

During the transition from the nineteenth to the twentieth century, the old institutions and ideas that had shaped the world and the West since the triple revolution began to show signs of strain and exhaustion, while a new undercurrent of disillusionment and dissatisfaction with established society began to gather force. The old order in the West was still sufficiently well-entrenched to hold up until 1914, but already it was being eroded, both from within and without, by the appearance of counterforces destined to overthrow it and form the foundation of life in the twentieth century. The essential feature of the generation preceding the First World War was precisely that it was a twilight time, during which the old nineteenth-century order found itself giving way, gradually but steadily, to the emerging twentieth-century order. This tension would finally be resolved by the war itself.

At the turn of the century, the average middle-class western European saw little to suggest that his civilization was in peril. Imperialist expansion had extended European influence to every corner of the globe. Britannia ruled the waves, Europe's predominance in world affairs was at an all-time high, and Europeans enjoyed unprecedented prosperity. For almost a century, the European powers had managed to avert a major war among themselves, and none seemed in the offing. Economically, too, Europe was supreme. Between them, Britain, Germany, and France controlled sixty percent of the world market for manufactured goods, and no country except the United States and Japan had escaped European economic domination. Europeans were proud of their scientific and technological superiority, which had made possible their ascendancy and inspired supreme self-confidence and optimism about the future. Europe's political and economic supremacy was matched by her cultural supremacy. The great European capitals—Paris, London, Berlin, Vienna, and Rome—were the cultural centers of the world. To them were drawn the creative elites in all fields, and from them emanated the influences that shaped the thought and attitudes of mankind throughout the civilized world. At the dawn of the new century, celebrated by the magnificent Paris Exposition of 1900, there seemed little reason to suppose that this situation would change. Nevertheless, danger signals were already evident.

Imperialism and its Impact

Three new powers, the United States, Russia, and Japan, all capable of challenging and supplanting western European hegemony in the non-European areas of the world, loomed on the horizon. All eagerly entered into competition with the western European powers for empire: the United States in the Caribbean and the Pacific, Russia in the Balkans and the Far East, and Japan also in the Far East. Even without their entry into the race for empire, however, it is unlikely that the non-European world would have submitted indefinitely to European imperialist subjugation. The Ethiopian defeat of the Italian invaders in 1896, the Boxer Rebellion in 1900 protesting the western takeover of China, and the stunning victory of Japan over Russia in 1904 were early signs of the anticolonial backlash to come.

An even graver threat to Europe's privileged position was the rivalry among the imperialist powers themselves. Britain came into conflict with France, Germany, and Holland over the partitioning of South Africa. Germany clashed with France over Morocco and with England over the much more serious issue of relative sea power. And Austria vied with Russia for influence in the Balkans. The Fashoda incident and the Spanish-American War of 1898, the Boer War from 1899 to 1902, the Russo-Japanese War of 1904–1905, the Agadir crisis of 1911, and the Balkan Wars of 1912 and 1913 were simply landmarks in the deterioration of international relations brought on by an imperialist rivalry that would culminate in the First World War. As the rivalry spread and increased in intensity, the original justifications for imperialism—the superiority of Western civilization and the responsibility of the great powers to spread its blessings throughout the world—were bolstered by the less high-minded claims of the racial superiority of whites and the struggle for existence and survival of the fittest, derived from Darwin. The great literary apologist of imperialism, Rudyard Kipling, and its great literary critic, Joseph Conrad, both had had long first-hand experience in the colonial world.

If imperialist expansion enabled the European powers to dominate world affairs, it also signified the displacement of the old structure of power by a new one. From the Congress of Vienna in 1815 to the Congress of Berlin in 1878, the governing idea of European political life had been that of a concert of nations, a concept based on a realizable balance of power among the major European states and designed to promote common European interests and equilibrium in the West. But by 1890 this concept was no longer feasible. The inequities, tensions, and divergent interests dividing the European powers had grown too great to be resolved within that now restrictive framework; the threat of the non-European powers to European supremacy also rendered the balance of power obsolete. Preeminence in European affairs could no longer be divorced from the question of preeminence in world affairs.

By 1890, there were in fact only two real poles of power in Europe: British sea supremacy and German preponderance on the continent. Around them crystallized the new alliance systems—the Triple Alliance of Germany, Austro-Hungary, and Italy, and the Triple Entente of Britain, France, and Russia—that would dissolve the old concert-of-nations concept and sunder the West into two increasingly opposed camps. This new division, all too reminiscent of the internecine conflict between Athens and Sparta that brought down ancient Greece, culminated in the holocaust of World War One and finally cost Europe its supremacy in world affairs. The rivalry for profit and power abroad and the deterioration of political relations at home turned out to be but two sides of the same coin.

Imperialism also undermined the traditional nation-state and nationalist ideology. Far-flung empires, geographically remote from their mother countries and encompassing populations widely different in social, cultural, and historical background, were incompatible, both in theory and practice, with the Western idea of the nation-state as a relatively homogeneous polity, defined by common institutions, a common language, and a common culture. Typically, imperialist powers ruled and exploited their subject peoples without absorbing them or extending citizenship and national rights to them, without even preparing them for eventual independence and friendly participation in international affairs. Imperialism, therefore, did not represent an extension of nationalism, but rather its negation. It gave rise to the supranational or transnational state that foreshadowed the vast intercontinental superpowers that would emerge after the Second World War. Although motivated by national self-interest, this new political structure could find little sanction in the nationalism of the past, which emphasized the cultural solidarity and political equality of the citizenry. The relationship of the imperialist power to its subject peoples was essentially that of a master to his slaves. And such a relationship found more appropriate sanctions in the myths of racism, in the innate superiority of the master civilization, and in a dog-eat-dog conception of life and politics.

All of this suggests the degree to which imperialism at the turn of the century had departed from the old structure of power. The new imperialist powers were not necessarily European and did not necessarily follow the European pattern of development. Japan's sudden emergence as a major force in world affairs dramatically exemplified how a nation with a completely different history and culture could selectively appropriate elements of the European tradition, graft them onto its own, and use the new power afforded by the borrowings to bolster the native structure and make it competitive with the West. The United States and Russia were Western but found themselves in conflict with the European powers and with each other. Nor were the European powers themselves of a kind. Britain and France were liberal-democratic countries, Germany and Austro-Hungary were authoritarian regimes, and Italy wavered between the two. Britain and France were naval powers; Germany and Austro-Hungary were land powers. Western Europe was industrial, urban, and middle class; Eastern Europe was still largely agrarian, rural, and peasant. If anything, the disparities within the international order during the imperialist era became more pronounced than ever before.

Imperialism, therefore, did not represent the Westernization of the world so much as it did the fragmentation of the Western tradition into elements adaptable to the emerging new world order: namely, the elements of science and technology, and elements inconsistent with or irrelevant to it; namely, Judaic-Christian religious beliefs, humanist culture, and liberal-democratic politics. The end result of imperialism was the polarization of all mankind into a few "have" nations, which flourished at the expense of the many "have-not" nations. Whole continents—Africa, Asia, and Latin America—fell under the control of a small clique of powers intent upon monopolizing the world's resources and markets. Large parts of Europe itself, namely, the fringe areas of Ireland, Spain, southern Italy, and the Balkans, were excluded from the material prosperity generated by overseas expansion. To be sure, the Western powers

The White (?) Man's Burden.

(Cartoon from *Life,* March 16, 1899).

dominated the imperialist rivalry. By 1900, within one generation, the European powers alone had gained control of one-fifth of the world's land area and one-tenth of its population. But imperialism's legacy to the twentieth century was more the growing disparity between the "haves" and "have-nots" than between the Western and non-Western peoples.

Imperialism marked the high point of the conflict between modernism and traditionalism, which, while not confined to the Western world, was far more advanced there than elsewhere by 1900. Until the advent of imperialism, most of mankind still lived, whether from choice or necessity, in traditional premodern ways. Imperialism succeeded in disrupting these long familiar patterns, tribal, agrarian, and religious, but failed to provide alternatives. The result was that most of the colonial peoples found themselves, and continue to find themselves almost a century later, worse off than before, without a past or future, manipulated from without and unstable within. In contrast, the great powers were those in which the forces of modernization—industrialization, urbanization, and the secularization of culture—either displaced tradition altogether, as in the liberal-democratic countries of Britain, France, and the United States, or else served to reinvigorate old interests and institutions, as in the authoritarian regimes of Germany, Japan, and Russia. There was nothing intrinsically Western about modernization. The fringe areas of Europe, Latin America, and the deep South of the United

States, all Western certainly, were scarcely touched by modernization, while non-Western Japan and partially Westernized Russia were well along the way to achieving it.

Throughout the world in the nineteenth century, where tradition was still capable of maintaining equilibrium and containing or accomodating innovation, modernization made least headway. But where the premodern order was already corrupt or in decline (or almost nonexistent, as in the United States) modernization made rapid progress. This was true in England and France in the early decades of the century, in Germany and Japan by mid-century, and in the United States and Russia by the 1880s. By 1900, modernization was an accomplished fact in all these countries and, by way of imperialism, was on the march throughout the world.

Industrialization Takes Command

The driving force of modernization was a new wave of industrialization during the 1880s. It differed from earlier technological progress in that it did not simply improve upon existing productive processes, but created entirely new industries, notably the electrical industry. Electricity was a new source of power, cleaner and more efficient, easier and more economical to produce, and with a greater potential and range of applications than power derived from coal and mechanical sources. Moreover, the development of electrical power depended far more than earlier industrial advances upon sophisticated scientific theory. The dynamo, a machine introduced in the 1880s to transform mechanical energy into electrical energy, represented a more difficult intellectual feat than such earlier inventions as James Watt's steam engine, the result of comparatively elementary practical observations. The dynamo would not have been possible without extensive experimental research and the mathematical formulation of the properties of electricity, magnetism, and light carried out by Michael Faraday, Clerk Maxwell, and many other theoretical scientists working in Western universities and laboratories. This new source of energy made possible electrical lighting, the electrification of transportation, the telephone and radio. All became realities by the first decade of the twentieth century, and have since become indispensable to civilized life and further technological progress. Not without reason did the distinguished contemporary American man of letters, Henry Adams, himself hostile to the emerging new order, regard the dynamo as the symbol of the modern age and its break with the past.

Other new industrial advances, no less remarkable than electrical power, were making their appearance by the turn of the century. Thermodynamics, the science of converting one form of energy into another, made possible the internal combustion engine, which in turn made possible the automobile and power-propelled airplane. The first rudimentary automobiles were seen on the roads of Europe and North America as early as the 1890s, and the Wright brothers demonstrated the first power-propelled airplane in 1903.

These developments gave impetus to the search for cheaper, more efficient fuels and lighter, more malleable metals. In 1897, the first diesel engine was manufactured. The steam turbine (forerunner of the gas turbine developed in the 1940s) was already powering electric generators and large ships. The chemical industry was producing the first synthetic products and experimenting with alloys important to the metallurgical industries. The American engineer Frederick Winslow Taylor, in his theory of "scientific management" conceived in the nineties, formulated the methods and goals of mass production, which Henry Ford put into practice in the first decade of the twentieth century. Just as important as the new inventions themselves were the more rapid pace of technological advance, the closer alliance between technology and the theoretical sciences, and the implementation of more systematic and specialized modes of production. For good reason, this new wave of industrialization, which made 1900 such a confident year, has come to be called a "second industrial revolution."

As with imperialism abroad, industrialization at home acted as a solvent of the old order and a catalyst of the new. By the end of the nineteenth century, the foundations of present-day urban and industrial society were laid. The new scientific, technological, and industrial advances, unlike the old, were large-scale undertakings, requiring enormous amounts of capital and the concentration of population and facilities into vast urban agglomerations. The result was a complete change in the complexion of advanced industrial countries. The small-scale entrepreneur was rapidly supplanted by the industrial baron with his boards of directors and trustees; the independent artisan was supplanted by the collectivized factory worker, performing his specialized function in a vast network of similar, interlocking functions. The small family business, common before 1880, gave way to the huge and complex trust and cartel, such as the Krupp Steel Works in Germany, Schneider-Creusot in France, Vickers-Armstrong in Great Britain, and John Pierpont Morgan's colossal United States Steel Corporation. In Germany alone, the number of industrial plants employing fifty workers or more doubled between 1880 and 1914; at the same time, those employing five or less declined by half. The total number of German industrial workers in 1914 was four times as great as in 1880. Villages burgeoned into towns and towns into cities. The Ruhr Valley in

Germany and the English Midlands were transformed into sprawling belts of industrial and urban concentration. The new industrial order offered the prospect of a higher material standard, but it also marked the rise of the now familiar spectacle of a collectivized and conformist, rootless and impersonal mass society.

An increase in the food supply and improvements in medicine and hygiene caused a sharp decline in the death rate and a rise in population, which swelled the influx into the cities. Whereas Europe's population had increased by only about 30 million between 1850 and 1870, it soared by about 100 million between 1870 and 1900, a figure which does not include the emigration of some forty percent of the overall increase. The overwhelming majority of this new population was absorbed by the towns and cities. In Germany, the number of cities with more than one hundred thousand inhabitants increased from eight in 1870 to forty-eight by 1910; Russia had sixteen cities of this size by 1900. In the United States, nearly half the population was concentrated on one percent of the available land, and one-eighth lived in the ten largest cities. Before 1850, only London and Paris had populations exceeding a million. By 1900 twelve more cities had reached that level. Four were European: Berlin, Vienna, St. Petersburg, and Moscow; three were North American: New York, Chicago, and Philadelphia; two were South American: Buenos Aires and Rio de Janeiro; and three were Asian: Tokyo, Osaka, and Calcutta. The giant metropolis had established itself as the center and symbol of the new worldwide industrial order, which, like imperialism, had sprung into existence within a single generation.

Emergence of Mass Society

All these changes, which occurred within so short a time span, were bound to have a profound impact on the social order. The new business classes, now in control of unprecedented wealth, emerged as new social elites, proud lords of vast industrial, commercial, and banking empires. In Europe, they tended to merge with remnants of the old landed aristocracies, still at the top of the social scale, to form a single, relatively homogeneous ruling class. This fusion typically came about through intermarriage between members of the two groups, and from social intermingling—education at the same schools, membership in the same social clubs, attendance at the same social events, and vacationing at the same spas and resorts. It was further enhanced by the ennoblement of such prominent industrialists and bankers as the Rothschilds, the Sasoons, and Ernest Cassel in England, the Krupp and Siemens families in Germany, the Rothschilds and Gutmanns in Austria, and the Franchettis in Italy. Many members of the old aristocracies in turn derived much of their wealth and influence from industry and commerce; examples would include Lord Derby of England's Stanley family, the princes Pless and Henckel-Donnersmarck in Germany, and the Hohenlohes in Bohemia. In the United States, where no such old aristocracy existed, the *nouveaux riches*—the Vanderbilts, Rockefellers, and Stanfords, Andrew Carnegie, J. P. Morgan, and Marshall Field—succeeded in becoming a new ruling aristocracy of wealth by their own efforts.

In some respects, the new elites resembled the old; both were arrogant and proud, privileged and exclusionist. In other ways, they differed, as old wealth often differs from new. What land, social position, and tradition had been to the old aristocracies, money, power, and influence were to the new. Often, especially in the United States, the business oligarchs took pride in being ambitious, self-made men of humble origin: virtues extolled in Horatio Alger's enormously popular books for boys. And, unlike the old aristocracies, who typically disdained business affairs and preferred living in the country to the city, the new elites prided themselves on their entrepreneurial skills and success. Although they owned lavish country estates and frequented exclusive pleasure resorts, they preferred to live, at least part of the time, in the cities close to their enterprises. Their city mansions, along New York's Fifth Avenue and Washington Square, San Francisco's Nob Hill, and the Bois de Boulogne and Avenue Foch in Paris, were prominent features of the changing urban landscape, symbols of success for all to see and envy. The new elites saw themselves as more industrious and resourceful than other men, better adapted to the struggle for existence, and living testimony of the survival of the fittest. They thought of themselves as the pillars of the new society and were indeed the single most powerful stimulus to the emergence of mass society. The industrialist and the imperialist, often one and the same, found their philosophical apologists in Charles Darwin, Herbert Spencer, John Dewey, and others who preached natural inequality, the glory of struggle and competition, elitism, the inevitability of progress, and the superiority of the practical and pragmatic approach to life.

Their critics saw them differently. Naturalist novelists, like Émile Zola in France and Theodore Dreiser in the United States, depicted them as ruthless exploiters, driven by an insatiable lust for riches and power at the expense of any and all. The astute contemporary observer of this emerging elite in the United States, Thorstein Veblen, depicted it in his classic study, *The Theory of the Leisure Class* (1899), as made up of unproductive parasites, vestiges of the past, characterized by their acquisitiveness and ostentatious display of unearned wealth merely to arouse envy ("conspicuous consumption" and "invidious comparison," he called it). Others, sympathetic to the old preindustrial order, like the Swiss historian, Jakob Burckhardt, and Henry Adams in the United States, viewed them as vulgar upstarts and philistines, a menace to civilization itself. The evolution of the new business oligarchy in Germany was brilliantly portrayed by Thomas Mann in his novel, *Buddenbrooks* (1901). In England its manners and morals were the subject of John Galsworthy's *The Forsyte Saga* (1922). Edith Wharton's many novels dealt with the life of the upper classes in the United States.

Further down the social scale, the middle classes were in the process of being polarized between the new business classes on the one hand and the rapidly expanding industrial proletariat on the other. As industrialization spurred the growth of large corporate structures and the centralization of wealth and power, the middle classes found their traditional economic independence, social homogeneity, and liberal outlook threatened. Either they were absorbed by the new order, becoming civil servants and professionals, managers and bureaucrats, or they were forced down the social scale into the ranks of the lower middle classes, who were being left behind by the new order.

What had started in the early nineteenth century as a relatively unified liberal class, claiming to represent the best interests of society as a whole, began to fragment by the end of the century and to serve an essentially antiliberal order, one that acknowledged no common interest except that of the strongest. At the upper end of the bourgeois hierarchy were the well-paid managers and directors, who tended to identify their interests with those of their employers. Toward the center were the professional groups and some intellectuals and bureaucrats, who tended to uphold traditional liberal values. At the bottom were the petty bourgeois, who were threatened with extinction or absorption by the industrial working classes and who were becoming disillusioned with liberalism altogether. This stratification, economic, social, and ideological, not only undermined liberalism and its supporters, but, in doing so, allowed anti-liberal forces to make rapid headway.

This erosion of liberalism was most advanced among the lower middle classes, whose existence was most threatened by industrialization. The more it worked against them, the more they became desperate, exasperated, and susceptible to reactionary doctrines and programs that promised to halt or reverse the processes responsible for their plight. They were hostile to the working classes, who threatened their precarious economic status; to large-scale capitalists, against whom they could not compete; and to intellectuals and Jews as conspicuous beneficiaries and defenders of liberal and radical values. Not surprisingly, twentieth-century fascism's largest and most enthusiastic body of supporters came from the lower middle classes. The plight and outlook of the petty bourgeois in Germany before the First World War was the subject of Heinrich Mann's novel, *The Patrioteer* (1918).

The upper echelons of the middle classes adapted to the new order by becoming its functionaries. Already the most educated element in Western society and the one that placed the highest value on education, they were admirably suited to meet the need of industrial society for large numbers of highly trained specialists. This new managerial class, the so-called white collar workers—administrators, civil servants, professionals, and others necessary to modern industrial production, although not themselves producers—quickly became, and has since remained, the fastest-growing segment of the wage-earning population in advanced industrial countries. Indispensable contributors to and beneficiaries of the order they served, the white-collar workers quickly supplanted the dying class of small-scale independent producers and entrepreneurs as the primary source of support and stability of advanced capitalist industrialization. Moreover, as most white-collar work could be performed as well by women as by men, the expansion of this sector of the economy presented a hitherto almost nonexistent opportunity for women to participate in life outside the home. In the long run, it acted as a solvent of the woman's traditional domestic role and the strength of the family unit, and as a stimulus to female discontent with a male-dominated society.

The demand for this new class of trained specialists also had a significant impact on education. The availability of education at all levels increased sharply after 1880 and its emphasis shifted from the arts and letters to the natural sciences and technology. Technical and research institutes were founded and received the right to grant recognized degrees, a right formerly reserved to universities. Germany and the United States, both rapidly developing into world powers, took the lead in providing this new practical education and applying it to science and industry. Other countries followed suit more slowly. But in all industrially advanced countries, higher learning was ceasing to perform its traditional function of providing an elite educated to intellectual and moral self-improvement; rather, it was becoming instead a means of economic and social advancement. More people from a broader range of social backgrounds could now take advantage of greater educational opportunity to serve themselves and society. In so revising its goals, higher education began to perform an indispensable service to scientific and technological progress and to play a leading role in the formation of mass society.

However, despite the practical value of a university education, the cost in money, time, and intellectual effort still restricted the number who could take advantage of it. In Europe as late as 1913, the number of university students ranged between seven and eleven for each ten thousand people. Moreover, the increasing subordination of education to practical demands aroused the concern of those still dedicated to traditional educational values and those critical of or hostile to the new order. In Europe, where the currents of traditional humanistic education still ran strong, such distinguished educators as Matthew Arnold, Jakob Burckhardt, and Friedrich Nietzsche voiced alarm at the new trend. Even in the United States, where the new education was more congenial to the national temperament and met less resistance from older educational traditions than in Europe, Henry Adams, speaking for many of America's educated around the turn of the century, lamented that his classical education at Harvard had ill prepared him for productive participation in contemporary affairs, and that he would have been better served by training in mathematics and the natural sciences. The new education was still elitist, but the educated elites were ceasing to be the conscience of society and becoming its servants instead.

At the bottom of the social scale were the industrial working classes, who had grown large and strong enough during the last quarter of the nineteenth century to effectively influence the new order. In the 1880s, the trade-union movement, in the face of much opposition, began to make headway in organizing workers and forcing employers to provide better wages and working conditions. Socialism also began to flourish and find political expression in the formation of such powerful parties as the German Social Democrats and the British Labour Party. In 1889, the newly created European Socialist parties formed an alliance called the Second International, a federation far more vigorous than the fragile First International, which had lasted from 1864 to 1876. Although the decisions of the International were not binding on the individual Socialist parties, the International did create the impression of a great, united, transnational movement working toward common goals.

By 1900 the industrial working classes of the Western world had every expectation that their condition would continue to improve indefinitely. Their ranks were growing, and the so-called revisionist Socialists, led by Eduard Bernstein, even imagined that socialism would soon emerge victorious through peaceful, legal elections. In reality, however, the more success labor enjoyed, the less inclined it was to oppose or disrupt the existing order. The trade unions, willing to work within a system in which their members were beginning to prosper, repudiated revolutionary ideology and confined themselves largely to "bread-and-butter" issues, such as the gradual improvement of wages and working conditions. The Socialist parties, heavily dependent on trade-union support at elections, also began to lose their original Marxist revolutionary fervor. Marx's earlier predictions of the imminent collapse of capitalism did not seem consistent with the general prosperity that prevailed between 1890 and 1914.

Moreover, the Socialist parties and organizations in industrially advanced western Europe had undergone a transformation from small and disciplined revolutionary elites into massive bureaucratic structures, subject to the same inertia, stratification, and rigidification as any other large-scale bureaucracy. Socialism itself began to fragment into those who wished to adhere to Marx's original revolutionary doctrines, revisionists inclined to reject revolution, anarchists fed up with Socialist inaction, and syndicalists who flourished in countries like Spain, France, and Italy where industrialization lagged behind and workers could hope to have their demands met only by direct and immediate action. As with the middle classes, the fragmentation of the working classes and their willingness to compromise served to strengthen the new order rather than to change or undermine it. And in August of 1914, most Socialist leaders, after having resolved to resist the war policies of their respective governments, capitulated and consented to a war which, by their own admission, could only serve the interests of the ruling classes.

New Discontents

The stability of the new order depended on its ability to extend the benefits of progress and prosperity to a majority of, and eventually to all of mankind. Its enormous success in fulfilling that goal between 1880 and 1914, despite the growing disparity between the "have" and "have-not" nations, between the extremes of wealth and poverty within the advanced countries, and between those at the top and the bottom of the social scale, earned that era the name *la belle époque.* There were, however, those who could not or would not share in the new order; those it dislocated, deprived, or disillusioned. Naturally, they became sources of discontent. Among them were various national groups, especially in central and eastern Europe, that had as yet failed to gain independence from reactionary regimes blocking their way to modernization; landed classes being forced out of existence by industrialization; elements of the clergy and aristocracy being superseded by new and more powerful privileged groups; women denied political and economic equality; youth and intellectuals repelled by the new order's excessive materialism and mechanization of life. They remained in the minority before 1914, but their existence was a constant reminder of the limitations and failings of the new order and a threat to its stability.

NATIONAL MINORITIES The question of national minorities was primarily a central and eastern European concern, although Ireland, the Rhine provinces of Alsace and Lorraine, and the Tyrol, all in Western Europe, also became trouble spots. Throughout the nineteenth century, the ascent to power of the great Western nation-states and the liberal ideal of national self-determination had inspired national minorities to struggle for political independence. The advent of imperialism and industrialization intensified the national question all the more as it widened the gap between the "have" and "have-not" peoples within Europe and threatened to sink national minorities to the status of mere colonials. The urgency of the issue was greatest in regions with highly mixed populations, most notably the long belt between Germany and Russia that stretches from the Baltic to the Black Sea, with its multiracial, multilinguistic, and multireligious population. The states most affected by nationalism were the Austro-Hungarian, the Russian, and the Ottoman empires, which jointly controlled the region. The issue was the same, in kind if not in degree, between the Irish and English in Great Britain, between the French and Germans in the Rhineland, and between the Italians and Austrians in the Tyrol.

The conflicting minorities in these areas of stateless nations and nationless states began to ground their struggle for liberation from foreign rule, and for statehood and territorial expansion, in a form of ethnic chauvinism evident in the imperialist rivalry abroad. Pan-Germanism, pan-Slavism, pan-Anglo-Saxonism, and Italian and French irredentism were all movements conceived to establish closer ties between mother countries and minorities of the same ethnic background outside their political jurisdiction. The effect of such ideology was to intensify the hatreds among the minorities themselves and to draw the great powers into their local disputes, thereby jeopardizing further the already precarious political status quo. These local disputes, between Germans and Czechs in Bohemia, between Serbians and Croatians in the Balkans, and between Rumanians and Hungarians in Transylvania, to mention but a few, reenacted on a small scale the worldwide competition for empire. For the mother countries and their client minorities, ethnic nationalism served as a justification for expansion. For the oppressed minorities, with no powerful sponsoring ally, ethnic nationalism served to resist expansion and to nurture a sense of national uniqueness. By the same token, this new form of nationalism offered the dominant minorities hope of entering the mainstream of modernization by incorporation into or alliance with a great power. And to the unsponsored minorities, it served to support and revitalize local folk traditions, as exemplified by the Gaelic revival in Ireland and by proposals for the cultural autonomy of minorities within a supranational state, recommended by the Austrian Social Democrats Otto Bauer and Karl Renner and other intellectuals concerned with the national question.

In all of this, the European Jews, who were heavily concentrated in Eastern Europe but nowhere a majority of the population, were an anomaly in that they could make no territorial claims and had no political sponsor; yet, they constituted a distinctive group. These factors made them especially vulnerable to racial hatred, and they served as a conveneint scapegoat for competitors, particularly where they played a prominent role in European commercial and cultural affairs. Anti-Semitism ran particularly strong in Vienna, the most nationally diverse of the major European capitals and a city where Jews were especially prominent in public affairs. But anti-Semitism was also strong enough in France to split the country between conservatives and radicals over the notorious Dreyfus affair in 1895. Most Jews, like most members of other national minorities, wished to enter and share in the new European main current. But the Jews, now victims of an intensified racism and no longer

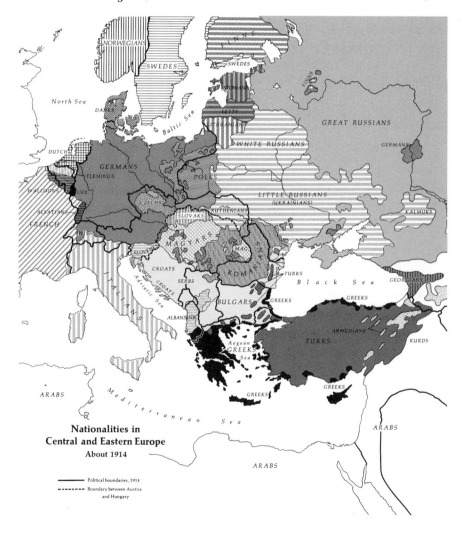

**Nationalities in
Central and Eastern Europe**
About 1914

————— Political boundaries, 1914
– – – – – Boundary between Austria
and Hungary

secure in or content with their traditional but stagnant ghetto existence, also experienced the first stirrings of nationalism in the form of Zionism, which called for the creation of a Jewish homeland in Palestine and found expression in Theodor Herzl's influential pamphlet, *The Jewish State* (1896).

Each national minority hated its oppressive foreign overlord, but it also hated other minorities. And these minorities could gain the support of the great powers only at the risk of general war. Their insistence upon statehood, each at the expense of the other and all at the expense of the ruling powers, was not only incompatible with the old order, but was also unrealizable within the new. Under the circumstances, their belligerent agitation, carried on vociferously in the press and by pamphlet, through secret societies and underground paramilitary organizations, served only to poison the atmosphere and prepare Europe for war.

FEMINISM   Another new discontent was feminism—a discontent that, like the national question, had its roots in the eighteenth century but came to a head during the generation before the First World War. Prominent women who had participated in the American and French Revolutions, such as Abigail Adams in America and Madame Roland and Mary Wollstonecraft in Europe, were among the first to assert the cause of equal rights for women in the name of the universal rights for which those revolutions had been fought. Although their demands were disregarded at the time, the movement for female emancipation gained momentum and received support from the influential Saint-Simonian social reformers, from the distinguished female novelist, George Sand, and from one of the nineteenth century's great liberal spokesmen, John Stuart Mill. Magazines devoted to women's interests began to appear, such as *La Femme Nouvelle* (1832–34) and *La Gazette Des Femmes* (1836–38). By mid-century, women were gaining greater educational opportunity, and a few, like Jeanne Derain in France, Louise Otto in Germany, and Lucretia Mott in the United States, had even entered politics.

By the 1880s, women were gaining a foothold in the professions and becoming a significant part of the rapidly expanding labor force. New leaders, including Lili Braun and Helene Lange, Beatrice Webb and Ethel Snowden, the Pankhurst sisters and Susan Anthony, assertive and often distinguished in public life, rallied to their cause. Feminism also found impressive literary advocates in Henrik Ibsen, George Bernard Shaw, and Gerhart Hauptmann. In 1888, the International Woman Suffrage Alliance was formed to advance the right of women to vote. The first countries to grant this right were New Zealand in 1893, Australia in 1902, and the Scandinavian countries in the decade preceding the war. Not until after the First World War did women win the right to vote in the major Western countries.

Suffragettes marching on Fifth Avenue in New York.
(The Granger Collection).

The surging Socialist parties endorsed feminism, as did the English Fabians and the French radicals, partly because of their commitment to social equality, and partly to win massive female support in their ideological conflict with capitalism. The classic Socialist statement on the female question was August Bebel's, *The Woman and Socialism,* which appeared in 1893 and was subsequently amplified by Friedrich Engels, Karl Kautsky, and Karl Liebknecht. The effectiveness of this endorsement was demonstrated by the enlarged enrollment of women in the various Socialist parties and the appearance of such outstanding female Socialist and social reform leaders as Rosa Luxemburg, Vera Zasulich, Beatrice Webb, and Emma Goldman. By 1900, feminism unquestionably had become an explosive issue, engulfing all advanced Western society and having far-reaching effects on some of mankind's oldest institutions and attitudes.

Despite the progress of feminism, in 1900 the vast majority of women were still economically dependent on and socially inferior to men. The advances made by women over the course of a century in education, employment, and politics, while impressive, were largely byproducts of the gains made by the social classes to which they belonged. Women constituted no independent interest or force in society. The progress of their struggle for full equality still depended on what society at large was willing to allow. And society was not yet willing to allow women to threaten its basic structure. Feminists were still far from having achieved their ultimate goal in 1914 and would continue to pursue it after the war. But nowhere was the tension between traditionalism and modernism more evident than in the condition of women in Western society at the dawn of the twentieth century.

YOUTH was a third group of discontented; their discontent focused chiefly on the mechanization and regimentation of life in the new industrial order. Throughout the Western world and especially in Germany, large segments of youth began to rebel during the nineties against its vulgar materialism and moral hypocrisy. Their protest took the form of a return to nature, a rediscovery of the virtues and gratifications of physical fitness and the outdoor life, and freer sexual behavior. Tramping in an uncrowded and uncontaminated countryside, engaging in physical exercise and sport, and abstaining from the artificial stimulants of tobacco and alcohol were ways restive youth chose to escape and combat the denaturalization and debilitation of people by mechanization. In protest against the regimentation of life by an artificial and restrictive social code, they came to the defense of instinct, spontaneity, and eroticism, whether in the form of nudism, premarital sexual relations, or, as in some cases, even homosexuality—all very shocking to their puritanical elders. This dissent was more than a mere manifestation of natural youthful restlessness and impatience with the older generation. It was dissent aimed at the very foundations of the new order and its dehumanizing effects, and although by no means confined to the young, it was most common among them.

These discontents were more pronounced in Germany than elsewhere because the conditions that caused them were more pronounced there. Germany in 1890 was, as it had been throughout the nineteenth century, basically an authoritarian, militaristic, bureaucratic society. The unification of Germany in 1871 and its rapid rise during the next twenty years to the status of a world power reinforced these characteristic features of German life. The haughty and imperious Wilhelm II, emperor from 1888 to 1919, was the very personification of German authoritarianism. Germans at every social level, intoxicated by their new power and prosperity, were only too eager to follow his example. Authoritarianism naturally ran strong among the ruling classes, its chief beneficiaries, and among the omnipresent military and bureaucracy, which were its chief embodiments. But it also pervaded the lower levels of society: schoolteachers, the clergy, and parents, with whom the young came into constant contact.

Authoritarianism at this level was the subject of Heinrich Mann's superb novel of 1905, *Professor Unrat,* on which the famous movie, *The Blue Angel,* was based; it told the story of a pathetic schoolteacher far down the pecking order, servile to his superiors, tyrannical toward his students, and miserable in his own personal life. Even leaders of the socialist opposition in Germany, men like August Bebel and Karl Liebknecht, had about them a paternalistic air, quite annoying to their counterparts in other countries. And the German universities, once strongholds of dissent but now mainly training centers for specialists and bureaucrats, could no longer serve discontented youth. Such circumstances obviously did not encourage independent thought and action.

The rapid industrialization of Germany also favored the growth of youth unrest. The industrialization that had taken England and France more than a century to achieve, Germany achieved and surpassed in the last three decades of the nineteenth century. There was insufficient time for the social structure to absorb its effects. Germany was still a *nouveau riche* country in 1890, and the German upper and middle classes manifested, to a greater extent than their English and French counterparts, the typical *nouveau riche* traits of boorishness, provincialism, and philistinism. German intellectuals—most of them the very opposite in every respect—never tired of denouncing such behavior. These qualities were not admired by sons and daughters; their parents' wealth now enabled them to seek "higher" values. Repelled by parents, teachers, and clergymen, they were more inclined to share the attitudes of the disaffected intellectuals, themselves displaced by the new order and bitterly hostile to it.

Most of these men, typified by Paul de Lagarde, Moeller van den Bruck, and the great poet Stefan George, held frankly ultraconservative and romantic views. They called upon German youth to reject the new order and revert to the supposedly more spiritual values of preindustrial Germany. Since the inception of Romanticism in the late eighteenth century, Germany had always been its true homeland. And since Romanticism was the first great movement to exalt youth, to proclaim its innocence, purity, and superiority to adulthood, to make virtually a cult of youth, there was nothing unusual about its appeal. Many of the German elders in 1890 had themselves responded in their youth to the romantic appeal of the student unions, known as *Burschenschaften,* which had been dedicated to the cause of German unification.

These were some of the conditions which prompted the founding of the German Youth Movement in 1901, whose members disconcerted their respectable middle-class parents by leaving home with knapsacks on their backs to rough it in the country as *Wandervögel* (wandering birds), as they called themselves. The movement spread quickly, and soon political parties, notably the Socialists, and even churches followed suit, seeing their advantage in sponsoring such groups. Outside Germany, youth's infatuation with nature and physical fitness found satisfaction in the Boy Scouts (founded in England in 1908), the Girl Scouts (founded in the United States in 1912), the Y.M.C.A. and Y.W.C.A., and in similar organizations. What differentiated the original German Youth Movement from all the others, however, was that it was organized *by* youth instead of *for* youth. And therein lay its significance. True, the program of the *Wandervögel* was totally unoriginal. Its members were largely indifferent to politics and posed no threat to the established order; they contributed nothing to culture, except to revive the folksong. In 1914, they patriotically went to war, a move that promptly smashed their splendid bodies and their dreams of a simple life close to nature, a disillusionment those who returned never recovered from. But the *Wandervögel* set a precedent by translating into a massive, even if harmless and ephemeral, social movement the idea of a youth counterculture, inspired by the earlier Romantic cult of youth and nature. Like the feminists, the young were developing a sense of themselves as forming a distinctive social constituency with its own needs, rights, and viewpoints. And, as with the feminists, this new self-awareness was to become a permanent force in Western society.

In countries where authoritarianism, intellectual pessimism, and the dislocations brought on by industrialization were less pronounced than in Germany, the energies of youth were more easily contained and channeled in socially acceptable ways. In France and the Latin countries, traditionalism still ran strong. Industry was less advanced and less disruptive; the family, the educational system, and the Catholic Church were still pillars of society. In England and the United States, where optimism and self-confidence abounded at the turn of the century, the energies of youth were easily linked to the national purpose and channeled into institutionalized sports and athletic competition, school clubs and college fraternities. Indeed, in the United States, youth was the very symbol of the national experience, and participation in sports and the rugged outdoors was a sign of virility and patriotism. As Kaiser Wilhelm embodied the qualities most detested by German youth, Theodore Roosevelt embodied those qualities of frontier ruggedness endearing to Americans and emulated by American youth.

Only when disillusionment with the new order began to set in—after the First World War and, even more, after the Second—did the attitudes of youth in the Western countries begin to approximate those of discontented German youth at the turn of the century. For French, British, and American youth, nature then began to seem a refuge and escape from society. This changing attitude found expression in the writings of the then youthful D. H. Lawrence, T. E. Lawrence, and others. To young

American writers especially, notably Ernest Hemingway and Thomas Wolfe, nature came to symbolize lost innocence, lost purity, lost youth itself.

The question of national minorities, feminism, and the youth movement were the characteristic discontents of the emerging new order. Few would have thought, before 1914, that any or all of them would ever become flaming issues. But it was disputes among the national minorities and between them and the great powers which helped plunge the Western world into war. And it was the failure of the new order to raise women and youth to the status of full partners in a common enterprise that kept their discontents alive and growing in scope and intensity. The common denominator of all three groups of discontents was precisely the frustration of rising expectations: expectations aroused by the new order itself with its watchwords of progress and prosperity, democracy and self-determination. But most people from all walks of life were far more preoccupied, during *la belle époque,* with the bright new horizons opening before them than with the still light winds of discontent.

CULTURE OF THE PREWAR ERA

Times of rapid transition usually spur cultural and intellectual ferment. Such times provide few ready-made answers to or attitudes toward the problems of a world in flux, a world that begs reinterpretation. The passing away of the old and the rise of the new creates a tension that demands an explanation, an evaluation, a resolution. The prewar era, one of the most creative in modern history, was no exception. No area of creative endeavor escaped the impact of the great transformation Western society was undergoing. And every area, literature and the arts, philosophy and social theory, the natural sciences and religion, experienced an extraordinary efflorescence. It was the age of the Fauves, Cubists, Expressionists, and Futurists in the arts; Joseph Conrad and D. H. Lawrence, André Gide and Marcel Proust, Thomas Mann and Hugo von Hofmannsthal in literature; Richard Strauss, Gustav Mahler, and Arnold Schönberg in music; the age of Friedrich Nietzsche, Henri Bergson, and Bertrand Russell in philosophy; Sigmund Freud and Carl Jung in psychology; Albert Einstein, Max Planck, and the Curies in the physical sciences; and many more too numerous to mention. But prewar culture was more than this impressive roster of names and movements. It was a culture that closed the gates to the past and opened those to the future.

The new culture gravitated around two poles: a preoccupation with decline and decadence on the one hand, and bold experimentation and innovation on the other. The two complemented each other: the denunciation of Western culture as exhausted and decadent spurred the search for new insights, values, and forms of expression; this search in turn reinforced the view that Western culture, liberal, rational, and humanistic, was indeed in dissolution. Both tendencies stemmed from the same source: the hostility of the early nineteenth-century romantic to emerging bourgeois society and his alienation from it—a rift that widened as the century wore on.

The first tendency manifested itself in a highly affected art-for-art's sake aestheticism, an ivory-tower intellectualism, and a disreputable infatuation with moral and spiritual decadence designed to shock the smug bourgeoisie. The second tendency found expression in the development of drastically new views about the nature of man, society, and the natural world. Almost all the leading contributors to the culture of the prewar era were dissatisfied members of the middle classes and critical of its privileged position and self-righteousness. Those preoccupied with decadence tended to be conservative critics of the new industrial order, while the innovators sought to invalidate the new order by transcending it. Common to all was disillusionment with the thought and culture of the now triumphant bourgeoisie.

Heralds of a Dying Order

By the end of the nineteenth century, the alienation of artists and intellectuals from middle-class society was so extreme and widespread that growing numbers of them found it impossible to reconcile themselves to it and futile to oppose it. Naturalism, decadence, symbolism, and expressionism were movements founded by men seeking either consolation or inspiration in the prospect of the decay and decline of Western civilization. In these movements the self-assertiveness and combativeness of the early nineteenth-century romantic turned to resignation and despair. Some intellectuals and artists sought to isolate themselves within society, as did the modest professors Walter Pater and Stephen Mallarmé, and the bureaucrat Joris-Karl Huysmans. Others deserted the Western world altogether—the brilliant young French poet Arthur Rimbaud, the great primitivist painter Paul Gauguin, and the sensitive American storyteller Lafcadio Hearn. They discovered in Africa, the South Seas, and Japan respectively the simplicity, authenticity, and regard for beauty and humanity they no longer could find at home. Still others—the vagabond painter Vincent van Gogh and the admitted homosexuals Oscar Wilde and André Gide—became social outcasts.

But whether introverts, escapists, dandies, or eccentrics, all deliberately chose to be social outsiders. Disillusioned with reality, they found themselves thrown back upon their own intensely private minds and imaginations, often feeding on their personal fantasies and manias. For them thought and art ceased to be ways of understanding and coping with reality and instead became ways to resist, flee, and counteract it. Whatever would shock and disconcert the hated middle classes pleased these self-proclaimed mavericks; hence, their esoteric cult of beauty and pure art inaccessible to philistines, their infatuation with crime, vice, and society's victims, and their complete contempt for established conventions and values. Whether they shut themselves up within their own private worlds or looked beyond the Western world for a better life in simpler surroundings, these aesthetes and intellectual iconoclasts typically considered themselves the final flowering of a fading civilization, unheeded heralds of a dying order.

NATURALISTS AND DECADENTS   The naturalist writers of the *fin de siècle* concerned themselves with the tension between man's physical and psychological nature and his social existence. They took pride in being scientific and realistic in their art, but their "slices of life" without personal commentary almost always ended in disaster or death. In reality, their supposedly scientific method was intended to give credence to a

Landscape with Cypresses near Arles. Painting by Vincent Van Gogh, 1888.

(Tate Gallery, London.)

Two Tahitian Women. Painting by Paul Gauguin, 1897. Return to primitivism in the arts.
(Courtauld Institute Galleries, London).

deeply pessimistic outlook. The individual is the helpless victim of forces, both internal and external, over which he has no control. Some leading naturalists, like Émile Zola and Arthur Schnitzler, emphasized the external social forces responsible for man's degradation. Others, like Guy de Maupassant and August Strindberg, emphasized the inner, irrational, self-destructive forces. But whether the stress fell on the antisocial nature of man, or on the antihuman effects of society, the end result was the same: man's defeat. The general public was shocked and outraged by the naturalists' overriding concern with social outcasts and sexuality. But far more significant than the subject matter itself was the pessimistic view that formed it, the view that natural man and artificial society are forever incompatible. Such a view directly contradicted the traditional Western liberal-humanistic claim that the two are not only compatible, but that society alone can guarantee the survival and fulfillment of natural man.

In sharp contrast to the naturalists, the decadents, notably J. K. Huysmans and Oscar Wilde, delighted in artificiality. Only, the artificiality that delighted them was in defiance of conventional moral and intellectual standards. It served to set them off from the rest of society, to insulate them and allow them to indulge their bizarre and exotic tastes.

What the decadents protested was not so much man's denaturalization as his deindividualization by modern society. The prototypes of the decadent personality—Des Esseintes in Huysmans' novel, *Against Nature* (1884), and Wilde's hero in *The Portrait of Dorian Gray* (1891)—were solitary eccentrics who indulged in decadence solely to cultivate and assert their individual personalities. These characters were designed to show that, if man loses himself by conforming to society's rules, he can rediscover or, more accurately, invent himself (since he lacks a discernible nature) only by defying those rules. Even naturalism concerned itself only with an impersonal, undifferentiated human nature and not with the unique individual, and in that respect it was little better than the social order it criticized.

In the viewpoint of the decadent, the true individualist had logically to end up a social outcast, a martyr to the cause of individuality, as Wilde himself ended up, attempting to live the scandalous life he wrote about. Characteristically, Wilde defended socialism in his essay, *The Soul of Man under Socialism* (1891) on the grounds that poverty obstructs and retards individual development. He also defended socialism because, in his day, it represented dissent, which the decadent automatically approved. "It is through disobedience that progress has been made, through disobedience and rebellion," Wilde wrote in this essay. The scandalous views and attitudes of the decadents had their intended effect of outraging the public. But, as with the naturalists, the real significance of the decadents was to protest society's violation of another fundamental tenet of the Western liberal-humanistic tradition: the sanctity of the individual, to which the decadent, society's enemy, now claimed to be sole and rightful heir.

SYMBOLISTS AND EXPRESSIONISTS, even more than naturalists and decadents, retreated from external reality into the realm of imagination alone. Theirs was a dream-world of moods and impressions and their art a revelation of the workings of the interior mind by means of archetypal images, symbols, and emotions. On their view, art and life are not only distinct but mutually exclusive. The symbolist hero of Villiers de l'Isle-Adams' celebrated prose poem, *Axel* (1890), exclaims: "Oh, the external world! Let us not be made dupes by the old slave, chained to her feet in broad daylight, who promises us the keys to a palace of enchantments when it clutches only a handful of ashes in its clenched black fist!"

This was the view of artists without a function in a world they believed was totally devoid of poetic values. In renouncing the world, they also renounced the mimetic aim of art, which had been characteristic of Western art from the beginning until and including the impressionists. For the writers, Paul Verlaine and Stephen Mallarmé, Ezra Pound and William Butler Yeats, Rainer Maria Rilke and Franz Kafka, and for the painters, Wassily Kandinsky, Edvard Munch, and Pablo Picasso, the goal of art was not to reproduce or criticize the world, but rather to recreate it imaginatively. Symbolism and expressionism, although less obviously antisocial and offensive to public taste than naturalism and decadence, were more radical movements in that they severed the artist from society altogether and made him responsible to no one but himself and his art. This new conception of the artist and his relation to society was expressed by the hero of Walter Pater's *Marius the Epicurean* (1885), who arrives at the conclusion "that the individual is to himself the measure of all things, and must rely on the exclusive certainty to himself of his own impressions. To move afterwards in that outer world of other people, as though taking it at their estimate, would be possible henceforth only as a kind of irony."

Not all those preoccupied with the decline of Western civilization belonged to avant garde movements. Some of the most significant art and literature concerned with this issue made no technical innovations and implied no antisocial attitudes. The popular novels of Joseph Conrad and the literary fantasies of G. K. Chesterton dealt with some of the most pressing moral and existential problems facing man in modern society. Hugo von Hofmannstahl enchanted Viennese audiences with plays and operatic libretti that nostalgically recalled the splendid past of the Habsburg monarchy, although Hofmannstahl himself foresaw and regretted that its days were numbered. And the stories of Thomas Mann, though they are populated by alienated artists and frustrated intellectuals and deal with the decline of all that was dear to Mann in Western culture, were written in a style that was witty and ironical, sophisticated and fastidiously conservative.

FRIEDRICH NIETZSCHE   Of all the heralds of decline, however, none was more significant or representative than Friedrich Nietzsche (1844–1900). He was the very prototype of the defiant solitary, embodying in his tormented life and writings the anxieties that Western artists and intellectuals were beginning to feel about the future of their civilization. Having matured in preindustrial Europe, Nietzsche was closer in spirit to the great classical, romantic, and idealist traditions of the past than his younger contemporaries; for them these cultural legacies were more artifacts than living realities, worthy of ironical treatment maybe, but not passionate dedication.

The scope of Nietzsche's critique encompassed the whole of Western civilization. In his early writings of the seventies, especially the brilliant essay, "The Birth of Tragedy" (1872), Nietzsche traced the origins of the malaise of the modern world all the way back to Greek antiquity, to the suppression of heroic pagan values by the onset of Socratic intellectualism, then Christian morality (which he called a "slave" morality), and, finally, to the emergence of modern "herd" man. The Greeks had achieved greatness, he believed, because they had temporarily succeeded in reconciling, in the form of tragedy, two antagonistic life forces or principles, which Nietzsche named the Dionysiac and Apollonian, after the mythical gods who represented them. The West went into decline, he argued, because the Apollonian forces of reason, form, and stability had gained the upper hand over the wild Dionysiac forces of will, instinct, and irrational myth. "Understanding kills action," he concluded in this essay, "for in order to act we require the veil of illusion."

Like the great interpreters of Greek civilization before him, Nietzsche regarded that civilization as the highpoint of human history, the norm and model of the good society. Also, like his predecessors, he used the Greek example as a stick to beat modern society, which had long since lost the capacity to emulate the Greeks. Unlike his predecessors, however, Nietzsche admired the Greeks not for their spiritual Apollonian qualities, but for their sensuous Dionysiac ones. His vision of a rebirth of tragedy and a new heroic age was predicated on a liberation of the Dionysiac forces and a return to the primordial fount of myth. "Every culture that has lost myth has lost, by the same token, its natural creativity.

History, no less than excessive intellection and ascetic morality, saps man's vital energy by depriving him of myth. The message of Nietzsche's essay, "The Use and Abuse of History" (1873), was that history, at least the modern linear concept of history, intimidates and lulls man into inaction, either because he feels that it is useless to oppose history, or because he feels that so-called progress is inevitable and therefore requires no effort on his part. In either case, history is just another form of understanding that kills action. According to Nietzsche, the only worthy conception of history is the Greek view of time as an endless, inevitable succession of cycles, an "eternal recurrence," which provides no grounds either for hope or despair. Instead, such a view is conducive to action because it offers man the opportunity to live his life so that it will be worthy of infinite repetitions. "To redeem what is past, and to transform every 'It was' into 'Thus would I have it!'—that only do I call redemption!" he declared in *Thus Spake Zarathustra* (1883–85). For Nietzsche, heroic man must make history and not be made by it. In order to do so, he must live, like Nietzsche's own mythical Zarathustra, in solitary defiance of the world. Iconoclasm and creativity are but two sides of the same coin. Rejection of history is the prerequisite to creativity, and creativity, the fruit of man's liberation from the past.

In his later writings of the 1880s and 1890s, Nietzsche called for a resurrection of the Dionysiac forces in the person of a "superman" capable of liberating himself and others from the corrupting influences of materialism, conformism, bourgeois self-seeking, and socialist do-goodism—a being "beyond good and evil," as he put it. The superman, exemplified by Zarathustra, is one in whom the spiritual and sensual forces are once again reconciled and given free rein, as in Greek tragedy. He is a man who uplifts others by the force of example alone, not by coercion or fake promises or grubby political maneuverings. This is what Nietzsche meant by the "transvaluation of values" and the "will to power." But his view of life was, by his own admission, a tragic one. For the superman must live with the knowledge that his existence, like everyone else's, is part of a fatalistic cycle—an existence enacted many times before and destined to be reenacted many times again. "Behold, we know what thou teachest: that all things eternally return, and our-selves with them, and that we have already existed times without number, and all things with us." The superman must live, therefore, knowing that his heroic mission to transform himself and the world in accordance with the Greek ideal can be no less ephemeral, no less a transitory moment in the overall course of human development, than was Greek tragedy itself.

Nietzsche was less a prophet of the new age than a last brilliant af-terglow of the old. His vision of the rebirth of the glory of ancient Greece was an inspiring but impossible dream: impossible because, as he himself realized, it could no longer serve as a call to action. Rather, it signified the typical predicament of the alienated *fin de siècle* intellectual; he could neither accept historical reality nor offer a feasible alternative to it. Nevertheless, his message was timely, forceful, and brilliantly argued. It influenced such diverse writers as Ibsen and Shaw, Gide and Mann, as well as Italy's fiery poet of sensual and heroic action, Gabriel D'Annun-zio. Nietzsche's distinction between the Dionysiac and Apollonian nur-tured naturalism and anticipated Freud. His vigorous defense of indi-vidual responsibility reverberated in the writings of the decadents and anticipated existentialism. And his insight into the source and function of myth bore fruit in the symbolist and expressionist movements and in the heroic political theory of Georges Sorel. In sum, Nietzsche was to the late nineteenth century what Rousseau had been to the eighteenth: a pivotal figure whose influence extended in every direction.

Discovery of Irrational Man

The proclamation of the bankruptcy of Western liberal, rational, and humanistic values went hand in hand with the proclamation of man as an essentially irrational being. This was largely the work of Henri Bergson (1859–1941), Sigmund Freud (1856–1939), and their many disciples—leaders in the upsurge of irrationalism whose teachings marked the highpoint of disenchantment with middle-class civilization. A century earlier, dissatisfied bourgeois intellectuals had championed reason in protest against a semifeudal social order that justified its existence by appeal to irrational doctrines and practices. Now they rushed to defend the irrational in man to protest what they considered the equally constrictive rationalism and scientism of the now no less privileged middle classes. In both cases, intellectual discontent was aroused once philosophical doctrines came to serve narrow ideological interests. Nietzsche had already proclaimed the primacy of blind will over the effete intellect and announced that thought is little more than a transparent rationalization of immoral, or amoral, acts that originate in the primal will. Such declarations inspired the characteristic view of the *fin de siècle* rebels against reason that intellect and instinct, will and idea, thought and action are not simply different but complementary facets of man's mental makeup; rather, they are polar opposites.

HENRI BERGSON and Freud both began as believers in the positivist science of their day. But both began to reject it when they found that it failed to explain phenomena peculiar to the human psyche. Bergson built his philosophy on a sharp distinction between the everyday clock-time of science and practical life and time as we actually experience it. Science measures and divides time quantitatively; time as experienced is constant change, an indivisible and intangible flow, a purely internal process that cannot be measured because it does not exist in space. Time never *is;* it is always *becoming.* Clock-time orders our experience of time, but it is not the experience itself. Hence, it is less real than time as experienced; in fact, it is non-existent in the sense that a description of a thing is not the thing itself. Real time, as distinct from the measurement of time, Bergson called "duration," to designate its fluidity, continuity, and indivisibility, its purely temporal, nonspatial, intangible characteristics. Consequently, real time can be experienced intuitively (immediately, directly, as a dynamic whole), but cannot be known intellectually—that is, by means of concepts properly applicable only to the external world of matter in space.

From these thoughts Bergson drew the conclusion that matter and mind are two entirely different realms, the one existing in space and the other in time. Matter is subject to the deterministic laws of science; but mind, which knows itself and its contents intuitively, is free. The mind's freedom is exemplified especially by memory, which is not merely the retention of a past perception, but is a qualitatively different phenomenon. A memory has no spatial existence, nor does it necessarily correspond to anything in space. Rather, it is an immediate experience, an image known intuitively, which may or may not resemble the original perception, but which, in either case, is something entirely different from it. Perception is a physical act, memory an intuitive act. One perceives a material object, but one remembers an immaterial image. In other words, memory creates; it does not merely record. And the mind's creativity, as demonstrated by memory, artistic imagination, religious experience, and other intuitive activities, is proof of man's freedom.

If men choose to think of themselves as bodies whose behavior is subject to the same deterministic laws governing other bodies, the choice to do so is still free, because it issues from the deeper real self, which is creative and enduring. Decisions are not merely reflex reactions to external stimuli; rather they create new situations. All the intellectual knowledge in the world will not tell a man how he should act, or even that he should act. The decision to act, and act in a particular way, originates from within, from the inner self that is free.

In his best known and most influential work, *Creative Evolution* (1907), Bergson interpreted evolution in the large as analogous to the development of individual consciousness. Both are expressions of the same universal life force (*élan vital*), which informs and unites every living thing, but which finds its highest expression in human intuition. What intuition is to consciousness, the *élan vital* is to evolution: the force that makes it creative and not merely recurrent. Intuition is the *élan vital* in its purest form. Moreover, evolution and the development of human consciousness are both self-creating processes in which change is the only constant. And because change is purely temporal and intangible, both processes defy scientific analysis, which can think only in terms of things and relationships in space.

Bergson rejected the mechanistic and teleological theories of evolution on the grounds that both, even if from opposite viewpoints, presuppose a preordained plan of development which precludes genuine creativity—that is, spontaneous and unpredictable expression. Evolution, like human consciousness, is not an orderly succession of phases, a cumulative process governed by fixed natural laws and moving toward some preestablished goal. Rather, it is an efflorescence of separate manifestations of a single creative force in a still unfinished universe, which man can influence by his free actions. Bergson's exalted conception of evolution was analogous to the work of a painter, whose separate brush strokes produce a single effect that he has freely chosen and is free to change, or abandon and start anew, if he so chooses.

It was only a short step from this vitalistic view of evolution to a form of philosophical mysticism, a step Bergson took in his last major work, *The Two Sources of Morality and Religion* (1932), and in his near conversion in later life from Judaism to Roman Catholicism. In this work, he treated morality and religion, at least in their pure "dynamic" manifestations, as psychological experiences in which man is most at one with the universal life force. It is this intensely emotional feeling of oneness with all life, and not social utility, that inspires the deeds of heroes, saints, and mystics, who are the highest expression of this emotion. Their lives, deeds, and teachings, far more than any logical argument, testify to the existence of God. And their selfless dedication to their fellow man testifies to the love that is born of such mystical communion with the universal creative spirit.

Bergson's importance in the history of modern Western thought was not due so much to the originality or significance of his contributions to philosophy as to his influence on the thought of the *fin de siècle*. His lectures first at the École Normale Supérieure and then at the Collège de France were enormously successful, and he inspired such diverse and brilliant talents as Georges Sorel, Marcel Proust, and his student, Charles Péguy. Others, like Wilhelm Dilthey and Max Scheler, William James and Ortega y Gasset, also expressed their indebtedness to him. His message could please those who looked upon Western civilization around 1900 as the very epitome of the creative urge—driven by a titanic Faustian impulse, as the German historian, Oswald Spengler, would say—and those who viewed it with contempt and wished to start anew, as Georges Sorel, leader of the syndicalist branch of socialism did. Bergson was hailed by pragmatists and vitalists, by socialists and Catholics, and by the French and non-French alike. His intuitionism found fertile soil in the symbolist movement, and his metaphysical and moral views bore no small resemblance to those of Tolstoy. And though his philosophy opposed the prevailing positivist conception of science, it anticipated the new physics, just then being formulated, which was also antipositivist and on the way to proclaiming the principle of indeterminacy and the reducibility of matter to energy.

No doubt Bergson's personal prestige and popularity and his impact on the Zeitgeist at the turn of the century were due in large part to the relief his philosophy gave from tedious materialism, crude positivist determinism, and ignoble bourgeois self-seeking. His views gave new life to belief in the primacy of the spirit, free will, heroic action, and the value and satisfaction of artistic creation. He was the first major thinker since the early nineteenth century to wage war against scientific determinism in the name of a metaphysics of freedom. And, if he did not win that war, he at least made irrationalism intellectually respectable once more. Whereas Schopenhauer, Kierkegaard, Dostoevsky, and Nietzsche had been social and intellectual outsiders whose irrationalism had been angry, pessimistic, and rebellious, Bergson was an insider who transformed their legacy with Gallic finesse into something joyous, optimistic, and constructive. If there is any connection between the philosophy he professed and the ideologies of the vicious, enslaving totalitarian movements of the twentieth century, the connection is neither personal nor direct, but one which attests that irrationalism in any form, no matter how benign or sublime, is in the last analysis a morally and intellectually irresponsible doctrine.

SIGMUND FREUD   If Bergson was the Prometheus of *fin de siècle* irrationalism, Freud was irrationalism's Sisyphus. Although little known at the time, Freud would displace him from the summit of intellectual prestige after the First World War. Bergson appealed to a generation bursting with energy and eager for intellectual confirmation of its Herculean drives and ambitions. Freud appealed to a generation broken, frightened, confused, and above all desperate for a satisfactory explanation of evil, which was conspicuously absent from Bergson's philosophy.

Freud, like Bergson, began to break with established scientific views when he discovered that they failed to explain certain behavior disorders, such as hysteria and neurosis, that seemed to have no physiological foundation or cause. Consequently, he gradually abandoned the physical explanation of nervous disorders and began to conceive the psyche as an autonomous sphere with its own structure and dynamic. During the 1880s, he found that patients could be treated successfully when persuaded, under hypnosis, to reveal unhappy forgotten events of their early lives. Because hypnosis did not work with all patients, Freud developed the technique of free association of ideas, which also helped dredge up painful past experiences. This technique resulted in relief from psychological pain and became the characteristic technique of psychoanalysis. It worked best when patients could be persuaded to relate their dreams, "the royal road to a knowledge of the unconscious activities of the mind," Freud concluded in his first major work which deals with the subject, *The Interpretation of Dreams* (1900).

Freud did not invent the concept or discover the existence of the unconscious; Schopenhauer, Nietzsche, and others had done so before him. But he was the first to claim to be able to demystify it and subject it to what he believed was scientific scrutiny, despite the obvious differences between his new analytical technique and the prevailing physiological approach to psychology, as represented most notably by his Russian contemporary, Ivan Pavlov. Because the unconscious mind is not directly observable, it cannot be studied by the same methods applicable to what is directly observable, a point that has always raised doubts about the scientific validity of Freud's theory. But because the unconscious holds the key to understanding the whole human personality, it takes precedence over the conscious mind and is the proper sphere of psychological investigation. This now well-known distinction between the mind's two strata was fundamental to Freud's theory. It allowed him to posit the source of mental anguish and anxiety otherwise inexplicable, and at the same time allowed him to believe that the rational mind, where the repressed contents of the unconscious crop up and cause problems, might be able to gain some measure of control over problems.

Unlike his irrationalist predecessors, Freud did not believe that the psychological pain arising from the conflict between the mind's two levels could ever be permanently abolished; however, he did think that this conflict could and should be alleviated. In this respect, his view of life was even more tragic than theirs. There was nothing in Freud's theory comparable to Schopenhauer's belief in the possibility of achieving a state of Nirvana-like quiescence, in which the turbulent will ceases to exist. There was nothing in it of Nietzsche's apocalyptic vision of a rebirth of tragedy in the form of a perfect harmony between the Dionysiac and Apollonian life forces. Nor did Freud share Bergson's glorification of the irrational *élan vital*, which finds sublime fulfillment in the "open" morality of heroes and in the "dynamic" religion of mystics. On the contrary, man, for Freud, is forever stretched over a Procrustes bed made up of the demanding and socially forbidden sexual drives of the unconscious id at one end, the stern moral prohibitions of the tyrannical superego at the other end, and the intermediary ego, badgered from both sides and saddled with the unenviable job of getting him through life in one piece.

The picture became all the grimmer when, after the war, Freud added aggression to his roster of unconscious forces that impel man. In *Civilization and its Discontents* (1930), he summed up his view thus: "Life, as we find it, is too hard for us; it brings us too many pains, disappointments and impossible tasks. In order to bear it we cannot dispense with palliative measures.... There are perhaps three such measures: powerful deflections, which cause us to make light of our misery; substitutive satisfactions, which diminish it; and intoxicating substances, which make us insensitive to it. Something of the kind is indispensable." For Freud, life is a Sisyphean burden, and the best we can do is bear it with stoic dignity, knowing that the inescapable furies that hound us, both from within and without, are taking their inevitable toll.

From his early discovery that the unconscious is the source of all motivation, Freud drew the conclusion that man is an essentially irrational creature, driven by forces wholly unknown to him. Our explanations of our actions are merely rationalizations of these forces which are sexual in nature. The importance Freud attached to sexuality, which later was to divide the psychoanalytical movement, resulted from his observation (1) that a person's first and primary impressions are sexual, (2) that sexual desires are the ones most frequently repressed, and (3) that sexual gratification is the epitome of the pleasure principle, which governs the id. The reality principle, which governs the ego, forces man to channel or "sublimate" the sexual drive in socially acceptable ways—a procedure learned largely in early life under parental guidance. This process of socialization inevitably entails some degree of frustration and repression, for the child's first love object is the parent of the opposite sex, while the parent of the same sex, as sole possessor of the child's love object, is guiltily regarded by the child with envy and hostility (Freud's famous Oedipus complex). The family, which creates this emotional conflict for the child—frustration followed by guilt feelings—is, therefore, the first and foremost agent of repression. The family's socialization of the child, whether relatively smooth and painless, or whether unusually frustrating and traumatic, establishes the pattern of behavior that the child will carry with him into the world as a mature person. Thus, Freud's theory contained a double determinism: the determination of actions by the unknown unconscious, and the determination of personality in infancy.

In his later writings, from *Totem and Taboo* (1913) to *Moses and Monotheism* (1939), Freud applied his findings about individual psychology to the larger issues of religion, society, and civilization. (These will be discussed in the next chapter in the context of postwar developments in the field of psychology in general.) But his main ideas were worked out many years before the First World War, in his writings on dreams, art, humor, and the psychopathology of everyday life. And these ideas were bound to offend an era tolerant of hypocrisy, bursting with self-esteem, and confident in the ability of reason to ameliorate the human condition. They could have little impact on a generation that applauded the optimistic reformers G. B. Shaw and H. G. Wells; that threw its humanitarian energies into pacifism, vegetarianism, and antivivisectionism; and that abhorred the naturalists' risqué views, which so closely resembled Freud's own.

Only when the great guns strung across Europe blasted *la belle époque* into oblivion did Freud's theories come front and center. This happened not because Freud was the greatest thinker of his time, nor even because he was the most brilliant and compelling protagonist of irrationalism, but rather because his theory was the *extreme* of irrationalism: thoroughly pessimistic, highly anti-intellectual, pseudoscientific, dogmatic, and more at variance with the traditional Western conception of man as a unique, rational, morally responsible being than any other secular doctrine before or since. As such, it became the consolation and catechism of a generation for which a terrible war had turned Western civilization into a burned-out wasteland.

Irrationalism in Political and Social Thought

At the turn of the century, traditional views still dominated political and social theory. In England, progressive liberal values, which now assumed a democratic and sometimes socialist complexion, were upheld by Herbert Spencer and the Fabian reformers. In France, old-time Enlightenment rationalism still ran strong among the victorious Dreyfusards and in the widely read writings of Anatole France. In Germany, a modified form of idealism prevailed in neo-Kantian and neo-Hegelian academic circles, and in the writings of the distinguished philosopher-historians Wilhelm Dilthey and Friedrich Meinecke. Marxism had made headway everywhere and was championed in its extreme revolutionary form by Lenin and the Russian Bolsheviks. But by 1900 a growing number of thinkers throughout the Western world were becoming increasingly interested in the role of the irrational in political and social affairs.

GEORGES SOREL, Bergson's countryman and admirer, was the central figure of a group of mainly French and Italian intellectuals, including Vilfredo Pareto, Gaetano Mosca, and Roberto Michels, who led the way in analyzing the irrational in political life. All of them rejected the liberal assumption that political thought and action are the outcome of reason tested by experience and held instead that they result from habit and lethargy, subconscious drives, or a restless will to power. All believed that politics is more a matter of might than right, and that political positions are merely rationalizations or myths used to justify the pursuit of power. All were political elitists who believed that government by the most capable was the best protection against misgovernment. And, although their opinions varied as to who should rule and how, all agreed that the ruling elite at any given time is the group which has established its right to rule by its demonstrated ability to seize and hold power. Understandably, such views were conceived and gained ground in countries where liberalism was shaky. But even in England, the avid liberal Graham Wallas warned, in his pioneering work, *Human Nature in Politics* (1908), that irrational impulses in politics must be recognized and brought under control if liberal views and values were to be preserved.

Sorel himself, originally a Marxian socialist, became intensely hostile to bureaucratic and parliamentary procedure, whether bourgeois or socialist. Such government, he believed, does nothing more than perpetuate itself and the status quo. Whether the instrument of a decadent, materialistic, uninspired bourgeoisie, by and for whom parliamentary government was invented, or whether in the hands of dissident minorities, like the supposedly revolutionary socialists, bureaucracy can never lead to action. It is a political dead end, a confession of ideological bankruptcy, which disqualifies it as an acceptable political practice. Only revolutionary violence changes the world, Sorel proclaimed in his best known work, *Reflections on Violence* (1908). And violence is never generated by appeals to reason or by elections and constitutions. Rather, it is a purely emotional response to an immediate situation aroused by a call for heroic action. Not all violence is heroic, but all heroism is violent in that it upsets the status quo and changes the world. In order to mobilize this latent potential, Sorel, by combining elements of Marx, Nietzsche, and Bergson, fathered the idea of the political myth.

Political programs, ideologies, and utopias, Sorel argued, are merely abstract intellectual constructions; they may serve as models for action but never as calls to action. That is the special function of political myths, which have no other purpose than to arouse collective passions. They do not describe, analyze, or propose courses of action, nor are they subject to debate, modification, or compromise. Political myths are nothing more or less than "expressions of a determination to act." In agreement with Marx, Sorel claimed that only the oppressed proletariat could be inspired to heroic deeds and great historical achievements. But the means he prescribed to achieve this result derived more from the irrationalism of Nietzsche and Bergson than from Marx's highly intellectualistic dialectic. Sorel's prescription was the exciting impromptu myth of the general strike, adopted by the syndicalist movement to arouse the workers to seize factories, paralyze the economy, confront the enemy in hand-to-hand street combat, and, ultimately, to form a new elitist working-class government.

Sorel's adherence to Marxist goals linked him with the political Left. But his frank irrationalism and emphasis on heroic action inspired Mussolini and obviously prefigured certain aspects of later fascism—not least Hitler's "big lie." Sorel's great miscalculation was to think that the working classes, whom he idealized as only nonproletarian political visionaries are prone to do, would embrace his theory, whereas in reality it eventually came to fruition chiefly among the petty bourgeois and their leaders whom Sorel detested. But, from irrational premises, what could be expected other than irrational results?

Whereas Sorel was an elitist of the Left, who hailed the liberation of popular passions, Pareto, Mosca, and Michels were elitists of the Right who looked to the ruling classes to hold the irrational impulses in check. All three closely identified the irrational in politics with mass society and democratic government, which resulted in their adherence to more or less antidemocratic political positions. Pareto, the most antidemocratic of all and a supporter of Mussolini's fascist regime before his death in 1923, argued in his major work, *The Mind and Society* (1916), that any society without a ruling class must succumb to instinct and passion, or what he called "residues" (habit and unconscious drives), which govern the conduct of the masses. The only sound approach to politics, he claimed, was the supposedly rational, scientific, "logico-experimental" method, inspired by Machiavelli, which enables elites to control and manipulate the masses by playing upon the "derivations" or rationalizations of their conduct. Elites must combine the craftiness of the fox with the bold assertiveness of the lion. They must follow a policy of calculated expediency, designed to meet each situation with the appropriate response and guided by the ultimate aim of consolidating their power, preserving continuity, and allowing only for controlled change.

Mosca, who refused to endorse Mussolini's regime, differed from Pareto chiefly in that he made room in his ruling class of the economically powerful for a body of "disinterested" public servants who, because of their peculiar talents and lack of large vested interests in any given political system, could genuinely reflect and reflect upon the broad interests of society as a whole. Michels, in turn, in his studies of the role and workings of political parties in modern society, proclaimed the "iron law of oligarchy," by which he meant the inevitable tendency of all political parties, regardless of whose interests they claimed to represent, to evolve eventually into closed, self-perpetuating elites. He, too, acquiesced in Mussolini's regime. Starting as analysts of the irrational in politics, all of them, Sorel and Pareto, Mosca and Michels, ended as advocates of irrationalism of one kind or another. In the process, however, they shed more light on the political movements and mechanisms of modern mass society than their more traditional and less perceptive liberal adversaries.

Dilemma of the Social Sciences

The growing preoccupation with decadence and with the irrational side of life in the emerging new order prompted social observers to take a fresh look at mankind's collective existence. If the traditional rational values of the West were indeed defunct and men were but creatures of irrational drives, was a science of society even possible? Was not the very concept of a science or logic of society a contradiction in terms? And if intellect was merely the façade of actions originating in the irrational subconscious, was it still possible to believe in the ultimate triumph of reason in human affairs, as Hegel and other influential philosophers had believed? Was it still possible to believe in the applicability of scientific concepts to social phenomena, as positivists since Comte had held? And if the new views now making their appearance rendered such old assumptions invalid, did not these views themselves pose an insuperable barrier to an objective analysis of social man? These questions troubled thinkers who still aspired to discern the significant patterns and designs underlying social developments, but who were no longer certain that it was possible to do so: thinkers like Ferdinand Tönnies, Émile Durkheim, and Max Weber, three of the great pioneers of modern sociology.

FERDINAND TÖNNIES (1855-1936) was among the first to point out this dilemma in his book, *Gemeinschaft und Gesellschaft* (1887), which contrasted the concept of community (*Gemeinschaft*), dominant before the advent of modernization, to that of society (*Gesellschaft*), characteristic of the triumphant new urban industrial order. Community was good, according to Tönnies, because it was based on the personal and deep-rooted, spontaneous, and natural relations between people typical of the family, the clan, and comparatively homogeneous rural groups. Society, on the other hand, was evil in that it favored the opposite: impersonal, superficial, coerced, and artificial human relations. This contrast between an ideal healthy social order and the real but unhealthy one went back at least as far as Rousseau and the romantics. But Tönnies was one of the first to give it a systematic sociological foundation, laying the groundwork for much important subsequent social research, especially in Germany, where the issue of modernization was just coming to a head.

However, if Tönnies' interpretation had the merit of casting new light on the impact of modernization on premodern social patterns and values, it also posed but failed to answer certain thorny methodological questions. If, for example, genuine community was possible only under premodern conditions of existence, how could it serve as either a model or a counterpoise to modern society? If it were not merely a vestige of the past, why had it failed to survive the transition which brought society to the fore? By the same token, if the relations Tönnies associated with society were as negative as he claimed, why had modern mankind allowed itself to fall prey to them? And if the relations he associated with community were as positive as he claimed, what, if anything, could be done to restore them? In short, how could fact be reconciled with value in the sphere of mankind's social existence? This question was Tönnies' chief legacy to modern social theory.

ÉMILE DURKHEIM (1858-1917), who ranked with Bergson as a leading influence on French thought before the war, attempted to resolve the question by appeal to the concept of equilibrium. Society, he reasoned, because it precedes and takes precedence over the individual, determines the standards, both moral and material, the individual must live by if he is to function at all. That which integrates the individual with society is good; that which does not is bad. This line of thought allowed Durkheim, in his pioneering theoretical work, *The Rules of Sociological Method* (1895), to distinguish between "normal" social phenomena, "social conditions that are most generally distributed," and the others, which he termed "morbid" or "pathological." In other words, Durkheim equated the normal with the average individual at any given time and the pathological with the "deviation from this standard of health." If perfect integration, personified by the completely socialized person, represented one pole, the desirable pole, of the social spectrum, "anomie"—a word Durkheim introduced into the sociologist's vocabulary, referring to a state of social breakdown and anarchy—represented the other, undesirable pole. The extreme expression of anomie, he concluded in his next major work, *Suicide* (1897), is the person who takes his own life because he fails to adjust minimally to prevailing social standards, finds himself completely isolated, and is, therefore, unable to find any reason or purpose in living.

Durkheim's was a sociology by consensus, reflecting his own personal dedication to democratic and utilitarian values derived from the Enlightenment. Unlike Tönnies, Durkheim believed that social normalcy is, by definition, the rule rather than the exception and that social norms at any given time embody humanity's highest collective achievement. He also believed that most people most of the time know what is good (as defined by society), know how to enact it, and are willing to compromise and exercise restraint in the pursuit of self-interest for the sake of preserving social stability. But, like Tönnies, Durkheim was deeply distressed by the increasing signs of social disintegration and anomie apparent in the emerging new social order of his day, as dramatically exemplified by the rising suicide rate. And although he did not, like Tönnies, condemn the new order out of hand—indeed, his definition of social normalcy by consensus did not allow him to do so—he did grow to share the German's nostalgia for an older, supposedly simpler and more integrated social existence. This nostalgia found expression in his last major work, *Elementary Forms of Religious Life* (1912).

Durkheim's dilemma was this: if integration is the sole criterion of a healthy society, what is to prevent the conclusion that a well-functioning totalitarian society is not a healthy society? This conclusion Durkheim personally would have abhorred. If, on the other hand, all deviations from the social norm, saints and sinners alike, are lumped together indiscriminately under the heading "pathological," what standard is left to judge society's health other than the purely functional one of integration, with all its amoral implications? If Durkheim had abandoned his distinction between the socially normal and the pathological, he would have deprived himself of what he considered an essential tool of scientific analysis. By holding to it, however, he deprived himself of the possibility of making any moral or value judgments about man's social existence, which, he himself believed, was the whole point of scientific enlightenment.

The root of this theoretical quandary was Durkheim's inadequate appreciation of the historical forces of change, some of which are, certainly, merely disruptive and ephemeral, although others contain the potential for new and lasting modes of social organization. As with Tönnies, Durkheim's view of society was unrealistically static and rigid. True, Durkheim marked an advance over Tönnies in that he passed from a merely descriptive classification of social phenomena to a more scientific and analytic approach. This aspect of his theory appealed to his many mainly French and Anglo-American successors, who shared Durkheim's faith in the fundamental soundness of existing social institutions and values and his faith in, if not man's fundamental goodness, at least his basic good sense. But Durkheim fared little better than Tönnies in synthesizing what exists with what they both alleged ought to exist in man's social existence. The result was a relativistic impasse from which Max Weber, the most profound and fruitful of the pioneers of modern sociology, sought to rescue the new discipline.

MAX WEBER   Any social science worthy of the name, Max Weber (1864-1920) maintained, must eschew value judgments of any kind. Sociology should never serve either to condemn or sanction society; it should always strive to be strictly "value-free," as he put it. In two famous lectures, "Science as a Vocation" and "Politics as a Vocation," both delivered in 1918, Weber took the anti-Marxist position that understanding and changing the world are two entirely different undertakings. The first is a matter of reason and intellect, the second a matter of will and action. To be sure, the two vocations can and should be complementary. A person cannot take an intelligent stand on public issues unless he is well informed, which is where sociology can make a worthwhile contribution; one is not likely to become well informed unless he is seriously concerned with public issues. Unfortunately, however, this happy conjunction is rarely the case. The reason, according to Weber, is that science can never answer the ultimate human and political question put by Tolstoy: "What shall we do, and how shall we live?" Whereas, in politics, said Weber: "to come out and take a stand is one's damned duty. The words one uses in a political meeting are not means of scientific analysis but means of canvassing votes and winning over others. They are not ploughshares to loosen the soil of contemplative thought; they are swords against enemies; such words are weapons. It would be an outrage, however, to use words in this fashion in a lecture or in the lecture-room."

This tension between the two apparently irreconcilable vocations of science and politics preoccupied Weber throughout his life and writings, although he formulated it explicitly only in his later years in the lectures mentioned. To him, it was not merely an academic question, it was a pressing personal and existential crisis; this, because Weber himself was one of the gifted few deeply involved in both callings. He was too concerned with moral and political issues ever to rest content being a passive, noncommittal observer of events. But he also had too much intellectual integrity ever to sink to the level of mere rhetoric in expressing his moral and political views. Moreover, he concluded that, generally, science and intellectualism in his day had so permeated all spheres of life in the Western world that, instead of contributing to responsible political and moral decision-making, they were actually undermining it by neglecting the human will and passions where such decision-making originates. It was precisely to check this ominous trend that Weber turned to social theory. But was a sociology possible that could address itself to the question of how we should live without sacrificing the highest standards of scientific objectivity and impartiality? This was the question on which Weber's theory turned.

Far more deeply steeped in history and philosophy, especially of the German variety, than Tönnies and Durkheim, Weber made these disciplines the basis of his thinking. In his wide-ranging studies, not only of German and Western civilization but of ancient and Far Eastern civilizations as well, Weber noted an apparently universal tendency whereby intellect and science win out eventually over spontaneity and spirituality, passion and poetry, heroism and myth: everything, that is, which gives life meaning in the early phases of society's development. But what, in the process, man gains in the way of efficiency, stability, and mastery over himself and his environment, he loses in the way of a sense of selfhood, purpose, and community with his fellow man. For while intellect and science can tell man how to do things and provide the means to do them, they cannot tell him what to do, or even that he should do anything at all. Intellect enables man to discover and dispel illusions, but it does not of itself offer him any alternative conception of a meaningful and satisfying existence. Intellect despiritualizes the world without respiritualizing it. The end result, rapidly approaching in the West, Weber believed, is a sort of social arteriosclerosis. An efficient but deadening, impersonal, aimless bureaucratic type of government takes command; everyday life becomes increasingly mechanized, routinized, and institutionalized; and men find their lives more secure but also more atomized and spiritually impoverished. Once society reaches this point, it can no longer cope with sudden change or crisis. Should either occur, society reverts to an older type of political authority characteristic of the early phase of its existence: the "charismatic" leader, the great man who wins allegiance by dint of a forceful personality, sweeping vision, or heroic deeds, as personified by Caesar, Napoleon, and other great leaders. Then a new cycle begins.

Much of Weber's theory was reminiscent of the early modern Italian thinker, Giambattista Vico, who also conceived the history of societies in terms of a cyclic process and deplored the "barbarism of intellect" characteristic of a society's late existence. Weber's theory was also reminiscent of Marx, whose dialectical materialism and historical determinism in some respects directly influenced his thinking. In contrast to both, however, Weber did not believe that there was anything inevitable or predetermined about this pattern of history, which is why, unlike Tönnies and Durkheim, he stressed the importance of moral and political responsibility. Men are free at any given time to make moral decisions and to try to alter the course of events by translating their choices into collective political action. Whether such efforts will succeed, only time will tell. But "all historical experience confirms the truth—that man would not have attained the possible unless time and again he had reached out for the impossible."

Nevertheless, Weber did believe that historical regularities are sufficiently constant and universal to enable the social scientist to analyze a society's structure and prospects at any given time. For example, the forms of political authority throughout history, notwithstanding the individual features of each particular government, have appeared regularly enough and have shared enough common characteristics to enable the social scientist to classify them into three types—charismatic, traditional, and legal—and to study them in relation to their social context. Choices may be arbitrary and irrational in origin and, therefore, beyond scientific analysis and prediction. But if choices are to become effective, they must find intellectual and institutional outlets that will enable them to thrive within a given social environment. In other words, there must be some logical consistency or "elective affinity" between the choice itself and the forms of social expression it assumes. Such elective affinities can be discovered by constructing "ideal types": abstract logical models that do not correspond exactly to anything real, but that allow the social scientist to determine the degree of logical integration of social behavior and to project its consequences.

Weber followed this procedure in his best known and still controversial work, *The Protestant Ethic and the Spirit of Capitalism* (1905), in which he attempted to show the logical relationship between two apparently unrelated phenomena: Calvinism and capitalism, the one religious and the other economic. While he did not claim that one caused the other, he did argue that each reinforced the other. Calvinism, with its emphasis on work, thrift, rational calculation, elitism, and mastery over the physical world—all for the spiritual purpose of glorifying God on earth—served as a sort of cocoon that protected and nurtured the chrysalis of capitalism. Capitalism in turn, which emphasized the same virtues for quite different, earthly reasons, served to strengthen the Calvinist movement and raise it to a high level of worldly success and influence.

Originally, this purely unintentional and unforeseen collaboration exemplified a high degree of logical integration. But it also hastened the rationalization of life in the Western world to a degree in which religion of any kind eventually would have no place. By the end of the eighteenth century, religion already was in decline. Disintegration of the collaboration had set in, and capitalism, now mature and triumphant and no longer in need of outside ideological support, proclaimed its independence and self-justification and assumed a profoundly irreligious complexion. In effect, Calvinism had nurtured its own gravedigger and the gravedigger of all religion. At the same time, capitalism's coming of age marked a new and more advanced stage in the rationalization of social life. But the price paid for this development was an impoverishment of spiritual life, bringing the Western world one step closer to the end of its turn-of-the-century historical cycle and the start of a new one, barring unforeseen circumstances.

Weber succeeded in incorporating Tönnies' moralism and Durkheim's functionalism into a single unified theory, which, he hoped, would help Western mankind create a healthier, happier society. But his premises seemed to lead only to discouraging conclusions. For if science does not and should not influence the decision-making process, if words used as weapons are out of place in the lecture room and the language of scientific analysis is out of place at a political meeting, what can motivate people to make more intelligent decisions? And if science does influence decision-making, should it not then recognize and acknowledge its share of responsibility for the course of events?

With the coming of war, Weber himself lost what little faith he still had in the capacity of Western mankind to improve its social existence. He continued, until his death, to insist upon vocational responsibility on the grounds that, when all else is lost, especially then, there is nobility and consolation in clinging to professional integrity, regardless of consequences. But if Hitler's rise to power could be interpreted as the terrible fulfillment of Weber's prophecy of the imminence of a new charismatic leader, it also testified to the limitations of a social theory which exempted scientists and intellectuals from political responsibility. Had Weber, then, rescued social theory from bias and relativism only to deliver it over to futility? He recognized this dilemma, but failed to solve it. In the long run, it proved to be one of the most weighty of the many problems Weber bequeathed future social theory.

A Quiet Revolution

By the 1890s, another intellectual upheaval was underway in the natural sciences. It went almost unnoticed at the time, but in the long run it would have a momentous impact on established ideas. It was the product of a number of advances in many different areas of research and experiment. Among the most important were Wilhelm Roentgen's discovery of X-rays, Pierre and Marie Curie's discovery that radium emits energy, Max Planck's quantum theory, according to which energy is emitted in discontinuous ejections rather than in a continuous flow, and Ernest Rutherford's transformation of nitrogen atoms into hydrogen atoms. By 1913, scientists had shown that the atom, earlier thought to be the solid and uniform, inert and indivisible building block of nature, was actually a whole new active universe unto itself; a sort of miniature solar system composed of a positively charged proton (its nucleus) surrounded by negatively charged electrons.

The most significant single advance was Albert Einstein's theory of relativity, formulated between 1905 and 1916. Its point of departure was the famous Michelson-Morley experiment, performed in 1887, which demonstrated that all motion is relative to something else, and since there is nothing in the universe that constitutes an absolute standard of measurement, there can be no absolute motion. Einstein went on to provide a unified theory, according to which there is no such thing as absolute space, time, or motion. Space, he demonstrated, is not filled with a weightless substance called ether against which motion can be measured, as earlier physicists had supposed. Consequently, there is no absolutely stationary space. All motion is relative to the speed at which the observer himself is moving.

Einstein also concluded that matter and energy are interchangeable, having calculated that mass varies according to the velocity at which it moves. This relationship he expressed in his now famous equation: $E=mc^2$ (energy equals mass multiplied by the square of the speed of light). The basic principle of relativity also yielded the conclusion that, just as mass and velocity are interrelated, so, too, are space and time. The two are not distinct entities, he held, but instead constitute a continuum, a four-dimensional space-time continuum. And Einstein's bold new theory of the curvature of space was dramatically confirmed in 1919, when a solar eclipse proved his prediction that light rays passing near the sun would be bent.

The "new physics," as it came to be called, eventually made possible such things as television, nuclear energy, the use of radioactivity, travel in outer space, and a host of other technological achievements indispensable to contemporary life. Since these achievements did not begin to materialize until a generation later, they will be dealt with at greater length in the next two chapters. But the immediate effect of the new scientific breakthroughs was to overthrow the older Newtonian conception of nature as a well-functioning, intelligible mechanism, and to replace it with a far more complex, bewildering conception, which seemed to defy the average intelligent person's everyday common-sense experience of nature. As against the older Newtonian view, the new physics proclaimed that nature is not uniform throughout, that the concept of causality is meaningless in science, that nature cannot be represented adequately within the framework of space and time, and that the scientific observer and what he observes are not two distinct and unrelated entities. Just as artists and intellectuals were in the process of uncovering previously unsuspected depths and complexities within the human sphere and questioning the capacity of reason to cope with them, so, too, physicists began to make similar revelations with respect to the external world and man's relationship to it. If such basics as space, time, and motion were mental constructions rather than concrete things, and were relative rather than absolute, what certainties remained?

THE FIN DE SIÈCLE AS PSEUDOMORPH

The *fin de siècle* bore the earmarks of a "cultural pseudomorph," a term popularized after the First World War by the controversial German historian Oswald Spengler. It was a term he borrowed from geology, describing a rock that retains its shape after its original elements have been leached out of it and new materials have replaced them. Applied to history, the term pseudomorph refers to civilizations that manage to retain their essential structure in the face of significant change and new infusions. Such was the West on the eve of the First World War, when Spengler conceived this analogy. For while the West experienced rapid and significant change in every area of life between 1880 and 1914, it also showed a remarkable ability during this time to absorb, withstand, contain, or disregard the forces of change that eventually would undermine it.

Imperialism, as we have seen, was not simply hyperactive nationalism. Rather, it represented a fundamentally new conception of politics, calling for indefinite expansion beyond established national boundaries and paving the way for the emergence of a new political entity: the modern superpower, which eventually would supersede the older nation-state. Yet, for a time, Western governments ingeniously succeeded in absorbing imperialism into the existing political framework by appealing to such slogans as the white man's burden and manifest destiny. And governments continued to think in terms of national integrity, a concert of nations, and an international balance of power, although imperialism implied their subversion in every way.

Industrialization, too, changed the complexion but not the basic structure of the West before 1914. Marxists confidently predicted that the new mode of production would necessarily bring socialism in its wake, whether by revolutionary or peaceful means. But it was the already-advanced capitalist countries that took and held the lead in industrialization and assimilated it to the existing social and economic structure. In some cases, industrialization actually revived dying social classes, such as the German Junker, the English lord, and the Japanese samurai. As for the new social classes that industrialization called forth—the large-scale entrepreneur, the urban proletarian, and the white-collar worker—they, too, despite their numbers and potential power, had curiously little effect for a time on the social and political status quo.

The new social discontents, voiced by workers and national minorities, testified to the growing inequities within and between nations. Those voiced by women and youth called into question some of mankind's oldest and most cherished notions: namely, that the family is the basic unit of society and that women and youth are social inferiors. These discontents also were either ignored, contained, or channeled in socially accepted ways. And if alienation and dissent became the rule rather than the exception among the boldest and most original artists and intellectuals of the day, they scarcely posed a threat to the existing order of things. Although strained by all these new developments, the structure of the Western world remained intact. And proud of its unprecedented power and prospects, the West drifted, with a serenity and self-confidence not to be known again in the twentieth century, toward the disaster of world war.

BIBLIOGRAPHY

General Works

The New Cambridge Modern History. Vol. 11: *Material Problems and World-Wide Problems, 1870–1898,* edited by F. H. Hinsley (Cambridge, 1962); vol. XII: *The Era of Violence,* edited by D. Thomson (Cambridge, 1960). See also the rev. ed. of vol. XII: *The Shifting Balance of World Power, 1898–1945,* edited by C. L. Mowat (Cambridge, 1968).

HALE, ORON J. *The Great Illusion, 1900–1914.* New York: Harper & Row, 1971.

HAYES, CARLTON J. *A Generation of Materialism, 1871–1900.* New York: Harper & Row, 1941.

MUNHOLLAND, J. KIM. *Origins of Contemporary Europe, 1890–1914.* New York: Harcourt, Brace & World, 1970.

Politics and Society

Cambridge Economic History of Europe. Vol. 6: *The Industrial Revolutions and After,* edited by M. M. Postan and H. J. Habakkuk. Cambridge: University Press, 1965.

BALFOUR, MICHAEL. *The Kaiser and his Times.* London: Cresset, 1964.

BARZUN, JACQUES. *Race, A Study in Modern Superstition.* New York: Harcourt, Brace & Co., 1937.

BEALE, HOWARD K. *Theodore Roosevelt and the Rise of America to World Power.* Baltimore: Johns Hopkins Press, 1956.

BOTTOMORE, T. B. *Classes in Modern Society.* London: Allen & Unwin, 1965.

BRIEFS, GOETZ A. *The Proletariat, a Challenge to Western Civilization.* New York: McGraw-Hill, 1937.

COBBAN, ALFRED. *A History of Modern France.* Vol. 3: *1871–1962.* Baltimore: Penguin Books, 1965.

COCHRAN, THOMAS C. and WILLIAM MILLER¡ *The Age of Enterprise.* Rev. ed. New York: Harper & Row, 1961.

COLE, GEORGE D. H. *The Second International, 1889–1914.* 2 vols. London: Macmillan & Co., 1956.

DUGAS, RENÉ. *A History of Mechanics.* Translated by J. R. Maddox. New York: Central Book Co., 1955.

FEIS, HERBERT. *Europe: The World's Banker, 1870–1914.* New Haven: W. W. Norton & Co., 1930.

GAY, PETER. *The Dilemma of Democratic Socialism: Eduard Bernstein's Challenge to Marx.* New York: Collier, 1952.

GOLLWITZER, HEINZ. *Europe in the Age of Imperialism, 1880–1914.* London: Thames & Hudson, 1969.

GREENE, THEODORE M. *Liberalism, its Theory and Practice.* Austin: University of Texas Press, 1957.

HOBSBAWM, ERIC J. *Industry and Empire.* New York: Pantheon, 1968.

HOLLINGSWORTH, THOMAS H. *Historical Demography.* Ithaca, N. Y.: Cornell University Press, 1969.

HYNES, SAMUEL. *The Edwardian Turn of Mind.* Princeton: Princeton University Press, 1968.

JENKINS, ROY. *Asquith: Portrait of a Man and an Era.* New York: E. P. Dutton & Co., 1965.

JOHNSON, DOUGLAS W. *France and the Dreyfus Affair.* London: Blandford, 1966.

KANN, ROBERT A. *The Habsburg Empire: A Study in Integration and Disintegration.* New York: Praeger, 1957.

KLEMPERER, KLEMENS VON. *Germany's New Conservatism: Its History and Dilemma in the Twentieth Century.* Princeton: Princeton University Press, 1957.

KOHN, HANS. *The Idea of Nationalism.* New York: Macmillan Co., 1944.

LANGER, WILLIAM L. *European Alliances and Alignments, 1871–1890.* 2d ed. New York: Vintage Books, 1950.

LLOYD, TREVOR O. *Empire to Welfare State: English History, 1906–1967.* London: Oxford University Press, 1970.

MASUR, GERHARD. *Imperial Berlin.* New York: Basic Books, 1970.

NEF, JOHN U. *War and Human Progress, An Essay on the Rise of Industrial Civilization.* Cambridge, Mass.: Harvard University Press, 1950.

ROSENBERG, ARTHUR. *Imperial Germany: The Birth of the German Republic.* Translated by J. Morrow. Boston: Beacon Press, 1964.

SEMMEL, BERNARD. *Imperialism and Social Reform: English Social-Imperial Thought, 1895–1914.* Garden City, N. Y.: Doubleday & Co., 1960.

SCHORSKE, CARL E. *German Social Democracy, 1905–1917: The Development of the Great Schism.* Cambridge, Mass.: Harvard University Press, 1955.

SHAFER, BOYD C. *Nationalism: Myth and Reality.* New York: Harcourt, Brace and Co., 1955.

SINGER, CHARLES J. et al., eds. *A History of Technology.* Vol. 5: *Late Nineteenth Century, 1850–1900.* Oxford: Clarendon Press, 1958.

STEARNS, PETER N. *European Society in Upheaval.* New York and London: Macmillan Co., 1967.

TAYLOR, ALAN J. P. *The Struggle for Mastery in Europe, 1848–1918.* Oxford: Clarendon Press, 1954.

TAYLOR, EDMOND. *The Fall of the Dynasties: The Collapse of the Old Order, 1905–1922.* Garden City, N. Y.: Doubleday & Co., 1963.

THORNTON, A. P. *Doctrines of Imperialism.* New York and London: Wiley, 1965.

TUCHMAN, BARBARA W. *The Proud Tower.* New York: Bantam Books, 1966.

WEBER, ADNA F. *The Growth of Cities in the Nineteenth Century.* Rev. ed. Ithaca: Cornell University Press, 1963.

WEBER, EUGENE J. *The Nationalist Revival in France, 1905–1914.* Berkeley and Los Angeles: University of California Press, 1968.

WRIGLEY, EDWARD A. *Population and History.* London: Weidenfeld & Nicolson, 1969.

ZELDIN, THEODORE. *France 1848–1945.* Vol. I: *Ambition, Love, and Politics.* Oxford: Clarendon Press, 1973.

Intellectual and Cultural Trends

ANTONI, CARLO. *From History to Sociology: The Transition in German Historical Thinking.* Translated by H. V. White. Detroit: Wayne University Press, 1959.

BOWRA, CECIL M. *The Heritage of Symbolism.* London: Macmillan and Co., 1943.

BROMBERG, WALTER. *The Mind of Man: A History of Psychotherapy and Psychoanalysis.* New York: Harper & Row, 1963.

CAUDWELL, CHRISTOPHER. *Studies in a Dying Culture.* London: John Love, 1938.

CURTIS, MICHAEL. *Three Against the Third Republic: Sorel, Barres, and Maurras.* Princeton, N. J.: Princeton University Press, 1959.

GRAÑA, CÉSAR. *Bohemian Versus Bourgeois: French Society and the French Man of Letters in the Nineteenth Century.* New York: Basic Books, 1964.

HANNA, THOMAS, ed. *The Bergsonian Heritage.* New York: Columbia University Press, 1962.

HARPER, RALPH. *The Seventh Solitude: Metaphysical Homelessness in Kierkegaard, Dostoevsky, and Nietzsche.* Baltimore: Johns Hopkins Press, 1965.

HEISENBERG, WERNER. *Physics and Philosophy: The Revolution in Modern Science.* New York: Harper & Row, 1958.

HITCHCOCK, HENRY. *Architecture: Nineteenth and Twentieth Centuries.* 2d ed. Baltimore: Penguin Books, 1963.

HOROWITZ, IRVING L. *Radicalism and the Revolt against Reason.* New York: Humanities Press, 1961.

HOUGH, GRAHAM. *The Last Romantics.* London: Duckworth, 1949.

HUGHES, HENRY S. *Consciousness and Society: The Reconstruction of European Social Thought, 1890-1930.* New York: Random House, 1958.

JACKSON, HOLBROOK. *The Eighteen Nineties. New* York: Alfred A. Knopf, 1925.

KLINGENDER, FRANCIS D. *Art and the Industrial Revolution.* Rev. ed. New York: Schocken, 1970.

LEA, FRANK C. *The Tragic Philosopher, A Study of Friedrich Nietzsche.* London: Methuen, 1957.

MASUR, GERHARD. *Prophets of Yesterday: Studies in European Culture, 1890-1914.* New York: Harper & Row, 1961.

PECKHAM, MORSE. *Beyond the Tragic Vision: The Quest for Identity in the Nineteenth Century.* New York: Braziller, 1962.

PEVSNER, NIKOLAUS. *Pioneers of the Modern Movement from William Morris to Walter Gropius.* London: Faber & Faber, 1936.

PRAZ, MARIO. *The Romantic Agony.* Translated by A. Davidson. 2d ed. London: Oxford University Press, 1951.

READ, HERBERT. *A Concise History of Modern Painting.* New York: Praeger, 1959.

SCOTT, JOHN A. *Republican Ideas and the Liberal Tradition in France, 1870-1914.* New York: Columbia University Press, 1951.

SHATTUCK, ROGER. *The Banquet Years: The Origins of the Avant-Garde in France, 1885 to World War One.* Rev. ed. New York: Random House, 1968.

SOROKIN, PITIRIM A. *Contemporary Sociological Theories.* New York: Harper & Row, 1928.

THAYER, JOHN A. *Italy and the Great War: Politics and Culture, 1870-1914.* Madison, Wis.: University of Wisconsin Press, 1964.

WEISS, JOHN, ed. *The Origins of Modern Consciousness.* Detroit: Wayne State University Press, 1965.

WHITROW, G. J. *The Structure of the Universe.* London: Hutchinson's University Library, 1949.

WHYTE, LANCELOT L. *The Unconscious Before Freud.* New York: Basic Books, 1960.

WILLIAMS, RAYMOND. *The Country and the City.* New York: Oxford University Press, 1973.

WILSON, EDMUND. *Axel's Castle.* New York: Charles Scribner & Sons, 1931.

ZWEIG, STEFAN. *The World of Yesterday.* New York: Viking Press, 1943.

IV

ERA OF
TOTAL WAR:
1914–1945

FIRST WORLD WAR AND ITS LEGACY

In August of 1914, Europeans marched to war enthusiastically for the last time, assured by their political and military leaders that it would be a short one, like the Austro-Prussian War of 1866 and the Franco-Prussian War of 1870/71. What ensued was a bloody conflict that lasted more than four years and ended with approximately twelve million men killed in action and twenty million more wounded, countless millions of civilians ravaged by disease, whole cities at the brink of starvation, and a swath of destruction through Belgium and France that extended from the English Channel to the Swiss border. It was a conflict that ended in mutual exhaustion rather than in victory or defeat, leaving a legacy of bitterness, resentment, and discontent such as to make another war almost inevitable.

The great issues which precipitated the war—the rivalry between Austria and Russia in the Balkans, the rivalry between France and Germany for supremacy in Europe, and the rivalry between Great Britain and Germany for supremacy at sea—were quickly forgotten in the heat of battle as the war developed into a life-and-death struggle for total victory at any cost by whatever means. The great battles are remembered not so much for what they accomplished as for their staggering casualties. The

Recruits at Southwark Town Hall, London, December, 1915.

(Radio Times Hulton Picture Library).

so-called Battle of the Frontiers at the war's outset cost the French three hundred thousand men. The British lost fifty thousand at Ypres in 1914. General Joseph Joffre's offensives through the summer of 1915, which gained nothing, cost the French four hundred thousand men. In the great battle of Verdun in 1916, the Germans and French each lost three hundred fifty thousand. And at the Somme in 1916, the Germans lost half a million, the British four hundred ten thousand, and the French one hundred ninety thousand. The slaughter was unprecedented and the military gains insignificant.

The war was detonated by the assassination of the Austrian Archduke Franz Ferdinand, heir to the Habsburg throne, in Sarajevo on June 28, 1914. The assassin was a member of the Black Hand, a Serbian organization dedicated to the unity and independence of the South Slav peoples. The Habsburg government, exasperated by the growing agitation of its national minorities for independence and fearful of Russian intervention in the Balkans, presented an ultimatum to the Serbian government that it could not possibly meet within the forty-eight hours allowed. Serbia turned to Russia for support, and Austria to Germany. In the following weeks the half-hearted efforts of these governments to pre-

Casualty at the Somme offensive 1916.

(Imperial War Museum, London.)

vent war, or at least to confine it to a local war, broke down and military mobilization began. The alliance systems, forged since the turn of the century, now went into effect. The Entente—France, Russia, and Britain—squared off against the Central Powers—Germany and Austria-Hungary. Between July 28 and August 4, 1914, Austria-Hungary declared war on Serbia; Germany declared war on Russia; and

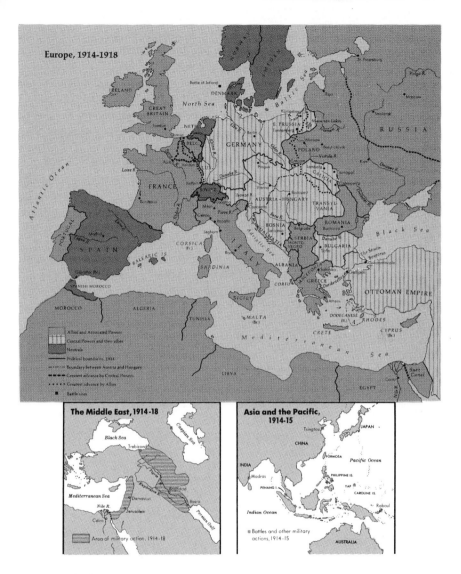

Europe, 1914-1918

The Middle East, 1914-18

Asia and the Pacific, 1914-15

France and Britain declared war on Germany. On August 4, German armies crossed the Belgian frontier and the war was on.

The German strategy, known as the Schlieffen plan after the general who had conceived it, was to win a quick victory against France in the West and then concentrate the whole German force against Russia in the East. The campaign began well for the German armies, under the command of Helmuth von Moltke, the nephew of Bismarck's famous general. By the end of August, they had smashed through Belgium, forced the French to retreat at Chalerois, and were heading south toward Paris. But the French army under General Joseph Joffre succeeded in stopping the German advance at the Marne River in early September and forced the Germans to retreat to the Aisne. The Battle of the Marne was a great victory for the French, because it denied the Germans their quick victory in the West. But it also guaranteed that the war would last much longer than either side had originally anticipated. The Germans then turned north to seize the Channel ports, which the British and French were determined to hold. Through most of November, the British defended them tenaciously at Ypres, the last major military engagement of 1914 on the western front.

The strategies, planning, and new technology designed to guarantee a quick victory were the very forces that prevented it, prolonged the war, and increased its destructiveness. The highly touted Schlieffen plan, aimed at knocking France out of the war quickly and enabling Germany to avoid a two-front war, failed in both objectives. The weakness of the French strategy was that their system of fortresses extending from Belgium south along France's eastern frontier proved woefully inadequate to resist a German offensive. Since neither side had prepared any alternative strategy in advance, the failure of these initial strategies left the combatants little choice but to fall back upon a "war of attrition" designed to produce victory by bleeding the other side to death.

By the end of 1915, operations on the western front were stalemated and the armies bogged down in trench warfare and murderous artillery barrages. The war on the eastern front also remained indecisive. After an initial Russian advance into East Prussia, the German armies, under the brilliant command of Field Marshal Paul von Hindenburg and General Erich Ludendorff, won a series of stunning victories over the poorly trained and armed Russian peasant armies, starting with Tannenberg in 1914. But final victory eluded the Germans and casualties were high.

As the conflict became stalemated, each side tried to break out of the impasse by broadening the war. In 1914, Turkey, much in debt to Germany for economic and military aid received before the war, joined the Central Powers. In 1915, Bulgaria, hoping to gain at Serbia's expense, did the same. Italy also abandoned neutrality in 1915 and came into the war on the side of the Entente lured by the promise of gain at Austria's expense.

The British, having failed in 1915 to strike at the Central Powers by sea from Gallipoli, extended operations to the Middle East, where they succeeded in arousing the Arabs against Turkish rule. The military exploits of Colonel T. E. Lawrence in the Middle East became almost legendary, and the campaign ended with the liberation of the Arabs from the Turks and the dissolution of the Ottoman Empire. Finally, in

1917, the United States, outraged by the sinking of the *Lusitania* two years before and by Germany's policy of unrestricted submarine warfare, entered the war on the side of Britain and France. That same year Russia was forced out of the war by its terrible military defeats and the outbreak of revolution at home.

The cost and length of the war soon forced the governments involved to take measures to regulate and control their economies and home fronts. Germany, most hard-pressed because of the effectiveness of the British blockade in cutting off supplies from overseas, led the way. Under the brilliant direction of industrialist Walter Rathenau, Germany's industry and eligible manpower were effectively harnessed to the war effort. Essential goods, such as food and fertilizers, that could no longer be imported or produced domestically, were replaced wherever possible by synthetic substitutes developed by German chemists. Other governments, less hard-pressed, followed suit more slowly. But as the war wore on and drained manpower and matériel, government intervention in the economy increased. Rationing and consignment of manpower and scarce goods contributed greatly to the war effort on all sides and demonstrated the capacity of governments to mobilize all of society's resources to a single end—a new lesson not to be forgotten or relinquished later. To these measures was added systematic propaganda—the deliberate distortion or falsification of events to sustain morale at home and to destroy the enemy's morale.

Such measures had the effect of obliterating the distinction between civilian and military life and forging a single, maximally efficient unit dedicated to the common goal of total victory, which the Germans called the union of *Volk* and *Front*. After the war, this vast increase of governmental powers in the Western nations was reserved for emergencies. But when life became a permanent emergency, from the Great Depression on, the war-time model of government control lay ready at hand to serve totalitarian and liberal-democratic regimes alike.

New technology also contributed to the scope and intensity of the war: the submarine, the airplane, the tank, poison gas, and the naval blockade. These instruments of destruction carried the battle, for the first time, above the ground and below the sea, and they made the battle on land and sea all the more deadly. But instead of breaking the deadlock, which was their intended purpose, these new techniques of warfare served mainly to intensify the conflict and to increase intransigence on both sides.

German victories over the Russians in 1915 allowed the new German chief of staff, Erich von Falkenhayn, to concentrate on the western front. In February of 1916, he launched a massive offensive at Verdun calculated to break the stalemate and destroy France's defensive line. The

French army, commanded by the inspiring General Philippe Pétain, barely managed to hold Verdun in one of the longest, bloodiest, and most critical battles of the war. When it ended in April, nearly seven hundred thousand on both sides were dead. Falkenhayn then launched the last great German offensive in June along the Somme against the new British army under the command of Sir Douglas Haig. The British succeeded in pushing the Germans back some fifty miles, but at the cost of suffering the worst casualty rates on either side of the war: sixty thousand the first day. By the end of 1916, morale on both sides was at its lowest and desertions began to occur. The now discredited Falkenhayn was replaced by the heroes of the eastern front, Hindenburg and Ludendorff; an angry French cabinet replaced Joffre with the younger and more offensively minded Robert Nivelle.

1917 opened with the decision of Hindenburg and Ludendorff to hold the line in the west and to concentrate on knocking Russia out of the war. They succeeded in both objectives. Nivelle was outmaneuvered in his April offensive in the Champagne, a defeat which left the French army on the brink of mutiny. The Austrians and Germans routed the Italian army at Caporetto in October. And during the summer, the Germans advanced, almost without resistance, against the badly weakened and demoralized Russian army into Russia itself, then in the midst of revolution. In March Nicholas II, the last Russian tsar, was overthrown and his government replaced by the provisional government of Alexander Kerensky, who promised his allies to keep Russia in the war. But after his army, under the command of his best general, Alexei Brusilov, was defeated by the Austrians in Galicia, the Russians could no longer effectively continue the war. On November 7, the Bolsheviks seized power and immediately sued for peace. The Germans demanded and received, over the protest of the new Bolshevik government, all of Russia's western provinces: Poland, the Ukraine, Finland, and the Baltic provinces. These were the terms of the harsh Treaty of Brest-Litovsk, which the Russians were forced to sign on March 3, 1918. Now the Germans were free once more to concentrate on the western front.

But the situation in the west had changed during the year. President Woodrow Wilson, who had won the 1916 election by his promise to keep America out of the war, was induced by three considerations to declare war on Germany on April 6, 1917. One was Germany's policy of unrestricted submarine warfare, adopted early in 1917, which took a huge toll on American and Allied commercial shipping. Another was Germany's attempt to arouse Mexico against the United States. The third was America's enormous financial and industrial investment in the Allied war effort. Moreover, a longing for peace was growing everywhere, including Germany, especially after the terrible but indecisive campaign at Passchendaele, during which foul weather and the use of mustard gas only added to the general misery. The German Reichstag even passed a peace resolution in July, which called for a peace without victory. But Kaiser Wilhelm II would not hear of it, and the Reichstag had no power to enforce its will. Instead, the Kaiser yielded to Ludendorff, who insisted on continuing the war, as he had yielded three years earlier to Moltke, who had insisted on war with Russia over the issue of Austria's ultimatum to Serbia. Nevertheless, the German government could no longer count on the whole-hearted support of the civilian population, and America's entry into the war tipped the balance in favor of the Allies.

Time was now of the essence if Germany was to win the war before American help arrived. Beginning in March 1918 Ludendorff and Hindenburg risked everything on a final offensive. At first it was successful, but the Germans lacked the reserves to win a decisive victory. A new French supreme commander, Ferdinand Foch, was appointed to coordinate the Allied defense. By the end of May, however, German forces had pushed to within thirty-seven miles of Paris. But they were now exhausted, and fresh American troops, under the command of John J. Pershing, were already arriving. In July, in a second battle of the Marne, the Allies were able to halt the German advance and launch a counteroffensive, remaining on the offensive until the end of the war.

Late in September, Ludendorff advised the Kaiser that only an armistice could save Germany. The eastern front was also collapsing. On September 30, Bulgaria concluded a separate armistice, and a month later Turkey did the same. In October, the Italians rallied and routed the Austro-Hungarian army at Vittorio Veneto. Austria, its army now destroyed, signed an armistice on November 3. The Germans were still in France in the autumn, but they had suffered severe defeats during the summer and could not hope to hold out against superior manpower and matériel. At home, morale had already collapsed and revolution was spreading throughout the country. Early in November, the German fleet at Kiel mutinied, and mutiny spread to other German seaports. Then revolution broke out in Bavaria. On November 9, the Kaiser abdicated; he fled to the Netherlands the next day. Finally, on November 11, Germany accepted Foch's armistice terms and the First World War came to an end.

When the great guns at last fell silent along the western front, it was obvious to all that the old practice of limited warfare and professional armies was gone. Gone was the old balance of power that had enabled Europe to live in comparative peace and stability for almost a century. Gone were the last remnants of dynastic rule: the Hohenzollern, Habsburgs, and Romanovs. Gone was the indisputable supremacy of

Europe in world affairs and the self-confidence of the middle classes. Gone, too, was respect for tradition, respect for the established order, and delight in the self-satisfied culture of old Europe. In short, with but few really wanting or expecting it, the nineteenth century had come to an abrupt end and the twentieth century had just as suddenly begun. The realization, and the widespread mood it evoked, that the war marked this great transition was expressed poignantly by D. H. Lawrence in a letter written to a friend in 1915: "When I drive across this country, with autumn falling and rustling to pieces, I am so sad, for my country, for this great wave of civilization, 2000 years, which is now collapsing, that it is hard to live. So much beauty and pathos of old things passing away and no new things coming. . . . No, I can't bear it. For the winter stretches ahead, where all vision is lost and all memory dies out."

Germany was more to blame for the war than any other country, as the German historian, Fritz Fischer, has shown in his controversial study, *Germany's Aims in the First World War*. Germany could have exercised more restraint in its pursuit of empire before the war and in its relations with France and Britain. Germany could have exercised more restraint in dealing with Russia over the issue of Austria's provocative ultimatum to Serbia, which was, after all, a local problem between the Habsburg government and its discontented national groups. Germany also could have shown more restraint in its conduct of the war, especially in the use of submarine warfare, and more responsiveness to the "peace offensive" of 1917. Nor was it necessary for Germany to have imposed such a harsh treaty on Russia in 1918, a treaty that served only to plant the seeds of a future conflict in Eastern Europe. Finally, the Kaiser could have exercised better judgment in weighing the advice of his politically irresponsible Junker military chiefs, notably Moltke at the beginning of the war and Ludendorff toward the end.

But to leave the question of war guilt at that would be one-sided and short-sighted. The First World War, more than most wars, resulted from many basic failings and abuses, miscalculations and false expectations, inequities, and discontents over a long period. The prewar imperialist rivalry was certainly a major cause of the war, as the distinguished British economist, John A. Hobson, foresaw as early as 1902 in his classic work, *Imperialism: A Study*. The addition of a unified and powerful Germany and Italy to the circle of imperialist powers, plus the pursuit by all of them of ever more dazzling profits, aggravated their rivalry after 1890 to the breaking point.

A decline in the quality of the political leadership after 1890 also played a role. No statesman of Bismarck's stature or ability followed him, and the delicate—too delicate—system of alliances he forged in Europe buckled after his passing. Nationalism everywhere degenerated steadily into aggressive jingoism and sabre-rattling. Fear of socialism, especially in Central Europe and among the lower middle classes everywhere, drove the bourgeoisie steadily to the Right, into the arms of a militaristic, autocratic aristocracy desperate to reassert itself in a final stand for survival, and into policies designed to divert domestic discontents abroad. The decision of the European socialist parties at the last moment to support their governments' war policies, rather than to stand united against war, also contributed to the course of events.

There were other factors as noted in the previous chapter. Among them were the decline of faith in religion and in reason, the failure of basic liberal tenets and institutions, and the difficulties encountered everywhere in adjusting tradition to the forces of modernization. There were the frustrations engendered by an overly specialized and mechanized daily routine as well as the alienation and irresponsibility of large numbers of artists and intellectuals throughout Europe. The discovery and adulation of the unconscious and irrational forces in the human makeup, delight in decadence among the socially dysfunctional, and ostentatious display and consumption among the affluent middle classes (brilliantly analyzed by Thorstein Veblen in *The Theory of the Leisure Class,* 1899) were among these factors. So, too, was the glorification of heroic action among the restless young, the emergence of elitist theories of politics and society, and the appearance of new and potent technology not easily assimilable to the existing framework of Western society. While none of these factors, nor all of them combined, made war inevitable, each brought war a step closer to reality and contributed to the general enthusiasm surrounding its outbreak. It was as if Europe were deliberately bent on self-destruction.

The Russian Revolution

By 1917, war-weariness and political discontent were spreading rapidly not only throughout Europe, but also, and especially, in Russia, which had suffered more than any of the other belligerents. Russia already had between six and eight million dead, wounded, or captured, and the country was starved, exhausted, and demoralized. Russia's desperate situation in the war was the immediate cause of the revolution that began with the overthrow of the Romanov monarchy in March, 1917 and ended with Lenin's seizure of power in November. But the causes and chain of events that explain why revolution succeeded in Russia, and nowhere else in Europe, began long before the First World War.

When Nicholas II became tsar in 1894, Russia was still the most backward of the European powers. Its government was the most purely autocratic: representative institutions scarcely existed; industrialization was just beginning; and the mass of Russians were still peasants, living in poverty as they had for centuries and unable to look forward to a better life. Russia's backwardness was dramatically demonstrated by its defeat in the Russo-Japanese War of 1904/05. The defeat led to workers' strikes and popular protests, which forced the tsar to enact reforms. One was the creation of a Duma, or national parliament; although the Duma lacked real power and did not represent the urban or rural poor, it proved nonetheless to be a significant concession. Another attempt by the government to bring Russia into the twentieth century was made by the tsar's capable prime minister, Peter Stolypin, whose agrarian reforms allowed the peasants to leave the *mir* (the traditional agricultural commune) and to buy their own land or emigrate to the cities to join the industrial labor force. But the assassination of Stolypin by a revolutionary in 1911 ended this brief period of moderate reform. For the next three years, Russia drifted under the leadership of an incompetent tsar and a German-born tsarina, whom Russians disliked for her alleged pro-German leanings and her loyalty to a conniving religious quack named Gregory Rasputin.

Most members of the Duma were moderates who supported the tsar's reform program, which had originally included universal male suffrage, parliamentary government, ministerial responsibility, and wide-ranging civil rights. Basically, they favored a constitutional monarchy on the Western European model. But outside the Duma were two popular clandestine revolutionary parties, more representative of the peasants and industrial working classes and more attuned to Russian political and social realities. One party, the Social Revolutionaries, had evolved from the nineteenth-century populist movement and sought to mobilize the peasants and improve their hard lot. The other party, the Russian Social Democrats, held Marxist views and based their program for revolution on the relatively small but rapidly expanding industrial working classes.

VLADIMIR ILYICH LENIN (1870–1924) belonged to the Russian Social Democrats and was responsible for dividing the party into two factions, beginning at its congress in 1903. Both factions believed that Russia could achieve socialism only through revolution. But the moderate Mensheviks, who accepted the orthodox Marxist position, believed that Russia would have to follow the path taken in the West and pass through a bourgeois phase of industrial growth and political reform before a revolutionary situation could develop that would lead to socialism. The smaller but more radical Bolshevik faction was headed by Lenin, who was already a hardened, professional revolutionary distinguished by his immense energy, shrewd intelligence, absolute discipline, and utter dedication to the revolutionary cause. Lenin was contemptuous of legality, peaceful compromise, and gradualism, all of which he considered the chief defects of the Menshevik position and of the socialist parties in the West. He knew that, according to orthodox Marxist theory, Russia was far from ready for revolution. However, he insisted that a party of disciplined revolutionaries need not wait for the theoretically "right" moment to strike, but should seize upon any revolutionary opportunity that presented itself. He believed that his party, and not the still-infant Russian proletariat, should form the vanguard of the revolution. In other words, Lenin believed—and here he made his own original contribution to Marxism—that Russia could and should make an immediate leap forward from a premodern to a socialist society without any intervening bourgeois historical phase.

Until 1917, the Bolsheviks remained a minority, overshadowed by the much larger and more influential Menshevik faction. Lenin himself was in exile in Switzerland and was growing increasingly discouraged by the course of events. But, in March of 1917, the tide began to turn in his favor. Russia had reached the breaking point. War-weariness, opposition to the tsar's conduct of the war and his indifference to the welfare of the masses, and the Duma's agitation for political and social reform led to a series of strikes and riots in the capital, Petrograd, climaxed by a mutiny of the troops garrisoning the city that resulted in the collapse of the monarchy. A provisional government was formed on March 12 by the Social Revolutionary Alexander Kerensky, who won the approval of the Allies by his promises to keep Russia in the war and to restore stability at home. Kerensky, however, was unable to keep either promise. His decision to continue the war was unpopular in his own country, especially after the Russian defeat against the Austrians in Galicia in the summer of 1917. And his government failed to meet the peasants' demand for more land, the workers' demand for more food and the enactment of sweeping socialist legislation. During the next eight chaotic months, while the provisional government lasted, peasants seized land, workers seized factories, soldiers deserted the army by the hundreds of thousands, and intellectuals voiced dreams of peace and progress.

The revolutionary opportunity, which Lenin had been awaiting for so many years, was at last presenting itself. In April, with help from the German government eager to see Russia knocked out of the war, by internal upheaval if necessary, Lenin returned home from exile with the promise of "peace, land, bread." He realized that the deterioration of Russia into chaos made it possible for even a small faction of revolutionaries to seize power, if it were disciplined, determined, and well-prepared. During the next seven months, Lenin was able to outmaneuver his liberal and socialist opponents by demanding an immediate end to Russia's participation in the war, land for the peasants, and a continuation of the proletarian revolution toward socialism. As conditions worsened and the provisional government continued to decline in popularity, Bolshevik influence increased, especially in the soviets (workers' councils). By October, the Bolsheviks were a majority in the Petrograd Soviet, and Leon Trotsky, who had earlier opposed Lenin, now joined with him and was elected its new chairman. On November 7, in a well coordinated action, Bolshevik forces seized the key points of Petrograd and overthrew the provisional government.

The new Bolshevik government immediately issued a peace decree, enacted land reform, and created a Council of People's Commissars to govern the state. But the Bolsheviks, although now in power, were still a minority party—they had not been elected and did not represent the majority of Russians. In the elections to the Constituent Assembly, held in late November, the Bolsheviks won slightly less than a quarter of the seats, while the Social Revolutionaries won a clear majority. Thus, if the Bolsheviks were to remain in power, they would have to rule dictatorially. This was not a difficult decision for Lenin, who had always scorned majority rule and parliamentary procedure. At stake, after all, was the future of the revolution that would spread from Russia to the rest of the world and liberate the exploited working classes. Weighed against that prospect, the necessity of governing Russia as a dictatorship seemed a small matter to the Bolsheviks. Lenin, therefore, openly proclaimed his government to be a dictatorship of the proletariat, which, although still a minority in Russia, was the only truly revolutionary class—the one, he believed, upon which the future of Russia and, ultimately, the world depended. On that justification, the Bolsheviks proceeded to suppress their political opponents and, finally, to dissolve the Constituent Assembly early in 1918. Ever since, Russia has been governed by a single party possessing absolute power.

It was one thing to seize power, quite another to consolidate it. The November revolution immediately plunged Russia into civil war, which caused new miseries for the Russian people. For the next three years, the Bolsheviks had to defend their victory against counterrevolutionary Russian forces (the Whites) and their foreign allies, including British, French, and American troops who were sent to try to prevent Russia from withdrawing from the war in Europe and to nip the new Communist regime in the bud. Fighting against superior odds under harsh conditions over vast distances—from Siberia in the east to Poland in the west—the Bolshevik forces, under the brilliant military leadership of the dynamic Trotsky, won the civil war in November of 1920. The Bolsheviks were successful largely for three reasons: Trotsky's organization and leadership of the Red Army, lack of coordination among the widely separated insurgent armies, and the widely held belief that the Whites were associated with the hated old regime and foreign military interven-

Lenin addressing a crowd in Moscow's Red Square on May Day, 1918.

(Culver Pictures, Inc.)

tion. The first Communist states was now an accomplished fact, and aroused hope and dismay around the world.

BEGINNINGS OF WORLDWIDE COMMUNISM The success of the November revolution put Lenin and his party in an excellent position to assume leadership of the Socialist parties throughout Europe. Even before the civil war ended, he summoned European Socialist leaders to Moscow to form a Third International to replace the Second that had collapsed when war broke out in 1914. The response of the Western European Socialists at the first meeting, held in March, 1919, was enthusiastic. Most of them were heartened by the Bolshevik victory in Russia, longed once more for a strong international organization, and believed that postwar Europe was ripe for revolution. But Lenin and his supporters, who expected the revolution to spread quickly to central and western Europe, were disappointed when this failed to happen. Moreover, Lenin was convinced at the time that a Communist Russia could not survive alone in a hostile world. Consequently, at the next meeting of the new International, held in July 1920, he demanded that the Socialist parties seeking membership accept his "Twenty-One Points," which called for strong party leadership and iron discipline. The constituent parties would have to expel their reformist elements, support the new

Russian government in its struggle against foreign intervention, prepare for a violent seizure of power in their own countries, and take a stronger stand against their antirevolutionary Social Democratic rivals.

Lenin's military program immediately divided the European Socialists. A majority refused to submit to the rigid discipline that Lenin had already imposed on his own party. They believed that dictatorship in the party and by the party would not be tolerated in western Europe, where Socialists were accustomed to democratic methods, and where the working classes were larger and more advanced than in Russia and therefore less in need of dictatorial party leadership. Most of the others submitted to Lenin's program, constituted themselves as Communist parties in their respective countries, and remained loyal to Moscow. Some Socialists left the movement disillusioned. By 1921, the split was permanent, and bitterness between the two unalterably opposed left-wing camps over the issue of party independence and organization has continued down to the present day. The split left the Third International, or Comintern, as it came to be called, little more than an arm of Soviet foreign policy. Not until the 1930s, during the crisis of the Great Depression and the spread of fascism, would the divided forces of international communism temporarily reunite.

Whether the Russian Revolution was inevitable or not is a question that has been debated since 1917 and is likely to be debated for some time to come. What is known with some certainty is why revolution succeeded in Russia and nowhere else in Europe. First, the monarchy was already discredited and had ceased to function even before it collapsed. This had also been true in France in 1789, but was not true of the monarchies of central Europe or the parliamentary governments of western Europe during and immediately after the First World War. Second, the provisional government was unable to stabilize the situation in Russia, which was not the case with the other war and postwar European governments. Third, the coalition of discontent was broader in Russia than in the rest of Europe; urban discontent coincided with massive land seizures by the peasants. Such a coalition had also existed in France in 1789, and would exist again in China in 1947 and in Cuba in 1958. But it did not exist in the rest of Europe either before or after the First World War. Fourth, Lenin and the other Bolshevik leaders, notably Trotsky and Stalin, were professional revolutionaries who possessed the determination and discipline to carry out revolution. Such leaders did not exist elsewhere. Fifth, the Russian people had to choose between the Bolsheviks and Whites during the civil war, and the vast majority felt they had more to gain from the Bolsheviks. Discontented elements in the rest of postwar Europe did not have to face such an alternative. Finally, the countries that might have prevented or suppressed revolution in

Russia were either defeated or else too war-weary to succeed. Therefore, contrary to Marx's original view that a communist revolution could succeed only in an advanced industrial society, it actually succeeded in the least likely country and has provided the model for all Communist revolutions since.

DISSOLUTION OF OLD EUROPE

1917 marked a major turning point: The entry of the United States into the war and Russia's withdrawal from it into revolution that year changed the whole complexion of the war and the whole course of Western history. United States participation in the war, while late and comparatively slight, sufficed to tip the balance in favor of the Allies and assure President Woodrow Wilson a predominant voice at the Paris Peace Conference in 1919. The harsh and humiliating Treaty of Brest-Litovsk, imposed by Germany on Russia in 1918, officially ended Russian participation in the war, pushed her western frontiers approximately two hundred miles eastward, and served to isolate her from general European affairs more than at any time since before the Napoleonic Wars. One of the few things that the Paris peacemakers could agree upon was that the newly emerging Soviet state and its influence must be contained—by a bloc of anti-Soviet buffer states in eastern Europe that came to be called the *cordon sanitaire.*

Wilson's position was governed by a desire to transform old Europe into a liberal-democratic united states of Europe. The Russian Revolution, under Lenin's leadership, represented a massive repudiation of and wholly new alternative to old Europe and Wilsonianism alike. Both positions had originated in old Europe: Wilson's in the flow of European ideas, institutions, and immigration upon which the United States was built; Lenin's, in the radical Marxist doctrines originally intended to apply to Europe and to societies following the characteristic European pattern of development, from which Marx himself had originally excluded Russia. But both positions, taken from their original context and adapted to new and dissimilar conditions, were now the property of two new poles of Western and world power. And, increasingly throughout the interwar period, Europe found itself torn between these two alternatives.

The rise of fascism in turn represented, among other things, a rejection of both positions and a desperate effort to restore European autonomy and hegemony. Fascism gained support by appealing to Europe's former greatness; to the severity and injustice of the peace treaties; to the nations most shaken by the war—Italy, Germany, Austria, and Hungary; to the social classes most threatened by the two new alternatives—the lower middle classes fearful of proletarianization, the upper middle classes fearful of democratization, and reactionary aristocrats and clergymen; and to racial superiority. The principal strength of fascism proved in the long run to be its most serious weakness as well. By 1939, it enjoyed the support, or at least the acquiescence, of the large majority of Europeans. But, by the very nature of its Europe-centered appeal, it could find little support in the much vaster non-European, non-Aryan world, in contrast to the more broadly oriented Wilsonian and Leninist positions.

Wilson's position was embodied in his Fourteen-Point program. Its two most important points were the democratic self-determination of all peoples, especially the newly emancipated peoples of eastern Europe, and a League of Nations empowered to mediate international disputes by public negotiation and legal process. In gaining these and other points in his program, Wilson was relatively successful in Paris. These were not new or unacceptable ideas in Europe, and it was thought that the support of the world's now most powerful nation might at last succeed in translating them into reality. With all the problems and bickering involved in implementing the first point, new political boundaries, which roughly corresponded to national lines, were drawn in Europe and provided an outlet for the long pent-up national aspirations of the peoples formerly subject to the Austro-Hungarian and Russian Empires. Poland, Rumania, Yugoslavia, and Czechoslovakia emerged as new states, as did Finland, Estonia, Latvia, and Lithuania.

The League of Nations might have met with success had not the United States Senate itself, reflecting the Americans' deep-rooted distrust of foreign involvements, refused in 1920 to ratify the Treaty of Versailles, mainly because it contained the clause providing for United States membership in the League. This rejection of Wilson's fondest hope dealt a harsh blow to him personally and to his high-minded political aim "to make the world safe for democracy." It also seriously undermined the efficacy of the League once it came into being in 1920.

Wilson had less success in curbing the understandably vengeful will of the British and French leaders, Lloyd George and Georges Clemenceau, who were determined to impose on Germany a punitive peace rather than the moderate one that Wilson alone advocated. Most of the war had been fought on French soil; France had lost almost one and a half million men, Britain almost a million, Italy about a half million, and the United States only a little more than one hundred thousand. For most Americans, the war had always been, as the popular song put it, "over there." The Germans, who themselves lost nearly two million men, had pinned their hopes on Wilson in suing for an armistice. What came out of the Versailles palace, however, was a far cry from the "peace without victory" that Wilson had originally called for. The representative of the newly formed German government, Matthias Erzberger, was simply handed a treaty he played no part in drawing up and which most Germans, right from the start, strongly protested.

The much debated and critical Treaty of Versailles left Germany intact (Wilson's work) but greatly diminished. Germany lost territory in the West to Belgium and France, including the long disputed province of Alsace-Lorraine and the industrially rich Saar Basin, which was placed under French administration until a later plebiscite returned it to Germany. Germany lost territory in the East to Poland, including the so-called Polish Corridor, which completely separated East Prussia from the rest of Germany. Germany also lost all its colonies abroad, which were eagerly gobbled up by Britain, France, and Japan. Also, the German-speaking seaport of Danzig was placed under the supervision of the League.

Germany was forbidden to build any offensive weapons, and its army

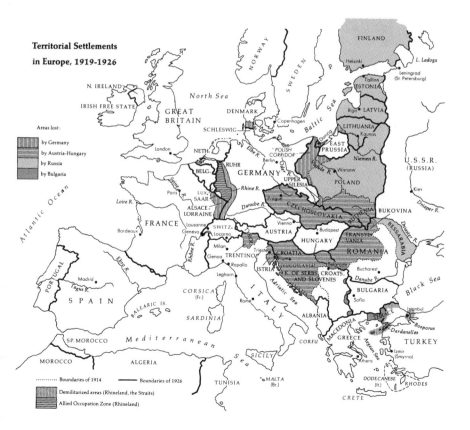

Territorial Settlements in Europe, 1919-1926

Areas lost:
- by Germany
- by Austria-Hungary
- by Russia
- by Bulgaria

········· Boundaries of 1914   ——— Boundaries of 1926

Demilitarized areas (Rhineland, the Straits)

Allied Occupation Zone (Rhineland)

was limited to one hundred thousand soldiers. Germany was also required to pay within two years the impossible sum of 5 billion dollars in war costs, a bill that France reset in 1921 at 33 billion dollars total, and to bear all the costs of occupation. Finally, there was the notorious "war guilt" clause of the treaty to remind the Germans ever after that they, and they alone, bore full responsibility for the war.

As harsh as the Treaty of Versailles was, it was not as severe as the Treaty of Brest-Litovsk, a fact conveniently forgotten in Germany. Its principal defect was that it was neither sufficiently severe to crush Germany forever nor moderate enough to reconcile Germans to its terms. In addition, it was inadequately enforced, as both Britain and the United States gradually withdrew their support, leaving France to face Germany alone once again. The terms of the treaty, especially the financial terms and the "war guilt" clause, were immediately denounced as dangerously unfeasible by the brilliant British economist, John Maynard Keynes, in his book, *The Economic Consequences of the Peace* (1919). Also in 1919, the distinguished British geographer, Halford J. Mackinder, in his *Democratic Ideals and Reality,* presented his new theory that land power is superior to sea power and that a great land force like Germany or Russia, should it gain control of the pivotal Eurasian heartland, could reach out from there by land for world empire undeterred by any sea power, no matter how mighty. Neither scholar was heeded at the time. And the Wilsonian position, or what was left of it by 1920, would have to stand or fall with the Versailles treaty with all of its defects.

The chief defect of Wilson's position was that it underestimated the economic and social difficulties of establishing a liberal-democratic order in Europe and overestimated Europe's willingness to be remodeled in the image and under the influence of the United States. Bolshevism's most serious failing was that it underestimated the appeal of nationalism and overestimated the readiness of the world, especially the West, to undergo revolution and accept communism, particularly if fomented by a Soviet Russia still considered backward and unstable. For a brief spell, in 1919, Hungary came under the Communist control of Béla Kun, and a Soviet republic was proclaimed in Bavaria. But these inroads were short-lived, serving mainly to alert the diplomatists in Paris to the threat of communism.

Wilson and the other peacemakers in turn almost completely ignored the question of the economic and social inequality within postwar Europe, especially the newly formed states in eastern Europe. Nevertheless, both positions, Wilson's and Lenin's, derived largely from old Europe and in competition for supremacy in the West in the wake of old Europe's dissolution, set the stage for the emergence of the United States and Soviet Russia as the two leading world powers and as the great rivals for global supremacy after World War Two. "World imperialism cannot live side by side with a victorious Soviet revolution—the one or the other will be victor in the end," Lenin proclaimed in 1919. The same year, Lloyd George warned the other allied statesmen: "Bolshevik imperialism does not merely menace the states on Russia's borders, it threatens the whole of Asia and is as near to America as it is to France."

The Twenties: Uncertain Peace

The early postwar years were marked by war-weariness, instability, and rapid economic disintegration. Only the United States, now the world's leading power and creditor nation, enjoyed an improved position, Europe floundered in the political and economic quandries resulting from the war and the peace treaties; meanwhile, Soviet Russia, wracked by civil war and resisted in its attempts to extend communism abroad, was forced to concentrate on internal stabilization and development.

Germany, now a republic, was the key to European recovery. But the government of the new Weimar Republic met with little enthusiasm either at home or abroad. Moreover, Germany suffered to a greater extent the hardships endured by all Europe at the time: rampant inflation and unemployment, declining production, massive bankruptcy of the formerly stabilizing middle classes, and bitterness over the war and the terms of the Versailles treaty. All of this served to increase political and social strife and to prepare the way for the rise of the extreme Right.

One of the early signs of things to come was the circulation of the "stab-in-the-back" explanation of Germany's defeat, an explanation in which the military falsely blamed defeat on the betrayal of the new civilian government that had signed the peace. Another was the formation of the Free Corps. These were groups of returning soldiers organized into irregular forces opposed to communism and responsible for the assassinations of such high-ranking government officials as Erzberger and Rathenau and for the 1920 Kapp *Putsch*, which temporarily drove the new government from Berlin. A third danger sign was the abortive attempt to overthrow the Bavarian government in 1923, the so-called Beer-Hall *Putsch*, organized by the illustrious Ludendorff and a then unknown excorporal named Adolf Hitler. The Treaty of Rapollo (1922), which restored diplomatic and economic relations between Germany and Russia, aroused the hostility of the western powers toward Germany even more than before. The most serious crisis came in 1923 when the French, now acting alone in enforcing the terms of the Versailles Treaty, marched into the Ruhr to collect war reparations. This move, which was met with passive resistance by German workers, brought the German economy to its worst state since the war and precipitated a government crisis that ended with the capable Gustav Stresemann becoming the new chancellor.

In Italy, as early as 1922, the first successful fascist regime was established under the leadership of the exsocialist, Benito Mussolini, who remained in power until his fall in 1943. However, despite all his bluster about representing a "new order," he proved to be largely an autocratic defender of the old entrenched conservative interests that supported him and an advocate of Italian expansion in the Mediterranean. The newly formed East European states, except Czechoslovakia and Finland, were mostly preindustrial, economically unviable, and only superficially democratic. They soon faltered and reverted to old autocratic forms of government.

Britain, although a victor, faced all the problems plaguing the rest of Europe plus new ones of its own. Economic life went from bad to worse until, in 1921, Britain found itself engulfed in serious depression. Although the situation began to improve the following year, the number of unemployed in Britain would never fall below a million until the outbreak of World War Two. The "dole," limited aid received under the Unemployment Insurance Act, was to become a permanent feature of British economic life. The Irish question, which had disturbed British politics for more than a century, also flared up again. The Easter Rebellion of 1916, aimed at achieving Irish home rule, was ruthlessly suppressed, and in 1921 a treaty was signed which divided Ireland into a northern Ulster state, which remained within the United Kingdom, and a southern Irish Free State with dominion status. This treaty, far from resolving the question, led to a renewed struggle for complete independence of the Irish Free State, which was finally achieved in 1937, and to future conflict between the two parts of Ireland. Britain also found itself embroiled in intervention in Russia and in colonial struggles in the Middle East.

France in turn, which had suffered most during the war, was spared the worst of the war's aftereffects. The prestige of France and the French army was high; in recognition, the peace conference was held in Paris. Alsace-Lorraine had been regained and represented a valuable addition to the French economy. Vigorous reconstruction of devastated areas was begun by means of reparations received and expected from Germany. And Clemenceau passed important legislation favorable to the now large and discontented working classes. Nevertheless, the French government, led by Poincaré, failed to achieve its goal of weakening Germany to the point where France could feel secure. The reparations received were less than expected slowing down the original pace of reconstruction and creating economic hardships. And the staggering loss of life, combined with a very low birthrate, made France inferior to

Germany in terms of potential military manpower. From the standpoint of achieving its primary objective—improving its political position from what it had been before the war—France was unsuccessful. By 1923, the French were forced to the painful realization that they could not go it alone in international affairs and would be unable to face a revived Germany alone in the event of a future war.

Two developments, the Dawes Plan of 1924 and the Locarno treaties of 1925, checked the process of postwar disintegration for a time and gave the Western world the only six years of relative normalcy it would know throughout the entire twenty-year interwar period. The Dawes plan fixed German reparations at a manageable amount; this action, combined with the stabilization of the currency and increase in exports, finally set Germany on the road to economic recovery. The Locarno treaties confirmed national boundaries as set forth in the Versailles treaty, admitted Germany to the League of Nations, and provided for a system of security for all signatories to be enforced by the League.

In 1925, Britain restored the gold standard, and the following year France stabilized its currency. The Kellogg-Briand Pact of 1928, which renounced war as a means to resolve international disputes, and the Young Plan of 1929, which again reduced German reparations and ended Allied occupation of the Rhineland, bolstered morale further. This spirit of international cooperation and internal stabilization was fostered by the leaders of all the major Western powers, and even the Soviet Union renounced war and came to agreements with the new states on her border.

But all of this, while encouraging, was inadequate to provide for a lasting peace or to survive a severe shock. The League lacked the means necessary to enforce its decisions and was further restricted by the fact that neither the United States nor the Soviet Union were members. Nor were the many pleas and proposals for international disarmament throughout the twenties backed up by provisions for effective enforcement. Moreover, the postwar recovery was limited largely to western Europe. The eastern European successor states continued to stagnate, as did most of southern Europe, with one after another of these states succumbing to some form of authoritarian rule. Even in western Europe, segments of the middle classes were so badly demoralized and impoverished by the war that they were neither willing nor able to guarantee the survival of traditional liberal, bourgeois values and institutions.

The European recovery was also heavily dependent on United States economic aid and diplomatic initiative—Dawes, Kellogg, and Young were all Americans, heirs to the waning Wilsonian vision of a world safe for democracy. European leaders—Baldwin of England, Poincaré of

France, and Stresemann of Germany—were aging conservatives, more interested in restoring the nineteenth century as far as possible than in coming to grips with the twentieth. And the democratic Weimar constitution of Germany, the lynchpin of European recovery, never gained the authority or support necessary to enable it to withstand assaults from the extreme Right and Left once Germany's new and shaky prosperity began to founder. The already precarious recovery of the Western world came to an abrupt and catastrophic halt with the Wall Street Crash of October 1929.

POSTWAR SOCIAL CHANGE

The First World War greatly accelerated the pace of technological and social change. Many products destined to become basic to twentieth-century life—the automobile, the airplane, and synthetic goods—were scarcely beyond the experimental stage in 1914. But the war placed them in such high demand that, by 1918, the industries producing them had come into their own and represented the wave of the future. Other industries, serving and served by them, quickly followed in their wake: the petroleum fuel industries, the improvement and extension of electrical power plants, and the communications industries: telephone, radio, and motion picture. More important than any one of these developments, however, and what made them all possible was the new method of mass production based on assembly-line construction, standardization of parts and equipment, and intensive specialization of labor. The implementation of mass production was especially rapid in the United States and in Stalin's Russia, countries large in area and population and rich in natural resources. Mass production hastened the flow of population from the countryside to the new industrial centers, which offered seemingly unlimited opportunities for a better material life. It swelled the ranks of skilled and unskilled labor, hastened the decline of the traditional, less specialized artisan and independent producer, and gave rise to a new managerial and bureaucratic class to oversee a system of production vastly larger and more complex than any previous system.

No industry owed more to mass production or exploited it more fully than the automobile industry, which set the pace and pattern of production for all other industries during the interwar period and did more than any other during that time to transform the very foundations of society. Henry Ford, who perfected the process of mass production in the United States, marketed the first Model T Ford in 1908. By the mid-twenties, the Ford Motor Company had sold more than 15 million

Model Ts. By the thirties, 26 million automobiles were registered in the United States and about 5 million in Europe.

During these years, Detroit emerged as the center and model of America's industrial heartland and provided all other industries with the example of a hierarchic system of huge, interlocking manufacturing plants related to each other like the different parts of an assembly line. By 1930, the automobile industry had become a leading index of national prosperity. The improvement of the automobile over the years, steady if not spectacular, stimulated developments in the metallurgical, fuel, and electrical fields, which subsequently benefited the aircraft and other industries. These developments were another indication of the extent to which the automobile cast its shadow over the whole of production. The automobile itself soon came to symbolize the speed and efficiency, the power and technological potential characteristic of the twentieth century and proved to be the single most potent solvent of older and more restrictive ways of life. It enabled the average person to enjoy, to share in, indeed, to identify himself with a world far more collectivized and impersonal, restless and uncertain than the prewar world.

Body Presses and Assembly of Chassis. Mural painting by Diego Rivera, c. 1932.

(From the collection of the Detroit Institute of Arts. Gift of Edsel B. Ford).

The automobile increased his mobility enormously and transformed totally the physical and social environment in which he lived. No technological development since the railroad so completely captured the public imagination and changed the complexion of everyday life.

The war also set in motion other social changes. One of the most significant was the movement of population on a massive scale. Almost two million Russians migrated from their homeland in the wake of the Bolshevik Revolution, most of them settling in Paris and other Western capitals, where the creative among them contributed much to Western cultural life during the interwar period. The reordering of the political map of Central and Eastern Europe forced the defeated powers to absorb large numbers of refugees, thereby adding to their hardships and discontents. Almost three-quarters of a million refugees fled to Germany from lands awarded to Poland, and another one hundred thousand entered Germany from Alsace-Lorraine. Hungary, which was much smaller and less able to absorb new population, received about four hundred thousand refugees. Greece and Turkey, long-time enemies, exchanged large populations, a procedure adopted on a smaller scale elsewhere but not always so successfully. France, the only country eager for immigration because of its declining birthrate and enormous loss of manpower during the war, received more than one and one-half million foreign workers during the twenties.

The flow of emigrants overseas, mostly to the United States but also to Latin America and the British dominions, grew at such a rate as to alarm the United States government into passing quota laws in 1921 and 1924. These laws worked against the countries of southern and eastern Europe, which produced the largest number of emigrants and were most in need of population escape valves for, despite the staggering loss of life during the war, Europe's population actually increased between 1913 and 1918 from 498 million to 534 million. But this increase occurred primarily in just those economically backward areas least able to accommodate a rising population. The United States quota laws had the long-range effect of bottling up this new population and thereby depressing the living standards of these countries even further.

All of this served to widen the gap between the "have" and the "have-not" nations and to add to the discontents leading to future war. Hundreds of thousands of average people all over Europe found themselves unable to live at home and unwanted abroad. The "stateless person"—the homeless, jobless refugee without a passport and without the protection of any government—became a common figure throughout the interwar years, one who personified in an extreme form the war's tragic effects on masses of humanity everywhere.

The war also generated widespread disillusionment, especially among the young, with the manners and morals of the prewar world. This disillusionment manifested itself in revolt against tradition and convention on all fronts: revolt against the family, religion, traditional attitudes toward sex and personal behavior, the subordinate role of women, revolt against the established order in general. Soldiers returned home bitter and restless. Others left home destitute, in search of a better life elsewhere, or were attracted by the excitement and glamor of postwar Paris, Berlin, and other cosmopolitan centers. Young Americans, in revolt against restrictive small-town life and against the babbittry of America's newly rich, became voluntary expatriates to Europe or congregated in Greenwich Village. Defiance and revolt manifested itself everywhere in bohemian dress and behavior, relaxed sexual standards, a taste for urban life and cosmopolitan culture, a preference for the jaunty over the genteel, women's demands for greater equality and independence, and in the enthusiastic acceptance of a uniquely and wholly twentieth-century style of life epitomized by the automobile, the motion picture, and jazz.

Culture of the Twenties

The turmoil of transition from the old order to the new reverberated in the culture of the twenties: a culture richer and bolder, more diverse and experimental than that of any other decade of the twentieth century. The creators of this culture, sickened and saddened by war, felt themselves to be a "lost generation," suspended between a moribund past and an uncharted future and bereft of faith in the traditional Western values of reason, progress, and humanism. This sense of loss, which fostered disillusionment and despair, permeated the work of almost every major writer, artist, and intellectual of the time. "I will show you fear in a handful of dust," T. S. Eliot somberly wrote of twentieth-century man in his famous poem, *The Waste Land* (1922).

New literary movements, notably Dadaism, Surrealism, and Expressionism, invented new ways of thumbing their noses at a civilization they considered senseless, hostile, and humanly bankrupt. Doom and gloom echoed also from much of the significant historical literature of the era: Oswald Spengler's *Decline of the West* (1918), Ortega y Gasset's *The Revolt of the Masses* (1930), and the early volumes of Arnold J. Toynbee's massive and prophetic *A Study of History*, which began to appear in 1934. Cubists and Futurists in the arts dismantled and reorganized visual reality almost beyond recognition. Igor Stravinsky and Darius Milhaud jumbled jazz and classical elements to produce a nervous, surging, often discordant music that defied conventional standards and offended respectable middle-class audiences; the atonal music of Paul Hindemith and the new twelve-note system of Arnold Schönberg and Alban Berg were altogether unfamiliar and incomprehensible to most music lovers.

Theologians of all faiths unanimously rejected an intellectual, moral interpretation of religion in favor of an intensely inward, mystical, near-apocalyptic approach inspired above all by the hitherto obscure nineteenth-century Danish forerunner of religious existentialism, Søren Kierkegaard. The primary preoccupations of this "lost generation" were the loss of selfhood, purpose, faith, the past, and a common sense of humanity. But if the Western world of the twenties aroused despair, iconoclasm, and protest, it also generated a bold and brilliant effort to chart this new and unexplored territory.

THE ARTS   The mood of the intelligentsia during the twenties found supreme literary expression in the novels of James Joyce and D. H. Lawrence, André Gide and Marcel Proust, Thomas Mann and Franz Kafka, Ernest Hemingway and F. Scott Fitzgerald, to mention but a few of the most significant writers. Each in his own way viewed the new order as devoid of human purpose or meaning and sought refuge or revitalization in intense introspection, in some sort of personal spiritual commitment, in nostaliga for the past, or in aestheticism. James Joyce, inspired by the psychological theories of Carl Jung, explored the multiple levels and complex symbolism of everyday life in his great epic, *Ulysses* (1922). This novel, which deals with a single day in the life of lower-class people of Joyce's native Dublin, gradually reveals itself as a symbolic reworking of the original *Odyssey,* with Leopold Bloom emerging as a modern Ulysses, Stephen Dedalus as his lost son Telemachus, and his wife, Molly Bloom, as Penelope. This reenactment translated into literature Jung's conception of a collective unconscious that preserves intact certain unchanging primal symbols and archetypes. It was intended to disclose what Joyce believed were universals of the human condition, giving significance to characters otherwise totally insignificant. As these human characteristics are psychic in nature and origin, Joyce chose as the means most effective to reveal them the then still new and experimental stream-of-consciousness technique, which he, along with Virginia Woolf and William Faulkner, succeeded in bringing to the forefront of modern literature. Dream and reality, fact and fantasy, the subjective and objective were so intertwined in their writings as to be almost indistinguishable. Paradoxically, however, this new style, which aimed to reveal the solidarity of all human life past and present by probing the hiddenmost recesses of the microcosmic psyche, served to accentuate the individual's utter insularity and the immensity of the abyss separating him from his physical and social surroundings.

D. H. Lawrence, who leaned more toward Freudian psychology, passionately denounced the denaturalization of man by modern society in one novel after another, beginning with *Sons and Lovers* (1913) and continuing in *The Rainbow* (1915), *Women in Love* (1920), *Lady Chatterley's Lover* (1928), and many other novels, short stories, poems, and essays. Lawrence, followed by Henry Miller and others, was uncompromising in his defense of nature and instinct over society and intellect. At his best, Lawrence was capable of evoking the life-giving beauty and majesty of nature and the power of instinct and emotion, especially the sexual drive, to ennoble and humanize life in a world deadened and impoverished by rapacious materialism, excessive intellection, and stifling institutions. At worst, he preached a frenzied irrationalism, hatred of mankind and its achievements, and a brand of "blood-thinking" congenial to fascism, which culminated in the nightmare, hate-filled world of Louis-Ferdinand Céline's *Journey to the End of the Night* (1932).

The subtle art of André Gide revolved around the tension between arbitrary social convention and individual conscience; the eccentric and solitary Marcel Proust devoted himself to rediscovering the past and its meaning by intense introspection and analysis of apparently insignificant personal memories in *Remembrance of Things Past,* a series of novels that appeared between 1913 and 1927. Thomas Mann, working within the German tradition of the philosophical novel, expanded his favorite theme of the opposition of spirit (the inner, creative spirit of high culture) and civilization (banal external reality) into a sweeping, intellectually brilliant explanation of the decline and exhaustion of the whole of modern Western culture in *The Magic Mountain* (1924). Franz Kafka, in one chilling tale after another written during his short and tormented life, depicted modern man as the plaything of a crazy politico-cosmic conspiracy that he can neither comprehend nor counteract. American writers in particular experienced and mourned the loss of innocence they thought America had known before the war. Gertrude Stein, Ernest Hemingway, F. Scott Fitzgerald, and many others sought in Europe refuge from the new America of easy virtue and heartless materialism, anti-intellectualism and provincial self-righteousness: an America savagely satirized at home by Sinclair Lewis and H. L. Mencken.

Poetry, too, reflected the decade's sense of loss and anxiety. Dada, a nonsense word adopted by a group of postwar writers convinced of the nonsense and vanity of everything—art and politics, morality and religion, even civilization itself—describes the nonsensical language they devised to expose and deride reality as they saw it. Tristan Tzara, one of the founders of Dadaism, wrote poetry by putting together words and newspaper clippings at random to produce the disjointed, montage-like effect that came to typify Dadaism. The Surrealists, led by André Breton, experimented with automatic writing, subconscious association, and dream-like imagery as the only way to discover and express the hidden meanings withheld by the superficial world of appearance.

Expressionism, which was centered in Germany and the most extreme of the new experimental movements, was formed by artists in all fields who viewed the world as a horrible sham and who sought to obliterate and smother it beneath a furious barrage of intensely emotional artistic outpourings. The Expressionist poets Georg Trakl and Ernst Stadler, the dramatists Georg Kaiser and Walter Hasenclever, and the painters Franz Marc and Oskar Kokoschka conceived art as a wholly subjective creation that must conquer and supplant the external world. However, the greatest poets of the time, T. S. Eliot, Paul Valéry, and Rainer Maria Rilke, did not adhere to any particular movement, but drew upon all sources that would help them discover and express new meaning in their "age of anxiety." Valery's *La Jeune Parque* (1917), Eliot's *The Waste Land* (1922), and Rilke's *Duinian Elegies* (1923) represent poetic landmarks in that search.

What was new and distinctive in all the important writers of the twenties, poets and novelists alike, was their search for new meaning, not in events themselves, but in the interior workings—conscious, subconscious, and emotional—of the isolated individual and the ways he relates to events. No novel of the twenties equalled the great social novel in the tradition of Thackeray, Balzac, or Tolstoy. No poetic work equalled the romantic flights of imagination in the tradition of Wordsworth, Hölderlin, or Pushkin. But in the exploration and discovery of the depths, complexity, and symbolic significance of the inner self, the literature of the twenties far surpassed anything written before.

The experimental groping for meaning and forms of expression appropriate to the new era extended to the other arts also. Painters were no longer content to portray the visual world merely as we passively perceive it; instead, they painted it, as we actively experience and structure it. A whole host of brilliant painters, centered mainly in Paris and Munich, developed a variety of non-representational forms designed to get at the underlying essences of things and their mental and emotional significance for the viewer. Pablo Picasso, Georges Bracque, and Piet Mondrian, founders of Cubism before the war, moved even closer to total abstraction afterwards. Edvard Munch and Ernst Barlach, Paul Klee and Wassily Kandinsky applied the intensely emotional spirit of Expressionism to painting.

In architecture, Frank Lloyd Wright, Walter Gropius, and Le Corbusier joined art and technology to create a style better suited to advanced industrial societies than the traditionalistic styles of the past. The result was a severely functional architecture, called Bauhaus in Europe, which rapidly gained acceptance throughout the Western world. The performance of Stravinsky's *Rite of Spring* in Paris in 1913 marked the beginning of bold innovation in the performing arts. Fresh themes and music, new techniques in staging, set design, and orchestration, brilliant new performers and dramatists, notably Diaghilev, Cocteau, and Pirandello, aroused controversy and had the effect of breaking down the traditional separation between performance and audience. Drama and dance, along with literature and the visual arts, had entered the twentieth century.

PHILOSOPHY   Intellectual life also underwent significant change after the war. Philosophy began to divide into two distinct and opposed camps: logical positivism and language analysis on the one hand, and phenomenology and existentialism on the other. Logical positivism, centered in England and the United States, rejected metaphysics, theology, and ethics in favor of the more rigorously verifiable truths of mathematics, logic, and the natural sciences. The other camp, which held sway on the continent, continued to concern itself, but in new ways, with metaphysics, ethical values, and human experience.

Two Cambridge philosophers, Bertrand Russell and Alfred North Whitehead, proclaimed the positivist position in their *Principia Mathematica* (1910–1914). They held that only the language of mathematics and symbolic logic enables philosophy to speak with clarity and precision, and that all statements not factual or verifiable by fact are senseless. A group of mathematically and scientifically inclined philosophers in Vienna, the so-called Vienna Circle, including Rudolf Carnap, Moritz Schlick, Otto Neurath, and others, found inspiration in Russell's ideas and propagated them first at home and then abroad as they fled oncoming fascism. Ludwig Wittgenstein, the most significant of the Vienna philosophers and one of the twentieth century's most original thinkers, contributed the theory, in his *Tractatus Logico-Philosophicus* (1921), that all thought is linguistic and that philosophy is nothing more nor less than a logical clarification of language and its use. Philosophy itself adds nothing new to knowledge; it is essentially a critique of language and the conditions under which language acquires and expresses meaning. Wittgenstein's pioneering work has since become the cornerstone of philosophy in the English-speaking world.

Philosophical idealism was kept alive during the interwar period by R. G. Collingwood in England, George Santayana in the United States, and Ernst Cassirer, who fled Germany when Hitler came to power. At the opposite pole, John Dewey's pragmatism continued to prevail in the United States. But, along with logical positivism, the most original and significant developments in philosophy during the twenties were the phenomenology of Edmund Husserl and the existentialism of Martin Heidegger.

The aim of phenomenology was to study reality as experienced, as it presents itself to consciousness, not as something which exists and can be known independently of our experience of it, as positivism held. Husserl's contribution was a technique for the detailed examination of the contents of consciousness and the way in which it structures reality. Following Husserl, who confined his analysis to the mind's cognitive functions, Heidegger extended the phenomenological approach to the whole of human experience in his *Being and Time* (1927), which became the cornerstone of modern existentialism. In it he concentrated on extreme emotional states, especially apparently groundless anxieties, which he considered most revelatory of man's true condition in the world. Heidegger's conclusion was that man finds himself in a world not of his making and devoid of any meaning other than what he confers on it by his own purely voluntary actions. Anxiety arises from fear of the death or nonbeing that will eventually overtake us all. Man can live a meaningful (authentic) life only by facing up to his inevitable annihilation and taking full responsibility for his own actions. He lapses into inauthenticity when he seeks to deny or disregard his destiny or to evade responsibility for his actions by shifting it elsewhere or by living in accordance with standards not his own. The two philosophical camps discussed here found new advocates in time and the split between them persisted and will be referred to again in the context of philosophy after World War Two.

SCIENCE AND RELIGION also developed in new directions after the war. The old Newtonian conception of nature, already in dissolution before 1914, gave way to a new model derived from Albert Einstein's theory of relativity, Max Planck's quantum theory, and Ernest Rutherford's research into the subatomic world. Together these major scientific breakthroughs, aided by new and improved technology, served to discredit the traditional commonsense materialist account of physical science as a realistic description of nature. As scientists began to probe nature's workings more deeply, far beyond the limits of ordinary sense experience, it became increasingly evident that the old explanation in terms of absolute space and time, substantial matter and causal determinacy, must be superseded by a model based on relativity and discontinuity, indeterminacy and uncertainty. The new science, far more abstract and sophisticated than the old, now claimed that matter is but a form of energy, that causality does not prevail at the ultimate level of physical reality, and that scientific explanations are not so much realistic descriptions of nature as conceptual constructs devised by scientists to describe and order their observations.

This new model, only implicit before 1914, came into its own during the twenties. Planck's theory that energy, especially at the subatomic level, does not manifest itself in a continuous, determinate flow or wave, but rather in discontinuous spurts or "quanta" led to the discovery by Werner Heisenberg and other physicists, between 1925 and 1927, that the behavior of energy particles is unpredictable. This finding, which Heisenberg called the principle of uncertainty, ruled out the possibility of discovering the exact position and momentum of energy particles and reduced their behavior to a matter of statistical probability. Heisenberg's work struck a hard blow to Newtonian science in that it replaced the mechanical model of nature by a mathematical model. Most physicists now concluded that the statistical laws of the new quantum theory were the ultimate laws of nature; they neither describe nor derive from any other fundamental laws of a deterministic sort.

Einstein further undermined Newtonian physics by showing that there is no fixed point of reference from which the movements of bodies in space can be calculated; rather, their movements are relative to the position of the observer. His theory of relativity, by refuting the absoluteness of space and time, cleared the way for a drastically new scientific picture of the world that conceived time as a fourth dimension and physical reality in terms of a four-dimensional continuum. Einstein's theory also furthered the view that science is not a realistic representation of an independently existing physical order, but is instead an intellectual construction adopted by virtue of its usefulness in predicting future observations on the basic of present ones. Astronomers, making use of Einstein's research into gravity and light from the standpoint of relativity theory, presented a picture of the universe as a system of galaxies expanding outward and away from each other from a particular point where all had originated. Rutherford, in turn, effected the first transformation of the atom in 1919, thereby refuting Newton's belief in the atom's stability. This achievement was followed by the atomic research which culminated in the production of the atomic bomb during World War Two.

Advances in the biological sciences, though not so dramatic, paralleled those taking place in physics. Indeed, the results of quantum physics suggested that a unified theory applicable to all material systems, organic and inorganic alike, might be possible by integrating the concepts of chemistry with those of physics. This approach led ultimately to the recent science of molecular biology, pioneered by Erwin Schrödinger and J. D. Watson shortly after the Second World War. The chief development toward that goal during the twenties was the perfection of the new science of genetics, pioneered by a nineteenth-century Bohemian monk, Gregor Mendel. Mendel's contribution to biology was his identification of genes as the source of hereditary characteristics and his account of genetic combinations and mutations. Mendel's findings were confirmed and improved upon by twentieth-century geneticists, who applied the statistical model used in physics to their experiments with the rapidly reproductive fruit fly. In genetics, as in physics, change seemed to occur in jumps rather than through a gradual, uninterrupted process of modification, and mathematics explained change in both fields better than any other method.

Progress in the understanding of the cell's composition and workings enabled scientists to learn more about the function of glands and hormones, vitamins, and antitoxins, information applicable to medical science. Penicillin was discovered in 1928, and cures for diphteria, yellow fever, and tetanus were also found during the interwar period.

Although the new science abandoned the old view of physical reality as a material mechanism explicable in terms of simple causality, most scientists continued to hold that science alone is capable of explaining nature without reference to any supernatural force or mystery. Indeed, the stunning successes and rapid progress of modern science served to reinforce that confidence. Nevertheless, some scientists and theologians were encouraged to believe that the new science, with its abandonment of determinism and acceptance of uncertainty, was more compatible with free will, moral autonomy, and religious faith than Newtonian science.

A far greater impact on religious thought during the twenties was the war itself. To theologians of all Western faiths, the spectacle of supposedly advanced societies tearing each other to pieces signified the collapse of liberal faith in secular progress and the bankruptcy of humanism and rationality. Their response was to seek to reverse the anthropocentric, rationalistic trend of religious thought dominant since the Enlightenment, which they now felt had compromised and finally betrayed true religion. Instead, theologians advocated a religion based on pure faith, man's sinful nature, his need of divine guidance, and the majesty but remoteness and unintelligibility of God. It was a religion not of this world; like so many reform movements of the past, it sought to return to the original faith. The leaders of this movement—the Catholic Jacques Maritain, the Protestants Karl Barth, Emil Brunner, and Rudolf Bultmann, and the Jewish religious philosopher, Martin Buber—were not, however, fundamentalists who believed literally in and upheld the Bible as the direct word of God. On the contrary, they were highly sophisticated thinkers who drew freely upon philosophy (especially existentialism), modern psychology (especially Jungian concepts), and social theory (especially pessimistic views), and who generally regarded the Bible as but a mythical, symbolical account of the metaphysical dimension of man's existence in the world. Paradoxically, the new theologians made liberal use of the secular tradition in order to refute it. In doing so, however, they infused their tragic view of life on earth and their defence of modern man's urgent need of God with an energy, emotional sincerity, and intellectual substance that gained support for their outlook far beyond strictly theological circles. The general retreat from liberal humanism was nowhere more extreme or evident in the years between the wars than in religious thought.

PSYCHOLOGY   More than any other intellectual development of the decade, psychology, and psychoanalysis in particular, vaulted into the center of attention. Scarcely any branch of cultural and intellectual life escaped its impact. Unlike any other interpretation of the human condition, psychoanalysis seemed uniquely of and for the twentieth century. It had few roots in the past and little concern for political and social affairs, concentrating instead on the interior life of the individual. Born of the same disillusionment with the world that characterized the era as a whole, psychoanalysis purported to explain human nature purely from within, as if the individual were a self-contained, static entity essentially uninfluenced by the changing world around him. Not only did psychoanalysis offer a new interpretation of existence; it also offered the hope that individuals could learn to understand themselves and regain a sense of personal identity and purpose, regardless of what happened in the world. This prospect naturally appealed to a highly collectivized, impersonal society in which the individual felt unable to control events, much less find meaning or consolation in them. Moreover, psychoanalysis combined just enough of the scientific, the exotic, and the iconoclastic, especially with regard to personal and sexual behavior, to give it wide public appeal. At the same time, it involved few of the risks, sacrifices, or commitments usually called for by serious political and social dissent.

The teachings of Sigmund Freud, the founder and leader of the psychoanalytic movement, assumed their final form after 1914, just when the movement's original unity was being undermined by an upsurge of conflicting views and claims to leadership which challenged Freud's own. Freud's early research into the origins of neurosis, the meaning of dreams, the subconscious sources of art and humor, the psychopathology of everyday life (slips of the tongue and the like) led him to the conclusion, which he took great pains to substantiate scientifically, that man is an essentially irrational creature, motivated by forces almost completely unknown to him and over which he has little control. The accounts people give of their conduct are largely rationalizations of its real, subconscious source: the libido or sexual instinct. Man becomes civilized either by repressing or channeling (sublimating) this instinct in the socially acceptable ways taught to him in early childhood within the family, the first and primary social group he encounters and totally depends upon. The pattern of behavior established at the beginning determines the individual's behavior thereafter. Thus, human personality is fixed long before a person reaches rational maturity and is so rigidly fixed that it can be restructured, if at all, only by long and intensive therapy. These claims of the subconscious determination of behavior and the formation of character during early childhood were the very heart of Freudian psychology and struck hard at the traditional Western conception of man as essentially rational, self-determining, and morally responsible.

After 1914, Freud added aggression to the sexual instinct as a primal motive force and began to extend this theory beyond the individual to society and culture in general. In *The Future of an Illusion* (1930) and other writings on religion, he argued that religion is a wish-fulfillment fantasy originating in guilt. *Civilization and its Discontents* (1930) argues that civilization as a whole is repressive in that it restrains instinct, but that this price must be paid if mankind is to avoid lapsing into a state of unleashed aggression. Freud himself unquestionably preferred civilization with all its oppressiveness, guilt-producing mechanisms, and restrictions on personal happiness to an uncivilized state where life is, as Hobbes expressed it almost three centuries earlier, "short, nasty, and brutish."

Freud also perfected his tripartite theory of human personality, according to which man is composed of an id, or unconscious reservoir of instinctual energy, an ego, which adjusts behavior to external reality; and a superego, the Freudian equivalent of moral conscience. Freud believed that although harmony between the three would be ideal, his own theory seemed to rule out the possibility of ever realizing it, either at the individual or collective level. It is true that Freud supported a few superficial social reforms, such as the liberalization of sexual mores and less authoritarian methods of raising children. But Freud himself remained stoic in attitude, viewing life as inherently tragic and offering no alternative. It is no accident that his often daring and original insights into the turmoil within and between men, once they were put into practice by the psychiatric profession, served far more to prepare people to adjust to the existing social order than to resist, renounce, or reshape it.

The first major rift within the psychoanalytic movement occurred when Carl G. Jung, Freud's would-be successor to its leadership, denied the primacy of sexuality in human development and claimed the existence of an all-embracing collective unconscious, which transcends the purely personal one. Each person retains in his subconscious unchanging archetypes of a mythical, symbolical nature shared by all men throughout time. Jung believed that therapy should strengthen these collective bonds by means of a mystical religious faith emphasizing the common spiritual humanity of every man—a view repugnant to the atheistic and scientific Freud. Alfred Adler in turn denied not only the primacy of sexuality but also that of the unconscious altogether, stressing instead the conscious efforts of the individual to compensate for his weaknesses and sense of inferiority and to enhance his power and stature in relation to other people.

In contrast to Jung and Adler, Wilhelm Reich emphasized, even more than Freud himself, the importance of sexual fulfillment to the well-being of both the individual and society collectively. Reich, unlike Freud, regarded society at large, rather than the immediate family, as the prime agent of psychological repression, and its chief means of repression, restriction on sexual freedom. His theory, developed during the thirties under the shadow of fascism, ascribed to sexuality a quasi-political function: sexual freedom and political freedom were but two sides of the same coin—a view revived by some social dissidents in the sixties. In his most extreme speculations, Reich conceived orgastic fulfillment as a sort of mystical experience, the one and only means by which the individual is able to merge momentarily with the vital forces at work in the universe at large. This experience of oneness with the cosmos was similar to that envisaged by Jung, although achieved in quite a different way.

Among nonpsychoanalytic psychologists, Ivan P. Pavlov, the Russian who pioneered the behavioral approach, spurned all psychoanalysis as pseudoscientific nonsense and adhered to a strictly physiological and quantitative method. Taking a position between psychoanalysis and behaviorism were the Gestaltists, represented by Wolfgang Köhler and Kurt Koffka. The Gestaltist approach concentrated on the individual's responses to present situations, rather than on the history of his psychological development or on the physiological foundations of psychological phenomena. Both of these latter approaches were overshadowed by psychoanalysis until after the Second World War.

SOCIAL SCIENCES   The social scientists also reflected the era's mood of despair and groping. The trend in history, sociology, and anthropology during the twenties was to challenge the prewar liberal-democratic faith in inevitable progress, the blessings of materialism, and the superiority of Western civilization. Historians Oswald Spengler and Arnold J. Toynbee warned of the impending collapse of the West and rejected the idea of linear progress in favor of a more cyclic and organic conception of civilizational development. They arrived at these conclusions by comparing civilizations with each other in terms of their inner consistency, their adaptability to change, and the vitality of their basic institutions and ideas, rather than in terms of what they do or do not contribute to material progress. From this standpoint, the Western world of the twenties appeared to be foundering.

The Spanish philosopher-historian, José Ortega y Gasset, denounced democracy and technology from a frankly ultraconservative, elitist standpoint in his *Revolt of the Masses* (1930). The American historian

Charles A. Beard, in his *Economic Interpretation of the Constitution of the United States* (1913), and the British historian Lewis Namier, in his *Structure of Politics at the Accession of George III* (1929)—both highly influential historians—interpreted significant historical persons and events in terms of the vested interests they served, whether consciously or not. Namier, especially, concentrated on the biographical backgrounds of history's decision-makers. He viewed them as little more than embodiments of vested interests and history itself as little more than the clash of these interests. French historians Marc Bloch and Lucien Febvre founded the most important historical publication of the interwar era, the *Annales d'Histoire Économique et Social* (1929), dedicated to the study of the supposedly more basic social and economic forces underlying political affairs. The growing impact of Marxism on Western historical and social theory manifested itself in the writings of Italian communist leader Antonio Gramsci and the German-educated Hungarian Marxist Georg Lukács. From many different standpoints, historians struck hard at traditional liberal pieties.

Karl Mannheim, the most original sociological thinker of the decade, reflected this trend in his *Ideology and Utopia* (1929), which interpreted ideologies as myths invented to sustain a social order and utopias as wishful dreams invented to justify a transformation of the social order. Mannheim's method, which he called the sociology of knowledge, did not deny the importance of ideas and intellectual systems, as the new social historians tended to do, but he did study them primarily from the standpoint of the social interests they served. In contrast to materialist and Marxist teachings, with which he otherwise agreed, Mannheim believed that only a "free-floating" intelligentsia, a class with no vested interests of its own, could hope to attain to truth and objectivity.

Anthropologists applied a similar method to the study of primitive peoples. Bronislaw Malinowski and A. R. Radcliffe-Brown, the founders of functional anthropology, concerned themselves with the role of institutions and rituals in contributing to the overall stability and equilibrium of the primitive societies they studied. Implicit in their approach was an organic conception of the good society, an essentially conservative bias in favor of equilibrium over change, even if change meant progress. Their intensive first-hand studies of tribal life in the South Seas, along with Margaret Mead's more popular *Coming of Age in Samoa* (1929), added much new knowledge and fruitful speculation about the early conditions of human existence. But these anthropologists also had the effect of fostering the old romantic notion that the "noble savage" is superior to civilized man, and a static social order superior to one that is dynamic.

The rich culture of the twenties served as a watershed between the

nineteenth and twentieth centuries. What remained of the past was fil-
tered out, and what resulted from bold experimentation with new concepts and techniques in the arts and sciences, in philosophy and social
theory, came to form the foundation of Western cultural and intellectual
life ever since. The chief stimulus to this creative ferment was the urge to
discover and define the forms of thought and expression most appropriate to the new conditions of life in the twentieth century. If any one
intuition guided this search, it was that human meaning and purpose are
not to be found in the world as given, but somewhere behind, beyond, or
below it—or else not at all.

THE GREAT DEPRESSION AND ITS IMPACT

The "roaring" twenties ground to a halt in the autumn of 1929 with the
Wall Street Crash which plunged the world into the most severe economic crisis in the history of capitalism. By 1932, its low point, unemployment had risen to thirty million, (thirteen million in the United
States alone), and world trade had shrunk by almost two-thirds. Economic slumps under capitalism were nothing new; economists both for
and against capitalism had long since come to expect them periodically.
What distinguished the Great Depression of 1929 from the others was its
duration, severity, and scope. This no one had anticipated, and no government was prepared to cope with it. There never was a real recovery
from this slump until 1939, when most countries had shifted to a wartime economy.

The crisis struck first and hardest in the United States. Because of
America's dominant role in world economic affairs, it spread rapidly
throughout the world, missing only Soviet Russia, which had been
excluded from international economic life since 1917 and was thus
spared. Underproduction, which resulted in unemployment and a de-
crease in trade, combined with overspeculation, which exhausted profitable investment opportunities, set the process in motion. But the economic factor most decisive in perpetuating the slump, once it started,
was the steep fall in the prices of primary products, in particular agricultural products and certain raw materials basic to industry, and the failure of these prices to recover. Had primary prices not fallen so sharply,
or had they recovered more quickly, the slump in industrial production
would not have been so great and the general crisis would not have been
so prolonged.

As it was, there was little to attract investment, and a vicious circle was
created: Declining investment meant declining production; declining
production meant declining employment; declining employment meant

declining consumption; declining consumption meant declining profit; declining profit meant declining investment; and so on. By the thousands banks that had speculated all too freely with their depositors' funds were forced to close their doors, thereby adding to the general panic, encouraging hoarding, and financially wiping out tens of thousands of low- and middle-income families. Internationally, agricultural countries were especially hard-hit and were forced to devalue their currencies and curtail their international payments. That these countries were no longer able to buy industrial goods harmed the industrial countries, who reacted by erecting trade barriers against foreign goods in order to protect their own industries. The situation was aggravated further by the sharp decline in American buying abroad and even more by America's recall of large loans, especially the recall of those made to Germany to help in postwar reconstruction. The overall result was a seemingly irreversible contraction of industrial production everywhere, a breakdown of the international economic system, and an increase in political tension and instability throughout the world.

For the United States, the depression was the most serious internal crisis since the Civil War. It seemed to strike from nowhere and caught the American people, lulled into euphoria by a decade of sensational prosperity, completely off guard. Without doubt, any Democrat could have defeated any Republican candidate for the presidency in 1932. But few could foresee then that the Democrat who did sweep to victory that year, Franklin D. Roosevelt, would write a whole new chapter in American history.

Right from the start, Roosevelt revived the old wartime model of government planning and control. He made use of all available means to wrest power from the financial and corporate moguls of Wall Street, Pittsburgh, and Detroit and to centralize it in Washington in the executive branch of the federal government. This he accomplished through his famous New Deal, a pragmatic, sometimes inconsistent, and overreaching program aimed at giving the White House ultimate control over the national economy. The flurry of legislation Roosevelt rammed through Congress during his first one hundred days in office—relief and public works programs, the Agricultural Adjustment Act, the National Industrial Recovery Act, the Tennessee Valley Authority, and federal support of cultural activities—formed the foundation of the New Deal. Equally important were Roosevelt's qualities of leadership: his seemingly boundless energy, despite physical paralysis; his ability to inspire confidence and appeal to the "little man"; his ability to calm and reassure the public through his regular "fireside chats" on radio; his willingness to cast aside pieties and to experiment, as he did with his whole-hearted application of Keynes' then-heretical economic theory that deficit spending and governmental "priming" of the economic pump are advisable in times of depression. The success and popularity of the New Deal with most Americans also reawakened a long dormant interest and pride in being American and in things American. The T. V. A. project, Rockefeller Center, Boulder Dam and many other dams, the great suspension bridges built during the thirties, most notably the George Washington in New York and the Golden Gate in San Francisco—these were not only magnificent engineering feats; they were also the embodiment of a native American aesthetic and a new national vitality.

Basically, Roosevelt was a conservative liberal who saved American capitalism by reforming it. But America was never to be the same again. Big government, costly government, government by bureaucrats, experts, and "brain trusts," government concentrated at the center and reaching into every area of public life—such government had come to stay. Henceforward, the United States was to be a welfare state. Still, compared to Britain's stagnation, France's decline, and Germany's drift towards barbarism, the New Deal was a striking success. Only Soviet Russia, driven mercilessly by Stalin towards the status of world power and fortress of communism, could claim a comparable success. The Soviet achievement did inspire widespread admiration, even among a relatively small but growing number of Western intellectuals disenchanted with capitalism in any form. But it came at the price of untold Russian suffering and sacrifice, submission to dictatorial rule, and the loss of basic human and civil rights. Still, as Wilson's vision found new life in Roosevelt's New Deal, Lenin's found new life in Stalin's ambitious economic five-year plans and his savage political purges.

Internationally, matters went from bad to worse. Roosevelt himself, like most other heads of government, frankly put national recovery above international cooperation. Between 1930 and 1933 many efforts were made to stem the tide, but all failed. In 1931 Britain, followed by one country after another, went off the gold standard, heralding the collapse of the international monetary exchange system. War debts either could not be paid or were openly repudiated. At the Lausanne Conference in 1932, the European delegates proposed that all war debts be cancelled, but the United States, by far the greatest creditor, refused.

Finally, in 1933 even the United States went off the gold standard, leaving the dollar, the last remaining stable currency, to fluctuate wildly on foreign exchanges. The last effort made to cope with the depression at the international level was the meeting of the World Economic Conference, held in London in 1933, which recommended, unsuccessfully, that the United States stabilize the dollar. Thereafter, governments concentrated on domestic recovery, regardless of international ramifications. As the world economic situation deteriorated, so, too, did the political. The Western liberal democracies, paralyzed, demoralized, and in dread of another world war, looked on passively as Japan invaded Manchuria in 1931, as Hitler came to power in 1933, as Italy invaded Ethiopia in 1935, and as civil war broke out in Spain in 1936.

THE RISE OF FASCISM

The First World War and its effects, the Russian Revolution, the disputed peace treaties, the severe social dislocations and discontents of the twenties, and finally, the Great Depression—these developments set the stage for the rise of fascism. Mussolini created the first fascist regime in Italy in 1922. In a second wave brought on by the Depression, fascism triumphed in Germany and in Central Europe. By 1939, most of Europe had succumbed to some form of fascism; only the Soviet Union, the traditionally liberal-democratic states of northwestern Europe, and Switzerland had not. Why did this happen? What did fascism stand for? Whom did it appeal to?

Ideologically, fascism arose in opposition to the other competing ideological movements of the interwar period: liberalism, communism, and the intermediary social-democratic and socialist parties. Historically, liberalism had flourished in advanced capitalist societies with large, stable middle classes. Communism had come into being in comparatively backward Russia, with no middle classes to speak of and no serious competing ideologies, except various forms of obsolete conservatism. Neither ideology was acceptable to most Europeans after the First World War. Liberalism had been in decline since the late nineteenth century for reasons discussed in the previous chapter: the imperialist rivalry, the emergence of antiliberal Germany and Japan as world powers, the enlargement of governmental controls over society, the appearance of a powerful new conservative business class, the growth of trade-unionism and socialism, and the disillusionment of many intellectuals with liberal values. Moreover, the United States, which had emerged from the war as the bastion of liberalism, began to isolate itself from the world after 1920 and to concentrate on its own affairs.

Europeans found communism, especially in its dictatorial Russian form, even less acceptable than liberalism. Communism emerged as a significant force in Europe after the Russian Revolution, but it could not hope to compete against Europe's still well-entrenched capitalist economies, trade unions, and variety of more moderate and flexible types of socialism. Communism was also opposed to private property, religion, nationalism, parliamentary government, and "bourgeois" culture—things still very dear to most Europeans. Moreover, as it became clear to Lenin and his followers in 1920 that the revolution would not spread quickly to the rest of Europe, the new Soviet state, like the United States, cut itself off from Europe and concentrated on its own internal development. Europeans from all walks of life could not help but be aware that both liberalism and communism, although they had originated in Western Europe, had found homelands elsewhere and were being turned against Europe. The social democratic parties, especially in Germany and Austria, were still popular with the middle classes after the war, but not as popular as before the war. They now faced stiffer competition from socialist, nationalist, and Catholic parties. And, like liberalism and communism, social democracy failed to appeal to just those social elements which would eventually rally to fascism: the lower-middle classes in the large cities and the small town and rural populations.

This ideological rivalry, and the inability of the competing ideologies to appeal to large segments of European society, was favorable to the growth of fascism. Its importance is evident from the fact that fascism, although typically a confused and incoherent ideology, made itself very clear on two points: its fanatical hatred of communism, and its complete contempt for liberalism and social democracy, both of which respected parliamentary government, democratic party politics, and civil rights. Fascism appealed to some members of every social class: large landowners, industrialists, professional people, civil servants, skilled and unskilled labor, farmers, war veterans, and the unemployed. It also appealed to some conservatives, socialists, and nationalists, and to Christians and nonbelievers alike. But fascism found its chief political support among those whom communism scorned and whom liberals and social democrats neglected: the lower-middle classes (small property owners, small businessmen, artisans, minor bureaucrats, pensioners, and schoolteachers) and marginal elements of society (embittered war veterans, disillusioned youth, political hotheads, the unemployed, and the unsuccessful). The lower-middle classes were the ones whose very existence was being threatened by the new industrial order of the twentieth century, the ones who were being crushed between big business and heavy industry on the one hand and organized labor and socialism on the other.

Although fascist leaders promised Europe a new social and economic order, their true intention was only to shore up the faltering old order by new means. One of their new means was the formation of authoritarian, elitist political parties, which would increase absolute control over all social classes and all spheres of life—parties that demanded absolute obedience from their members and, once in power, from every member of society. Their primary objective was to impose what Hitler called

Gleichschaltung—a leveling process aimed at bringing every member of society under the control of the party and into conformity with its will. Another new fascist technique was the systematic use of terror and violence, intimidation and assassination, not only as a way to seize and consolidate power, but also as a way to keep society in a constant state of fear and submission. Fascist leaders would stage massive political rallies and military parades to whip up crowd frenzy and rally mass support. They made political, religious, and ethnic groups (especially the Jews) their scapegoats, although such groups did not necessarily pose any threat to fascist regimes. But scapegoats served as convenient outlets for hatred and frustration; fascists could use scapegoats, making them appear the common enemy, to solidify strife-torn societies. Fascism also produced a new type of political leadership: the Italian Duce, the German Führer, and the Spanish Caudillo. The fascist leader was not a business-like bureaucrat, nor a dedicated revolutionary, nor an autocrat or dictator in the aristocratic tradition of Napoleon and Bismarck. Instead, he set himself up as a symbol of the national will, a folk hero through whom the masses could live vicariously, and a perfect embodiment of the fascist ideals of infallibility, sublime mission, and violent action.

BENITO MUSSOLINI (1883–1945) was the son of a blacksmith and Adolf Hitler (1889–1945), the son of a minor customs official. Both fought and were wounded in the First World War and loved to pose in later life as military heroes. Mussolini, the better educated of the two, was influenced during his student days by Nietzsche's philosophy, which exalted the will to power, and by Bergson's philosophy of intuition and heroic action. But he was especially impressed by Georges Sorel's syndicalist variety of socialism, which was more anarchist and opposed to organized political activity than orthodox Marxism, and which appealed to workers in the less advanced industrial areas of France, Spain, and Italy, workers who lacked political power and organization. Mussolini became a socialist before the war and rose to the prominent position of editor of the official socialist newspaper, *Avanti!* Hitler was a failure and a drifter in his youth. Hitler spent part of his youth in Vienna, where he was forced to take menial jobs and where he grew to hate the Jews who played a prominent role in that city's commercial and cultural life. Hitler's war experience gave him a purpose in life and a sense of camaraderie with his fellow soldiers. And he emerged from the war convinced that he would someday avenge Germany's defeat and humiliation, which he apparently associated with his own personal misfortunes.

Mussolini was expelled from the Italian Socialist party in 1914, when, in defiance of their policy of neutrality, he advocated Italy's entry into the war on the side of the Allies. He had by then been drawn to the cause

Hitler and Mussolini in Venice, 1933.

(Wide World Photos).

of the nationalists, who demanded the annexation of territory in the Trentino area of the Austrian Alps, where Italians formed a sizeable minority of the population. The war and its bitter aftermath convinced Mussolini that Italy was ripe for a political party that would combine both socialist and nationalist objectives. Italy, although on the winning side, had suffered terrible losses in the war and had been denied the Austrian territory promised by England and France in persuading Italy to enter the war on their side. Moreover, the war had left Italy resembling a defeated nation. Inflation was higher than anywhere else in 1919 and 1920. Strikes and riots had broken out in the northern industrial cities, and peasants had seized land in the agricultural south. The liberal government of the cautious Giovanni Giolitti failed to bring the situation under control. Moreover, in 1919, a band of war veterans, led by the nationalist poet, Gabriele D'Annunzio, occupied the disputed city of Fiume on the border between Italy and the newly formed state of Yugoslavia. When the two governments agreed a year later to make Fiume an international city, Italian troops drove D'Annunzio and his followers from the city, thereby increasing the bitterness that most Italians already felt.

It was under these conditions that Mussolini formed his Fascist party in 1919. Originally, the party consisted of only a small band of old-time syndicalists and veterans who called for immediate change by violent action. But, as conditions worsened and government inaction continued, the party quickly began to grow. Many of D'Annunzio's followers joined the fascists after their expulsion from Fiume. From them, Mussolini formed his first combat units and his *squadristi,* which gained attention by beating up socialists, liberals, and trade unionists and destroying their homes, headquarters, and printing presses. The party now began to receive financial support from landowners and factory owners who approved of these methods.

The 1921 elections made matters worse by returning a parliament divided between Liberals, Socialists, Catholics, and Fascists. The Fascists were able to win thirty-five seats. The socialists, although the largest single party in the new parliament, were not large enough to control it nor were they willing to form a coalition with any of the other parties. The chronic weakness of the government, along with Mussolini's election to parliament, contributed to the growth of the Fascists and emboldened them further. Throughout 1921 and the first half of 1922, the Fascists, using terrorist tactics on a large scale, succeeded in gaining control of most of the industrial north. The Fascists themselves were now chiefly responsible for making Italy ungovernable. By the autumn of 1922, they threatened to march on Rome itself. To avert this, King Emmanuel III appointed Mussolini prime minister and requested him to form a new government in accordance with the constitution. Technically, Mussolini had risen to Italy's highest political office in accordance with the constitution. In reality, he had done so by force and obstruction.

Once in office, Mussolini began to consolidate his personal power. Because the Fascists held only thirty-five seats in parliament, he proceeded cautiously at first, allowing some freedom to the press, labor unions, and opposing political parties. In 1924, however, one of the Socialist leaders in parliament, an outspoken opponent of Mussolini named Giacomo Matteoti, was murdered by Fascist thugs. Most of Mussolini's opponents in parliament resigned in protest. Fearful that the Matteoti affair would force him out of office, Mussolini struck back at his enemies. He mobilized the militia, the police, and his black-shirted *squadristi* to suppress the labor unions, muzzle the press, and crack down on his political opponents, who either emigrated, were imprisoned, or were forced to keep silent. By 1926, all political parties except the Fascists were abolished and Mussolini, called Il Duce, or the leader, was dictator.

Now that he possessed absolute power, Mussolini set about transforming Italy into what he called a "corporate state." By this he meant a state in which the Fascists would control the government, the large landowners and industrialists would control the economy, and both would control labor and the professions. This objective Mussolini accomplished by 1934. Simultaneously, he launched massive public works programs and rearmament of Italy, which eliminated unemployment, stimulated the economy, and earned him the reputation abroad of being a strong but able leader. In 1929, after sixty years of hostility between the Catholic Church and the Italian government, Mussolini reached an agreement with Pope Pius XI, who agreed to recognize the duce and his government in exchange for the independence of the Vatican from any secular control and a privileged role for the Church in Italian public education. The latter point produced friction between the Vatican and the duce, who was an atheist by conviction and feared the possibly anti-fascist educational influence that the Church might exercise over Italian youth. Nevertheless, this agreement, called the Concordat, held up and was popular with the Italian people. By 1930, Mussolini was secure at home and popular abroad. Soon he would be prepared for foreign expansion.

ADOLF HITLER'S rise to power was slower than Mussolini's. In 1919, he joined an obscure right-wing political group that called itself the National Socialist German Workers' Party. Among its members were the famous General Erich Ludendorff and such future high-ranking Nazi leaders as Hermann Goering, an ace pilot during the First World War, and Josef Goebbels, the party's fervid propagandist. In 1920 the party adopted a twenty-five point program that was a mixture of extreme nationalism, anti-Semitism, and anticapitalism. It denounced the Versailles treaty, called for Germany's annexation of Austria, and demanded economic reforms favorable to the hard-pressed lower-middle classes.

Hitler's party was only one of several nationalist parties holding similar views at the time. Divided they were weak, but united they would have made a formidable political force. With that in mind, Hitler decided to make his bid for power in the autumn of 1923, a year of great economic hardship and political instability in postwar Germany. Hitler chose November to lead a street march in Munich, known as the Beer Hall *Putsch*, which he hoped would overthrow the Bavarian government and then develop into a general revolution that would overthrow the harried national government. But the mistimed *Putsch* was quickly quelled, and Hitler received a short prison sentence. There he wrote *Mein Kampf*—a hodgepodge of racial hatred, nationalistic revenge, anticommunism, and terrorist political tactics—which would subsequently become the bible of the Nazi movement. The Weimar government managed to stabilize itself by 1924, and Hitler's party seemed on the way to extinction. But the seeds for its revival were scattered throughout Germany.

The Great Depression brought the National Socialist party back to life. Germany's unemployed rose to a figure (six million in 1932) second only to that of the United States, upon whom Germany heavily depended for loans that were no longer forthcoming. Party membership began to soar in 1929. Tens of thousands of jobless were recruited into Hitler's private army of brown-shirted Storm Troopers, corresponding to Mussolini's black-shirted *squadristi* and employing the same gangster methods on Communists, Social Democrats, Jews, and other "enemies of the German people."

In the 1930 elections, the Nazis increased their strength in the Reichstag (national parliament) from twelve to one hundred seven seats, and the Communists increased theirs to seventy-seven seats. The election left the center parties weakened and unable to gain parliamentary majorities; meanwhile, the Nazis and Communists battled each other in the streets. In the July 1932 election, the Nazis replaced the Social Democrats as Germany's largest single political party. In the November 1932 election, the Nazis lost slightly. But German big business now came to Hitler's aid, agreeing to pay his party's election debts and the Storm Troopers' wages in exchange for Hitler's noninterference in German industry.

The last step in Hitler's rise to power was near. On January 30, 1933, the aging President Paul von Hindenburg, on the advice of conservative intriguers in the government eager to make a backstairs deal with Hitler, appointed him chancellor of the German Reich. The election in March 1933 gave the Nazis and their conservative business and aristocratic allies a near majority in the Reichstag.

Hitler had come to power in the wake of Germany's defeat in the war, a humiliating peace treaty, a malfunctioning government, the worst depression in modern times, widespread unemployment, and communist political gains. Like Mussolini, whom he admired and emulated, Hitler had achieved his goal, technically, by legal means. In reality, and even more blatantly than Mussolini, he had done so by violence, the exploitation of anti-Semitism and anticommunism, and connivance with sympathetic conservative politicians and industrialists. Once in power, however, Hitler was able to consolidate his dictatorship more quickly than Mussolini because of his party's strength in parliament and its acceptance by a divided and demoralized electorate.

A fire, set by a retarded young Dutch Communist apparently acting alone, destroyed the Reichstag building in February 1933. This provided Hitler with a convenient opportunity to crush the Communists and to suspend all civil rights indefinitely. A month later, he was able to force passage of the Enabling Act by a now acquiescent Reichstag purged of Communists. The Enabling Act granted him full dictatorial powers for the next four years and effectively removed all remaining official obstacles to Hitler's totalitarianization of Germany. He used the act to persecute his political enemies, Jews, and recalcitrant Christian clergymen. It also made him secure enough to purge his own party of left-wing elements in 1934, in a bloody liquidation known as the "Night of the Long Knives." Local governments were deprived of power, and rival political parties were forbidden. Culture, education, the press, trade unions, and churches were placed under strict government controls. The civil service and judicial system were purged, and concentration camps were set up; through them a half million Germans passed, even before they were transformed into death camps for Jews and other racially "inferior peoples."

In 1933 Hitler withdrew Germany from the international Disarmament Conference and from the League of Nations. In 1935, he publicly denounced the disarmament clause of the Versailles treaty, a clause he was violating anyway by his military buildup. The same year, the notorious Nuremberg Laws, which forbade Jews marrying or having sexual relations with Aryans, were passed, foreshadowing Hitler's barbarous "final solution to the Jewish question." Upon becoming chancellor, Hitler also immediately set about curing the economy by means of massive public works programs and rearmament. These programs succeeded in putting Germany on the road to economic self-sufficiency, full employment, and a restoration of national pride. By 1935 Hitler, like Mussolini, was securely in power. Both were popular with the majority at home, respected abroad, and prepared for territorial expansion.

OTHER FASCIST REGIMES More moderate Fascist regimes came to power in the poor and industrially backward Catholic countries of Portugal, Spain, and Austria. Traditional conservative interests—large landowners, wealthy business classes, and established military cliques—were more firmly entrenched in these countries than they were in Italy and Germany. Consequently, they were better able to control social discontent without conspiring with upstart demagogues equipped with private armies, bizarre ideologies, and propaganda techniques calculated to whip up mass hysteria. Conservatives in these Catholic countries were mainly interested in restoring social and economic stability and in preserving their own privileged position in society. Their ideal was a hierarchical society in which everyone would know his place and keep it. What they feared most was change of any sort, especially revolutionary change from the Left. Accordingly, the type of fascism that appealed to them was a moderate version of Mussolini's clerical-corporate state: a state in which the Church and business class would enjoy a privileged position under the protection of one-party conservative rule.

In 1933 the Portuguese minister of finance, somber and pious Antonio de Oliveiro Salazar, was able to quietly impose such a regime on his country and to remain in power until shortly before his death in 1970. In

1939 General Francisco Franco succeeded in imposing such a regime on Spain, but only after his victory in the bloody Spanish Civil War. He, too, remained in power until his death in 1975. Austria began drifting toward clerical-corporate fascism in 1932, first under Engelbert Dollfuss, who was murdered by Nazi conspirators in 1934, and then under his more cooperative successor, Kurt Schuschnigg, who tried to steer a perilous, and finally doomed, course between growing Nazi sentiment in Austria and resistance to German annexation.

Encouraged by the victory of fascism in Italy and Germany, small but rigorous fascist movements sprang up also in the liberal-democratic countries of western Europe. The largest and most active of these Fascist minorities was in France. The Fascist league known as the *Croix de feu,* headed by a retired army officer named François de la Rocque, claimed nearly a million members. The *Parti populaire français,* headed by a former Communist mayor, Jacques Doriot, was smaller but more outspoken in its defense of authoritarian nationalism and in its opposition to the French republic, communism, and the Jews. Fascism in France reached its peak in February 1934, when a massive right-wing demonstration against the government nearly resulted in the overthrow of the French Republic itself. The election of Léon Blum's Popular Front government in 1936 put French fascism on the defensive. But it remained strong enough to divide and demoralize France as the threat of another war with Germany increased. And it gained a new lease on life under the four-year German occupation that began with the fall of France in June 1940.

The Fascist minority in Britain was much smaller and less significant than in France. In contrast to fascism on the continent, British fascism was more an outgrowth of the depression and frustration with parliamentary government than of military defeat, frustrated nationalism, or disillusionment with Western culture. The leader of British fascism was Sir Oswald Mosley, a former Labour party member, who founded the British Union of Fascists in 1932. His party's popularity reached its peak in 1934, with a membership of approximately twenty thousand. But by 1936 the party was in decline, appealing mainly to Jew-baiting rowdies in the working-class East End of London.

Fascism in Belgium and Holland was largely the product of frustrated nationalism (the Flemish minority movement in Belgium), disgust with parliamentary government (Léon Degrelle's Rexist movement in Belgium), and anticommunism (Anton Mussert's National-Socialist League in Holland). All these movements, which were encouraged and in some cases financed by Italy and Germany, enjoyed some success in the early thirties, but receded as fear of Nazi Germany grew in the Low Countries.

Fascism offered a solution to every kind of discontent. To the threatened elites (industrialists and large landowners), it promised to suppress the political Left and labor unions and to guarantee a managed economy in which they would continue to play the leading role. To the desperate lower-middle classes, fascism promised economic security and rescue from further economic and social decline into the ranks of the industrial proletariat. To ultranationalists and war veterans, it promised national unity and glory and positions in the party. To the unemployed, it promised jobs. To the intellectually disillusioned and socially maladjusted, it offered a purpose in life: a sense of belonging to a mighty cause. And to all, fascism offered psychological satisfaction by its promise of action—immediate action—not talk, nor theory, nor parliamentary debate, nor wait-and-see tactics. Liberalism and communism, although far apart on the ideological spectrum, stood for clearly stated goals and appealed to classes that formed the backbone of twentieth-century industrial society: the bourgeoisie and the proletariat. Fascism, on the other hand, was more a program of calculated disorder, designed to perpetuate the crisis conditions that first vaulted it to power. And its most enthusiastic recruits came from the desperate fringe elements of twentieth-century society.

The Popular Front: Fascism's Opposition

Organized opposition to fascism began in France with the formation of the Popular Front in 1934. This coalition was made up of Communists, Socialists, and middle-class Democrats alarmed by Hitler's victory in Germany the previous year and by the massive right-wing demonstration that nearly toppled the French Republic in February 1934. This idea of a united front against fascism originated with the French Communists, who persuaded Stalin, now head of the Soviet Union, to support it. Such a broad coalition was something new because, ever since the divisive meeting of the Comintern in 1920, the Communists had refused to cooperate with nonrevolutionary Socialists and "bourgeois" Democrats, who in turn deeply distrusted the Communists for their hostility and allegiance to Moscow. But now a common enemy brought them together in an uneasy alliance, and only in those countries where the threat of fascism was paramount—France in 1934 and Spain in 1936.

In 1934 the Soviet Union had shown signs of reversing its earlier policy of intransigence by joining the League of Nations in an effort to improve the Soviet Union's international position. A year later, Stalin agreed to support the Popular Front in order to gain western European allies in the event of war between the Soviet Union and Germany. At the same time, he concluded security agreements with France and Czechoslovakia. Stalin's apparent reversal made the idea of a Popular Front palatable to Socialists and Democrats, who were willing, under the circumstances, to meet the Communists half way and who were not unaware of the rapid growth of communism throughout Europe during the depression.

Popular Front candidates won a resounding victory in the French election of 1936, the most important election held in Europe between the wars. Since the Socialists emerged as the leading party in the new Chamber of Deputies, their leader, Léon Blum, became premier of France—the first socialist and the first Jew to hold that office. Blum seemed well suited to lead a coalition government. He was honest, tolerant, forceful, cultured, and deeply dedicated both to individual freedom and social justice. But almost immediately, Blum faced problems that would force him from office only a year after the election. The problems of pulling France out of the depression, meeting workers' demands for better wages and working conditions, and halting the advance of fascism were difficult enough. In addition, the conservatives hated Blum because he was too revolutionary (and Jewish as well); the Communists refused to cooperate with him because he was not revolutionary enough. This combination of difficulties finally caused Blum's fall and the collapse of the Popular Front in France.

The Popular Front began on a successful note. Within days of taking office, Blum settled a nation-wide strike of more than two million French workers. The agreements he arranged between labor and business to end the strike provided for a forty-hour working week, a minimum wage scale, paid vacations, and the right to collective bargaining. These agreements, called the Matignon Agreements and resembling the American New Deal on a smaller scale, were Blum's most successful and lasting achievement. But France's economic plight continued, and the Matignon Agreements, which were costly concessions to labor, only intensified the hostility of France's conservative business class to Blum's leadership.

Worse yet was the division of the Popular Front and French public opinion over the Spanish Civil War, which broke out a month after Blum took office. The chief reason for the existence of the Popular Front was to fight fascism, but it was over this very issue that the Popular Front foundered. The crisis began when the recently formed Spanish Republican government requested arms to put down a rebellion of right-wing generals. The Communists and some Socialists supported French aid to the Spanish Republic. But the moderate wing of the Popular Front threatened to dissolve the coalition government if France became involved in the Spanish conflict, even though a rebel victory would mean a third Fascist country bordering France. Conservatives and Fascists, now more furious than ever with Blum because he sympathized with the Republican cause, threatened civil war in France if he came to the aid of the Spanish "Reds." ("Better Hitler than Blum" was their slogan). Moreover, the conservative British government, insisting upon strict neutrality, warned France not to interfere.

Blum tried, unsuccessfully, to steer a middle course. He did not wish to risk civil war at home, a very real threat in 1937, or to weaken France's alliance with Britain. Thus, he refused aid to the Spanish Republic. But, gambling that the Spanish government would survive if the rebels also received no outside help, he joined with Britain and other European states in forming a Non-Intervention Commission to blockade foreign aid to both sides in the conflict. The blockade was half-hearted and ineffective from the start. The insurgents received large supplies of men and material from Mussolini and Hitler, and the Republican forces received substantially less aid from the Soviet Union. Blum, now discredited in the eyes of both wings of his government, resigned in June 1937. A year later, when Edouard Daladier became premier, the Popular Front was a thing of the past. It lived on only as an ideal, which the French Resistance would revive under the German occupation.

The Spanish Civil War

The Spanish Civil War (1936-39) began as a revolt against the Popular Front government elected in 1936 to defend the faltering Spanish Republic proclaimed in 1931. The Spanish Popular Front was even more diverse than the French. In addition to Socialists, Democrats, and a small number of Communists, it included groups which were more typically Spanish. One of these groups, the Syndicalists, who were predominantly workers concentrated in the industrial north, rejected parliamentary politics and demanded sweeping socialist reforms by direct action: paralysis of the economy and government by general strikes and the seizure of factories and businesses. Another group, the Anarchists, who were predominantly peasants concentrated in the agricultural south, saw the solution to their exploitation and grinding poverty in the seizure of land and the creation of a grass-roots agrarian communalism. (United by the war, these two groups became known as the Anarcho-Syndicalists). A third characterically Spanish component of the Popular Front were the Basque and Catalonian separatists, who demanded extensive autonomy for their culturally unique and economically more advanced provinces.

As in France, the one thing more than any other that brought these diverse groups together was their fear that the five-year-old Republic, which had sharply polarized Spain from its inception, would succumb to fascism as the similarly feeble Portuguese and Austrian republics had succumbed a few years earlier. Opposed to the Popular Front were the well-entrenched enemies of the Republic: wealthy landowners, the powerful Spanish clergy, conservative nationalists, and the army. When the more radical wing of the Popular Front attempted to follow up the 1936 election victory with a social revolution—land seizures, violent general strikes, outrages against churches and the clergy, and the murder of political opponents—the enemies of the Republic launched a counter-revolution led by General Francisco Franco in July 1936.

Franco's professional armies quickly gained control of the south and west of Spain and pushed the hastily trained and poorly equipped Republican forces back into the more modern industrial northeastern region enclosed by the Republican strongholds of Madrid, Valencia, and Barcelona. There the battle lines were drawn. As the war began to settle into a stalemate in the autumn of 1936, Mussolini and Hitler, at Franco's request, came to his aid with troops, tanks, artillery, and planes. After France's refusal to aid the Republicans, they had no choice but to appeal to Stalin, who assisted them on a smaller scale. But Stalin's agents also sought to dominate the Republican coalition, causing a bitter internal struggle between the Communists and the Anarcho-Syndicalists. The Communists, with their superior discipline, organization, and growing prestige, succeeded finally in gaining control of the coalition after a bitter three-day street battle with Anarcho-Syndicalists in Barcelona in May 1937. As in France, the Communists in Spain were not interested in a domestic social revolution; their sole interests were to defeat fascism, to win converts to Communism and friends for the Soviet Union, and to arouse the neutral western governments to assist the Spanish Republic.

When it became apparent that Communist intervention in Spain only made the western governments more suspicious of the Soviet Union and its possibly expansionist intentions in western Europe, Stalin abandoned the Republican cause in 1938 and gave up the whole four-year-old idea of collective security and Popular Fronts. Stalin's withdrawal enabled Franco to win the Civil War in 1939, but only after a prolonged bloody conflict, in which brutality on both sides, especially Franco's, aroused public opinion in the Western world against him and against fascism in general.

As the Spanish Civil War grew into an international conflict, it aroused political passions both within Spain and abroad as few wars have done. Tens of thousands of volunteers from abroad, mostly dedicated anti-Fascists and leftist intellectuals, streamed into Spain as International Brigades (including the Lincoln Brigade from America) to fight on the Republican side. Among them were George Orwell, André Malraux, Franz Borkenau, and Ernest Hemingway, whose books on the war are now literary classics. A much smaller number of volunteers, mostly militant anticommunists, served under Franco. One of their chief literary spokesmen was the South African poet Roy Campbell. One reason for this remarkable response from abroad was the volunteers' long pent-up frustration with their governments' inaction and appeasement of fascism. For many, especially Italian and German political refugees, the war presented their first opportunity to strike back personally at fascism. Another reason was the widespread belief, generated mostly by the Communists and only partly true, that the Popular Front was fighting for democracy. Indeed, many volunteers were convinced that democracy was at stake not only in Spain, but also in the countries from which they came. A third reason was the growing realization everywhere that the Spanish Civil War was only the prelude to a wider conflict, and that the sooner the battle lines were drawn, the better. But as the Popular Front fell prey to internal strife, as the war tipped in Franco's favor, as the atrocities committed by both sides mounted, and as the war became increasingly mechanized, much of the original political idealism of the foreign volunteers turned to cynicism and disgust.

The Civil War left Spain wounded, exhausted, and divided—the first victim of the Second World War. More than a half million Spaniards had died, and Franco had imprisoned and drove into exile many hundreds of thousands more. Relations among the western European states, and between them and Soviet Russia, were more strained than ever. Both sides now had good reason to distrust each other. Fascism had won another great victory, and its leaders became bolder than ever. They now had good reason to believe that they could advance at will. The Popular Front, which had achieved its greatest success in Spain in 1936, died in the ruins of Madrid in March 1939.

RUSSIA UNDER STALIN

When Lenin died in 1924, it was not certain who would succeed him. The most likely candidates were Leon Trotsky, the hero of the Revolution and the civil war, Gregory Zinoviev, chairman of the Comintern, and Nikolai Bukharin, the party's leading theorist. They, like Lenin himself, were well-educated, widely travelled, and cosmopolitan in outlook. All of them, especially Trotsky, believed that, despite the setbacks suffered by communism abroad between 1919 and 1923, the Russian Revolution would eventually expand to the rest of Europe and then the world.

Joseph Stalin (1879-1953), on the other hand, was poorly educated and had almost no experience of the world beyond Russia. His role in the party had been confined at first largely to clandestine activities, such as raids on banks to raise party funds, and later to organizational affairs. But what he lacked in education, sophistication, and vision he made up for in shrewdness, determination, and ruthlessness. A poverty-stricken youth and many years in tsarist prisons had hardened Stalin into a man whose ability to survive and whose will to power, as events would show, exceeded that of his competitors.

In 1924, Stalin held the key post of party secretary, which he used to consolidate his political power. One of his strengths was that his opponents, who considered him their intellectual inferior, underestimated his ability to seize and hold power. But his main strength lay in the fact that he reflected growing opinion within the party that the consolidation of communism in Russia should take precedence over the extension of communism abroad. Immediately after Lenin's death, Stalin used these strengths to divide his opponents and eliminate them one at a time. Trotsky was the first to go; with Zinoviev's help Stalin had him removed from the powerful office of war commissar in 1925. Next, Stalin turned against Zinoviev himself; with the support of sympathizers newly appointed to the Politburo (the party's steering committee), he had Zinoviev dismissed from the chairmanship of the Comintern.

By now, it was too late for Stalin's opponents to unite against him. In 1927, the tenth anniversary of the Revolution, Stalin was powerful enough to have Trotsky and Zinoviev, whom he denounced as "deviationists," expelled from the party itself. Stalin was now indisputably head of the Russian Communist party, which meant head of Russia as well. He alone would now determine party policy. Two years later, the still popular Trotsky was forced into exile, where he publicly denounced Stalin as a traitor to the Revolution and gained a large international following of anti-Stalinist, "Trotskyite" Communists. This most dangerous of Stalin's political enemies was murdered by a Stalinist agent in Mexico in 1940.

Stalin's rise to power meant the victory of his program to bring communism to Russia first. The 1917 Revolution had transformed Russia politically but had left the economy much as it had been under the last tsar. Stalin's plan was to create a Communist economy and transform Russia into a world power as quickly as possible. He intended to do this by collectivizing Russia's huge peasant population, a move intended to increase agricultural production and release manpower for a rapid industrial development. This enormous task was complicated by Stalin's determination to pursue both objectives simultaneously and without foreign aid.

Collectivization began in 1928. But most peasants, especially the wealthier, landowning *kulaks,* fiercely resisted consolidating their small holdings into large collectives and leaving their farms to work in far-off factories. Stalin responded with force. Between 1929 and 1933, millions of *kulaks* and other uncooperative peasants were either killed or transported to forced labor camps in remote regions of Siberia. Millions more died in the famine of 1932/33. But by 1934 the unwilling peasants had been forced to accept collectivization.

The first of Stalin's industrial five-year plans also went into effect in 1928. All available manpower, capital, and technology were harnessed to the construction of factories, dams, and whole new industrial cities, some of which were located deep in the Russian interior, where they were less exposed to foreign invasion. The five-year plans, which continued until the Second World War, also took a heavy toll in human suffering. Wages were low, hours long, working conditions poor, living conditions drab, and food and consumer goods scarce. But from 1929 to 1939, Russia rose from fifth to third in the world in overall production trailing only the United States and Germany. The transition of Russia's economy from capitalism to communism had also been achieved.

In 1934 the assassination of one of Stalin's trusted advisors served as a pretext for him to begin a new political purge. A series of trials that began in 1935 and culminated in 1937 and 1938 eliminated almost all the remaining old Bolsheviks leaders, including Zinoviev and Bukharin, who were shot, and many high-ranking army officers and party bureaucrats, especially those with political connections or experience abroad. The trials made such a mockery of the Western world's sense of justice that many observers, Communists and non-Communists alike, who previously had sympathized with the Soviet experiment, now found Stalin and Russian communism repugnant. But the purge extended far beyond the government into Russian society itself. Millions perished in the purge, and millions more were deported to Siberia's forced labor camps, which Aleksandr Solzhenitsyn later depicted, in all their horror, in his famous work, *The Gulag Archipelago* (1974).

When the purge ended in 1939, Stalin was as supreme in Russia as Hitler was in Germany, although the two dictators used their power to different ends. The misery that the Russian people suffered under Stalin during the thirties was enormous. Weighed against this suffering was Stalin's success in transforming Russia into the first Communist state and a major world power free of the unemployment and economic stagnancy plaguing the Western world. A new generation that knew no alternative to Stalin's leadership and therefore accepted it had grown up since the Revolution. His considerable achievement was a great source of patriotic pride to this new generation and would unite the Russian people, despite their sufferings, behind Stalin during the terrible war that lay ahead.

Culture of the Thirties

Events of the thirties produced an abrupt politicization of cultural and intellectual life, in contrast to the aestheticism and experimentation, the inwardness and comparative indifference to political and social issues characteristic of the previous decade. The depression and the rise of fascism aroused new concern with these issues and everywhere polarized the creative elites to the Left and Right. What both sides had in common was their deep disillusionment with capitalism, a disillusionment that now began to find cultural and intellectual outlets.

The new totalitarian regimes immediately clamped tight controls on thought and expression and silenced or drove into exile those who would not submit. As early as 1929, the Nazi ideologist, Alfred Rosenberg, founded a Militant League for German Culture dedicated to opposing the cosmopolitan, modernist, allegedly "decadent" culture that had flourished in Germany and throughout the West during the twenties. Once in power, the Nazis ruthlessly suppressed all art with non-Aryan, Communist, pacifist, or international overtones and officially sanctioned only easily intelligible art that praised the heroic and primitive, supposedly Germanic, virtues. Schools, academies, and museums were purged accordingly; racially "inferior" peoples were naturally deprived of any role in cultural affairs; opponents were either driven into exile or silenced. All the arts and communications media were brought under the control of Josef Goebbels' Propaganda Ministry, and everyone associated with the arts and their dissemination was forced to submit. Hitler's cultural policy reached its apogee in 1937 with the opening of the Nazi-style House of Art in Munich and the consignment of all undesirable works to a nearby Degenerate Art Exhibition, which, to the credit of German taste at the time, was far better attended than Hitler's own philistine display.

In 1929 Stalin also began to crack down on the freedom of cultural expression in Russia, bringing to a close an era of rich creativity in literature and the performing arts. "Socialist realism" was declared the official Soviet style. Although based on different assumptions, Socialist realism differed little in execution from Hitler's own dictatorial cultural formula. It opposed innovation and foreign art, especially German and Western art, and exalted in simplistic and hackneyed fashion the virtues of the proletariat, communism, and the heroism of the Russian masses. In 1932, the government abolished all independent cultural organizations and replaced them with state-controlled Unions of Soviet Writers, Composers, Artists, and Architects. Between 1936 and 1938, control of all cultural activity passed to a new state Committee on Art Affairs, which was authorized to denounce deviationists and opponents of official policy. Among the most distinguished victims of socialist realism were Russia's great filmmaker, Sergei Eisenstein; writers Isaac Babel and Boris Pilnyak; the dramatists Vsevolod Meyerhold and Nikolai Okhlopkhov; and the composer, Dimitri Shostakovitch—these were but a few of the countless thousands forced to toe the party line, attacked in the press, silenced, murdered, or driven to suicide.

Nor did Italy produce much of artistic worth during Mussolini's long and comparatively less severe regime. Most of his enemies had been dealt with long before 1930, and those who remained tended to acquiesce. The great Italian Communist leader, Antonio Gramsci, one of the few potential threats to Mussolini's regime, was imprisoned in 1926 and not released until shortly before his death in 1937. Italy's most famous man of letters in the twentieth-century, the moderately liberal Benedetto Croce, was forced out of public life into seclusion, where he managed to finish his last major writing, *History as the Story of Liberty* (1938). But potentially more dangerous than such isolated individuals was the powerful and generally unsympathetic Catholic Church, which Mussolini had to deal with and which acted as a curb to any bid on his part for absolute control over the spiritual life of the Italian people, even after his Concordat with Pope Pius XI in 1929. Mussolini's principal contribution to culture was his enthusiastic endorsement of a monumental but unimaginative pseudoclassical style of architecture, aped by Hitler and Stalin, which served to enhance the totalitarian image of infallible imperial authority.

In the liberal-democratic countries of the West, artists and intellectuals were politicized by the depression and subsequent attempts at social reform and by the Spanish Civil War and the ever-growing influx of anti-Fascist refugees. Leftist intellectuals in France, joined by older humanists like André Gide, and sympathetic émigrés like Heinrich Mann, rallied to the Popular Front and the Spanish Republican cause. They channeled their efforts principally through the Communist-led Association of Revolutionary Writers and Artists, which was founded in 1932 to defend Western culture against fascism. This new alliance of the arts and politics was productive of some of the decade's most outstanding creative achievements. Among them were the novels of the then Communist, André Malraux, who dealt with the first Communist bid for power in China in *Man's Fate* (1933) and with the heroism of the Republican forces in Spain in *Man's Hope* (1938). In both novels, the political man of action as hero replaced the passive, introspective literary hero of the previous decade. The last volumes of Roger Martin du Gard's *The Thibauts* eloquently pleaded for socialism and pacifism, although they ended on a note of despair. Jules Romains' *Verdun* (1938), another political novel, was one of the great successes of the age.

The poets Louis Aragon and Paul Eluard, who converted from surrealism to communism, added to the ferment by putting their poetry in the service of revolution. The Paris International Exhibition of 1937 displayed Picasso's huge mural, *Guernica*, a stirring evocation of the horrors of war inspired by the German bombing of the Spanish Basque town of that name. The best French films of the decade were also products of the artistic Left: René Clair's *A Nous la Liberté* (1931), Jean Vigo's

L'Atalante (1934), and Jean Renoir's *La Grande Illusion* (1937). The influential French Right, which scorned liberalism and Blum's government and despised communism, found expression in the Action Française group of writers and in the novels of Henry de Montherlant and Louis-Ferdinand Céline.

In England, a forceful anti-Fascist movement grew up around such organizations as the Artists' International Association, the General Post Office Film Unit (G.P.O.), the Group Theatre, the Euston Road school of painters, and the magazine *New Writing*. What they all aimed at was a photographically accurate social realism, as exemplified by Christopher Isherwood's novels dealing with the decline of German society before and under Hitler and George Orwell's *Homage to Catalonia* (1937), the classic account of the Spanish Republican cause and its subversion by Stalinist forces. The new poets, W. H. Auden, Stephen Spender, and C. Day Lewis, in contrast to the mystical, metaphysical, esoteric poetry of T. S. Eliot and Ezra Pound, expressed their viewpoints on contemporary social issues in plain everyday language. Even the distinguished Catholic novelists Evelyn Waugh and Graham Greene turned to a realistic, if satirical, portrayal of the contemporary secular world and its failings, injustices, and general tawdriness. The British Right was represented by a small but brilliant group of literary figures, including Wyndham Lewis, D. H. Lawrence, T. S. Eliot, and W. B. Yeats.

In the United States, the Group Theater and the New York Congress of American Writers accommodated left-wing artists and performers. The thirties were also the heyday of the proletarian novel and the novel of social protest in America, although these were rarely written from an orthodox Marxist standpoint. Such were the novels of John Dos Passos, John Steinbeck, James T. Farrell, Nelson Algren, and the brilliant social satirist Nathanael West. The most ambitious work of fiction attempted by any writer in English during the thirties was John Dos Passos' *U.S.A.*, a trilogy of novels published between 1930 and 1936 that criticized modern American society more from an anarchist than a communist perspective; like much of the literature of social protest of the time, it was written in a severely documentary, camera-lens style calculated to heighten its realistic effect. Dos Passos' novels, as well as most American literature of social protest during the thirties, were inspired more by native American experiences than by ideological borrowings from abroad, although these were not insignificant and made their way into the mainstream by way of the growing influx of political refugees. A new crop of writers—William Faulkner, E. E. Cummings, Robert Frost, and Eugene O'Neill—in contrast to their cosmopolitan predecessors, found inspiration in American life, as did the painters Reginald Marsh, Georgia O'Keefe, Charley Sheeler, Ben Shahn, and Edward Hopper.

The American film industry was enriched by the talents of the newly arrived directors from Central Europe: Erich von Stroheim, Ernst Lubitsch, and Fritz Lang, in whose footsteps Clifford Odets, Orson Welles, Franchot Tone, and other graduates of the new American left-wing theater followed. The Theater Project's best-known production, Marc Blitzstein's *The Cradle Will Rock* (1937), showed the influence of Bertolt Brecht who, along with Kurt Weill, had created the brilliant social satire, *The Three Penny Opera* (1928), before fleeing Germany. Both men found political asylum in the United States, where they continued to contribute much to the American stage and screen until Brecht's return to East Germany after the Second World War. The American painters Ben Shahn, Jackson Pollock, Willem de Kooning, and Mark Rothko were influenced by the politically revolutionary Mexican painters Diego Rivera, José C. Orozco, and David A. Siqueiras, who executed a number of politically inspired murals for United States capitalist institutions while in exile from their own country.

Roosevelt's New Deal further activated cultural ferment by extending federal support to unemployed writers, composers, artists, and theater groups, most notably the Theater Project. While such aid enabled many to propagate left-wing views in the arts, it had the long-term effect of curbing the trend to the Left and gaining valuable support for Roosevelt's program to reconstruct American capitalism. Discounting T. S. Eliot and Ezra Pound, both of whom had departed America for Europe many years before the depression, there was no clearly defined, coherent cultural Right in America during the thirties. Generalized conservative views, aimed more at modern industrial civilization than at radical ideology per se, were voiced by some writers, mostly of the American deep south, such as Thomas Wolfe and William Faulkner, Allen Tate and John Crowe Ransom.

In sum, the culture of the thirties developed around the ideological polarization between Left and Right. Both camps seemed to agree that the existing social order, liberal, democratic, and capitalist, was in an advanced state of decline and contained little worth saving. Both advocated radical change. The Right favored the imposition of stability and the restoration of European hegemony in world affairs by means of militaristic, totalitarian regimes; the Left advocated the creation of an international socialist order that would eradicate the inequities and tensions of the existing system. In quality, the output of the Left was generally far superior to that of the Right. While it is true that Communist influence and leadership predominated in the left-wing camp, it was by no means unanimous or uncontested. On the contrary, Communist insistence on controlling the French and Spanish Popular Fronts, plus the growing realization among initially sympathetic Western intellectuals that Stalin's regime differed little from the Fascist regimes in harshness, did as much as anything to divide and disilluion the non-Communist factions of the Left. By the late thirties, this disillusionment, inflated by the shock of the Nazi-Soviet Pact, threw the Left into disarray, confusing and immobilizing even the most ardent Communists. Still, both ideological camps regarded the coming war as the final struggle to determine which would control the future. As it turned out, both were premature in predicting the collapse of the West and badly underestimated the will and resources of middle-class capitalist societies to survive another war and carry on. But such ideological speculations would have to be put aside until the contest was settled, for a second time, on the battlefield.

THE GATHERING STORM

Fascist expansion began with Japan's invasion of Manchuria in 1931, in defiance of the League of Nations of which Japan was then a member. The Japanese government, which had come under military control in the 1920s, decided upon expansion on the grounds that Japan required an empire in the Far East if it was to free itself from economic dependence on the Western world, provide an outlet for its surplus population, and prevent its rivals, China and the United States, from becoming dominant in Asia and the Pacific. The other members of the League—Britain, France, Germany, and Italy—failed to deal with the aggressor. Japan's invasion of Manchuria, and the League's delay in censuring it, naturally encouraged aggression elsewhere and discredited the League; Japan, along with Germany under the new government of Hitler, withdrew from it in 1933. Japan had embarked on a course of expansion that six years later would lead to war with China and, finally, to involvement in the Second World War. The slack in Japan's economy, caused by the world depression, was now taken up by the task of equipping large armies on the Asian mainland and preparing for unlimited military operations.

Mussolini made the next move. Judging that it would be easier to gain territory in Africa than in Europe, he launched an invasion of Ethiopia in 1935. He had not forgotten that primitive Ethiopia had inflicted a humiliating defeat on an invading Italian army in 1896. And he had not forgotten that Britain and France had failed to keep their promise of allowing Italy to expand at Austria's expense after the First World War. Once again, the League of Nations failed to act effectively. The League enacted economic sanctions against Italy—strong enough to infuriate Mussolini but not strong enough to impede his invasion. Once again, Britain and France protested the invasion but failed to act decisively.

The Ethiopians fought bravely, but they were no match for Italian planes and poison gas.

The League's ineffective sanctions and British and French protests served only to push Mussolini into an alliance with Hitler, which he had previously resisted, and to discredit the League and the whole idea of collective security. With the formation of his alliance with Hitler in 1936, Mussolini also withdrew his protection of Austria against German intervention, thereby removing the only serious obstacle to its eventual annexation by Hitler.

Hitler made his first move while the Ethiopian campaign was still in progress. In March 1936, one year after his denunciation of the disarmament clause of the Versailles treaty, Hitler sent troops into the Rhineland, which the Versailles treaty and the Locarno Pact of 1925 had declared a demilitarized zone. Hitler's remilitarization of the Rhineland served to test his popularity at home and his credibility abroad. On both counts he was successful. The German public approved; the French and British protested but did nothing. The same year Hitler joined with Mussolini to form the Berlin-Rome Axis and with the Japanese government to form the German-Japanese Pact. Armed with these new alliances, Hitler and Mussolini, in a bold new show of foreign intervention, sent aid to Franco in his revolt against the Spanish Republic, a move the dictators welcomed as an opportunity to test their new weapons. If Germans had any remaining doubts by the end of 1936 as to Hitler's intentions, both domestic and foreign, his dreaded Gestapo, headed by Heinrich Himmler, and his private army of fanatically devoted Storm Troopers were there to dispel them.

No sooner was Franco's victory in Spain guaranteed than Hitler invaded and annexed Austria without a fight in March 1938. Just days later he demanded the Sudetenland, a strategic province of Czechoslovakia with a mainly German-speaking population. Determined to keep the peace, Neville Chamberlain, British prime minister since 1937, and Daladier of France, who had replaced Blum, agreed to appease Hitler once more, even though the loss of the Sudetenland would leave Czechoslovakia defenseless. Its cession to Hitler, over outraged Czech and Russian protests, was negotiated at the notorious Munich meeting on September 30, 1938, and Chamberlain returned home with his illusory promise of "peace in our time." The assumption behind this concession was that Hitler would at last be satisfied with the acquisition of territories which were after all predominantly German-speaking. But Hitler, apparently amazed at the ease with which he could bamboozle Western statesmen with his bluster, flagrantly violated the Munich treaty only six months later when he absorbed the remainder of Czechoslovakia. Not to be outdone, Mussolini clamored for the annexation of the

French territories of Nice, Corsica, and Tunisia and proceeded to annex the tiny country of Albania on Good Friday of 1939.

The last great bombshell fell on August 23, 1939, when Germany and Russia, sworn enemies, signed the mutual nonaggression Nazi-Soviet Pact, which shocked world opinion and caused Western Communists and sympathizers to desert the party in flocks. The Russians justified the pact on the grounds that it gave them more time to prepare for eventual war with Germany, and that in any case the Western powers had proved useless as allies and even desired war between Germany and Russia. The Germans cynically justified the pact on the grounds that it would serve their expansion in eastern Europe and eventually against Russia herself. Scarcely a week later, on the morning of September 1, 1939, Germany invaded Poland. On September 3rd, Britain and France, awakened to reality at last, declared war on Germany. Appeasement and dread of another all-out war had reached their limits in the West. The Second World War had begun.

SECOND WORLD WAR

Hitler's decision to invade Poland was based on two considerations: his eastern front was temporarily secure by the terms of the Nazi-Soviet Pact signed in August; his enemies in the West seemed unwilling and unable for the time being to involve themselves in another world war. Under these conditions, Hitler judged that his chances for success would never be better. Either the Western powers would not go to war for Poland's sake (they had not done so for the sake of Spain or Czechoslovakia) or, if they did, he would be able to crush Poland quickly with Russian help and then concentrate his whole force against France and Britain. There would be no divisive two-front war this time; Hitler's strategy of lightning warfare (*Blitzkrieg*), to be carried out by highly mobile Panzer divisions and concentrated aerial bombardments by the Luftwaffe, would ensure that his plan of attack would not bog down into enervating trench warfare. The first two years of the war seemed to bear out Hitler's thinking as he and his allies won one sweeping victory after another.

The invasion of Poland gave the world its first look at Hitler's devastating but efficient *Blitzkrieg*. As German planes pounded the cities, terrifying and confusing the civilian population, Panzer divisions raced across the flat Polish terrain easily beating back the much smaller Polish forces made up mostly of old-fashioned cavalry and slow moving infantry. Behind the tanks came the German infantry to consolidate their hold on the conquered territory. The German advance was so swift and thorough that it even surprised Stalin, who, nervous about having German armies on his border, ordered the Red Army to advance into Poland on September 17. Warsaw, devastated by aerial and artillery bombardment, fell on September 27, and the invasion of Poland ended less than six weeks after it began. All of this happened, as Hitler had expected, before Britain and France could make a move. Hitler and Stalin divided Poland between them with Hitler taking the larger share. But Stalin took the opportunity to occupy the Baltic states of Lithuania, Latvia, and Estonia, which restored Russia's western frontier to approximately what it had been before the 1918 Treaty of Brest-Litovsk.

Stalin also demanded territory from Finland to protect the vulnerable Soviet city of Leningrad, situated only twenty miles from the Finnish border. But Finland, unlike the other Baltic states, was an advanced industrial country with a modern army, and it resisted Stalin's demands. So, without declaring war, Stalin ordered the Red Army to invade Finland on November 30, 1939, beginning what came to be called the "winter war." At first the Finns, assisted by a severe winter, were able to hold their own and inflict huge casualties on the poorly equipped and commanded Red Army. But eventually the superior manpower of the Soviets began to tell, and Finnish resistance was broken in March 1940. Stalin gained the territory he demanded. But his victory over the Finns, whose brave resistance aroused admiration everywhere, pushed Finland into joining with Germany against the Soviet Union in 1941.

In April 1940 Hitler struck again, this time in Scandinavia to cut off British and French aid to Finland. During the winter war, the British and French had prepared to land a large force in Norway to assist the Finns against the Russians and close Norwegian waters to German shipping. But before the Anglo-French force arrived, the Germans swept up through Denmark and parachuted troops into Norway. Tiny Denmark, taken by surprise, offered no resistance. Norway fell after only a few weeks of sporadic fighting, and Sweden was spared a German attack by declaring itself neutral.

When the war began, the British and French expected the Germans to attack western Europe immediately as they had in the First World War. But the western front remained quiet throughout the first eight months of the war. The long delay worked to Germany's advantage, because it lulled French and British troops into a false sense of security, and they began to refer to the war as a "phony war." The commander of the French armies, General Maurice Gamelin, prolonged the delay by adopting a defensive strategy that had worked for the French in the First World War. He kept his armies behind the Maginot line, which was a system of forts that the French had built along their eastern border to repel a German invasion. The only weak point in the Maginot line was the heavily wooded Ardennes area, through which the French believed no modern army could pass. The Ardennes is where Hitler launched his surprise attack on France and the Low Countries on May 10, 1940.

The German attack caught the French and British completely off guard. Ten Panzer divisions under General Guderian crossed the Ardennes and broke through the French lines at Sedan. As German planes bombed and strafed French roads and supply lines, Guderian's tanks, followed by the infantry, fanned out and drove south toward Paris. Simultaneously, the Germans launched an attack against Holland and Belgium, both of which had declared themselves neutral, and neither of which was prepared to resist a German assault. German planes smashed the Dutch port city of Rotterdam, and Holland fell on May 14, just four days after the attack began. The Belgians, who, until the attack came, had refused to coordinate their defense with the French, held out until May 27. The Germans now had part of the divided French and British forces bottled up in Belgium and the rest retreating toward Paris. On June 4, a massive British flotilla, which included almost every British boat that could float, miraculously evacuated approximately 330,000 British and French troops from the beaches of Dunkirk on the Belgian coast. A week later, Mussolini declared war on France in anticipation of a certain German victory.

The fall of France was now only a question of time. The French had not prepared themselves for German *Blitzkrieg*, and when it came, they reacted too slowly. As the Germans advanced toward Paris, the French, deprived of a large part of their forces by the Dunkirk evacuation, began to lose heart and to resign themselves to defeat and occupation. When the Germans triumphantly entered Paris in mid-June, Daladier resigned as premier in favor of the popular Marshal Pétain, the aging hero of the First World War. Pétain immediately sued for an armistice, which left northern France under a German occupation that would last four years and the rest of France under a compliant government, known as the Vichy government, headed by Pétain himself. Charles de Gaulle, a young tank commander, and a few other patriotic Frenchmen who opposed Pétain's armistice escaped to London, as the Polish, Norwegian, Dutch, and Belgian heads of government already had done, and formed a French government in exile to continue the fight against Hitler.

Within six weeks, Hitler's armies achieved what the German armies a generation earlier had failed to achieve in four years: the defeat of France, which fell on June 22, 1940. This was by far Hitler's most impressive and satisfying victory to date. His defeat of an army that had been regarded for twenty years as the best in the world shocked and amazed the world, including the Führer himself, who had not counted on such a quick victory and had not fully prepared his next move. Had Hitler been willing or able to stop there, his record of conquest would have eclipsed even that of the mighty Bismarck. But so long as Britain and his Russian ally of convenience remained undefeated, and so long as the threat of United States intervention hung over him, he could not hope to consolidate his conquests permanently. In any case, drunk with victory and lacking Bismarck's restraint and statesmanship, Hitler had no intention of stopping.

The fall of France and the Low Countries left Britain alone to face the German onslaught in Western Europe. The veteran political leader, Winston Churchill (1874–1965), who had been criticizing his government's policy of appeasement and demanding more energetic preparation for war, succeeded Chamberlain as prime minister in May. Churchill's forceful personality and stirring speeches in Parliament during the summer and fall of 1940 rallied the British people to his leadership and prepared them for the difficult battle ahead. He promised them eventual victory, but at the price of unremitting "blood, toil, tears, and sweat."

Hitler's plan was to invade Britain by a massive naval assault across the English Channel. In preparation for the assault, he summoned the Luftwaffe to soften British defenses. Goering's planes pounded London and British industrial and military targets relentlessly between August and October of 1940. But the British had two advantages. One was the new invention of radar, which could detect the German air raiders in advance. The other was their small but superior Royal Air Force (RAF), which inflicted heavy losses on the Luftwaffe. The German air raids caused widespread death and destruction, but they failed to drive the RAF from the skies or to destroy civilian morale. Even before the London blitz ended in November, Hitler decided to call off the invasion of Britain. The Battle of Britain, as it was called, was his first setback. After the battle, Churchill praised his courageous RAF pilots with his now famous words: "Never in human history have so many owed so much to so few."

Denied in the West and faced with the prospect of a long war, Hitler decided in December that now was the time to invade Russia, which was rich in grain and petroleum. But before he could launch the attack, he was forced to come to the rescue of Mussolini, who had rashly invaded Greece in October and had been repulsed. Mussolini had been faring poorly ever since he became involved in the war. The British were beating back his attack in Egypt and were crippling his navy in the Mediterranean. Hitler himself no longer regarded Mussolini as an important ally and had denied him Nice, Corsica, and Tunisia, which Mussolini had wanted for his belated and insignificant participation in the defeat of France. Now, the Greeks had forced his bungling army to retreat to Albania.

Once again, *Blitzkrieg* produced quick results. In April, German forces simultaneously overran Greece and Yugoslavia, which had changed from the Axis to the Allied side a month earlier. Before the end of April, both countries capitulated. The Allies now could not threaten Hitler's drive to the East from the Balkans. The other south-central European states—Rumania, Hungary, and Bulgaria—were already allied with Germany. Hitler also sent General Erwin Rommel's tank force to reinforce the Italians in Lybia and aroused Iraqi rebels against the British and French in Syria. Hitler had lost valuable time, but now he was ready to deal with Russia.

On June 22, 1941, exactly one year after the fall of France, the German invasion of Russia, the largest invasion of all time, was launched along a two thousand-mile front. For several months it seemed that Hitler might win his greatest victory and secure all Europe. The Russian armies suffered staggering losses and fell back hundreds of miles, and the Germans advanced to the gates of Russia's two largest cities: Moscow and Leningrad. But the early onset of a severe winter, stubborn Russian resistance, and overextended German supply lines forced Hitler to suspend the offensive until spring. The time lost aiding Mussolini the year before began to tell. Japan's surprise attack on Pearl Harbor on December 7, 1941 plunged the United States into the war; the Red Army, under General Georgi Zhukov, simultaneously launched an unexpected counteroffensive. Hitler now faced both the two-front war he had always sought to avoid and a powerful new American army.

Through the winter of 1941/42, the Russians began to dislodge the Germans from their advanced positions and drive them back in severe fighting. The British and Americans struck at German and Japanese naval power, carried out bombing raids on industrial cities in northern Germany, and began to prepare for an eventual invasion of the strongly fortified European continent. Stalin demanded the immediate opening of a second front by his Western allies to ease the pressure on his own overburdened armies. But Churchill and Roosevelt, fighting against two widely separated enemies over vast distances, were not yet prepared for such an undertaking. Moreover, their alliance with Stalin was strained by distrust and suspicion on both sides. Nevertheless, time was on the side of the Allies. The Germans and Japanese could not hope to match their combined manpower and productive capacity, once they were fully mobilized. The turn of the tide became apparent in the closing months of 1942, when the German offensive in the East was permanently halted at the great battle of Stalingrad, the Japanese advance in the Pacific was checked, and British and American victories in North Africa began the encirclement of Hitler's Fortress Europe.

As the war expanded, the German occupation of Europe became more severe. During the first two years of the war, the years of quick and easy victories, the occupation had been relatively mild in all countries except Poland. Hitler detested the Poles as "racially inferior" and began to repopulate their relatively poor country with "superior" German Aryans. However, the western European countries were a different matter. They were economically advanced and, therefore, useful to Hitler; and their populations (except for the Jews) were, conveniently, at least partially Aryan. As their cooperation, or at least peaceful acquiescence, served the war effort, Hitler did not wish to offend them unnecessarily. Many western Europeans in turn preferred Hitler's "New Order" to a Europe open to communism and Soviet influence. Some preferred occupation to a continuation of warfare. Others did not believe that the Allies could defeat the Nazis.

Once the invasion of Russia began, however, it became necessary to increase production and manpower and to ration food and other essential consumer goods. The governments of the occupied countries were forced to pay a large share of the rapidly rising war costs. Hundreds of thousands of non-Germans were drafted to fight on the Russian front. Millions of war prisoners, mostly Poles and Russians, and workers from all of the occupied countries were conscripted to toil in German factories under conditions of slave labor. The Nazi occupiers also aroused needless hostility by alienating local officials and replacing them with hated "collaborators" such as Vidkun Quisling in Norway, whose name has since become synonymous with political betrayal. Acts of disobedience were punished by the execution of innocent hostages, and the dreaded Gestapo regularly resorted to torture and death to enforce submission and to extract information.

But Hitler's most atrocious policy was his systematic extermination of six million Jews, two-thirds of the Jewish population of prewar Europe, and millions of other "racially inferior" Eastern Europeans. "The final solution to the Jewish question" began in earnest in 1942 and was carried out during the next three years by Heinrich Himmler's fanatical SS (*Schutzstaffeln*) detachments. Millions of men, women, and children were gassed, incinerated, and covered over in mass graves in Auschwitz, Treblinka, Dachau, and many other extermination camps whose names sicken the memory. They were murdered not for anything they did, but simply for what they were by the accident of birth. The more able-bodied Jews were worked to death or used as human guinea pigs in medical experiments. Stalin's forced labor camps had at least some rational justification, since they opened up new areas for development and contributed something to the economy. Hitler's death camps served no rational purpose whatever and even detracted from the war effort by diverting badly needed men and material from the fronts. But racism and terrorism had served Hitler well in the past. And he guessed, correctly it seems, that most people (there were courageous exceptions) would put up with any hardship, provided that something worse lay in store for "racial inferiors."

All of this was a far cry from what initially sympathetic and acquiescent Europeans expected of the Nazi New Order. As the occupation grew harsher in 1942, local resistance groups sprang up in almost all of the occupied countries, from France to Poland and from Norway to Greece. The Communists, who had remained inactive while the Nazi-Soviet Pact lasted, immediately took the initiative in organizing resistance groups once the invasion of Russia began. Many non-Communists also joined: Catholics, Socialists, workers, patriots, and leftist intellectuals. The resistance revived the old Popular Front coalition of Communists and non-Communists united by a common enemy.

The resistance movements were strongest in countries like Norway, Yugoslavia, and Greece, where the terrain was suitable for guerilla warfare, and in Poland, where the occupation was harsh enough to unite the civilian population against it. Where the occupation remained comparatively mild—in Denmark and Czechoslovakia, for example—there was little resistance until the end of the war. And where the civilian population was divided between a cooperative resident government and a rival government in exile, like France, resistance developed more slowly. Underground resistance groups appeared in Italy and Germany as well, once the war began to go against these countries. As the resistance movements grew and became more active during the last two years of the war, they gained great prestige as brave fighting units, as symbols of national opposition to fascism, and as prospective focal points for the postwar reorganization of Europe.

In 1943, the Allies took command. The turning point for the Russians was the battle of Stalingrad, the costliest battle of the war, which they finally won in February 1943 after five months of savage fighting. The Red Army, which rapidly regained prestige lost by Stalin's signing of the Nazi-Soviet Pact and his winter war against the Finns, now began to push the Germans back in terrible fighting with huge losses on both sides. The turning point for the British was the battle of El Alamein, where General Bernard Montgomery's forces finally halted Rommel's advance into Egypt. The turning points for the Americans were the battles of Midway and Guadalcanal in the summer of 1942, which halted the Japanese advance in the Pacific. An American army, commanded by General Dwight D. Eisenhower, landed in North Africa in November, and the British, Americans, and Free French forces loyal to De Gaulle cleared North Africa of the Germans and Italians.

In July 1943 Allied forces landed in Sicily. The Germans fought hard to defend the island, but the Italians offered only token resistance. They were tired of the war, sick of constant defeats, and disgusted with Musso-

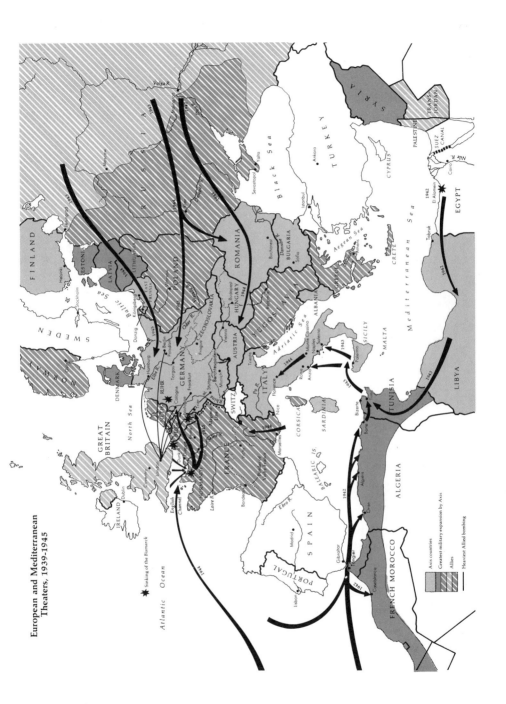

European and Mediterranean
Theaters, 1939-1945

lini and the domineering Germans. On July 25, just after Sicily fell, Mussolini was deposed and Italy surrendered. The Italians, under Mussolini's successor, Marshall Pietro Badoglio, hoped that by surrendering they could save their country from being turned into a new battleground. But the Germans rushed in reinforcements, rescued Mussolini, and turned Italy into an occupied country. For the next year and a half, the Germans in the north fought bitterly to prevent the Allies in the south from advancing, and the Italian people suffered all the miseries of a long war.

Stalin, Churchill, and Roosevelt met together for the first time in November 1943 at Teheran to coordinate their final drive against Hitler. The two western leaders agreed with Stalin that it was necessary to open a major second front to relieve German pressure on the Russian armies in the East. Stalin preferred a British and American invasion of France. But Churchill, who feared that Stalin meant to swallow up all of eastern Europe, proposed attacking Germany through the Balkans, which he called the "soft underbelly of Europe." Roosevelt, who was more concerned with military than with political considerations at the time, sided with Stalin on the grounds that an invasion of France would be the quickest and most direct way to strike at Germany. Churchill was persuaded, and the three leaders agreed to launch a cross-Channel invasion of France in the spring of 1944.

On June 6, 1944, D day, the long-awaited Allied invasion of France began with a massive amphibious landing on the Normandy coast. The Germans resisted tenaciously on all fronts: in the East against the advancing Russians; in Italy against the British and American armies reinforced by French troops from North Africa; and now in western Europe against a combined Allied force commanded by General Eisenhower. German resistance was fierce enough to postpone defeat for another year. But the encirclement of Germany now began to close with few setbacks. Rome had fallen on June 4, and the Allies were able at last to make headway against the Germans in Italy. The Russians were beginning their drive to Berlin. Eisenhower's armies were fighting their way off the Normandy beaches into northern France. And a secondary attack was being prepared in the south of France. The Germans were now fighting to save what remained of a European empire mightier than any of the past. The Allies were fighting for no less than total victory and unconditional surrender. A band of conspirators close to Hitler, hoping for more favorable peace terms, attempted to assassinate him in July 1944. But the attempt failed, and the now crazed Führer was more than ever determined to fight to the end.

The Allied leaders met once more before the war's end at Yalta in February 1945, where their growing differences became apparent. Stalin insisted upon and was grudgingly granted control of Eastern Europe, which in any case he already occupied. Roosevelt was more amenable to this concession than Churchill, because he was eager to gain Soviet acceptance of his Wilsonian idea for a postwar United Nations inspired by the failed League of Nations. Roosevelt hoped that this concession to Stalin would sustain the alliance and ensure good relations between the three Allied powers even after the war. The varying positions of the three leaders at this conference (since then hotly debated) were all reasonable at the time. None really wished to jeopardize their alliance before the war even ended. Churchill, always an imperialist and outspoken anti-Communist, was naturally concerned above all with the potential threat of a powerful and expanded Soviet Union to the security of Europe and to British interests abroad. The more internationally minded Roosevelt, who had less to fear from Russia as an immediate threat to the United States and its sphere of influence, was reluctantly willing to pursue good relations with Stalin for the sake of international peace and stability. Stalin, for his part, was absolutely determined to prevent any future western invasion of his devastated and exhausted country by gaining control of Eastern Europe, which had already been used three times to invade Russia. The alliance held up, but the seeds of the coming Cold War were sown at Yalta.

Within three months of the Yalta Conference, the war in Europe came to an end. The once mighty German armies, now diminished, exhausted, and in retreat, could no longer sustain the superior military onslaughts from all sides, the devastation of industrial centers and terrorization of the civilian population from the air, and the harassment of enlarged resistance forces now fighting in the open. It was too late for Germany's few newly developed jet aircraft and V1 and V2 rocket-bombs to affect the outcome. In December 1944 Hitler launched one last desperate counteroffensive through the Ardennes, where the Germans had overwhelmed the French four and a half years before. At first, the attack forced the Allies back and opened a large bulge in their lines— hence, the name Battle of the Bulge. But after a few weeks of fierce fighting, the Allies repelled the attack, which only delayed their advance.

By the time the first American troops crossed the Rhine into Germany late in March, the Red Army was already at the outskirts of Berlin. Roosevelt did not live to see the end of the war; he died on April 12, the day after the Americans reached the Elbe. Rather than surrender, Hitler committed suicide on April 30, just as the Red Army was forcing its way into a Berlin that lay in ruins. Churchill urged the Americans to take Berlin and Prague before they fell to the Russians. But Eisenhower, in keeping with Roosevelt's policy of cooperation with the Russians, refused. The Germans surrendered to Eisenhower on May 7, thus ending the Second World War, which had lasted for six terrible years. But Berlin and Prague were occupied by the Russians.

The Allied leaders met again in July and August in Potsdam, where Stalin won new concessions, including the advantageous Oder-Neisse boundary for Poland, which Russia now controlled, and the promise of ten billion dollars in reparations. Germany and the city of Berlin were partitioned into zones of Allied occupation, pending a final peace settlement that was never reached. Europe itself divided into two camps during the next two years as the Western allies drifted steadily apart from Soviet Russia and into a state of Cold War.

The fierce Pacific war came to an abrupt and dreadful end in August 1945 when the new American president, Harry S Truman, made the difficult decision to drop the first newly developed atomic bomb on Hiroshima on August 6 and another on Nagasaki three days later. The Japanese surrendered formally on September 2 to General Douglas MacArthur, commander of the American forces in the Pacific.

The scale of death and devastation in this most destructive of all wars makes the statistics seem almost senseless. Approximately 30 million were dead in Europe alone, and twice that number were homeless. Poland had lost twenty percent of its total population (including Jews), Yugoslavia ten percent, the Soviet Union between 10 and 12 million, and Germany more than 5 million. Hundreds of cities and towns lay in ruins, and transportation and communications systems were all but inoperative. Many countries were on the verge of starvation. Poland, Yugoslavia, Italy, and the Ukraine were kept going only with aid from the United Nations Relief and Rehabilitation Administration. Germany and Austria were able to survive only with the help of the occupying powers. Even victorious Britain and France, by the standards of any previous war, looked like defeated nations. In the summer of 1945, after six years of war, Europe was faced with disease, famine, and economic collapse.

How had supposedly civilized peoples allowed all this to happen? Was it due to a civilization that had temporarily failed to function? Or was there something inherently wrong with that civilization? These frequently asked questions, and the various answers given to them, would divide the world and the West, politically and ideologically, during the grim postwar and cold war years.

BIBLIOGRAPHY

General Works

GILBERT, FELIX. *The End of the European Era, 1890 to the Present.* New York: Norton, 1970.

HARRIS, RONALD W. *The 20th Century: An Historical Introduction.* New York: Harper & Row, 1968.

HUGHES, HENRY S. *Contemporary Europe: A History.* 3d ed. Englewood Cliffs, N. J.: Prentice-Hall, 1971.

PAXTON, ROBERT O. *Europe in the Twentieth Century.* New York: Harcourt Brace Jovanovich, 1975.

First World War

ALBRECHT-CARRIÉ, RENÉ. *The Meaning of the First World War.* Englewood Cliffs, N. J.: Prentice-Hall, 1965.

DEHIO, LUDWIG. *Germany and World Politics in the Twentieth Century.* Translated by D. Pevsner. New York: W. W. Norton & Co., 1967.

FELDMAN, GERALD D. *German Imperialism, 1914–1918.* New York: Wiley, 1972.

FISCHER, FRITZ. *Germany's Aims in the First World War.* Translated by J. Joll. London: Chatto & Windus, 1967.

HOLBORN, HAJO. *The Political Collapse of Europe.* New York: Alfred A. Knopf, 1951.

LAFORE, LAWRENCE. *The Long Fuse.* Philadelphia and New York: J. B. Lippincott Co., 1965.

ROTH, JACK J., ed. *World War I: A Turning Point in Modern History.* New York: Alfred A. Knopf, 1967.

TUCHMAN, BARBARA. *The Guns of August.* New York: Macmillan Co., 1962.

TURNER, LEONARD C. F. *Origins of the First World War.* London: Edward Arnold, 1970.

Russian Revolution

CARR, EDWARD H. *The Bolshevik Revolution.* 3 vols. London: Macmillan and Co., 1950–1953.

DANIELS, ROBERT V. *Red October.* New York: Charles Scribner & Sons, 1967.

NETTL, J. P. *The Soviet Achievement.* New York: Harcourt, Brace & World, 1967.

ULAM, ADAM B. *The Bolsheviks: The Intellectual and Political History of the Triumph of Communism in Russia.* New York and London: Collier, 1965.

WOLFE, BERTRAM D. *Three Who Made a Revolution.* Boston: Beacon Press, 1948.

Dissolution of Old Europe

BIRDSALL, PAUL. *Versailles Twenty Years After.* New York: Reynal & Hitchcock, 1941.

EPSTEIN, KLAUS. *Matthias Erzberger and the Dilemma of German Democracy.* Princeton, N. J.: Princeton University Press, 1959.

KEYNES, JOHN M. *The Economic Consequences of the Peace.* New York: Harcourt, Brace & Howe, 1920.

MANTOUX, ETIENNE. *The Carthaginian Peace.* London: Oxford University Press, 1946.

MAYER, ARNO J. *Politics and Diplomacy of Peacemaking.* New York: Alfred A. Knopf, 1967.

NICOLSON, HAROLD. *Peacemaking, 1919.* London: Constable, 1934.

WALTERS, FRANCIS P. *The League of Nations.* 2 vols. London: Oxford University Press, 1952.

The Twenties: Uncertain Peace

CARR, EDWARD H. *The Twenty Years' Crisis, 1919-1939.* London: Macmillan and Co., 1939.

―――. *International Relations Between the Two Wars.* London: Macmillan and Co., 1948.

CRAIG, GORDON and FELIX GILBERT, eds. *The Diplomats, 1919-1939.* Princeton, N. J.: Atheneum, 1953.

FELIX, DAVID. *Walter Rathenau and the Weimar Republic: The Politics of Reparations.* Baltimore: Johns Hopkins Press, 1971.

GATZKE, HANS W., ed. *European Diplomacy Between Two World Wars, 1918-1939.* Chicago: Quadrangle Books, 1972.

GREENE, NATHANAEL. *From Versailles to Vichy: The Third French Republic, 1919-1940.* New York: Thomas Y. Crowell Co., 1970.

MAIER, CHARLES S. *Recasting Bourgeois Europe: Stabilization in France, Italy, and Germany in the Decade after World War I.* Princeton, N.J.: Princeton University Press, 1975.

SETON-WATSON, HUGH. *Eastern Europe Between the Wars, 1918-1941.* 3d ed. New York: Harper & Row, 1967.

SONTAG, RAYMOND J. *A Broken World, 1919-1939.* New York: Harper & Row, 1971.

Postwar Social Change

CARR, EDWARD H. *The New Society.* London: Macmillan & Co., 1951.

GRAVES, ROBERT and ALAN HODGE. *The Long Week-End: A Social History of Great Britain, 1918-1939.* Rev. ed. New York: Norton, 1963.

HALPERIN, SAMUEL W. *Germany Tried Democracy.* New York: Thomas Y. Crowell Co., 1946.

KULISCHER, EUGENE M. *Europe on the Move: War and Population Changes, 1917-1947.* New York: Columbia University Press, 1948.

LANDES, DAVID S. *The Unbound Prometheus.* Cambridge: University Press, 1969.

ORTEGA Y GASSET, JOSÉ. *The Revolt of the Masses.* New ed. New York: W. W. Norton & Co., 1957.

WILLIAMS, RAYMOND. *The Long Revolution.* London: Chatto & Windus, 1961.

―――. *Communications.* Rev. ed. London: Chatto & Windus, 1966.

Culture of the Twenties

ADORNO, THEODOR W. *Philosophy of Modern Music.* Translated by A. G. Mitchell and W. V. Blamster. New York: Seabury Press, 1973.

ALLEN, WALTER. *Tradition and Dream.* Harmondsworth: Penguin Books, 1964.

ARON, RAYMOND. *The Opium of the Intellectuals.* Translated by T. Kilmartin. New York: W. W. Norton & Co., 1962.

BENDA, JULIEN. *The Treason of the Intellectuals.* New ed. Translated by R. Aldington. New York: W. W. Norton & Co., 1969.

BERGONZI, BERNARD. *Heroes' Twilight.* London: Constable, 1965.

BLACKHAM, HAROLD J. *Six Existentialist Thinkers.* London: Routledge & Kegan Paul, 1953.

FOWLIE, WALLACE. *The Age of Surrealism.* New York: Swallow Press, 1950.

GAY, PETER. *Weimar Culture.* New York: Harper & Row, 1968.

GRAVES, ROBERT. *Goodbye to All That.* Rev. ed. Garden City, N. Y.: Doubleday & Co., 1957.

GREENBERG, CLEMENT. *Art and Culture.* Boston: Beacon Press, 1961.

GURVITCH, GEORGES and WILBERT E. MOORE, eds. *Twentieth-Century Sociology.* New York: The Philosophical Library, 1946.

HEIM, KARL. *The Transformation of the Scientific World View.* New York: Harper, 1953.

HEISENBERG, WERNER. *Physics and Philosophy: The Revolution in Modern Science.* New York: Harper, 1958.

HUGHES, HENRY S. *Oswald Spengler: A Crucial Estimate.* New York: Charles Scribner & Sons, 1952.

JOEDICKE, JURGEN. *A History of Modern Architecture.* Translated by J. C. Palmes. London: Architectural Press, 1959.

JOLL, JAMES. *Three Intellectuals in Politics.* London: Pantheon, 1960.

KRAFT, VIKTOR. *The Vienna Circle.* Translated by A. Pap. New York: The Philosophical Library, 1953.

LAQUEUR, WALTER. *Weimar: A Cultural History, 1918–1933.* New York: G. P. Putnam's Sons, 1974.

LEVITAS, G. B., ed. *The World of Psychoanalysis.* 2 vols. New York: Braziller, 1965.

MEYER, LEONARD B. *Music, the Arts, and Ideas.* Chicago: University of Chicago Press, 1967.

MYERS, ROLLO H., ed. *Twentieth-Century Music.* Rev. ed. London: Calder & Boyars, 1968.

NASH, ARNOLD, ed. *Protestant Thought in the Twentieth Century.* New York: Macmillan Co., 1951.

READ, HERBERT. *Concise History of Modern Painting.* London: Thames & Hudson, 1959.

RIEFF, PHILIP. *Freud: The Mind of the Moralist.* New York: Viking Press, 1959.

ROAZEN, PAUL. *Freud and his Followers.* New York: Alfred A. Knopf, 1971.

SCHRÖDINGER, ERWIN. *What Is Life?* Cambridge: University Press, 1944.

TATON, RENÉ, ed. *Science in the Twentieth Century.* Translated by A. J. Pomerans. London: Thames & Hudson, 1966.

WILSON, EDMUND. *Axel's Castle.* New York: Charles Scribner's Sons, 1931.

The Great Depression

GALBRAITH, JOHN K. *The Great Crash, 1929.* Boston: Houghton Mifflin Co., 1955.

GERSCHENKRON, ALEXANDER. *Bread and Democracy in Germany.* Berkeley and Los Angeles: University of California Press, 1943.

HODSON, HENRY V. *Slump and Recovery, 1929–1937: A Survey of World Economic Affairs.* London: Oxford University Press, 1938.
KINDLEBERGER, CHARLES P. *The World in Depression, 1929–1939.* Berkeley: University of California Press, 1973.
LEWIS, WILLIAM A. *Economic Survey, 1919–1939.* London: Allen & Unwin, 1949.
ORWELL, GEORGE. *The Road to Wigan Pier.* London: Gallancz, 1937.
REES, GORONWY. *The Great Slump: Capitalism in Crisis, 1929–1933.* New York: Harper & Row, 1971.

Fascism

ARENDT, HANNAH. *The Origins of Totalitarianism.* New York: Meridian Books, 1958.
BUCHHEIM, HANS. *Totalitarian Rule. Its Nature and Characteristics.* Translated by R. Hein. Middletown, Conn.: Wesleyan University Press, 1968.
CARSTON, FRANCIS L. *The Rise of Fascism.* London: Batsford, 1967.
FRIEDRICH, CARL J., ed. *Totalitarianism.* Cambridge, Mass.: Harvard University Press, 1954.
NOLTE, ERNST. *Three Faces of Fascism.* Translated by L. Vennewitz. New York: Holt, Rinehart & Winston, 1966.
ROGGER, HANS and WEBER, EUGEN, eds. *The European Right.* Berkeley and Los Angeles: University of California Press, 1966.
WEISS, JOHN. *The Fascist Tradition.* New York: Harper & Row, 1967.
WISKEMANN, ELIZABETH. *Europe of the Dictators, 1919–1945.* London: Collins, 1966.

Italy

CASSELS, ALAN. *Fascist Italy.* New York: Thomas Y. Crowell Co., 1968.
CHABOD, FEDERICO. *A History of Italian Fascism.* Translated by M. Grindrod. London: Weidenfeld & Nicolson, 1963.
FINER, HERMAN. *Mussolini's Italy.* London: Gollancz, 1935.
SALVEMINI, GAETANO. *Under the Axe of Fascism.* New York: Viking Press, 1936.
TANNENBAUM, EDWARD R. *The Fascist Experience: Italian Society and Culture, 1922–1945.* New York: Basic Books, 1972.

Germany

BRACHER, KARL-DIETRICH. *The German Dictatorship.* Translated by J. Steinberg. New York: Praeger, 1970.
BULLOCK, ALAN. *Hitler: A Study in Tyranny.* London: Odhams Press, 1952.
FEST, JOACHIM. *Hitler.* Translated by R. and C. Winston. New York: Harcourt Brace Jovanovich, 1974.
HERZSTEIN, ROBERT E., ed. *Adolf Hitler and the Third Reich, 1933–1945.* Boston: Houghton Mifflin Co., 1971.

JARMAN, T. L. *The Rise and Fall of Nazi Germany.* New York: Signet, 1956.

KOGON, EUGEN. *The Theory and Practice of Hell.* Translated by H. Norden. London: Secker & Warburg, 1950.

MASER, WERNER. *Hitler: Legend, Myth, and Reality.* Translated by P. and B. Ross. New York: Harper & Row, 1973.

MOSSE, GEORGE L. *The Crisis of German Ideology: Intellectual Origins of the Third Reich.* New York: Grosset & Dunlap, 1964.

————, ed. *Nazi Culture.* New York: Grosset & Dunlap, 1966.

NEUMANN, FRANZ. *Behemoth: The Structure and Practice of National Socialism.* Rev. ed. New York: Harper & Row, 1966.

STERN, FRITZ. *The Politics of Cultural Despair.* Berkeley and Los Angeles: University of California Press, 1961.

The Popular Front

BROWER, DANIEL R. *The New Jacobins.* Ithaca, N. Y.: Cornell University Press, 1968.

DALBY, LOUISE E. *Léon Blum: Evolution of a Socialist.* New York: Yoseloff, 1963.

GREENE, NATHANAEL. *Crisis and Decline: The French Socialist Party in the Popular Front.* Ithaca, N. Y.: Cornell University Press, 1969.

KRIEGEL, ANNIE. *The French Communists: Profile of a People.* Translated by E. P. Halperin. Chicago: University of Chicago Press, 1972.

LARMOUR, PETER. *The French Radical Party in the 1930's.* Stanford, Calif.: Stanford University Press, 1964.

The Spanish Civil War

BRENAN, GERALD. *The Spanish Labyrinth.* 2d ed. Cambridge: University Press, 1960.

BROUÉ, PIERRE and EMILE TÉMIME. *The Revolution and the Civil War in Spain.* Translated by T. White. London: Faber & Faber, 1972.

CARR, RAYMOND, ed. *The Republic and the Civil War in Spain.* New York: St. Martin's Press, 1971.

JACKSON, GABRIEL. *The Spanish Republic and the Civil War, 1931-1939.* Princeton, N. J.: Princeton University Press, 1965.

PAYNE, STANLEY G. *The Spanish Revolution.* New York: W. W. Norton & Co., 1970.

THOMAS, HUGH. *The Spanish Civil War.* New York: Harper & Row, 1961.

Russia Under Stalin

CONQUEST, ROBERT. *The Great Terror: Stalin's Purge of the Thirties.* New York: Macmillan Co., 1968.

LEWIN, MOSHÉ. *Russian Peasants and Soviet Power.* Translated by I. Nove. London: Allen & Unwin, 1968.

MEDVEDEV, ROY. *Let History Judge: The Origins and Consequences of Stalinism.* Translated by C. Taylor. New York: Alfred A. Knopf, 1971.

MOORE, BARRINGTON JR., *Soviet Politics: The Dilemma of Power.* Cambridge, Mass.: Harvard University Press, 1950.

TUCKER, ROBERT C. *Stalin as Revolutionary, 1873–1929: A Study in History and Personality.* New York: W. W. Norton & Co., 1973.

ULAM, ADAM B. *Stalin: The Man and his Era.* New York: Viking Press, 1973.

The Gathering Storm

EUBANK, KEITH. *The Origins of World War II.* New York: Thomas Y. Crowell Co., 1969.

ROWSE, ALFRED L. *Appeasement: A Study in Political Decline, 1933–1939.* New York: W. W. Norton & Co., 1961.

SALVEMINI, GAETANO. *Prelude to World War II.* London: Gollancz, 1951.

SCHUSCHNIGG, KURT. *Austrian Requiem.* Translated by F. Von Hildebrand. New York: G. P. Putnam's Sons, 1946.

TAYLOR, ALAN J. P. *The Origins of the Second World War.* London: Hamilton, 1961.

WHEELER-BENNETT, JOHN H. *Munich: Prologue to Tragedy.* New York: Duell, Sloan and Pearce, 1948.

―――. The Nemesis of Power: *The German Army in Politics, 1918–1945.* New York: St. Martin's Press, 1954.

WISKEMANN, ELIZABETH. *The Rome-Berlin Axis.* New York: Oxford, 1949.

Culture of the Thirties

CAUDWELL, CHRISTOPHER. *Studies and Further Studies in a Dying Culture.* New York: Monthly Review Press, 1971.

CAUTE, DAVID. *Communism and the French Intellectuals.* New York: Macmillan Co., 1964.

CROSSMAN, R. H. S., ed. *The God that Failed.* London: Hamilton, 1950.

HUGHES, HENRY S. *The Obstructed Path: French Social Thought in the Years of Desperation, 1930–1960.* New York: Harper & Row, 1966.

KOESTLER, ARTHUR. *Arrow in the Blue.* New York: Macmillan Co., 1953.

―――. *The Invisible Writing.* New York: Macmillan Co., 1954.

―――. *Darkness at Noon.* Translated by D. Hardy. London: Cape, 1940.

LUKÁCS, GEORG. *Realism in our Time.* Translated by J. and N. Mander. New York: Harper & Row, 1964.

SYMONS, JULIAN, ed. *The 1930's.* London: Cresset, 1960.

WOOD, NEAL. *Communism and British Intellectuals.* London: Gollancz, 1959.

The Second World War

BLOCH, MARC A. *Strange Defeat.* Translated by G. Hopkins. London: Oxford University Press, 1948.

CALVOCORESSI, PETER and WINT, GUY. *Total War.* New York: Pantheon Books, 1972.

CHURCHILL, WINSTON S. *The Second World War.* 6 vols. Boston: Bantam Books, 1948–54.

DAWIDOWICZ, LUCY S. *The War Against the Jews, 1933–1945.* New York: Holt, Rinehart & Winston, 1975.

FEIS, HERBERT. *Churchill, Roosevelt,Stalin: The War They Waged and the Peace They Sought.* Princeton, N. J.: Princeton University Press, 1957.

LIDDELL-HART, BASIL H. *The History of the Second World War.* New York: G. P. Putnam's Sons, 1971.

MICHEL, HENRI. *The Shadow War: The European Resistnace, 1939–1945.* Translated by R. Barry. New York: Harper & Row, 1972.

TREVOR-ROPER, HUGH R. *The Last Days of Hitler.* New York: Collier, 1947.

WERTH, ALEXANDER. *Russia at War, 1941–1945.* New York: Avon Books, 1964.

WILMOT, CHESTER. *The Struggle for Europe.* London: Collins, 1952.

WRIGHT, GORDON. *The Ordeal of Total War, 1939–1945.* New York: Harper & Row, 1968.

SINCE THE SECOND WORLD WAR: THE CONTEMPORARY EXPERIENCE

THE COLD WAR, 1945–1953

The most important results of the Second World War were the emergence of the United States and the Soviet Union as superpowers and the political and ideological conflict between them that in 1947 came to be known as the Cold War. These developments had been set in motion by the First World War and the Russian Revolution. But neither the United States nor the Soviet Union had been prepared between the wars to assume the role of world leader. Russia was in the midst of its third Five-Year Plan when the Second World War broke out, and Stalin signed the Nazi-Soviet Pact in 1939 to gain badly needed time to prepare for an eventual German invasion. Roosevelt, although personally sympathetic to Britain and France, had promised to keep America out of the war, and American public opinion remained predominantly isolationist until Japan's surprise attack on Pearl Harbor in 1941. During the war, the Allies were too preoccupied with defeating Hitler to formulate any long-range postwar objectives. Only toward the end of the war, at the Yalta and Potsdam Conferences in 1945, did the question of the postwar reorganization of Europe and the underlying differences among the Allies came to the fore. By then, it was clear that the political future of the West and the world would depend largely on Moscow and Washington and the relations between them.

Stalin's primary concern in 1945 was the security of the Soviet Union, which could only be guaranteed, he insisted at Yalta and Potsdam, if the Eastern European countries bordering the Soviet Union were friendly, But these countries had been created by the peace treaties that ended the First World War precisely to serve as an anti-Soviet buffer zone. Poland had attempted to seize the Ukraine during the Russian civil war and had been used twice by the Germans as the invasion route to Russia. Moreover, Finland, Rumania, and Hungary had joined the Germans in making war on Russia in 1941. Once the Red Army succeeded in ridding Eastern Europe of the Germans and occupying it, Stalin had no intention of relinquishing control over this volatile region and returning to the prewar status quo.

Between 1945 and 1947, Moscow permitted coalition governments, called National Fronts, to be established in Eastern Europe; they were made up of Communists, Social Democrats, and popular agrarian peasant parties. These National Front governments attempted to combine a policy of cooperation with the Soviet Union with a comparatively large measure of national autonomy and freedom. But in 1947, as relations between Stalin and his wartime allies rapidly deteriorated, he decided upon tighter control of eastern Europe. All of the countries occupied by Russian troops—Poland, Czechoslovakia, Hungary, Rumania, Bulgaria, and East Germany (known after 1949 as the German Democratic Republic)—were brought under one-party Communist governments controlled by Moscow. Under these new regimes, which called themselves Peoples' Democracies, the countries of Eastern Europe were quickly absorbed into the Soviet political, economic, and military system. The only country to escape this fate was Yugoslavia, headed by Marshal Tito, the Communist leader of the Yugoslav partisans, who had liberated his country without Russian assistance, and who successfully resisted in 1948 Russian interference in his own one-party Communist government. Tito's success in adopting an independent course infuriated Stalin and made him all the more determined to prevent any other Eastern European country from defecting from his newly formed Soviet bloc.

Roosevelt pinned his hopes for the reorganization of the Western and world political order on the continuation of the wartime alliance and on the ability of the United Nations, which came into being in 1945, to mediate international disputes. Roosevelt was willing to concede Soviet domination of Eastern Europe, which was after all an accomplished fact by the end of the war. But he expected in turn that Stalin would accept the principle of international consultation and cooperate with his wartime allies in the recovery of postwar Europe. He also expected that Britain and France would cooperate with the United States in the reconstruction of Western Europe.

However, much changed between Roosevelt's death in April 1945 and the Potsdam Conference in July, which was attended by Truman. For one thing, Churchill, who had mediated effectively between Stalin and Roosevelt throughout the war, was voted out of office and was replaced at the conference by the Labour leader, Clement Atlee. The appearance of two new inexperienced political leaders at Potsdam only heightened the mutual distrust between them and Stalin. The tension was also increased by the fact that Stalin had adamantly refused to yield to the Anglo-American demand to include some members of the Polish government in exile in the new Communist government of Poland unilaterally chosen by Stalin himself. A third change was that the United States had successfully exploded its first experimental atomic bomb the day before the conference began, which gave Truman a strong hand in the negotiations. But the primary source of tension at Potsdam was the old ideological conflict between capitalism and communism and the emerging political rivalry between the two new superpowers for global supremacy in the wake of the violent collapse of the European powers and Japan.

The immediate issue, which most seriously divided Moscow and Washington, was the reorganization of postwar Germany. All of the Allies agreed that Germany must be demilitarized and its wartime leaders punished. All agreed that Germany must be occupied and pay reparations. But they differed over the amount of reparations and the future status of Germany. Russia and France demanded heavy reparations and a permanently weakened Germany. Britain and the United States favored milder reparations and a restoration of Germany to economic self-sufficiency and eventual political participation in general European affairs. Just before the Potsdam Conference, the four Allied powers moved into their respective occupation zones, agreed upon at the Yalta Conference. They had also agreed at the Yalta Conference that Berlin, which lay within the Soviet zone, would be occupied jointly by all four Allied powers.

A single unified Allied Control Commission was supposed to coordinate the four occupation zones. But almost immediately they went their separate ways. The Soviet occupying authorities proceeded to strip their Eastern zone of most of its industrial equipment, planning to use it in the reconstruction of their own ravaged country. They also operated their zone as a self-contained economic entity, which violated the agreement that Germany was to be treated as a single economic unit. The United States retaliated by reneging on Roosevelt's promise to the Russians at Yalta that they could draw reparations from the American zone. The Americans also moved to strengthen their zone in Berlin and the American presence there. Early in 1947, the British and Americans, over Russian protests, united their zones into a single economic unit, and a year later France joined them. In 1948—again, over Russian protests—the three Western Allies agreed to work toward a political constitution for all of Western Germany. By now, even the pretense of a unified four-power occupation had come to an end.

The German crisis came to a head in the summer of 1948, when the Russians, retaliating against the plan of the Western Allies to form a separate West German government, cut off all ground transportation to Berlin. The Western Allies responded by organizing a massive airlift into Berlin that lasted almost a year, until the Russians called off the blockade. Berlin itself had little military or strategic value. But it was, and would remain, important as a symbol. To the Russians, the presence of the other three occupying powers in Berlin, which lay deep inside Soviet-occupied Germany, symbolized Western hostility to the Soviet Union and a thorn in the side of the Soviet zone. To the Western Allies, the Berlin airlift symbolized their joint cooperation in Germany and their determination not to be bullied. The airlift was successful, but it greatly intensified the cold war. Any hope for the unification of Germany was now extinguished. The western Federal Republic of Germany became a sovereign state in September 1949. The eastern German Democratic Republic was proclaimed a month later.

The conflict between the United States and the Soviet Union in Germany was only one episode in the rapidly escalating cold war. As the Russians tightened their hold on Eastern Europe and began to shift from a defensive to an expansionist foreign policy, the Americans intervened increasingly in Western Europe, the eastern Mediterranean, and eventually everywhere throughout the noncommunist world. This permanent American involvement in Western European and world affairs was further stimulated by the fact that Britain and France were no longer strong enough to resume their role as world powers. The British, who had been fighting the Communists in Greece since 1944, were forced to turn over to the Americans the responsibility of protecting Greece and Turkey from increasing Soviet and domestic Communist pressure. In requesting funds from Congress in March 1947 to aid these two strategically important countries, Truman took the opportunity to issue a statement that became, and has since remained, the cornerstone of American foreign policy. The Truman Doctrine, as it was called, committed the United States publicly to "support free peoples who are resisting attempted subjugation by armed minorities or by outside pressures"—which meant in effect American intervention anywhere in the world that threatened to come under Communist control.

The economic counterpart of the Truman Doctrine was the Marshall Plan, a massive aid program designed to hasten Europe's postwar recovery, conceived by Secretary of State George C. Marshall. Originally, the

Marshall Plan offered aid to all European countries, regardless of ideology, provided that the recipient countries would coordinate their proposals to make maximum use of the American assistance. The Soviets viewed the Marshall Plan simply as a cold war maneuver aimed at drawing any nation that accepted it into the American sphere of influence. Accordingly, most of the Eastern European nations refused to participate. The exceptions were Poland and Czechoslovakia. When they agreed to participate, the Soviet Union quickly stepped in to prevent it. Thus, when the Marshall Plan went into effect in 1948, it was a strictly Western European program, which benefited the recipient countries enormously during the four years it remained in effect. But the Marshall Plan, and the Soviet reaction to it, also served to harden the lines between East and West.

By the end of 1947, both superpowers viewed the cold war as a crusade. The Russians accused the Americans of encirclement and of obstructing the Soviet Union's legitimate defensive foreign policy. The Americans accused the Soviet Union of expansionism and repression of the countries it occupied. The Russians were alarmed by the stiffening attitude of the Allies in Germany and by the Truman Doctrine, the Marshall Plan, and American military aid to Greece and Turkey. They retaliated, late in 1947 and 1948, by replacing all multiparty regimes in Eastern Europe with one-party Communist rule and setting up the Berlin Blockade. These actions alarmed the United States and Western Europe into forming a military alliance against the Soviet Union in 1949. This alliance of twelve states, called the North Atlantic Treaty Organization (NATO), faced 250 Russian divisions in Eastern Europe, which organized into the Warsaw Pact in 1955. By 1950, Europe was permanently divided into two armed camps on the brink of a third world war.

The cold war expanded beyond Europe in June 1950, when Communist North Korea invaded South Korea, which was supported by the United States. Truman immediately sent military aid to the South Koreans, which led to American involvement in an Asian land war that would last three years. Public opinion in the non-Communist world at first approved the American intervention; it seemed to show America's willingness to defend its allies. The United Nations voted to support the intervention, and several Western European countries sent troops to assist the American forces.

However, once the North Koreans were driven back and the Americans invaded their territory, causing Communist China to intervene, Europeans began to have second thoughts. They feared that the Korean War might escalate into a world war, which would involve them against their will. The Korean War was also having an inflationary effect on their recovering economies. In addition, the United States, appearing ever more militant, began to urge the rearmament of Germany. The idea of rearming Germany only five years after Hitler was distasteful to most Germans as well as to other Europeans. American economic aid to Europe was also becoming increasingly military aid. But because the Western European countries were economically dependent on the United States, they reluctantly agreed to form a new multinational military organization, called the European Defense Community (EDC), which would include German forces. The EDC only increased tension within Europe and between Europe and America. However, since none of the participating countries were willing to relinquish authority over their armed forces, the EDC proved unsuccessful.

The Korean War marked a new low in East-West relations. The Kremlin was becoming convinced that Washington was planning a war against the Soviet Union itself. The aging Stalin was becoming suspicious of everyone around him. He accused several doctors, most of whom were Jewish, of trying to poison Soviet leaders. He accused Jewish Communist leaders of sympathizing with Israel and its Western supporters. Between 1950 and 1952, Stalin again purged the Eastern European governments of leaders suspected of ideological deviations. The purge of the Czechoslovak government was especially severe. In Western Europe, conservatism and militant nationalism were gaining ground. Anti-Communist feeling was reaching almost hysterical proportions in the United States. Loyalty oaths were required of government employees. The House Un-American Activities Committee (HUAC), chaired by the rabid anti-Communist, Senator Joseph R. McCarthy, conducted widely publicized hearings that ruined the lives and careers of hundreds of decent and loyal American citizens and poisoned the American political atmosphere for many years to come. In a trial that has remained controversial since it took place in 1950, Julius and Ethel Rosenberg were convicted of passing atomic secrets to Soviet agents and were the first in American history to be executed for treason. By the end of 1952, it seemed, on both sides of the iron curtain, that a third world war was inevitable.

European Recovery

When the Second World War ended, most Europeans did not want to return to the prewar political and economic order, which the war and the depression had discredited. At the same time, they were far too war-weary and preoccupied with survival to think in terms of sweeping social change or experimentation. Most Europeans in 1945 yearned for peace, security, reconciliation, democracy, the restoration of individual freedom, and governments willing and able to achieve these goals.

POLITICAL RECOVERY   Many Europeans expected that the resistance movements, which had led the fight against fascism and were at the height of their popularity in 1945, would provide Europe's postwar political leadership. The resistance movements, inspired by the Popular Front of the thirties, had successfully unified Communists, Socialists, liberals, and Christians in a common cause. Their leaders also were young and dedicated to the ideals of social justice, individual rights, reconciliation between social classes, and nonsectarian politics.

The resistance movements, however, had little impact on the reorganization of postwar Europe. The only exceptions were Yugoslavia, where the partisan leader, Marshal Tito, became and remained head of the government, and France, where De Gaulle briefly headed the postwar provisional government until he resigned in 1946. One reason why the resistance movements quickly faded from the political scene was that their leaders were politically inexperienced and no match for professional politicians under the new and unfamiliar conditions of peacetime. Many resistance leaders were not politicians at all and only wished to return to private life. A second reason was that the resistance movements, although popular, remained minorities and did not reflect the broad range of public opinion. Many Europeans in 1945 were disgusted with politics and politicians in general, regardless of ideology. Another reason was that the old antagonisms between Communists and non-Communists within the resistance movements began to reemerge once the war was over. Finally, any possibility of Europe's steering an independent course disappeared when the cold war opened in force in 1947.

The resistance movements failed to provide new leadership. But they did inspire the idea of cooperation among the three political groups which dominated postwar Europe: the new Christian Democrats and the older Communist and Socialist parties. The Christian Democrats were strongest in Italy, France, and southern Germany. They appealed especially to Catholics, who wished to unite their religion with social and economic reforms. The religious emphasis of the Christian Democrats enabled them to gain the support of Christians of all social backgrounds, workers and bourgeois alike, many of whom regarded Christianity as the only effective ideological bulwark against communism. The Christian Democrats also appealed to conservatives, whose parties had been discredited by the war, and who viewed the Christian Democrats as the lesser of the existing political evils. Under Konrad Adenauer, a mayor of Cologne in the 1920s and a proven anti-Nazi, the Christian Democrats governed West Germany from 1949 to 1969. The Italian Christian Democratic party, led by Alcide De Gasperi until 1953, controlled every Italian government for thirty years after the liberation. The Christian Democratic party in France, called the Popular Republican Movement (MRP), was founded in 1944 by followers of De Gaulle and remained powerful until the early fifties.

The Communists emerged from the war for the first time as a major force in Western European politics. One reason for their popularity was the prestige they had gained as leaders of the resistance. The hardships of the war and postwar economic deprivations also pushed large numbers of Western Europeans into the Communist camp, especially the poor and the working classes, who were no longer content with moderate Socialist solutions to their problems. Communism also appealed to many intellectuals and young people, who were disillusioned with capitalism and parliamentary politics, and who generally knew communism only in its moderate wartime form as an anti-Fascist force working with non-Communist anti-Fascists for national liberation. Moreover, the Western European Communist parties, in accordance with Soviet policy, put aside social revolution and participated, until 1947, in coalition governments, which included Socialists and Christian Democrats, just as Communists participated in the coalition National Front governments of Eastern Europe. With the escalation of the cold war in 1947, Communists were forced out of the French and Italian national governments, which allowed these governments to come under the control of the conservative Christian Democrats. But the Communist parties remained strong in both countries, and communists continued to be elected to local offices.

ECONOMIC RECOVERY   The most pressing problem Europeans faced after the war was the awesome task of economic recovery. Although military casualties had been higher in the First World War, the Second World War took a much heavier toll on the civilian population and its productive capacity. Most major European cities, industrial centers, and transportation and communication systems lay in ruins in 1945. Hunger and famine were widespread throughout the continent, and mass starvation was averted in such countries as Italy and Yugoslavia only through emergency aid provided by the occupying powers and United Nations relief agencies. Millions of homeless refugees and prisoners of war were forced to take refuge in dismal displaced persons camps. The numbers of uprooted were swelled by millions of Germans expelled from their ancestral homes in the Sudetenland and east of the Oder-Neisse line. In many parts of Europe, goods were so scarce and inflation so rampant that people resorted to barter. The black market flourished. Some members of the resistance movements viewed the end of the war as an opportunity to take revenge on wartime collaborators. Gangs of homeless youths, who had known little but violence and poverty in their young lives, roamed the streets of large cities. Europeans on both sides of the ideological divide were also growing anxious about their political future. But the overriding concern of most Europeans in 1945 was survival, and few thought at the time that life would return to normal within the generation.

The economic recovery of Europe, like its political recovery, took place within the context of the cold war. Between 1945 and 1947, before the cold war opened in force, the pace of reconstruction was very slow. Without outside help, European governments could do little to check inflation, control the black market, stabilize currencies, regulate wages and prices, or stimulate production. Not until the United States initiated the Marshall Plan in 1947 did Western Europe begin to emerge from the economic chaos that engulfed it. Moreover, Western Europeans still possessed the technological know-how and knowledge of managing an advanced industrial society that enabled them to rebuild their economies more swiftly and successfully than anyone had originally anticipated. During the seven years that the Marshall Plan remained in effect, from 1947 to 1954, Western Europeans were able to turn every dollar of the $12 billion provided by the United States into six dollars of capital formation. By 1954, Western Europe was well on its way to prosperity. By contrast, the Eastern European countries, which were burdened by heavy reparations to the Soviet Union and the reintegration of their economies into the Soviet bloc, would not experience a measure of prosperity until the 1960s. Thus, the very conditions under which the economic reconstruction of Europe took place served to widen the gulf between East and West.

The Great Depression and the Second World War convinced most Europeans that some degree of government planning and regulation was necessary to achieve world peace and social and economic stability. Most agreed that the well-being of society could no longer be left up to volatile and expansionist free market economies. Consequently, welfare governments came into being throughout Western Europe during the early postwar years. The British electorate soundly defeated Churchill's Conservative government in 1945 and voted in Clement Atlee's Labour party, which remained in power until 1951.

The first priorities of the new British government were full employment, a comprehensive social security system, a national health program, and nationalization of the basic coal, steel, and transportation industries. But postwar Britain faced problems that any government would have found difficult. One major difficulty was that the two world wars had greatly reduced Britain's accumulation of overseas investment and had left the country short of capital to pay for the food, fuel, and raw materials that it had to import. Heavy military expenditures to preserve overseas possessions also held back Britain's economic recovery. Another difficulty was that the British people were less willing than they had been during the war to suffer the shortages and sacrifices necessary to keep their economy solvent. The obsolescence of industrial equipment and the lack of willingness and capital to replace or improve it also hindered Britain's economic recovery. The authority of the Labour government was further weakened by frequent strikes in basic industries, and by constant Conservative opposition to its policies.

All of these difficulties enabled the Conservatives to win the 1951 election and subsequently to return the steel and road transport industries to private enterprise. But the Conservatives retained most of the welfare programs initiated by the Labour party, and the coal and railroad industries remained nationalized. Even these changes, however, did little to solve Britain's underlying economic problems.

The continental Western European countries were more successful than Britain in dealing with their postwar economic problems. For one thing, the more complete destruction of their industrial facilities left them little choice but to rebuild from scratch, using the most modern technology. For another, the more desperate plight of their populations acted as a stimulus to greater cooperation among the social classes and political parties. The continental countries of Western Europe were also better able to provide for their own agricultural needs, and their economies were less dependent on imported raw materials. Their military expenditures were also lower than Britain's—in fact, almost nothing in defeated Italy and West Germany. Not least, they had at their disposal an abundant supply of cheap and willing labor.

France, Italy, and West Germany used American aid to modernize their industrial equipment and to create mixed economies based on extensive government planning and stimulation of the private sectors of the economy. Immediately after the war, the French Provisional Government nationalized the coal, steel, and utilities industries, the largest insurance companies, the Bank of France, and the Renault automobile firm. Nationalization ended in 1946, however, and the governments of the Fourth Republic, which lasted from 1946 to 1958, left most production in private hands. Government planning agencies were created to coordinate the public and private sectors of the economy and to encourage growth in basic industries. Extensive welfare programs, started during the Popular Front era, were also enacted. Under the leadership of the Christian Democrat Robert Schuman, who became prime minister in 1947, France raised its level of production by 1952 fourteen percent higher than what it had been in 1938. Despite the many changes of government in postwar France, state planning and welfare became and remained permanent features of French life.

In Italy, the state exercised even greater control over the economy than it did in France and Britain. It also enacted the most far-reaching welfare programs in all of Western Europe. De Gasperi's Christian Democratic government refrained from nationalizing industries, but it retained regulatory power over the whole economy. The most serious problem of postwar Italy was the poverty and economic backwardness of the south, which the government attempted to remedy by breaking up some of the large estates and redistributing the land to the peasants. This reform fell far short of De Gasperi's original intention, since it provided for the needs of only a small number of the landless poor. But it was an important first step in improving the economy of the agrarian south and bringing it into line with the industrial north. By 1952, production and income levels in Italy, as in France, stood well above what they had been before the war.

The most dramatic postwar recovery occurred in West Germany, which within a decade rose from rubble to become the wealthiest nation in Western Europe. The "economic miracle," as the Germans called it, was carried out by the Christian Democratic government of Konrad Adenauer, chancellor from 1949 to 1963, and his able economics minister, Ludwig Erhard. Several factors, not all of them purely economic, contributed to this remarkable revival. One was that the Germans were an energetic and disciplined people accustomed to efficient, although paternalistic, government and efficient bureaucratic management. These qualities had played an important role earlier in the rise of Germany to the status of world power and would serve the Germans well again in rebuilding their country after the Second World War. Another stimulus to West Germany's rapid recovery was that most Germans, regardless of their political allegiances under the Third Reich, associated the Nazis with defeat and national disgrace. They were eager, therefore, to put that reputation behind them as quickly as possible and acquire a new and internationally respectable reputation. Most Germans also realized in 1945 that they could no longer steer an independent course. The division of Germany and the conditions of the cold war left West Germany little choice but to integrate into the Western bloc.

In contrast to the other major Western European countries, the Germans, who had lived under rigid Nazi economic management, were eager to return to a competitive private enterprise system. Instead of imposing controls, therefore, Adenauer's government adopted a system of incentives to encourage private investment and rewards for overtime work. At the same time, the government expanded the social security programs, begun under Bismarck, and increased government planning and public investment. But the heart of West Germany's recovery was the revival of its mighty industrial capacity, which was left largely in private hands. Under the conditions of the cold war, West Germany's Western allies, especially the United States, encouraged this development, and they abandoned their efforts to limit the German economy and to break up its giant economic units. They also left the lower echelons of the trained prewar bureaucracies largely intact. The West Germans were also not burdened by military development, colonial wars, or unrealistic reparations. By the mid-fifties, West Germany emerged as the economic showplace of Western Europe, appearing in sharp contrast to impoverished East Germany, which was headed, between 1945 and 1969, by the Moscow-trained Communist party secretary, Walter Ulbricht.

The Korean War and the rapid economic recovery of Western Europe encouraged a trend toward conservative government, which became apparent in the elections of the early fifties. In the British election of 1951, the Conservatives narrowly defeated the Labour party, and Winston Churchill returned to power for the last time. In the French election of the same year, the MRP and the Socialists lost ground to parties of the Right. In the Italian and West German elections of 1953, the Christian Democrats remained dominant, but they had become increasingly the parties of the wealthy business and landowning classes and had abandoned their former interest in political and economic reform. In the United States, the Republican presidential candidate, Dwight D. Eisenhower, was elected in 1952 after twenty years of Democratic administration. This swing to conservatism did not signify a revival of the desperate reactionary forces of the 1930s. Rather, it was a reaction to the worsening relations between East and West, a manifestation of American political and economic penetration of Western Europe, and a vote of confidence in the modified form of capitalism under which the Western world was prospering for the first time since the Great Depression.

Co-Existence and Prosperity, 1953–1963

Several events occurred in 1953 that had the effect of easing international tensions. One was the death of Stalin, which kindled the hope, on both sides of the iron curtain, that relations between East and West might now improve. Another was the Soviet Union's production of a hydrogen bomb, which broke the United States' monopoly on nuclear weapons and aroused the hope among Europeans that the new balance of terror, as some called it, would reduce the chance of war between the superpowers. The three-year-old Korean War also came to an end in 1953, and Senator McCarthy's shrill campaign against communism subsided. Perhaps the most psychologically reassuring development that year was the acceleration of the postwar recovery into an economic boom, which gave Western Europeans a new sense of self-confidence and well-being. These events by no means eliminated international tensions—the cold war has continued to wax and wane down to the present day. But they did open up, for the first time since the Second World War, the prospect of peaceful coexistence and a new era of stability and prosperity.

The relaxation of the cold war and the economic boom that started in the early fifties reinforced the trend in the Western world toward conservative government. Western Europe of the fifties and early sixties was the Europe of Winston Churchill and his Conservative successors: Anthony Eden, Harold Macmillan, and Alec Douglas-Home in Britain; of Alcide De Gasperi and his Christian Democratic followers in Italy; and of Konrad Adenauer in West Germany. In France, the collapse of the unstable Fourth Republic at the end of the fifties brought back to power the paternalistic war hero, Charles de Gaulle, who would rule France under an authoritarian constitution from 1958 to 1969. For the United States, the fifties was the era of Eisenhower's Republican administration, which was more inclined than Truman's previous Democratic administration to accept the political status quo in Europe.

Conservative governments were popular in the West because of their ability to foster and sustain prosperity and their appeal to the revived middle classes. In Britain, Churchill and his Conservative successors retained most of the nationalization and social welfare legislation enacted by the postwar Labour government. But they also eliminated unnecessary economic controls and austerity measures caused by the war. This combination of social welfare programs, government control of basic industries, and the lifting of restrictions on private enterprise resulted in the first real prosperity that Britain had known since 1914. The return of prosperity enabled the Conservatives to remain in power for thirteen consecutive years, during which time the Labour party steadily declined.

In West Germany, the "economic miracle" enabled Konrad Adenauer and his Christian Democrats to increase their plurality with each election, and they achieved an absolute majority in the election of 1957. Under Christian Democratic leadership, the West German economy emerged as the most powerful in Western Europe and served as an example and endorsement of relatively unrestricted capitalism. During the Korean War, West Germany became a member of NATO and in 1955 was permitted to rebuild its armed forces. Faced with sweeping Christian Democratic election victories, the declining Social Democratic party abandoned its Marxist heritage and in 1959 adopted a new program, accepting the remilitarization of Germany and deemphasizing class conflict and the nationalization of German industry. In 1956, Adenauer felt secure enough to outlaw the Communist party, depriving a minority of its right to be represented in government at all for the next thirteen years.

In contrast to Britain and West Germany, Italy and France were pushed toward conservatism by a series of government crises that disrupted both countries during the fifties. Both countries had multiparty political systems; in neither was a single party strong enough to win a clear parliamentary majority or to form a stable coalition government.

The Christian Democrats were by far the strongest party in Italy, but they were too weak to govern alone. After De Gasperi's death in 1954, five coalition governments came and went in as many years. The Christian Democrats were also plagued by internal dissent. One faction, headed by the party's most dynamic leader, Amintore Fanfani, favored an alliance with Pietro Nenni's Socialist party, which had broken with communism after the Hungarian uprising in 1956 and grew into Italy's third largest party. The other faction, supported by business interests and the Vatican, steadfastly resisted Fanfani's proposal for an "opening to the Left," which could have produced a secure coalition government with a popular reform program. Instead, the conservative faction preferred to rule with the support of the right-wing Monarchists and Neo-Fascists. The conservative faction held the upper hand until 1960, when a series of left-wing demonstrations, protesting the government's authoritarianism and tolerance of neo-fascism, toppled the ministry. Fanfani was now able to form a new government with a slightly broader political base. But the Socialists did not become full participants in the government until 1963. The main effect of this belated opening to the Left, however, was to intensify the factionalism that would continue to plague Italian politics throughout the sixties.

Political strife also divided France under the Fourth Republic. Conservatives came to power in France in the election of 1951. But they were not strong enough to rule alone, and they encountered constant opposition from the Communists and Socialists. Moreover, France was embroiled in colonial wars in Indochina (1945–54) and in Algeria (1954–62), which sapped the country's resources and increased political tension. France's humiliating defeat in Indochina in 1954 created a crisis that brought Guy Mollet's Socialist party to power in the election of 1956. But the Socialists were no better able to rule alone than the Conservatives; the Conservatives, embittered by the French defeat in Indochina, were determined to avoid a repetition in Algeria. The death blow to the Fourth Republic came in 1958 when the French army in North Africa seized control of Algiers in defiance of the legitimate government in Paris. In the midst of this crisis, the ever-popular De Gaulle emerged from retirement and declared himself ready to form a new government.

De Gaulle was the one man who could provide unity, and it was unity above all that most of the French people wanted after twelve years of political strife and instability. De Gaulle was a vigorous leader deeply dedicated to restoring France to prosperity and national greatness. In 1962, he broke the Algerian insurrection and extricated France from the last of its colonial involvements. Now he was free to move forward with the economic and technological modernization of his country.

De Gaulle also believed in a united and independent Europe strong enough to stand up politically, economically, and militarily to the two superpowers—a Europe in which France would play the leading role. In pursuit of this rather unrealistic goal, he proposed a close alliance with Adenauer, developed an independent nuclear research program, gradually withdrew France from NATO, and in other ways sought a more independent French policy within the Western coalition. But the price France paid for unity and the pursuit of national greatness under De Gaulle was acquiescence to authoritarian government that ruled more through bureaucracy than through parliamentary process and the decline of France into political apathy and conformity.

As conservatism gained ground in the West during the fifties, even the semi-Fascist dictatorships of Spain and Portugal became respectable. Both countries had remained neutral during the Second World War. But Franco and Salazar had both sympathized with Hitler, for which they were widely criticized abroad. At the end of the war the United States, Britain, and France had publicly called for the overthrow of Franco. On the other hand, Portugal, despite Salazar's Fascist leanings, had provided the Allies with military bases in the Azores during the war, and was therefore permitted to become a founding member of NATO in 1949. By 1953, however, in exchange for military bases in Spain, the United States extended economic aid to Franco and also to Salazar. In 1955, Spain was admitted to the United Nations, but not to NATO. With American economic aid, the two dictators began to improve the stagnant economies of their impoverished countries, although both countries continued to lag far behind the rest of Western Europe. Economic improvement in turn awakened the desire for political freedom. But both dictators remained firmly in control of their countries until shortly before they died. Not until the seventies, therefore, could the movement for political change in the Iberian peninsula gain momentum.

THE EUROPEAN ECONOMIC COMMUNITY   The eclipse of Europe in the Second World War, the rise of the superpowers, and the pressures of the cold war all contributed to the movement for Western European integration that developed after the war. In the interest of peace and stability, many Europeans in the late forties were willing to subordinate their traditional national loyalties, which had caused so much conflict in the past, to the ideal of some larger European unity. Among them were the distinguished statesmen Robert Schuman, who became French prime minister in 1947; the Belgian socialist leader Paul-Henri Spaak, who also became prime minister of his country in 1948; and the British Labour government's foreign secretary, Ernest Bevin. With Western Europe's return in the early fifties to conservative government, which revived traditional nationalism, especially in France and Britain, much of the original enthusiasm for a fully integrated Western Europe died. Spaak's proposal in 1949 for a Council of Europe to unify Western Europe politically came to nothing; the proposal for a European Defense Community was defeated in 1954. In the economic sphere, however, integration proved highly successful.

The first practical steps toward integration were the Marshall Plan and NATO, which required the coordination of all the participating countries. The next important step was Robert Schuman's proposal in 1950 for a European Coal and Steel Community (ECSC), which came into being a year later and included France, Italy, West Germany, Holland, Belgium, and Luxembourg. The ECSC in turn laid the foundation for the crowning achievement in the economic unification of Western Europe: the European Economic Community, better known as the Common Market, which went into effect in 1958 and included the same member countries as the ECSC. The Common Market transformed an area almost the size of the United States, with a population of about 175 million people, into a free-trade area, within which goods, capital, and workers could move freely. It gave an enormous boost to production and trade among the participating countries and greatly accelerated Western Europe's economic recovery. It allowed millions of workers from poor areas, such as southern Italy, to migrate and work in the prosperous countries of West Germany and France. The Common Market also produced a degree of coordination and harmony among the member countries unknown in the past.

But the movement for European integration, and the Common Market especially, also created problems. The Common Market excluded Britain and the other "fringe" countries of Western Europe—Denmark, Norway, Sweden, Switzerland, Austria and Portugal. They in turn formed the unsuccessful European Free Trade Area in 1959 in response to the Common Market. In this respect, the Common Market acted as a divisive as well as a unifying organization, causing friction between France and Britain and threatening to exclude Britain from general European affairs.

The movement for European unity, since it was confined to Western Europe, also had the effect of hardening the lines between East and West. Neither the Soviet Union nor the United States could have permitted the integration of both parts of Europe without jeopardizing what each considered essential to its national security. The Common Market also encouraged political and economic centralization and decision-making by bureaucracies instead of by elected officials. It gave rise to a large and complex multinational bureaucracy, headquartered in Brussels, which was beyond the control of elected national parliaments and public pressure. And it stimulated the growth of huge corporations, such as the Krupp firm in West Germany and the Saint-Gobain-Péchiney conglomerate in France, that wielded enormous economic power and influence over political and social policy. Thus, although the Common Market was an overwhelming success, especially during the first decade of its existence, it also helped to shape an environment which would stir discontent in the late sixties.

AFTER STALIN   The death of Stalin in 1953 shook the Soviet political structure and reverberated throughout Eastern Europe. After a quarter of a century of rule by a man more powerful than any tsar, it would take the Soviet state another five years to produce a new political equilibrium equipped to deal with the changing realities of the postwar world. Stalin's immediate successor was Georgi Malenkov, who ruled together with other top Soviet leaders, since none of them was strong enough to dominate the rest. Malenkov's policy was to increase the production of consumer goods, which the Russian people had been denied under Stalin, and to relax the economic exploitation of the Eastern European satellite states. But opposition within the party to these departures from orthodox Stalinism forced Malenkov to resign in 1955. He was succeeded by Marshal Nikolai Bulganin, who returned to the Stalinist emphasis on heavy industry and armaments production. In 1955, the Soviet Union formed a military alliance with its satellites, called the Warsaw Pact—the eastern European response to NATO. The Soviet Union also sought to improve its relations with Yugoslavia, which Stalin had earlier denounced for refusing to submit to Soviet control. Gradually, both by choice and necessity, Soviet leaders were beginning to move away from orthodox Stalinism.

The turning point of the post-Stalinist era came when the secretary of the Communist party's Central Committee, Nikita Khrushchev, publicly denounced Stalin as a tyrant at the Twentieth Party Congress in 1956. His attack on the man, who stood second only to Lenin in the pantheon of Soviet leaders, took the Communist world completely by surprise; it signaled the start of an internal "thaw" that allowed Soviet citizens greater freedom to criticize their regime than they had ever known under Stalin. Khrushchev, who now emerged as the strong man of the Soviet government, relaxed restrictions on writers and artists, reemphasized the production of consumer goods, and replaced the rigid and often inefficient centralized economic planning system with more flexible regional planning bureaus. His de-Stalinization policy also aroused the hope in the Eastern European countries that they might now enjoy more political and economic autonomy, and in the West that there might be a relaxation of the cold war.

De-Stalinization was Khrushchev's response to several postwar pressures on the Soviet Union that could no longer be ignored. One was the realization that an advanced technological society could not be governed solely by untrained party bureaucrats. An educated elite of scientists and economic planners had emerged after the war; their talents and policy recommendations had to be taken into account if the Soviet Union was to keep pace with the West. Something also had to be done about closing the growing gap between the prosperous West and the East, which in the mid-fifties still languished in poverty under repressive puppet regimes. If the Soviet bloc was to remain stable, some concessions had to be made to the mounting demands for more personal freedom and a higher standard of living. Finally, if the Soviet leaders were to carry through these de-Stalinization measures, it was in their interest to improve relations with the West. They began by meeting with Eisenhower and Western European leaders at the first cold war "summit conference" in Geneva in 1955. Little was accomplished there, but it was the first time that the leaders of the two superpowers had met face to face since the Potsdam Conference ten years earlier.

Stalin's death in 1953 was greeted in Eastern Europe by workers' uprisings in Czechoslovakia and East Berlin, which the Russians put down by force. Warned by these events, however, the Soviet government under Malenkov began to grant some political and economic leeway to the Peoples' Democracies. Eastern European reactions to Khrushchev's denunciation of Stalin were even more severe. A wave of popular anti-Soviet demonstrations spread over Poland and Hungary in 1956; workers, intellectuals, and students demanded a more flexible and national variant of socialism. The Polish situation was settled peacefully when the Russians permitted the return to power of Wladyslaw Gomulka, who had been out of favor since 1947 for advocating a Polish way to socialism. Gomulka, without alarming the Russians unduly, halted the forced collectivization of land, reinforced civil rights, and improved his government's relationship with the Catholic Church. In Hungary, however, the demonstrations flared into open rebellion, and Soviet tanks and troops repressed it by force. Budapest was shelled, three thousand Hungarians were killed, and two hundred thousand others emigrated to the West. Western governments protested the Soviet action vigorously, but they did not interfere. The events of 1956 showed that the Soviet Union was willing to make some concessions to Eastern European demands for more autonomy within the Soviet bloc, but that it was not willing to allow any of its satellites to go the way of independent Yugoslavia.

The bloody suppression of the Hungarian uprising outraged public opinion in the West and revived the old divisions and distrust between Western and Russian Communists. In retaliation against the West, Khrushchev returned to a more aggressive foreign policy and to sterner controls at home. In 1958, after he was securely installed in power as Soviet premier, he began once again to put pressure on Berlin by threatening to permit the East Germans to close the city to Western traffic. This pressure culminated in the building of the Berlin Wall, which permanently divided the city. The incident of an American U-2 plane shot down over the Soviet Union also heightened international tension and undermined the second cold war summit conference held in Paris in 1960. Relations between the superpowers deteriorated further when Khrushchev began constructing missile sites in Cuba in 1962. Nevertheless, Khrushchev's new militancy did not signify a return to Stalinism. The Russian and Eastern European peoples were allowed to enjoy a measure of prosperity and civil freedom they had not known under Stalin; cultural and economic exchanges between East and West were increasing. Neither superpower seriously wished to risk another world war in an age of deadly nuclear weapons. With the passing of the Cuban missile crisis, East and West settled down once more to a relationship of uneasy coexistence and an era of economic development.

Emergence of the Consumer Society

To the generation that had lived through the Great Depression and the Second World War, economic security and material comfort became more important than ideology and class loyalty. Weary of sacrifices and

American supermarket. Photo: Burt Glinn (Magnum).

deprivation, postwar Western society plunged into consumption. The economic boom that began in the early fifties was made possible only by sustained mass consumption—by an apparently inexhaustible demand for housing, automobiles, television sets, home appliances, and other consumer goods of every sort. Automobile production in Europe almost tripled between 1950 and 1960. West Germany led the way with a yearly output of just under 3 million passenger cars. Britain and France produced between 1.5 and 2 million each, and Italy topped the million mark in 1963. In the United States alone, the number of registered passenger cars increased from 40 million in 1950 to more than 83 million in 1971. Mass consumption in turn was made possible by welfare programs and state planning, which generated confidence in the economy and reduced the necessity of saving against emergencies. The longer prosperity lasted, the more firmly the ideal of the consumer society took root.

The demand for a high standard of living was not new, but the ability of the advanced industrial countries to satisfy this demand on such a large scale was. The steep rise in productive capacity was due largely to the pace of technological development, which increased rapidly after the Second World War. The war itself had spurred the invention of new technology. Radar, rocketry, and jet propulsion had been introduced during the European campaign, and splitting the atom had made it possible to tap a whole new source of energy.

The cold war kept the superpowers in competition for technological superiority, which resulted in space travel and the production of frightening new weapons. The development of other sophisticated technology—computers, automation, and advances in the communications, transportation, electronic, and chemical industries—also increased the productive capacity of the industrialized countries.

These developments, and a host of other technological achievements that have changed the face of contemporary society, were made possible by a close working relationship between government, science, and industry that evolved under stress during and after the war. Wider technical education and the profit incentive also hastened the invention and application of new technology, which in turn increased production and provided new jobs. By 1960, Western Europe, which occupies only about three percent of the world's land surface and contains only about nine percent of the world's population, produced twenty-five percent of the world's industrial output and accounted for forty percent of world trade.

The rapid pace of technological change that gave rise to ever larger, costlier, and more complex production systems also necessitated a much larger number of technicians and managers to operate them. These people were well-educated, ambitious, and loyal to the governments and industries they served; their special skills enabled them to become increasingly important in economic and political decision-making. They were recruited from all social classes on the basis of talent. Because of their diverse backgrounds, they did not as a group adhere to any particular social or political philosophy. In contrast to previous educated elites, they tended, as they rose on the social scale, to lose interest in such questions and to dismiss ideological debate as irrelevant. For them, the important questions were how to improve production and increase prosperity, questions they believed had little to do with the relative merits of capitalism and communism as competing ways of life. The technicians and managers were rewarded for their services, not with positions of leadership, for which their specialized educations did not prepare them, but with high salaries, status, and prestige. Accordingly, they tended to view these rewards as the ultimate social values; and their prominence enabled them to promote these values throughout society. This same trend was occurring in the Communist countries of Eastern Europe, although on a lesser scale. If they were to equal and eventually surpass production in the West, as Khrushchev predicted in 1960, the Soviet and other Communist governments were forced to raise up a privileged class of technical experts.

As the demand for specialized knowledge grew after the war, more emphasis than ever before was placed on mass education. The number of universities, colleges, and technical schools, along with the number of enrollments, increased rapidly during the fifties and sixties. The number of college and university students in the United States climbed from 2 million in 1946 to 6.3 million in 1967. During the same period, their proportion increased from twenty-two percent to forty-six percent of those between the ages of eighteen and twenty-one. Between 1950 and 1965 enrollment in British, French, and West German universities almost tripled; in Italy it more than doubled. Access to institutions of higher learning was made easier by low fees, government subsidies, and low-interest loans. This expansion of higher education, which extended to all social classes, had a democratizing effect. But it also served, more than ever before, as a means to economic advancement, and higher education in the consumer society thus fostered social and intellectual conformity.

Not everyone, however, shared equally in the upsurge of consumption. It was most pronounced in the United States and in the industrially advanced countries of Western and Central Europe; the Mediterranean countries lagged behind and, although their standard of living rose between 1955 and 1965, the gap between them and the northern industrial countries widened. The migration of 2.75 million laborers from Spain, Portugal, southern Italy, Greece, Turkey, and Algeria to the industrial centers of Britain, France, West Germany, Switzerland, and Scandinavia indicated just how great the gap was between the rich countries and poor regions where little was done to eliminate the conditions of poverty. The level of consumption in Eastern Europe also remained far below that in the West, although the gap began to close in the early sixties as the Communist countries placed new emphasis on the production of consumer goods.

Within the industrially advanced countries, the general standard of living rose dramatically, but the distribution of wealth remained uneven and actually grew still more uneven during the period of prosperity. In 1971 the wealthiest 1.2 percent of the American population owned 33 percent of all personal wealth. The wealthiest 1.2 percent of the British population owned 21.44 percent of all personal wealth. In Germany, 1.7 percent of the population owned 35 percent of the total national wealth. And in France, where economic inequality was greatest, 10 percent of the population had retained about 75 percent of the national income since 1954, while the poorest 10 percent had received only about 5 percent. These figures show that general prosperity could coexist with a concentration of ever greater wealth in proportionally fewer hands.

This economic disparity reinforced social disparities: between owners and wage-earners, between the educated and uneducated, between those with and without social status, and between those who could afford the products of the consumer society and those who could not. The general prosperity of the fifties and early sixties effectively concealed these inequities. But once the economies of the industrially advanced countries began to falter in the late sixties, the inequities surfaced in the form of widespread social unrest, disillusionment, and criticism of the values of the consumer society.

The emergence of giant corporations contributed greatly to the uneven distribution of wealth. The old national trusts and international cartels reappeared after the war as national monopolies and international conglomerates. Their growth was encouraged in some countries, especially Germany and Japan, by direct government subsidies and in others, such as the United States, by generous tax allowances. The economic penetration of the world's capitalist economies by the United States and the formation of the Common Market also stimulated the growth of giant corporations. Their more sophisticated technology, management, and marketing techniques made them more powerful than any economic organizations of the past.

By the late fifties, such corporations were able, individually, to monopolize critical sectors of the economy and, collectively, to dominate the economy as a whole. In Belgium, for example, the Société Générale had under its control in 1959 fifty to eighty percent of all bank deposits, more than sixty percent of the insurance companies, seventy percent of all trade in ferrous metals, more than forty percent of the iron and steel industries, thirty percent of coal, and twenty-five percent of electrical energy. By 1970, the two largest German companies accounted for forty percent of the total national industrial production and one-third of its work force. The merger of Edison with Montecatine in Italy created one of the world's most powerful chemical combines. More business mergers took place throughout the world in 1966 alone than during the whole previous decade. On the one hand, these vast corporations could produce cheaply and efficiently. On the other, they dealt a hard blow to free enterprise and gave rise to powerful private oligarchies.

CONFORMITY AND COMMUNICATIONS   Conformity was also a marked feature of the consumer society. Prosperity curbed criticism, and the pressures of the cold war discouraged ideological deviation in East and West alike. Big government, big corporations, and mass education geared to economic and social advancement also contributed to the standardization of attitudes and values. The rapid growth of a popular commercial culture after the war crowded out what little remained of traditional high-brow and folk cultures. The mass media, most of all television, were particularly effective in shaping public opinion. The object of television, radio, and the contemporary press was to impress the mind more quickly, effortlessly, and lastingly than words; this they accomplished by their impact on the senses and use of shock techniques. But the mass media were subject to intense social, political, and financial pressures; therefore, they lacked the independence and incentive to be objective. The mass media brought the world directly into the home, but in the process transformed the home into an instrument of acculturation to the commercial and political values they served. In this respect, the mass media counteracted the effects of formal education, where students learned at their own level and had time to absorb and reflect upon what they were learning.

As with other powerful corporate interests, the mass media developed into monopolies. In Europe, television and radio became for the most part state services regulated by self- and official censorship. The media in the United States were dominated by a few giant networks and news services. After the war, many of the small and medium size newspapers in France came under the control of the Hachette and Havas organizations. In West Germany, the conservative Axel Springer clique gained control over nineteen newspapers with a total circulation of about 18 million. In Italy, only five newspapers in 1970 reached more than two hundred thousand readers each. Many of the major British newspapers were amalgamated during the sixties by the Lord Rothermere, Lord Thomson, and Cecil King groups. In the Soviet Union and Eastern Europe, all the media were state controlled. Whether privately or state controlled, however, the mass media represented a revolution in communications that enabled them to exert unprecedented influence over public opinion.

EXPANDING POPULATION   The growth of population and migration to the cities increased at a rapid rate throughout the world during the third quarter of the twentieth century. From 1825 to 1930, world population increased at a rate between four and seven percent from about 1000 million to 2000 million. Between 1930 and 1960, it increased at a rate between fourteen and twenty percent to 3000 million. Despite the frightful loss of life in the Second World War, the population of Western Europe alone rose by twelve percent between 1940 and 1955. This growth was due largely to improvements in medicine, hygiene, and agricultural production, which reduced infant mortality and increased life longevity.

The expanding economies of the industrially advanced countries were able to absorb this population increase. A rising standard of living, more effective methods of birth control, and greater educational and social opportunity in these countries also encouraged the trend toward later marriage and smaller families. The economies of the underdeveloped countries, however, failed to keep pace with their population growth. The pattern of early marriage and large families has continued in these countries, and their population growth has soared. India, for example, which has followed a pattern similar to that of much of Asia and Latin America, experienced a rate of population growth that reached a staggering high of twenty-one percent in the 1950s, higher than any rate of increase recorded for Western Europe in the previous century and a half. In relation to the industrialized countries, the underdeveloped countries, which include most of the earth's population, have grown poorer, and the gap between them continues to widen.

As the world's population increased, many more migrated to the cities. During the postwar era of prosperity, the cities of Europe and North America grew rapidly while the rural population remained stationary or even declined. Old cities became overcrowded to the bursting point, and new industrial centers sprang up where none had existed before, as in Asian Russia and in the south and southwest of the United States. As advanced technology made it possible to increase agricultural production with less manpower, more rural population was freed, indeed forced, to migrate to the cities. This was as true in Eastern Europe and Russia, where the forced collectivization of the land and the industrial programs of the Communist governments produced an influx of workers into the cities, as in the West, where the small farmer was displaced by large agricultural corporations and government planning. This rural depopulation had the economic advantage of moving people into higher-paying occupations and making agriculture more efficient and productive. But it also reduced the importance of a traditional way of life that for centuries had acted as a stabilizing influence on society. As in the past, the cities offered new opportunities and set the styles and patterns of consumption; now, however, no segment of society escaped their influence.

The population increase and the growth of cities also gave rise to serious material, social, and psychological problems. Overcrowding turned the cities into great urban sprawls. The industrial heartland of Western Europe, made up of Britain, the Netherlands, Belgium, France, parts of West Germany, and northern Italy, became almost barren of agriculture and reached a population density four times that of the United States. Unplanned and unstructured urban agglomerations sprang up in the industrial regions of the United States: around the lower Great Lakes, between Boston and Baltimore on the Atlantic Coast, and between Los Angeles and San Diego on the Pacific coast. The cities suffered from congestion, pollution, and a decline in the speed, efficiency, and economy of transportation. Municipal services declined. City centers and established neighborhoods deteriorated. Crime rates rose, and social and racial tension mounted. These conditions in turn increased the city dweller's sense of helplessness, anxiety, and insecurity.

As the costs and stresses of city living climbed, many of those who could afford it moved to the suburbs. This movement deprived the cities of a productive and prosperous part of the population and the tax base it provided. The suburbs were not a new or improved form of urban living; rather they were random growths governed by the desire for escape or refuge. The suburbs were simply the fallout of the metropolitan explosion. The exodus to the suburbs during the fifties and sixties hastened the disintegration of the cities and added to their waste of space, destruction of the natural environment, strain on transportation facilities and dependence on the automobile, and social and psychological dislocation.

Revolt Against Colonialism

Europe's decline in the Second World War and the rise of the superpowers ended five centuries of European expansion. The European colonial powers—Britain, France, the Netherlands, Belgium, and Portugal—emerged from the war too weak and discredited in the eyes of the non-European world to regain or remain in control of their overseas possessions. The cold war weakened their position further, by spreading ideas of national self-determination throughout the world. One by one the subject peoples of Asia and Africa demanded and achieved independence, either peacefully or by force. Between 1945 and 1960, no less than forty countries with a combined population of approximately 800 million—one-quarter of the world's inhabitants—revolted against colonialism and won independence.

IN ASIA   The liquidation of Europe's colonial empires began in Asia, where nationalist movements galvanized by the Second World War already existed. The great subcontinent of India, where Mahatma Gandhi and Jawaharlal Nehru had led a national movement between the wars, gained its independence from Britain peacefully in 1947. The same year, after severe internal fighting between Hindus and Moslems, the predominantly Moslem northern portion of India became the independent state of Pakistan. Ceylon gained its independence from Britain a year later, and Malaya followed in 1957. All four newly independent Asian states became members of the British Commonwealth. After two years of fierce fighting, the Dutch lost Indonesia, which became independent in 1949 under the nationalist leader, Achmed Sukarno.

The French fought an even longer and more bitter war to regain control of Indochina from the Communist national liberation leader, Ho Chi Min, who came to power after the Japanese defeat and immediately proclaimed the former French colony the Republic of Vietnam. The Indochina war lasted from 1946 to 1954, when the French suffered a crushing defeat at Dien Bien Phu and were forced to depart. During the early postwar years, the United States opposed the Indochina war and colonialism in general. Its opposition stemmed partly from moral indignation and partly from self-interest, in that former colonies would be open to American political and economic influence. But the victory of the Communists in China in 1949 and the outbreak of the Korean War in 1950 alarmed the American government into supporting the French in the Indochina war as part of its effort to contain communism throughout the world. Toward the end of the war, the United States was providing the French army in Indochina with up to eighty percent of its supplies. After the French defeat in 1954, a conference of foreign ministers in Geneva partitioned Vietnam into a northern sector under the control of Ho Chi Min and a southern sector under a government sponsored by the United States. The same year the United States and Britain formed the Southeast Asia Treaty Organization (SEATO), a defensive alliance modeled on NATO, which included most of the non-Communist countries of Southeast Asia. Under the pressures of the cold war, the revolt against colonialism increasingly took the form of a confrontation between traditional elites supported by the United States and national liberation movements supported by the Soviet Union and China.

IN THE MIDDLE EAST   Syria and Lebanon, which had been French mandates since the First World War, gained their independence peacefully from France in 1945. Britain granted independence a year later to its mandate of Transjordan, which was renamed Jordan in 1948. Palestine, also a British mandate, was a more difficult matter: Jewish refugees from Hitler's holocaust began arriving in Palestine soon after the war and supported the long-standing Zionist demand for a Jewish homeland in Palestine. The Arabs violently opposed the idea of a sovereign Jewish state in their midst carved out at their expense. Under pressure from both sides, in 1947 the British referred the Palestine question to the United Nations, which recommended the termination of the mandate and the partition of Palestine into separate and sovereign Arab and Jewish states.

On May 14, 1948, as the last British troops were leaving Palestine, David Ben-Gurion proclaimed the Republic of Israel. The surrounding Arab countries immediately launched a war against the new Jewish state, which Israel won. But hostilities persisted, and Arab leaders encouraged unreconciled Palestinian refugees to continue their struggle to regain their homeland. New wars broke out between Israel and her Arab neighbors in 1967 and 1973; again Israel won, but a lasting peace was not achieved. After their first defeat, the Arabs found an inspiring new leader in the energetic Gamal Abdel Nasser, who came to power in Egypt in the early fifties. In a show of strength against the Western powers, which supported Israel, he nationalized the Suez Canal in 1956. Britain, France, and Israel coordinated an attack to recapture control of the canal zone. When both superpowers and the United Nations protested, however, the attack was called off and Nasser closed the Suez Canal to international traffic. This humiliating setback ended European dominion in the Middle East. The Arab countries, under Egyptian leadership, continued to improve their international position by playing the superpowers off against each other and using oil and economic boycotts as weapons to weaken support for Israel.

IN AFRICA   Most of the African colonies gained their independence peacefully in the late fifties and sixties. Some became independent only after prolonged violence. The East African colony of Kenya was torn by strife between the black nationalist Mau Mau and the white settlers, who were aided by the British, before its independence was negotiated in 1963. In the Union of South Africa (a self-governing dominion within the British Commonwealth) and Rhodesia, where white settlement was larger than in the other British colonies, the whites refused to share power with their huge black majorities. In order to preserve white rule, both territories declared themselves independent republics: The Union of South Africa in 1961 and Rhodesia in 1965. As the surrounding colonies became independent, these two bastions of white supremacy increasingly became targets of black African nationalism. In 1960, Belgium reluctantly gave up the mineral-rich Congo, which immediately fell into a state of civil war that lasted almost a decade. After 1961 Portugal was the only country still using military force to maintain control over its colonies; after more than a decade of sporadic fighting, Mozambique and Angola finally won their independence from Portugal by force in 1975.

The French fought hard against Moslem rebels to retain possession of their North African colonies of Tunisia, Morocco, and Algeria. The most important of the three by far was Algeria, which was the largest area of French settlement abroad, having a French population of about a half million. Many had lived in Algeria for three or four generations and, like the whites in South Africa, felt they had as much right to the land as the native population. When the Algerian revolt broke out in 1954, the French were determined to avoid another defeat like the one they had suffered in Indochina just a few months earlier. In order to concentrate their forces in Algeria, they agreed to the independence of Tunisia and Morocco in 1956. But there was no quick victory in Algeria.

As the war dragged on, it drained French manpower and resources and damaged France's prestige abroad. The French and Moslem rebels both committed atrocities that shocked world opinion. Frantz Fanon's widely read book, *The Wretched of the Earth* (1959), endorsed by Jean-Paul Sartre, bitterly denounced French and Western colonialism and pas-

Soldiers of the FLN in Algeria, 1962. Photo: Marc Riboud (Magnum). Revolt against colonialism.

sionately defended the cause of the Moselm rebels. The Algerian war became so unpopular in France itself that it precipitated the fall of the Fourth Republic in 1958 and the election of De Gaulle, who promised to end it quickly. French public opinion was so divided, however, that it took him another four years to reach the agreement, on the Moslem rebels' terms, that gave Algeria independence in 1962 and ended the longest and bloodiest African colonial war.

CONTINUING ECONOMIC DEPENDENCE   Although the successful revolt against colonialism gave the newly liberated peoples a new sense of dignity as well as political representation in the United Nations, political independence did not end their economic dependence on the Western powers, which continued to monopolize the world's markets and resources. Many of the newly emerging nonwhite nations, especially in Africa, were poorly prepared for independence and economic self-sufficiency. For a short time during the 1950s some observers thought that India, Egypt, and Yugoslavia might emerge as the nucleus of a neutral Third-World bloc, which would act as a counterpoise to the American and Soviet blocs. But the poverty of these countries and the growing gap between the world's rich and poor peoples precluded this possibility. In 1964, the United Nations Conference on Trade and Development (UNCTAD) was created to tackle the problems of economic growth in the third world. Many individual Western states in the 1960s also began to provide economic and technical assistance. Despite this aid, however, the gap between the Third World and the rest of the world widened. In 1970, the gross national product per capita in almost sixty sovereign countries was less than $250 a year. Approximately 1.5 billion people had less than $100 a year to spend, whereas ten percent of the world's population (mostly white) enjoyed eighty percent of the world's income.

Erosion of the Postwar Equilibrium, 1963–1975

The early sixties were the high point of the postwar era. The European and American economies flourished, and the Common Market was becoming an economic rival of the United States. Western Europe no longer depended on American aid, and De Gaulle, for one, felt confident enough to advocate a unified independent Europe "from the Atlantic to the Urals." After the Cuban missile crisis of 1962, tensions between the superpowers subsided to their lowest point since the cold war began. In 1963, the United States and the Soviet Union signed a partial Nuclear Test Ban Treaty, and a "hot line" telephone was installed between the White House and the Kremlin to reduce the chance of unnecessary future confrontations. Also, the worst of the colonial wars ended in 1962, when Algeria gained its independence from France, and relations between the former colonial powers and the newly independent nations began to improve.

However, changes began to occur in 1963 that threatened to undermine the postwar equilibrium. One was the assassination of John F. Kennedy, who had narrowly defeated the Republican candidate, Richard M. Nixon, for the presidency in 1960. Kennedy was young, appealing, and intelligent; he inspired a sense of national purpose beyond containing communism that had been missing from Eisenhower's eight-year-long administration. Kennedy's victory was part of a reaction to conservative government that was beginning to take place throughout the Western alliance. His death shocked and saddened the American people; the controversy surrounding his assassination, which was never resolved to everyone's satisfaction, opened a wound that never fully healed. The assassination of his politically aspiring brother Robert, and of the black civil rights leader Martin Luther King, Jr., five years later, in the midst of the painfully divisive Vietnam war, reopened the wound and aroused the suspicion in some circles that all three assassinations were part of a right-wing conspiracy. Whatever the facts, the controversial deaths of these distinguished leaders planted the seed of distrust in government, a seed that grew during the Vietnam war and was kept alive in the seventies by the Watergate scandal and other revelations of government misconduct.

KHRUSHCHEV'S FALL   A year after President Kennedy's death, Khruchchev was quietly ousted from power. Several setbacks caused his downfall. He had suffered a diplomatic defeat in his confrontation with Kennedy over Cuba. He faced mounting economic problems at home, especially low agricultural production. And, most important, he was at the center of the Sino-Soviet split, which began in 1960 with China's public denunciation of Khrushchev's policy of coexistence with the West. China's leader, Mao Tze-tung, accused the Russians of betraying international communism and of occupying Chinese territory along their 2000-mile-long border. Mao also claimed that the Chinese system of peasant communism was superior to the Soviet system and more applicable to the poor agrarian countries of the Third World.

After the signing of the Nuclear Test Ban Treaty in 1963, China accused Russia of capitulating to United States imperialism and the two countries broke off all relations. A year later, the Chinese tested their first nuclear bomb. By the end of the decade, Chinese and Soviet troops were skirmishing along their common border in Central Asia. The Sino-Soviet split threatened to divide the Communist world and indirectly fostered the movement toward greater national autonomy in Eastern Europe. Most of the Communist countries supported the Soviet

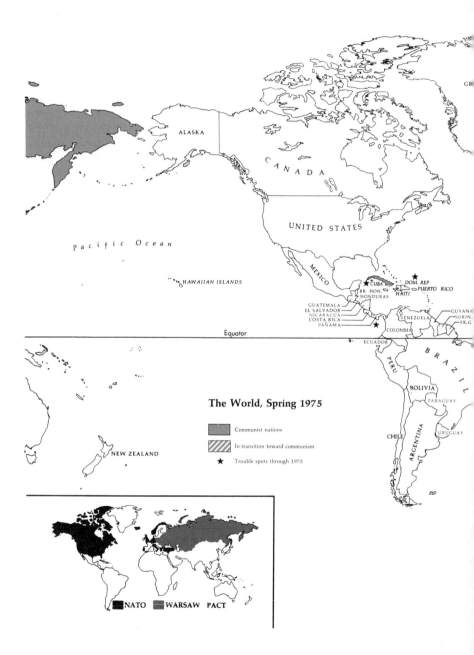

The World, Spring 1975

Communist nations

In transition toward communism

★ Trouble spots through 1975

NATO WARSAW PACT

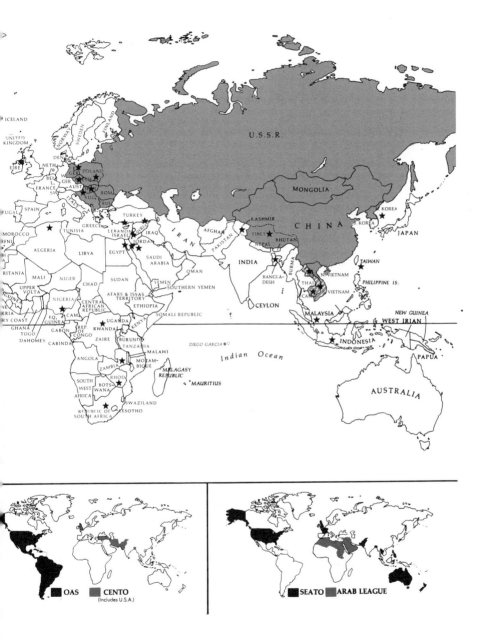

ICELAND

UNITED KINGDOM

NORWAY SWEDEN FINLAND

EIRE

NETH. DEN.

BEL. GER. POLAND

FRANCE L. WEST GER.

SW. AUST. ROM.

SPAIN ITALY YUG. BUL.

TUGAL

MOROCCO TUNISIA GREECE TURKEY

IFNI ALGERIA LIBYA LEBANON SYRIA IRAQ IRAN AFGHAN.

RITANIA ISRAEL JORDAN

MALI NIGER CHAD EGYPT SAUDI ARABIA OMAN PAKISTAN

UPPER VOLTA NIGERIA SUDAN YEMEN SOUTHERN YEMEN

NE CENTRAL AFARS & ISSAS INDIA

ERIA CAM AFRICAN TERRITORY

RY COAST FQ. GUINEA REPUBLIC ETHIOPIA SOMALI REPUBLIC

GHANA GABON UGANDA KENYA

TOGO REP. OF RWANDA

DAHOMEY CABINDA CONGO BURUNDI

ZAIRE TANZANIA

ANGOLA ZAMBIA MALAWI

MOZAM-BIQUE

SOUTH RHOD. MALAGASY REPUBLIC

WEST BOTS-AFRICA WANA

SWAZILAND

REPUBLIC OF LESOTHO

SOUTH AFRICA

U.S.S.R.

MONGOLIA CHINA KOREA KOREA JAPAN

KASHMIR TIBET NEPAL BHUTAN BANGLA-DESH BURMA TAIWAN

CEYLON THAI. N.VIETNAM PHILIPPINE IS.

CAM. S.VIETNAM

MALAYSIA

INDONESIA NEW GUINEA WEST IRIAN PAPUA

Indian Ocean

DIEGO GARCIA

MAURITIUS

AUSTRALIA

OAS CENTO
(Includes U.S.A.)

SEATO ARAB LEAGUE

Union, although tiny Albania and a small number of Communists in France and Italy took China's side. But for the first time since 1917, the Soviet Union faced competition for leadership of the Communist world.

Khrushchev's successors, Aleksei Kosygin and the more dominant Leonid Brezhnev, continued the process of de-Stalinization. They increased production of consumer goods and permitted profit and planning at the local level to stimulate economic growth and efficiency. They were also the first Soviet leaders to turn to the West for financial and technical assistance. The Soviet government concluded several foreign contracts in 1966, including one with Fiat that would triple Soviet automobile production in the next five years.

Strategic Arms Limitation Talks (SALT) between Soviet and American leaders got under way in Helsinki in 1969, and led to the first nuclear arms non-proliferation treaty signed by Secretary Brezhnev and President Nixon in 1972. Brezhnev negotiated a huge wheat purchase from the United States in 1972 and the next year concluded agreements for American capital investment. He also further relaxed Soviet control over the Eastern European economies, which stimulated productivity and encouraged more contact between East and West. The most dramatic result of this relaxation was the emergence of East Germany as the world's tenth industrial producer.

The new regime was not so generous, however, in tolerating dissent. There had been some relaxation of restraints on intellectual freedom after Stalin's death. But criticism of the regime by Soviet writers and scientists increased sharply during the mid-sixties—in some cases beyond what the regime considered permissible. Two dissident writers, Andrei Sinyavsky and Yuli Daniel, were brought to trial in 1966 and sentenced to deportation. Aleksandr Solzhenitsyn, the regime's most outspoken critic, was expelled from the state-controlled Russian Writers' Union in 1969 and forbidden to travel to Sweden in 1970 to receive his Nobel Prize for literature. After the publication abroad in 1974 of *The Gulag Archipelago,* his scathing indictment of the treatment of political prisoners in Soviet labor camps, Solzhenitsyn himself was imprisoned briefly and then, under pressure, emigrated to the West. The physicists Andrei Sakharov and V. F. Turchin and the historian Roy Medvedev criticized the restraints on intellectual freedom and travel to the West in a letter widely circulated among educated Russians in 1970. Soviet leaders reacted harshly to these criticisms and confined some of the dissidents to mental institutions. The regime also fostered a new wave of anti-Semitism, as a means to divert popular lassitude and disgruntlement, and made life difficult for the rising number of Soviet Jews who wished to emigrate to Israel and the West.

Thus, in 1967, the fiftieth anniversary of the Bolshevik revolution, the

Soviet Union still faced serious problems: the emergence of a hostile China, mounting demands in Eastern Europe for greater autonomy, an uneasy détente with the West, and economic difficulties and a rising tide of dissent at home. Consequently, when the new Czech leader, Alexander Dubček, took steps to liberalize his government in 1968, Soviet leaders cracked down. They were alarmed by Dubček's abolition of censorship, his decentralization of administration, and his attempts to make the government more national and democratic. After censorship was abolished, some Czechs went further than Dubček himself was willing to go. They demanded a multiparty system, withdrawal from the Warsaw Pact, and complete intellectual and artistic freedom. At first, Brezhnev tried to curb Dubček peacefully, hoping to avoid a repetition of the Hungarian uprising in 1956. But when Dubček, spurred on by his supporters, refused to back down, Soviet troops and tanks, assisted by units from other Warsaw Pact countries, occupied Czechoslovakia in August, 1968. Brezhnev justified the occupation on the grounds that a threat to socialism in one country was a threat to socialism in all countries. The occupation of Czechoslovakia outraged public opinion in the West, and alienated many Communists. But no Western government interfered, just as none had interfered in Hungary twelve years earlier. Dubček was removed from office in 1969, and his democratic reforms were dismantled. A year later, he was expelled from the party, along with five hundred other members. The Russians had had their way in Czechoslovakia. But their reversion to Stalinist methods to deal with the situation indicated that Soviet control over the communist world had eroded during the sixties.

STRESS IN WESTERN EUROPE   The postwar equilibrium also came under stress in Western Europe in 1963 when, after more than a decade, the long tenure of conservative governments began to come to an end. The Christian Democrats suffered setbacks in West Germany and Italy in 1963, and the Labour party returned to power in Britain a year later. Konrad Adenauer, who had grown increasingly authoritarian during his fourteen years as chancellor, was replaced in 1963 by Ludwig Erhard, the architect of Germany's "economic miracle." Under Erhard, the Christian Democrats remained in power until 1969. In 1966, however, Erhard's weakened party formed a coalition with the revived opposition Social Democrats under the leadership of the dynamic Willy Brandt, the former mayor of West Berlin who now became foreign minister. The Social Democrats won the election of 1969, and Brandt became Germany's first Social Democratic chancellor in nearly forty years.

Brandt's first priority was to improve relations with Eastern Europe, especially East Germany, which Adenauer and the Christian Democrats had adamantly refused to recognize. In 1970, Brandt signed a treaty with the Soviet Union, marking a major diplomatic breakthrough and earning Brandt the Nobel Peace Prize. The treaty ratified Germany's existing boundaries, pointed to a settlement of the Berlin question, and paved the way for closer relations between West Germany and Eastern Europe. Brandt also opened negotiations with East German leaders to improve relations between the two Germanies. In 1972, for the first time in eleven years, West Germans were permitted to visit East Germany for up to thirty days, although East Germans were still forbidden to visit West Germany. Shortly thereafter, the two Germanies agreed to mutual diplomatic recognition, and both were admitted simultaneously to the United Nations in 1973. During the worldwide recession of 1973–74, West Germany's seven percent inflation rate was the lowest in Western Europe. Brandt was suddenly forced out of office in 1974 by the discovery of an East German spy on his office staff. His successor, Helmut Schmidt, continued Brandt's policies, although he lacked Brandt's vision and personal appeal.

In Italy in 1963 the Christian Democrats formed a coalition with the Socialists that lasted five years. But this opening to the Left, long advocated by Fanfani, did little to solve Italy's growing economic and social problems. Discord within and between the two parties prevented the new government from dealing effectively with high inflation, poverty in the south, workers' discontents in the north, massive aid to education, and the regulation of urban growth. In the 1968 election, the Socialists lost heavily to the Communists, whose strength had been growing steadily. Although the government performed poorly, Communist leaders at the local level gained a reputation for efficient administration, honesty, and constructive action. The Communists emerged from the 1968 election as Italy's second largest party, and could now challenge the Christian Democrats for national leadership. The government faced a new emergency the next year. Italy's northern industrial centers were shaken by strikes and riots protesting inadequate housing and congestion caused by the massive influx of workers from the economically depressed south.

By the turn of the decade, Italy was rapidly becoming ungovernable. The Christian Democrats remained in power, but their support was dwindling and the Communists were gaining strength. During the economic recession of the early seventies, Italy's rate of inflation soared to twenty percent, the highest in Western Europe. New governments were formed, but they failed to reduce imports or Italy's enormous deficit in international payments. In 1974, the city of Rome declared itself bankrupt. The government requested and received a huge loan from West Germany. In the 1976 election, the Communists made their strongest showing and for the first time gained a voice in the national government. The question was whether it was not already too late for any government to cope effectively with Italy's apparently insoluble economic and social problems.

In Britain the Labour party, headed by an Oxford economics professor, Harold Wilson, returned to power in 1964, after thirteen years of Conservative government. Wilson's first priority was to expand the social welfare programs that had gradually eroded under Conservative rule. He renationalized the steel industry, democratized secondary education, enlarged social security, reinvigorated public housing construction, restored a full system of public medical care, and enacted tax reforms. These measures were popular but expensive. The money to pay for them depended upon a high rate of economic growth, but Britain's economic growth was impeded by outdated industrial equipment, poor business management, low worker productivity, frequent strikes, and a balance of payments deficit and overvalued currency inherited from the Conservatives. In 1967, Wilson had no choice but to devalue the pound and reduce military commitments abroad, dealing another blow to Britain's sagging prestige. The economy improved temporarily, but because of public apathy and a low voter turnout, the Conservatives won an upset victory in the 1970 election. During the recession, the British economy deteriorated rapidly, and Britain's admission into the Common Market in 1973 did little to solve its underlying economic problems. The Labour party under Wilson returned to power in 1974, but now Wilson was unable to cope with a fourteen percent rate of inflation and declining industrial production.

The bulwark of conservatism in Western Europe during the sixties was De Gaulle, who had come to power in 1958 because of his ability to provide France with stable government and a thriving economy. After liquidating the Algerian War in 1962, the last and costliest of France's colonial wars, and weathering the political crisis that followed, De Gaulle emerged as Western Europe's strongest and most influential leader. His call for a Europe independent of American control, his role in making the Common Market an economic rival of the United States, and his conciliatory policy toward France's former African colonies pleased many Europeans. But De Gaulle's haughty manner, his old-fashioned nationalism, his adamant refusal to admit pro-American Britain into the Common Market, and his unrealistic plan to make France the leader of an integrated Europe "from the Atlantic to the Urals" aroused the distrust of the other members of the Western alliance, especially Britain, and eventually undermined his popularity at home. De Gaulle's declining popularity became evident in the 1965 presidential election, in which his skillful opponent, François Mitterrand, won enough votes with his strong Socialist and Communist support, to force a runoff election. De Gaulle won the rematch, but by only a small margin.

De Gaulle's downfall began in May 1968 when angry students demonstrated against the inadequate facilities and rigid examination system of the French universities and their role in propagating "bourgeois" culture. Although these issues precipitated the demonstrations, underlying them were the students' pent-up disgust with the consumer society as a whole and distrust of the older generation. The student activists incorporated something of the spirit of the youth movement at the turn of the century, the anarcho-syndicalism of the thirties, and the Maoist doctrine of popular revolution. But they lacked leaders, a program, and mass support. The May protest in Paris was a genuinely spontaneous movement, in which the political parties played no part. The police clashed with the students, and the demonstrations flared into pitched battles on the Left Bank around the Sorbonne. The conflict quickly spread to industry, where sympathetic workers went on strike over the quite unrelated issues of higher wages and better working conditions. By the end of May, 10 million people were on strike throughout France. The economy was paralyzed, and the surprised government found itself involved in a major political crisis.

De Gaulle acted when he realized that the students' discontents and the workers' demands were fundamentally incompatible. Most workers wanted to improve their position within the system; the student activists wanted a social revolution. De Gaulle offered the workers a large wage increase, which they accepted early in June, thereby depriving the student movement of its mass support. Public opinion also turned against the students as the effects of the disrupted economy began to be felt. De Gaulle called for an election within the month, and the backlash of an angry public enabled him to win it by a landslide. De Gaulle had weathered the storm, but his reputation was badly damaged. A year later, the seventy-nine-year-old president, the last of the major wartime Allied leaders, resigned from office. The student uprising had not produced a social revolution, but it had demonstrated the vulnerability of a highly technological consumer society and had shaken off its self-confidence.

De Gaulle's successor was his former prime minister, Georges Pompidou, who continued to rule on behalf of the Gaullist majority, but in a more open and conciliatory manner than his predecessor. De Gaulle's attempt to create an independent nuclear force and his substantial wage increase to the workers after the May uprising had been costly. To pay for these programs, Pompidou devalued the franc and enacted austerity measures. He also set about to reform the universities and appease the workers. His most important decision in international affairs was to lift the French veto on Britain's admission to the Common Market. After his death in 1974, the presidency was won by another conservative, Valéry Giscard d'Estaing, who continued Pompidou's policy of seeking social peace at home and reconciliation abroad. Conservatism also remained intact throughout the sixties in Portugal and Spain. Salazar was succeeded in 1968 by Marcello Caetano, who remained in firm control of the government until he was overthrown in 1974 by army officers convinced that Portugal's future depended upon ending its long and costly colonial war in Africa. The new military government was quickly divided between Left and Right, with the long-suppressed Left determined to gain a voice in Portugal's political life. In Spain, after Franco's death in 1975, power passed to the young Prince Juan Carlos de Borbón, who faced the enormous task of making a peaceful transition from the previous dictatorship to a moderate democracy. As in Portugal, the transition was threatened by a collision between well-entrenched conservative interests and a resurgent Left allied with Basque and Catalonian separatists. The future of both countries remained uncertain in 1975.

UNITED STATES AND THE VIETNAM WAR   In the United States, the most critical political development of the late sixties was the Vietnam War. The United States became deeply involved in 1965 under Kennedy's successor, Lyndon B. Johnson. Kennedy had provided the unstable and unpopular South Vietnamese government limited aid to carry on its defense against the Communist north, but he had indicated, shortly before his death in 1963, that he would not involve the United States in a full-scale land war in Southeast Asia. Before becoming Kennedy's vice president in 1960, Johnson had served with distinction in the Congress almost continuously since 1937; his views on domestic and foreign policy had been formed during the Roosevelt and Truman administrations. His campaign slogan in the 1964 presidential election, which he won by a landslide, was the Great Society, by which he meant a renewal of Roosevelt's New Deal at home and a firm commitment to the Truman doctrine abroad. In 1965, the United States faced a serious ideological dilemma. If it stood aside when revolt broke out in Third World countries, it risked seeing them fall under Communist, or at least anti-American, control. If the United States intervened, as it did in the Dominican Republic in 1965, it angered liberal public opinion and local nationalists.

By 1965, the United States had spent hundreds of millions of dollars trying to bolster a series of pro-Western governments in South Vietnam that failed to resist the infiltration of Viet Cong guerrillas from the Communist north. The American commitment was so great, as militant American leaders argued, that withdrawal would have meant a heavy blow to American prestige and possibly the loss of all Southeast Asia to communism. By increasing its military commitment, the United States exposed itself to the charge of being an imperialist power and precipitating another Korean War. In addition, prosperity and the trend toward peaceful coexistence between the two superpowers had weakened the Western alliance. France in particular, under De Gaulle, was asserting its political independence within the Western alliance, developing its own nuclear weapons, reducing its involvement in NATO, and extending diplomatic recognition to Communist China. And nowhere in Europe did the American proposal for a multilateral nuclear force arouse much enthusiasm. Under these conditions, American leaders felt more strongly than ever that the United States alone was responsible for defending the non-Communist world. Ignoring the lesson of France's defeat in Vietnam a decade earlier, the United States came to South Vietnam's aid with a half million troops and billions of dollars in weapons.

American leaders believed that they could succeed where the French had failed. As it turned out, Vietnam was the longest and most unpopular war in American history. Not since the Civil War had the United States been so deeply divided, bewildered, and embittered, or had its prestige abroad been so low as in the late sixties. The war generated violent extremes of pro- and antiwar sentiment and shook American society to its very foundations. The crisis reached its peak between 1966 and 1968, when violent antiwar demonstrations and counterdemonstrations, ghetto rioting, student and youth rebellions, police retaliation, disbelief in government, and contempt for law and authority flared across the country.

The controversial American involvement in Vietnam seemed to provide a sanction for political violence and social upheaval at home. Thousands of American young men refused to perform military service, and thousands more deserted after induction. Many found political asylum in foreign countries, especially Canada and Sweden, which were outspokenly critical of the war. These defectors, approximately forty thousand in all, did not receive amnesty when the war ended. In Europe, American prestige sank to its lowest point since the Second World War. Opposition to the Vietnam War grew so great that Johnson decided not to run for reelection, despite the popularity of his domestic programs. The 1968 election was won by the Republican candidate, Richard M. Nixon, who promised to end the war quickly with honor. But the war dragged on two years longer, during which American planes secretly bombed Viet Cong bases in neighboring Cambodia. The war finally came to an end in 1970, when the frustrated American leaders concluded a hasty peace that was tantamount to defeat. After the Americans withdrew, South Vietnam quickly fell to the Viet Cong. Five years of fruitless fighting left the United States with fifty thousand dead, a sluggish and inflated economy, an overvalued currency, a nationwide drug-addiction problem, and a deeply demoralized public.

The Americans' troubles did not end with the settlement of the Vietnam War. Two years later, members of Nixon's reelection committee were discovered breaking into Democratic party headquarters at the Watergate complex in Washington. The Watergate break-in developed into the biggest American political scandal since the Teapot Dome scandal of the early twenties. High-ranking government officials were indicted, convicted, and imprisoned. Nixon himself, threatened with impeachment proceedings, resigned from the presidency in 1974, after winning the 1972 election by a landslide. His successor, Gerald R. Ford, immediately pardoned him, although Nixon had not admitted guilt and had not formally been charged with any crime. Ford's pardon averted legal action against Nixon, thus, arousing controversy, which hung over Ford's administration and played a part in his defeat in the 1976 election to the Democratic candidate, James E. Carter, who campaigned on the issue of trust in government.

In 1973, the United States was also plunged into its worst economic recession since the Great Depression of the thirties. The recession, which was aggravated by steep increases in the price of imported oil, lasted two years and quickly spread to the world's other capitalist economies. In 1975, the situation began to improve. The United States was pulling out of the recession, and Vietnam and Watergate were fading into unpleasant memories. But the United States did not fully regain the moral, political, or economic authority that it had enjoyed a decade earlier.

Social Discontents of the Consumer Society

Three interrelated social issues came to a head during the late sixties and early seventies and disrupted almost every advanced industrial society: the discontents of youth, women, and minority groups.

YOUTH   By the early sixties, a new generation that had not experienced depression and world war was coming of age; it had grown up under conditions of prosperity and rapid technological change. The world of the sixties was so drastically different from the prewar world and the pace of change so much more rapid that the new generation felt it had little to learn from the old. Young people in the sixties were also better educated and more mobile than any previous generation; thus, they tended to be more aware and critical of the world's injustices, inequities, and hypocrisies. Moreover, they found little to inspire them in the consumer society, which the older generation had welcomed as the end of two decades of hardship and sacrifice.

In the past, young people had usually been able to find outlets for their energy and enthusiasm in idealistic political, social, religious, or cultural movements. But few such outlets existed in the consumer society that proclaimed "the end of ideology," practiced "consensus politics," and encouraged the commercialization of culture. To young dissidents, the consumer society seemed bland, crass, callous, and conformist; they were unable to discover in it any valid personal or collective purpose in life. They distrusted the middle classes *and* the working classes, the bourgeois societies of the West *and* the Soviet style of communism in the East.

Ignored or rebuffed by their own societies, they turned for ideological inspiration to the oppressed Third World and to such leaders as Mao and Castro. But they were mainly concerned with the deteriorating quality of the societies in which they lived: societies which drafted them to fight wars they thought unjust, educated them to perpetuate institutions they had no hand in shaping, and preached values they did not share. Paradoxically, it was the consumer society itself that provided youth with the means to rebel against it: prosperity, education, and a permissive social and moral environment.

The young channeled their discontents at first into a vague and unfocused search for new lifestyles, which expressed their hostility to the consumer society but also their dependence upon it. These new lifestyles took the form of eccentric dress and grooming, libertarian sexual behavior, a taste for exotic spiritual experiences (such as Zen Buddhism, mysticism, and the occult), experimentation in communal living, the consumption of expensive mind-altering drugs, and the creation of a novel youth-oriented popular culture, as epitomized by the music of The Beatles. Except for the use of illegal drugs, all of this, while in defiance of the status quo, could be accommodated by it.

It was the long and agonizing Vietnam War that galvanized youth activists for a time into a surprisingly effective movement of political and social dissent. The youth movement proved capable of mounting mass protest demonstrations and risking direct confrontations with the police in the streets and on university campuses. It produced its own New Left politics and asserted its solidarity with the oppressed everywhere, especially the oppressed of the Third World. It produced its own leaders in Daniel Cohn-Bendit and Rudi Dutschke in Europe, Mario Savio and others in the United States. And it found influential intellectual sympathizers in Jean-Paul Sartre, Herbert Marcuse, and Noam Chomsky. The youth movement failed to upset the status quo or even to hasten the end of the Vietnam War. But it did send a series of shock waves that could not quickly be forgotten through the advanced industrial countries. The youth movement also helped to reinstate radical dissent, after a long lapse, as a force to be reckoned with and a tenable course of action.

FEMINISM   Women also became more active during the sixties in protesting their traditionally inferior status. They had already made some progress toward social equality during the previous century and a half. After the French Revolution, women for the first time gained certain basic civil rights: freedom of speech and thought and the right to own property and conclude valid contracts. In the mid-nineteenth century, the first women's colleges were founded, and women began to enter the labor force. By the late nineteenth century, women in some countries were gaining political rights: the right to vote and to stand for political office. The Socialist parties and trade unions recognized their political and social equality with men. And the suffragette movement of the early twentieth century, the first movement organized by and for women, turned the feminist cause into a general public issue. But so long as women remained economically dependent and tied to the home, they could not hope to achieve full emancipation in a male-dominated society.

As with youth, it was the consumer society that enabled women to progress further toward full participation in society on an equal footing with men. More educational opportunity, the trend toward smaller families, labor-saving technology in the home, a more liberal attitude toward divorce, and a rapid expansion of white-collar work, which women could do as well as men—all gave women a new opportunity to break out of the age-old pattern of economic dependence and social inferiority. Between 1900 and 1960, the percentage of women working in white-collar occupations in the United States increased from 24.5 to 45.7 in a sector of the economy that more than doubled in size during the same period. By the sixties, the proportion of women in the total labor force in some European countries was even higher: between fifty percent to sixty percent in the Soviet Union, Sweden, and Austria, and even as high as between twenty-five percent and thirty percent in the more traditionalistic and less industrially advanced Mediterranean countries. It is true that most of this participation in the economy was at the lower levels: secretarial and sales work, technical assistants, and the like. However, this gain represented a significant step toward economic independence and emancipation from codes of behavior, values, and expectations created for women but not by them.

By the early seventies, the traditional image of women in the industrially advanced societies was clearly in decline. But what their new image would be was not so clear. Older attitudes toward women persisted, and the woman's special role in the family still prevented the full social equality of the sexes.

MINORITIES   The plight of oppressed and the excluded minorities also became an issue during the sixties. Racial discrimination and poverty produced the civil rights movement in the United States. As late as 1960, between one-quarter and one-fifth of all American families (approximately 40 million persons) still lived on less than $4000 a year. Most lived in such economically depressed areas as the Appalachian region and in the slums of the large cities. A quarter of these poor were nonwhite, although nonwhites comprised only eleven percent of the population. The average employed black person in 1960 earned only slightly more than half of what the average white earned; twice as many blacks as whites were unemployed. Half of New York City's one million blacks lived below the minimum subsistence level. Poverty and racial discrimination reinforced each other, and the growing gap between rich and poor only exacerbated race relations.

During the sixties, the pent-up resentments of black people against this discriminatory pattern burst forth in a grass-roots drive for civil rights. A black Baptist minister, Martin Luther King, Jr., emerged as the head of a movement to combat racial prejudice in the Deep South. He preached civil disobedience as the best way to destroy segregation, and his work in bringing about the desegregation of the public transportation system in Montgomery, Alabama, won him the Nobel Peace Prize in 1964. Other groups, which included thousands of students and northerners, also joined in the struggle and organized "sit-ins" and "freedom rides" through the South to test federal regulations prohibiting discrimination. Often these actions led to violent confrontations with local police, but repeatedly, such actions resulted in the breaking down of legal racial barriers. The civil rights movements soon spread to the North, where sympathetic whites joined blacks in protesting discrimination in employment, housing, and de facto school segregation.

The nationwide impact of the civil rights movement became evident when two hundred thousand people, black and white, participated in a peaceful march on Washington in 1963 to demand racial equality. A century after the emancipation of the slaves, the conscience of the United States had at last been awakened to the plight of the black minority. When local police used clubs and tear gas to break up a peaceful black demonstration in Selma, Alabama, in 1965, thousands of northerners descended on Selma to show their support for the blacks' objectives.

The racial problem, however, could not be eliminated by demonstrations or even by laws. It would remain until underlying economic conditions and social attitudes had changed, and that would take time. Some blacks doubted that these conditions and attitudes would ever change. Some black leaders disliked and distrusted the white majority so intensely that they actually favored segregation and preached black nationalism. Inspired by the civil rights movement, other ethnic minorities, notably the Latin Americans and American Indians, also began to take renewed pride in their native cultures and in the contributions they had already made, or were capable of making, to the American mainstream. Like the blacks, they now protested the economic deprivation and social inferiority they suffered at the hands of the white majority. During the sixties and early seventies, these ethnic minorities made some progress, both by peaceful and violent means, in their struggle for full equality in American society. But their struggle was still far from over in 1975.

OTHER DISCONTENTS   Western Europe experienced a rising tide of worker and student discontents, which culminated in the national crisis in France in the summer of 1968. Workers went on strike to protest the monotony of their jobs and wages that did not keep up with the steep rise in inflation that was beginning to threaten Western Europe's prosperity in the late sixties. Student activists, like their American counterparts, disrupted universities to express their frustration with and hostility toward the whole structure of the consumer society. Government efforts to cope with these actions only sharpened the conflict to the point where parliamentary systems could scarcely function. For example, inflation and rising unemployment in Italy touched off a series of strikes and demonstrations that repeatedly brought the country to a standstill after 1969 and made it almost ungovernable by 1974. A nationwide coal miners' strike in 1972 paralyzed the British economy. Britain's first civil servants' strike and another miners' strike a year later brought down Prime Minister Edward Heath's Conservative government in the election of 1974. The paralysis of the French economy in 1968 by the temporary coalition between students and workers forced De Gaulle out of office the following year. Radical student groups kept West German universities in a state of unrest after 1967 and contributed to the fall of the Christian Democrats in 1969. Strikes and student demonstrations against low wages and government repression in Spain disrupted the last years of Franco's regime.

Social friction was sharpened also by the presence of more than two million mostly poor foreign workers in Western Europe's industrial centers, where they often worked for low wages and were treated as social and racial inferiors. Their labor was in demand, but the host countries made little effort to integrate them. By the early seventies, it was open to question whether Western European consumer societies could sustain a high rate of economic growth and whether prosperity alone could continue to guarantee their stability.

Western Europe also experienced a revival of deep-rooted linguistic and religious antagonisms. In Belgium, the old hostility between the Flemish majority and the dominant minority of French-speaking Walloons flared up again and forced the Belgian government to resign in 1968. A more serious situation developed in Northern Ireland when the

Catholic majority, which suffered discrimination in employment, housing, and education, clashed with the dominant Protestant minority in 1969. The British government sent troops to restore order, but the conflict expanded into a civil war that continued into the seventies with no solution in sight. At the same time, calls for home rule went up in Scotland and Wales. Basque separatists committed terrorist acts to back up their long-standing demand for independence from Spain. Catholic Croatian separatists also renewed their campaign for independence from Yugoslavia, where the Greek Orthodox Serbs were dominant. This resurgence of linguistic and religious loyalties was partly a reaction to economic and social inequities. But it was also a reaction to the indifference of consumer societies to the civil rights and cultural identities of minority groups.

At the end of the third quarter of the twentieth century, the consumer society was still intact. But for many it was losing its luster.

INTELLECTUAL AND CULTURAL TRENDS

The Postwar Mood

The Second World War shattered European intellectual and cultural life and disrupted the international exchange of artistic and scientific ideas. Most European universities, libraries, and research centers lay in ruins in 1945, and many leading writers and intellectuals were either dead or in exile. After Hitler's rise to power, there had been a great exodus of the educated and creative from Germany and other Fascist countries to Britain and America. New York and London after the war supplanted Berlin and equaled Paris as cultural centers of the Western world. Fascist governments had rigidly controlled culture and education and had suppressed whole areas of learning and free expression. Even in Italy, where repression had not been as severe as in Germany, not one novel or film, not one artistic or musical creation of the first rank appeared during Mussolini's regime. The intelligentsia in Nazi-occupied countries had been ruthlessly suppressed and, in Poland, even systematically liquidated. Stalin had turned Soviet Russia into a cultural wasteland and worse was yet to come. The direst forebodings of the most far-seeing minds of the prewar years seemed to have come to pass. Blanket bombings, concentration camps, and wholesale exterminations boggled the mind and imagination and seemed to make nonsense of religious faith, humanistic culture, and pride in human reason. What had Auschwitz and Hiroshima to offer in the way of inspiration, hope, or even satire?

The immediate postwar mood was reflected in such historical writings as Alfred Weber's *Farewell to European History* (1946), Arnold Toynbee's *Civilization on Trial* (1947), and Romano Guardini's *The End of the Modern World* (1950). It was reflected in a general distrust of faiths, ideologies, and institutions of any sort, and in the trend among artists and intellectuals to express their thoughts, feelings, and attitudes in the form of personal statements. Carlo Levi's *Christ Stopped at Eboli* (1945), Ernst Wiechert's *The Forest of the Dead* (1946), and many other writings of the time were first-hand accounts of events personally experienced, and they achieved an effect that no conventional work of fiction could match. The postwar Western world favored modes of thought and art, notably existentialism and Freudian psychology, which focused on the isolated individual and his abandonment—modes which served to brace the individual for survival in a failed and fallen world no longer trustworthy. This despair found expression in Jean-Paul Sartre's play *No Exit* (1944), in which the most famous line is "Hell is—other people!" and in the bleakness and desolation of Samuel Beckett's *Waiting for Godot* (1952), in which the two protagonists helplessly await the time when "all will vanish and we'll be alone again, in the midst of nothingness;" or, again, in Max Frisch's *The Chinese Wall* (1946), where a character muses: "A slight whim on the part of the man on the throne, a nervous breakdown, a touch of neurosis, a flame struck by his madness, a moment of impatience on account of indigestion—and the jig is up. Everything! A cloud of yellow or brown ashes boiling up towards the heavens in the shape of a mushroom, a dirty cauliflower—and the rest is silence, a radioactive silence."

War-weary Europeans, who had already experienced and registered the shock of global war a generation earlier, were not immediately interested in reading or writing about it again. No war novel of the calibre of Henri Barbusse's *Under Fire* (1917) or Erich M. Remarque's *All Quiet on the Western Front* (1928) appeared in Europe after the Second World War. The best war novels were written by Americans: Norman Mailer's *The Naked and the Dead* (1948), Joseph Heller's *Catch 22* (1961), and others. It was the American writer and reader who seemed to be discovering for the first time that modern warfare, whatever else it may do, breeds incredible cruelty and wastefulness, vicious behavior and pathological personalities, and generally brings out the worst in men.

Europeans were more interested in giving vent to the long-stifled urge to free expression, criticism, and artistic innovation. In the formerly fascist countries especially, this intellectual liberation assumed the form of "demythologizing" and debunking the recent past. This was a principal preoccupation of Group 47, a literary group founded in West Germany in 1947 that included some of Germany's best postwar writers: Günter Grass, Heinrich Böll, Uwe Johnson, and others. The Group 47 writers, like the resistance-bred intelligentsia of France and Italy and the

Angry Young Men of England, took it upon themselves to act as the conscience of society. Determined to exorcise the hold of the past on the present, all of these groups turned to exposing the guilt and hypocrisy of the generation responsible for the war and to denouncing its unregeneracy and return to power after the war. This development already foreshadowed the generational conflict that would burst forth again in the mid-sixties. The postwar mood manifested itself also in the rash of harshly realistic films made in Italy and elsewhere, which depicted the aftermath of war plainly and without adornment or moralizing, as if to show that the truth honestly presented was grim and painful enough to speak for itself.

While Europe was breaking free of suppression and government control of cultural and intellectual life, the leaders of the Soviet Union emerged from the war determined to maintain a tighter control over thought than ever before. Andrei Zhdanov, a powerful member of the Politburo and a favorite of Stalin, set the tone of Soviet cultural affairs during the early postwar years. He called for internal indoctrination and discipline in the cold war and ruthlessly set about purging Soviet realism, the official style of the Soviet Union and its satellites, of all alien "bourgeois" influences. The result was a policy of rigid repression and regulation in marked contrast to the rich and exploratory cultural trends in Russia during the interwar years. With Stalin's death in 1953, a mild relaxation of Zhdanov's policies set in, but nothing like a return to pre-Stalinist conditions has since taken place.

The United States, chief beneficiary of the exodus of artists and intellectuals from Europe, rose for the first time in its history to a position of cultural and intellectual leadership after the war. Its universities and research centers attracted students and educators from throughout the non-Communist world. The theories of Freud, Weber, Sartre, and other leading European thinkers began to gain wide acceptance in the New World, mainly by way of émigré professors and intellectuals who found their way to educational institutions and other cultural establishments across the land. Films made in Italy, Sweden, and England began to be shown widely in American commercial and art theaters; the names of Roberto Rosselini, Vittorio de Sica, and Ingmar Bergman quickly became, in the United States as well as in Europe, bywords of excellence in filmmaking.

American architects learned from such resettled European masters as Walter Gropius and Mies van der Rohe; American music gained from the talents of Paul Hindemith, Arnold Schönberg, and Igor Stravinsky. American theater audiences enjoyed the works of Sartre, Camus, and Jean Anouilh of France; Max Frisch and Friedrich Dürrenmatt of Switzerland; Samuel Beckett and John Osborne of Great Britain; as well as the works of Germany's most famous contemporary playwright, Bertolt Brecht, and the Rumanian-born Eugène Ionesco. Thomas Mann completed his masterpiece, *Doctor Faustus* (1948), in California, and American readers formed a ready market for the writings of newer European authors. What remained of parochialism in the mainstream of American cultural and intellectual life faded quickly in the early postwar years. The McCarthy purges—the belated American counterpart of the Zhdanov heel in the Soviet Union, although not nearly so severe—checked this trend but failed to reverse it. The internationalization of the American cultural and intellectual scene became an accomplished fact by the early fifties.

The flow of ideas and talents was not in one direction, however. The Europeanization of America was matched and surpassed by the Americanization of Europe. The American literary greats, Ernest Hemingway, F. Scott Fitzgerald, and William Faulkner, began to be more widely read in Europe; American painters, including Jackson Pollock and Ben Shahn, gained notice in European art circles; and American composers and musicians, many trained by émigré European teachers in the United States, began to perform and compete favorably with their counterparts abroad. The writings of certain selected American authors critical of life in the United States, among them Theodore Dreiser, Sinclair Lewis, and the early John Dos Passos, became available even in the Soviet Union. European institutions of higher learning began to introduce courses in American culture and society. Public and private exchange programs made it possible for American students and scholars to study and represent the United States abroad. The attention of Europeans began to focus seriously for the first time on the colossus across the Atlantic.

But the real impact of America on Europe came from popular culture, science, and technology. The boom in production of inexpensive paperback books, phonograph records, and art reprints broadened the exchange and consumption of cultural output on both sides of the Atlantic. Hollywood products, although inferior to the best European films, were widely viewed by Europeans of all backgrounds and gave mass audiences some notion, no matter how trivial or distorted, of life in America. Popular American magazines and journals began to make their appearance abroad, and jazz and popular music were heard everywhere. There was also the living presence of large American occupying forces and a renewal, on a larger scale than ever before, of the American tourist trade. European businessmen and industrialists began adopting American production and marketing techniques, and American fads and fashions made rapid headway in a society long deprived by war and austerity. Moreover, only the United States possessed the wealth and resources to support the elaborate and costly facilities that the demands of science in the postwar world required; as training centers and outlets for foreign scientists, they bound Europeans even closer to the American influence. The reconstruction of Western culture, as with politics and economics, was a truly hemispheric development, far more fluid, homogenized, and broadly based than ever before. The role of the United States in this reconstruction was that of assimilator, developer, and disseminator.

In all advanced industrial countries a change in the social function of the arts and sciences began to occur. Because of the economic burdens and political tensions, as well as the growing collectivization of public affairs and the greater complexity and costs of maintaining a cultural sphere, especially during the early postwar years, the arts and sciences could not get along without outside support. In the United States, private foundations provided grants, scholarships, fellowships, and other forms of financial assistance. In Europe such aid usually came from government or other public agencies, such as the Council of Industrial Design and the Arts Council in Britain and the French Ministry of Culture. Although this aid was indispensable, the motives behind it were not altogether disinterested. The Communist countries openly proclaimed that culture should serve national and ideological objectives. American foundations enjoyed tax concessions and prestige and naturally exercised some control over what and whom they supported. During the McCarthy era, American financial support of the arts even came to be regarded as part of the "free world's" creed. Nor was cultural subsidization in Europe entirely free of bias, especially in the awarding of prizes for literary and intellectual achievement.

In the postwar world the free-floating independent writer and artist, the modest but self-supporting theater and opera company, and the private scientist working mainly with his own resources were becoming as obsolete as the nineteenth-century artisan at the advent of mass industrialization. But the new situation posed a pressing and still unresolved problem. If the creative talent accepted his new public role, did he not risk degenerating into a panderer or lackey? If he rejected it, did he not risk depriving himself of any social function whatever? This problem became apparent as there emerged a purely commercial culture on the one hand and, on the other, a modernist trend in the arts that was so esoteric as to be incomprehensible to all but an initiated few.

Dominant Philosophical Trends

Two distinct trends in philosophy emerged after the war; one dominated in the English-speaking world and the other in continental Europe. The first was concerned primarily with a logical analysis of human knowledge (logical positivism) and the language in which knowledge is expressed and communicated (linguistic philosophy). Its leading exponents were Ludwig Wittgenstein, Gilbert Ryle, and Karl Popper in England, and Willard Quine and Nelson Goodman in the United States. The other trend, existentialism, which flourished in France, was more concerned with the nature of human existence and an analysis of the human condition. More imaginative but less disciplined than philosophy in the English-speaking world, existentialism, by the very nature of its venture, penetrated far beyond the purely philosophical sphere and became an omnipresent component of the postwar mood. Its leaders— Jean-Paul Sartre, Albert Camus, Maurice Merleau-Ponty, and Simone de Beauvoir—joined wide-ranging intellectual interests and a strong sense of personal commitment with great literary ability in a way unique among philosophical thinkers. Thus, they were able to reach a broad public not necessarily trained nor interested in purely academic questions.

LOGICAL POSITIVISM AND LINGUISTIC PHILOSOPHY, although not fundamentally in conflict with each other, represented two distinct spheres of interest. Both were anti-metaphysical and insisted upon rigorous investigation and verification, and both regarded the correct analysis of language and its use as philosophy's prime objective. But, whereas the logical positivists considered formal logic to be the criterion of correctness and considered the propositions of mathematics and the natural sciences the most perfect form of thought and expression, the linguistic philosophers denied logic this privileged role and concentrated instead on ordinary language—on how language actually is used rather than on how it supposedly ought to be used. The language philosophers held that all specialized uses of language can be translated into ordinary language and that the task of philosophy is to make explicit and clarify the rules of language as they evolve in practice.

The idea that meaning is not a logical relationship between language and the world but rather is a socially established custom was the work of Ludwig Wittgenstein (1881–1951) and his followers. Language, Wittgenstein believed, serves all sorts of communicative purposes besides the bare assertion of scientifically verifiable facts. It also serves many nonassertive or nondescriptive functions, such as the expression of gesture, emotions, and other psychological states. Scientific meaning is only one category of meaning within a much larger system of speech functions, each of which is valid according to its purpose. The misuse of language arises not from making nonassertive statements, but from confusing or misapplying the various categories of meaning as established by society.

In his last great work, *Philosophical Investigations,* published in 1953 shortly after his death, Wittgenstein used his theory of language to attack the old Cartesian dualism between a purely subjective and unknowable sphere and a purely objective knowable sphere of existence. Language, he claimed, spans the two realms. It expresses and exhausts all meaning, both subjective and objective. All that can be known about anything can be expressed in language; nothing that language cannot express, and express clearly, can be said to exist. The language we use to understand mental life, our own as well as that of others, is as public, no more or less so, as the language we use to understand the physical world.

Gilbert Ryle, in his *Concept of Mind* (1949), carried this line of thought even farther. Ryle held that to talk about mental life is simply to talk about the dispositions of human organisms. There is only one world, that of things and people existing in space and time, all of which are accessible to the senses and expressible in clear language. Linguistic philosophy thus pointed the way toward a purely behavioral approach to human existence.

Despite the criticism of language philosophers that positivism was too formal, restricted, and biased in its approach to knowledge and language, the logical positivists, Popper and Quine notably, continued to hold that logic and science are normative for all meaning. Only logic and science, they claimed, enable us to distinguish truth from error, perception from illusion, and knowledge from mere opinion. Even Wittgenstein conceded that philosophy does not add anything new to knowledge, but simply explicates what is already known and accepted. Whereas the language philosophers were hostile to any general principles in philosophy, the logical positivists held that logic and science can serve to eliminate falsehood from linguistic convention and contribute to the formation of a logically coherent and verifiable body of beliefs. Science, they believed, is entitled to this privileged role because, unlike metaphysics or any other category of meaning, its theories can be tested, refuted if mistaken or inadequate, and improved upon by new hypotheses and observations. But both schools of thought agreed that all meaning is contained in language and that the task of philosophy is to explicate the basic rules of language and purge it of its misuse.

EXISTENTIALISM, although a prewar development like logical positivism and linguistic philosophy, came to the fore after the Second World War. It represented a resurgence of older philosophical traditions primarily concerned with human and social issues and the active role of the intellectual in society. These traditions, which began with the Enlightenment and were revived by the war, were more deeply entrenched in continental Europe than on the Anglo-American periphery. The long Nazi occupation of France and other countries was a direct daily reminder to their inhabitants that the war was not only a life-and-death struggle between contending governments and peoples, but also a struggle about basic human values and the shape of the future. The occupation, especially in divided and demoralized France, posed acute problems of political and ethical behavior on an almost daily basis. The French and other resistance movements became nuclei of the most committed anti-Fascist forces, including freedom-loving intellectuals who looked upon their involvement as an opportunity to translate their philosophical views into action and to work for the reconstruction of man and society. Among them were the leaders of existentialism, Sartre, Camus and others, whose writings during and after the war bore the heroic stamp of their experience in the resistance.

Sartre's *Being and Nothingness* (1943), the classic statement of modern French existentialism, built on the early work of the German philosopher Martin Heidegger. Sartre set forth in this work the basic stock of existentialist views to be found, sometimes in modified and revised form, in Merleau-Ponty's *Phenomenology of Perception* (1945), Simone de Beauvoir's *Ethics of Ambiguity* (1947), and Albert Camus's *The Rebel* (1951). These works proclaimed the absurdity or meaninglessness of the world, the absolute freedom of the individual, the anxiety inherent in human existence due to the lack of any external guides or norms, and the ever present danger of acting in "bad faith"—that is, the individual's refusal to take full responsibility for his actions or his ascription of the causes of his actions to some outside source. Existentialism radically rejected any sort of determinism, whether social, psychological, or metaphysical, and any theory of human nature as given or fixed. Sartre insisted that the individual is a completely self-determining being who is totally and solely responsible for his acts. Man chooses his own existence by his enacted decisions and, in doing so, creates his nature. How we choose to exist precedes and determines what our nature will be. The individual does not only choose for himself, however. In choosing for himself, he chooses for all because the future is never predictable in advance; it always remains open and is decided by those who can make their will prevail at any given time.

Merleau-Ponty emphasized, even more than Sartre, that man is not a detached observer of the world around him, a being who passively contemplates or imposes arbitrary constructions upon it. Rather, he held, man is a subject dialectically related to his surroundings, who constantly endows the world with meaning based on his interactions with it. In his political philosophy, as set forth in *Humanism and Terror* (1947), Merleau-Ponty proclaimed that, while everything political that succeeds is not necessarily good, the political good must succeed in order to be good—as if to emphasize that knowing the good and enacting it by whatever means necessary, even terror, are but two inseparable aspects of a single project. The claim that the end does not justify the means is only an excuse not to act. Merleau-Ponty, Sartre, and other existentialists, although critical of Marxist philosophy and the Communist party, sympathized with Communist objectives and sought to reconcile that sympathy with their primary existential views. At bottom, however, existentialism was an interpretation of the human condition and a code of behavior conceived by and for the solitary individual in a senseless, indifferent, and hostile world. The charged atmosphere of French intellectual life in the early postwar era, the personalities and concerns of the existentialists in particular, and their collaborations and conflicts, were richly documented by Simone de Beauvoir in her novel, *The Mandarins* (1953).

If philosophy in the English-speaking world during the early postwar years defined its sphere of interests rather narrowly and took little interest in general human problems, this was due in part to the fact that the war had left it and its self-confidence relatively intact. Philosophy had but to get on with the business of advancing knowledge, scientific knowledge especially, which was the wave of the future and in which the Anglo-American world now held indisputable leadership, and with perfecting the instrument of language in which knowledge is expressed. In continental Europe, where the war had threatened the very foundations of civilized life, the result was far less faith in progress, reason, and science as panaceas for the ills of society. European philosophers, therefore, naturally turned to problems bearing on the nature of human existence and its vicissitudes. The war's effect on Marxist philosophy in turn, which won many new adherents and sympathizers in the West, was to strengthen its conviction that the capitalist world was all the closer to final collapse.

Science and Religion

The division within Western philosophy was paralleled by the traditional division between science and religion, which became even more pronounced after the war. Science moved further toward toward pure materialism; religion, toward pure fideism. It is true that the older uncritical optimism of scientists and public alike in the unmixed blessings of science was shaken by the destructive potential and abuse of some scientific achievements. The case of a distinguished nuclear physicist J. Robert Oppenheimer, who opposed the development of the hydrogen bomb, exemplified the deep personal, political, and moral conflicts which the contemporary scientist encountered in the course of his work but which his strictly scientific expertise did not prepare him to resolve. "We are all sons of bitches now!" Oppenheimer's colleague, Bainbridge, is

The Apollo II lunar module ascent stage, photographed from the command service module during rendezvous in lunar orbit. The Earth rises above the Lunar horizon. Photo: NASA.

reported to have remarked while witnessing the explosion of the first experimental atom bomb in New Mexico in 1945. And other recent scientific advances—space exploration, automation, cybernetics, the transplantation of vital organs and genetic manipulation, chemical and electrical healing techniques, the prolongation of the lives of the very sick and aged—all these advances and more posed a host of ethical and social, political and economic problems inseparable from the achievements themselves. Willingly or not, scientists were forced after the war to consider more seriously than ever before the implications of their work.

The various religions have also made some attempts to come to grips with public affairs in recent times. The war generated widespread disillusionment with institutionalized religion in any form, and many questioned the relevance of religion to public life and personal conduct. Among Catholics especially, there has been a great deal of concern about the state of the Church and its relevance to the modern world. Pope Pius XII was widely criticized for his silence and inactivity during the Second World War, but the larger question was whether the Church could go on without opening itself to new influences and modifying some of its basic tenets. Just after the war a small group of left-wing French Catholic priests tried to win back the allegiance of the working classes by joining their ranks, engaging in strenuous manual labor, joining Communist-sponsored trade unions, and participating in Communist demonstrations. The prestige of these worker-priests grew far beyond their numbers. But, because their activities came into conflict with the Church, their recruitment was halted in 1951 and their activities ceased altogether in 1959. Although this movement of worker-priests failed, it helped pave the way for subsequent attempts to liberalize the Church and make it relevant to contemporary society and its problems.

When Angelo Roncalli, a man of humble origin and a cardinal with wide experience of the world, became Pope John XXIII in 1958, he attempted to introduce sweeping reforms within the Church. His encyclicals aimed at adapting the Church to modern social and political developments. After only three months in office, he announced his intention of convoking an Ecumenical Council, only the third in the history of the Church since the Council of Trent in the sixteenth century. The Council, which finally began in 1962 and lasted until 1965, dealt with many matters of Church organization and policy, including the relationship of the Roman Catholic Church to other religions, the functions of priests and bishops, and the role of the laity within the Church. It appeared for a time that the Council might result in a fundamental liberalization and democratization of the Church. This prospect was dampened, however, when John XXIII died in 1963 and conservative forces within the Church began to regain the upper hand.

John's successor, Paul VI, continued to work for Christian unity and better relations with other faiths. But Protestants were antagonized by the Church's refusal to deviate from the doctrine of papal infallibility, its disapproval of mixed marriages, and other established tenets. The Church also remained firmly opposed to artificial birth control, the marriage of priests, and the granting of full absolution to Jews for the alleged crime of deicide. Some liberalization did result from the Council, such as allowing heterodox authors to defend themselves instead of automatically condemning them, but it fell far short of the reforms that were originally anticipated. The Protestant religions have generally adapted, or at least acquiesced, more readily to the processes of secularization. For Jews, the founding of the state of Israel in 1948 provided a new focus of Jewish life throughout the world.

However, despite these attempts on the part of science and religion to relate more closely to the world at large and its problems, the two have continued to go their separate ways. The sciences have continued to hold to a more or less purely materialistic conception of the physical universe in general and of human life in particular. In the 1950s the discovery of the DNA molecule in our hereditary makeup, which enables molecular biologists to explain and control genetic processes, resulted in discovering the link between living and nonliving matter. And the rapid ascendancy of the behavioral sciences and cybernetics since the war has bolstered the traditional scientific conception of the human organism as only a machine—a highly complicated machine with vast possibilities, but a machine all the same.

In religion, the vital force in recent years has been the trend, most prominent among Protestant theologians, to conceive religion as a purely personal spiritual or moral act of faith. This trend, which drew freely from existentialism, is reflected in the writings of Karl Barth, Karl Jaspers, Paul Tillich, and other Protestant religious thinkers. It is widespread also among average people of all religions in search of some sort of personal spiritual faith, but who are distrustful of institutions and official doctrines. Dietrich Bonhoeffer, a German protestant clergyman executed by the Nazis at the age of thirty-nine, exemplified this trend in an extreme form. In his view, secularization had displaced religion as a cultural force. In doing so, however, secularization had cleared away all interests and preoccupations extraneous to true Christianity and had made it possible for Christianity to return to its one and only valid vocation: man's encounter with Christ. For Bonhoeffer, Christianity was neither an institutional involvement nor a metaphysical doctrine. It was a purely personal experience sustained by prayer alone, a commitment applicable to but not dependent on the state of the secular world.

The Social Sciences and Psychology

Among Western social scientists and historians after the war there was a widespread reaction against all sweeping philosophies of history and prophetic theories of social change, such as those of Spengler, Marx, and others that had been prominent before the war. It was felt that such theories, far from being objective and accurate, served only to foster totalitarian thought and action of one kind or another. The philosophers, R. G. Collingwood and Karl Popper, from very different standpoints, led the way by denying that the methods of the natural sciences were applicable to the historical disciplines. Both men—Collingwood in his posthumously published *The Idea of History* (1946) and Popper in *The Open Society and its Enemies* (1945) and *The Poverty of Historicism* (1957)—claimed that the peculiar characteristics of man, his rationality and moral autonomy, precluded the possibility of studying the human record by the same means used to understand the mindless, mechanically ordered, predictable operations of nature. Following suit, most historians, other than Marxists, have in the main abandoned the search for grandiose schemes and have sought instead to enlarge the scope of historical knowledge, attain the maximum of accuracy and thoroughness, develop an interdisciplinary approach to their subject, and broaden their horizons to include the non-Western parts and peoples of the world.

Sociologists and political scientists also, many disenchanted with Marxism and inspired by Max Weber's ideal of a "value-free" science of society, have eschewed criticism and dissent in favor of predominantly descriptive theories of the workings of politics and society. In the United States, Talcott Parsons and Robert Merton led the way by advocating a functional approach to sociology, one that regards the established order of things as normative and social conflict as pathological. This school of thought held that the task of sociology is to show how society could function most efficiently—that is, with a maximum of stability and continuity based on norms established in practice—and that the social sciences should refrain from passing value judgments on society's institutions, beliefs, or prospects. The distinguished American political scientist, Robert Dahl, who strove for a theory completely free of ideology, confined himself to a purely neutral description of the ways in which power is acquired, distributed, and utilized.

In Europe, Joseph Schumpeter argued against Marxist economic theory—capitalism, he claimed, not only was not in decline but was actually more vigorous than ever. Marxist predictions of the inevitable collapse of capitalism had proven wrong, he held, because the vast new technocratic and managerial classes spawned by capitalism had a strong interest in its survival and the proven ability to streamline and rationalize its operations along Weberian lines. Schumpeter's proof was the emerging neo-capitalist system of great corporations capable of sustaining themselves by their functionally superior organizational techniques.

Along with Schumpeter, Raymond Aron, Daniel Bell, and others analyzed industrial society as the basic structure of all economically advanced countries, regardless of ideological differences. Industrial society, they held, is the common denominator and governing factor of both the neo-capitalist welfare states of the West and the controlled economies of the Communist world. This view implied the fundamentally optimistic conclusion of an eventual convergence of all industrially advanced nations and a corresponding decline of ideological and social conflict. Others more ideologically inclined, including Albert Camus and Hannah Arendt, defended classical liberalism not so much because they thought it the established tradition of the modern Western world or functionally superior to any known alternative, but rather because individualism better meets the needs of modern man and is more in accordance with the human condition as seen from a more or less existentialist perspective.

All these theories, in effect if not by intent, served to sanction the postwar status quo and reflected a renewed optimism and confidence in the ability of the Western world to recover and carry on. Throughout the fifties the voices of dissent among academic social theorists were few and far between. Not until the late fifties and especially the sixties, when a new wave of social discontent and upheaval was experienced, did those who questioned the very premises of liberal society and capitalism come to the fore: C. Wright Mills, Herbert Marcuse, C. B. Macpherson, Claude Lévi-Strauss, Noam Chomsky, and many other social critics, some of whom belonged to the New Left.

Psychology rapidly gained wide acceptance after the war and partly as a result of the war. Faith in the ability of psychology to discern and remedy the ills of contemporary man and society filled the void left by the loss of faith in religion, ideologies, and institutions. Psychoanalysis in particular, which had only a limited appeal before the war, gained ground rapidly after it, especially in the United States, which now bore the burden of unprecedented world power and experienced the full impact of the strains and tensions, the dislocations and anomie engendered by late industrial society. In its various revised forms, however, psychoanalysis ceased to be the comprehensive critical analysis of civilization's oppressiveness that it was in its original Freudian formulation. Psychoanalysis in the fifties became principally a therapeutic technique designed to help the unhappy or maladjusted individual, usually of the affluent middle classes, adapt to his social environment as given—not criticize, resist, or reject it. From a doctrine of dissent, psychoanalysis thus evolved into a therapy conducive to conformity. As such, it served the needs of an emerging new human type described by David Riesman in *The Lonely Crowd* (1950) as "other-directed": the type of person who accepts the established order and shapes his life in accordance with the expectations and preferences of others, in contrast to the older "inner-directed" type, who pursued his own inwardly conceived goals, whether they were socially accepted or not.

The behavioral approach to psychology, which sought to apply the strictest scientific standard to its analysis of human behavior, also forged ahead after 1945. Proceeding from a positivist assumption, behavioral psychology denied that human behavior is demonstrably different in kind from animal behavior. Behaviorists sought to demonstrate an essential continuity between the two and to develop theories applicable to all orders of higher organic life. They were primarily interested in the more elementary areas of human behavior, such as perception and learning. These were the areas in which the behavioral approach proved most successful, since they most closely resembled the same areas of behavior among all other higher animal orders, and also because they were more susceptible to scientific investigation and quantification than the more complex and less accessible areas of the human psyche from which meaning and value, language and abstract concepts derive.

B. F. Skinner, a rigorous adherent of the behavioral position, conceived all behavior, human and animal alike, in strictly mechanistic terms; behavior, he held, was no more than a direct, observable process of stimulus and response. The greater complexity of human responses to external stimuli is not due to the intervention of any unobservable internal factors, Skinner argued, but only to a more complicated nervous system, which is as subject to observation and quantification as the stimuli and responses it mediates. On this view, even rationality and language, traditionally thought of as distinctly human attributes, are nothing more than products of conditioning. Language, for example, is simply an accumulated possession acquired by conditioning, from which it seems to follow that sufficiently sophisticated machines can be constructed capable of learning languages and translating one into another—a project that has been attempted but so far has proved unsuccessful. However, new technological developments, notably computers, which have duplicated and even improved upon complex human mental processes, have given impetus to the behaviorist position. Skinner himself, in his *Walden II* (1948), went so far as to present a fictional utopian community composed of people whose behavior was totally conditioned to bring about complete social adjustment and harmony.

A third approach to psychology, the Gestaltist, which was intermediary between psychoanalysis and behaviorism, also gained ground after 1945. In opposition to behaviorism, Gestalt psychologists, led by Wolfgang Köhler, denied that organisms respond to their environment in a merely passive, mechanistic manner. Rather, they contended, organisms encounter situations already possessed of various expectations and anticipations by means of which they structure and synthesize the often incomplete and disorganized array of external stimuli impinging upon them. On the Gestalt view, the organism is not merely a passive subject conditioned by an environment over which it has no control. Instead, the organism is an active agent which determines, by means of its anticipations, what Köhler called the "requiredness" of the environment. Behavior, then, is not merely a reflex reaction to external stimuli, but a constant process of adjusting expectations to what situations seem to require at any given time. In contrast to the psychoanalytic approach to understanding behavior, the Gestaltists denied that the organism, the human organism above all, is solely or even primarily a product of its past and that it is necessary to know the organism's past in order to understand and predict its present and future behavior. More important than the organism's past experiences are its present expectations in ever changing situations; certain courses of action may appear more appropriate than others in terms of fulfilling the organism's expectations. The organism does not act as it does because of what it is or has been, but because of what it anticipates in the situation in which it finds itself. For the Gestaltist, the only important thing to know is what the organism anticipates upon entering a situation and whether and how its anticipations can be fulfilled in that situation.

Although none of these interpretations of human behavior posed any threat to postwar Western society, all served as points of departure for the doctrines of dissent in psychology which emerged in the late fifties and sixties: in the writings of Herbert Marcuse, Norman O. Brown, Ronald D. Laing, Noam Chomsky, and the structuralist approach to psychology.

The Two Cultures

In 1959, the distinguished British novelist and scientist, Charles P. Snow, published a lecture he delivered that year entitled "The Two Cultures," which immediately became and has remained controversial ever since. The controversy provoked by this publication was, by the author's own admission, due more to the timeliness than to the originality or profundity of its thesis, which was simply that a vast abyss of mutual incomprehension, indifference, and even outright hostility had developed between literary intellectuals and scientists. Snow, unique in that he was active in both cultures and concerned to represent each fairly and impartially, nevertheless blamed the literati for the fissure between the two, dubbing them "natural Luddites."

It was no accident that this fissure, long in the making in Western culture, surfaced first in Britain. On the continent, the traditional literary culture was still too well entrenched, and science not yet sufficiently advanced to pose a threat to it. In the United States, the opposite was true: the literary culture there had never succeeded in sinking such deep roots as to pose a threat to the practical, optimistic mentality on which Americans have always prided themselves. In the Soviet Union, where all spheres of culture were closely supervised by the regime, the issue never arose, at least not publicly. But in Britain, even before the Second World War, such prominent figures in literary life as T. S. Eliot and F. R. Leavis had already publicly expressed deep concern about the function and value of literature in the modern world. Moreover, Britain possessed both a vital literary culture and an equally vital scientific culture capable of challenging the literary intellectuals' hold on the moral imagination of the educated public.

The significant point in Snow's argument was that the literary culture, by its indifference or active resistance to what he believed were the essentially humanitarian and optimistic goals of science, had deeply divided Western culture from within and had distorted its historical perspective. His view implied further that the future belonged to science and that literature had the choice either to endorse science and assimilate and propagate its values, thereby reuniting Western culture, or else to forfeit its claim to be the moral consciousness of society.

Not long after the publication of Snow's lecture, Marshall McLuhan, the distinguished and controversial theorist of communications with a wide following among the young, carried Snow's argument a step further. In *Understanding Media* (1964), McLuhan enthusiastically proclaimed the end of the era of the printed word altogether—along with its associated features of privacy and individuality, ratiocination and logical consecutiveness—and the start of an era of electronic media destined to transform the world into a collectivized "global village" habituated to and bound together by an all-encompassing network of instantaneous and simultaneous electronic communications. Whether this assessment of the internal disunity of contemporary Western culture was correct or not is debatable. What is not debatable is the disunity itself.

For the first time in modern history, science and electronic technology are in a position to challenge literature for leadership of Western culture as a whole; for the first time, literature finds its cultural leadership jeopardized. Whatever the outcome, this cultural flux and reordering has become an integral part of the contemporary Western experience, not unlike the tension between the sacred and secular cultural traditions that developed during the late Middle Ages and Renaissance. The merit of the debate about the two cultures was that it at least identified the crucial issue: whether the traditional Western conception of man as a unique, rational, morally responsible individual, dating back to the Greeks, would survive; and, if so, how.

Ferment in the Sixties

The social unrest of the sixties was matched by a new ferment in intellectual and cultural life. The whole spectrum of creative activity was in revolt against the detachment and complacency, the amorality and self-righteousness of the previous decade. Indicative of the new trend in intellectual life was the emergence of the so-called structuralist school of thought, which was centered in France but extended far beyond.

STRUCTURALISM was less a philosophy in the conventional sense than a method applicable to all areas of human inquiry: the social and natural sciences, language, literature, and philosophy itself. The characteristic feature of structuralism was that it rejected the study of any field of human activity as merely a succession of isolated events to be recorded and classified (the diachronic approach) in favor of a method concerned with the logical and psychological relations that bind coexisting events into a unified system or structure (the synchronic approach). That is, structuralism favored a vertical, in-depth approach to the study of human activity in contrast to a horizontal and cumulative approach. A structure is not merely a collection of unrelated elements and their properties; it is a coherent self-contained, abiding whole; it contains no extraneous ephemeral elements and is governed by its own mechanisms of self-regulation and transformation. The task of the researcher is to discover, beneath the diachronic succession of events, the synchronic structure and the mechanisms according to which it subsists and functions. Ferdinand de Saussure (1857–1913) first applied this method to linguistics, the area in which structuralism has established itself most firmly. His work in linguistics has since been carried forward by Roman Jakobson, Noam Chomsky, and other linguists. Roland Barthes and Tzvetan Todorov are leading figures in the application of structuralism to literary analysis; Jacques Lacan and Jean Piaget in its application to psychology; and Michel Foucault and Louis Althusser in its application to philosophy and social thought.

Of all the structuralists, Noam Chomsky, working in linguistics, and Claude Lévi-Strauss, working in anthropology and ethnography, have probably made the greatest impact on contemporary thought in general. Chomsky, in opposition to the behavioral theory of language, evolved his own theory based on the observation that anyone who uses language can construct and understand sentences which neither he nor anyone else has ever encountered before. This creative power, which manifests itself very early in life, distinguishes all human languages from the systems of communication used by other species, systems which are closed and allow for the transmission of only a finite and comparatively small set of messages but do not allow for the variation or construction of new meanings.

Human language is unique in that an indefinite number of sentences can be formed from a finite vocabulary and a limited set of grammatical rules, just as a finite system of musical notation can yield an apparently indefinite number of musical compositions and variations. This unique quality of human language Chomsky explained by the "generative" property of grammar and its rules, which are common to all human languages, despite their surface diversity, and which constitute the "deep structure" of language. Only because all languages do have such a common "deep structure" is it possible to translate one into another. From this line of thought, Chomsky concluded that language cannot simply be a habit induced by conditioning, as the behaviorists maintained, or else grammar would lack its "generative" property. On the contrary, language must be the expression of certain unique innate dispositions common to the whole human species. Chomsky found further support for his views in the fact that all languages, primitive and civilized alike, are of approximately equal complexity; no language is really more primitive or closer to systems of animal communication than any other, regardless of the different stages of historical development of the peoples speaking them. All this gave support to the moral conviction of the essential and unique unity of mankind, a conviction held by Chomsky and by the structuralists in general. Chomsky himself became the most distinguished intellectual spokesman of the New Left during the Vietnam War and one of the most outspoken critics of American policy in Southeast Asia and elsewhere.

Lévi-Strauss applied the structuralist linguistic model to his study of primitive societies, which he viewed as complicated codes of communication rather than as bodies of historically evolved institutions, practices, and attitudes representative of mankind in an early transitory stage of development. Using this model, he drew the conclusion, in *The Savage Mind* (1962), that primitive thought is not inferior to civilized thought; it is not merely a childish, naive, superstitious prelude to the more advanced mental development of civilized man. It only seems so from the (biased) perspective of civilized man, who fails to perceive primitive life, especially those aspects of it which appear to him most primitive and irrational, as actually a coherent system, which is essentially communicative or linguistic in character and, thus interpreted, every bit as complex, sophisticated, and self-sufficient as civilized life. Myth, for example, is not simply a body of superstitious notions predating science and logic. Rather, it is an appropriate way of explaining events by peoples without history and without need of history (that is, without a literary tradition or a linear conception of time). If anything, Lévi-Strauss regarded primitive ways as superior to civilized ways. Primitive ways are the product of a culture that is integrated with nature and therefore humanly satisfying; civilized ways derive from a culture which is alienated from nature and therefore wanting.

Above all, Lévi-Strauss argued that primitive life is not simply a bygone phase in the course of human development. All primitive cultures, interpreted as systems of communication no better or worse than any other, manifest the universal structural characteristics of the human brain at work in the creation of culture in general. From this standpoint, Lévi-Strauss could entertain the hope that the primitive experience might still be latent somewhere in the recesses of mankind's collective unconscious and might one day reassert itself should the burdens, restrictions, and frustrations of civilized life finally become intolerable. In effect, Chomsky and Lévi-Strauss both turned the structuralist concept of the basic unity of mankind against the Western faith in progress and sense of superiority, which they regarded as a sham. Their findings led them to believe that the true politics of structuralism was Marxism.

Herbert Marcuse, another distinguished leader of the New Left, added to the intellectual ferment of the sixties from a more traditionally radical standpoint. From his early association with a group of radical intellectuals in Germany in the 1930s, he developed into one of the most persistent and outspoken critics of the neo-capitalist industrial and social order. However, Marcuse's Marx was not primarily the rigid economic determinist or theorist of class warfare that the Old Left knew. His Marx was the philosophical dissenter, the humanist, the analyst of the alienation and degradation of man under capitalism. Marcuse's main objects of attack were the vast, impersonal corporate structures that absorb individuals into a faceless, mechanized mass of functionaries, the overspecialization and trivialization of labor, the manipulation and deception of the public by government and privileged interests, the crass materialism and waste of human and material resources, the pollution of the natural environment, and the deterioration of the quality of life in general in contemporary capitalist societies. But his once utopian confidence that mankind, given the opportunity, would rebel against this state of affairs gave way in later life to despair prompted by the staying power of the system he never ceased to condemn and by its ability to appease, with a profusion of consumer commodities, those whom he believed it exploits and degrades morally and mentally.

Marcuse was also one of the first, along with Norman O. Brown, Erik H. Erikson, and Ronald D. Laing, to rediscover Freud as a great critical analyst of civilization comparable to and compatible with Marx. All of these critics subscribed more or less to the view that the psychopathology of man, as analyzed by Freud, is the product of an alienated society, as analyzed by Marx. Marcuse held that the new conditions of material abundance make it possible to overcome the repressiveness of civilization, which is born of economic scarcity, by giving freer reign to Freud's pleasure principle—that is, by transforming work into play and granting greater freedom to the erotic and sensual drives in everyday life.

Brown held that social repression and the neuroses it produces can be overcome only by reestablishing the continuity between man and nature that is present at the infantile stage of life, when what Freud called "polymorphus perversity"—or unrestricted sexual interest in the whole human body in contrast to the adult confinement of sexual interest to the genital areas—prevails. Erikson's research into the ways in which children acquire their sense of identity led him to criticize society's methods of raising and educating children.

Laing claimed that psychiatrists all too often ignore the social situations within which mental disorders occur, with the result that their diagnoses more often than not induce the disorders they are supposed to explain. Schizophrenia, for example, is inseparable from the socioeconomic environment within which it occurs. To treat the two as separate only falsifies the diagnosis, upholds established standards of behavior it condemns by way of distorted psychiatric diagnoses—a neat but vicious circle. Laing's studies of the family, the primary social unit where all behavior patterns are formed, reveal a complicated, sometimes bewildering, system of game- and role-playing that often results in what Laing called "binds" or "knots": unsolved fantasy situations which the family members carry over into their relations with others. The family is the breeding ground of all behavior, both acceptable and unacceptable, and therefore bears the chief responsibility, which it was not intended or suited to assume, for mankind's general social behavior. All of these theories obviously implied a drastic reordering of society.

CREATIVE FERMENT IN THE ARTS   The arts also added to the creative ferment of the sixties. Literature, the performing arts, and the visual arts all made renewed efforts to subject the real world to close critical scrutiny and to bridge the gap between serious and popular culture. Beginning with Federico Fellini's *La Dolce Vita* (1960), a realistic exposé of the decadence and immorality of the Italian upper classes, filmmakers—Michelangelo Antonioni, Jean-Luc Godard, Ingmar Bergman, and Andy Warhol among many others—began to introduce more social, psychological, and intellectual significance into their films. The sixties witnessed the production of the rock-musical, *Hair* (1968), the most successful of several theatrical productions that praised the new youth culture and invited audience participation in the performance. The theater of the absurd, the popular plays of Edward Albee and Harold Pinter in particular, effectively exposed some of the inanities of contemporary life, not by sneering at them from afar, but by enacting them, with all their humor and horror, onstage for public consumption. Pop and op art, in reaction to the excessive aestheticism of nonrepresentational painting, made greater use of everyday objects and new technology to create new visual effects and to infuse the visual arts with greater social significance.

The "new novel" of Michel Butor and Alain Robbe-Grillet carried realism to its extreme by depicting contemporary life as a world of men and objects utterly devoid of meaning or significance. The not-so-new novels of Saul Bellow and John Updike, Iris Murdoch and Doris Lessing, portrayed people trying desperately, but not very successfully, to wrest some meaning from the contemporary world. All along the line, the arts broadened their functions and reached into every area of life. And the whole spectrum of creative ferment in the sixties, philosophy and the social sciences as well as the arts, succeeded in subjecting most of the basic myths, taboos, and sacred cows of contemporary Western society to a more intense critical scrutiny than at any time since before the Second World War.

PROSPECTS

Where do we stand now in the face of an unknowable future? The postwar world, the West in particular, has experienced a pace and diversity of change so unprecedented that times within living memory already seem strangely remote and antiquated. So much of the past seems irrelevant today as to suggest that we have indeed entered upon a *post*historical phase of development: a phase in which our historical consciousness, so long a distinctive and vital component of the Western experience, seems to be receding into insignificance. If there is anything common to the diverse and often conflicting intellectual and cultural currents that have come to the fore since the war, it seems to be just this absence of historical-mindedness, whether due to indifference or to outright hostility to the past. All former generations depended to a greater or lesser extent on the past: for guidance in dealing with the present and anticipating the future; as a store of valued traditions, institutions, and ideas; for its wealth of experience useful to mental and moral maturation; even for temporary refuge from seemingly insoluble problems and solace for irreplaceable losses. Are we no longer in need of these dependencies? Have history's functions been usurped, replaced, or exhausted? Has the new world order, and modern technology in particular, succeeded at last in creating an environment so wholly different and self-contained as to have severed us from the past and imprisoned us in the present?

Or may we anticipate another renaissance? For renaissances are also a distinctive and persistent feature of the Western experience. Time and again, from antiquity to modern times, the West has undergone these rebirths—breakings of the cake of custom, sweeping dismantlings and reorganizations of social forces, fundamental upheavals in thought and action, reopenings of clogged channels to the past, spiritual pilgrimages to the origins of our collective existence—in brief, reactivations of the historical consciousness. Even now we see, here and there in everyday life—in the so-called "camp" culture, in the fads and fashions in dress and popular culture hearkening back to bygone days, in the taste among the discontented young for old-time political anarchism—a sort of spiritual groping among the remmants of the recent past for at least some echo of or intimacy with what has gone before. The new world order is awesome not only in its potential and promise, but also in the problems and dangers it poses. As we encounter the future, the chief questions may well be whether this new world order will permanently paralyze the vital forces that are deeply rooted in the Western past and of which the new world order is itself a product, and whether the West will petrify and become extinct as other remarkably advanced past civilizations have done. Or can these forces be rehabilitated to shape the new world order into the fulfillment of age-old dreams and hopes that would mark, not the end of the Western experience, but yet another phase in its continuing development?

BIBLIOGRAPHY

General Works

BARRACLOUGH, GEOFFREY. *An Introduction to Modern History.* Baltimore: Pelican, 1967.

BULLOCK, ALAN, ed. *The Twentieth Century.* London: Thames and Hudson, 1971.

CROUZET, MAURICE. *The European Renaissance since 1945.* Translated by S. Baron. London: Thames and Hudson, 1970.

LAQUEUR, WALTER. *Europe since Hitler.* Baltimore: Penguin Books, 1972.

WILLIS, FRANK R. *Europe in the Global Age: 1939 to the Present.* New York: Dodd, Mead, & Co., 1968.

The Cold War

FEIS, HERBERT. *From Trust to Terror: The Onset of the Cold War, 1945–50.* London: A. Blond, 1970.

FONTAINE, ANDRÉ. *History of the Cold War.* 2 vols. Translated by D. D. Paige. New York: Pantheon, 1968–69.

GADDIS, JOHN L. *The United States and the Origins of the Cold War, 1941–1947.* New York: Columbia University Press, 1972.

GRAEBNER, NORMAN A. *Cold War Diplomacy: American Foreign Policy, 1945–1960.* Princeton, N. J.: Von Nostrand, 1962.

HOROWITZ, DAVID. *The Free World Colossus: A Critique of American Foreign Policy in the Cold War.* Rev. ed. New York: Hill & Wang, 1971.

ULAM, ADAM B. *The Rivals: America and Russia since World War II.* New York: Viking Press, 1972.

WHEELER-BENNETT, JOHN W. and ANTHONY NICHOLLS. *The Semblance of Peace: The Political Settlement after the Second World War.* New York: St. Martin's Press, 1972.

European Recovery

KINDLEBERGER, CHARLES P. *Europe's Postwar Growth.* Cambridge, Mass.: Harvard University Press, 1967.

KNAPP, WILFRID F. *Unity And Nationalism in Europe since 1945.* New York: Pergamon Press, 1969.

MORGAN, ROGER. *Western European Politics since 1945.* London: Batsford, 1972.

POSTAN, MICHAEL M. *An Economic History of Western Europe, 1945–1964.* London: Methuen, 1966.

PRICE, HARRY B. *The Marshall Plan and its Meaning.* Ithaca, N.Y.: Cornell University Press, 1955.

WILLIS, FRANK R. *France, Germany, and the New Europe, 1945–1967.* Rev. ed. Stanford, Calif.: Stanford University Press, 1968.

Coexistence and Prosperity

ARDAGH, JOHN. *The New French Revolution: A Social and Economic Survey of France, 1945–1967.* New York: Harper & Row, 1969.

ARCHER, MARGARET S., ed. *Contemporary Europe: Class, Status and Power.* New York: St. Martin's Press, 1971.

BELL, DANIEL. *The End of Ideology.* Glencoe, Ill.: Free Press, 1960.

BOGDANOR, VERNON and SKIDELSKY, ROBERT, eds. *The Age of Affluence, 1951–1964.* London: Macmillan and Co., 1970.

BROWN, JAMES F. *The New Eastern Europe: The Khrushchev Era and After.* New York: Praeger, 1967.

DAHRENDORF, RALF. *Society and Democracy in Germany.* Garden City, N. Y.: Doubleday & Co., 1969.

FEJTÖ, FRANÇOIS. *A History of the Peoples' Democracies: Eastern Europe since Stalin.* Translated by D. Weissbort. New York: Praeger, 1971.

GALBRAITH, JOHN K. *The Affluent Society.* Baltimore: Penguin Books, 1962.

GAMARNIKOW, MICHAEL. *Economic Reforms in Eastern Europe.* Detroit: Wayne State University Press, 1968.

GREGG, PAULINE. *The Welfare State: An Economic and Social History of Great Britain from 1945 to the Present Day.* Amherst: University of Massachusetts Press, 1969.

HUGHES, HENRY S. *The United States and Italy.* Rev. ed. New York: W. W. Norton & Co., 1965.

IONESCU, GHITA. *The Politics of the European Communist States.* New York: Praeger, 1967.

KITZINGER, UWE W. *The European Common Market and Community.* New York: Barnes & Noble, 1967.

LEONHARD, WOLFGANG. *The Kremlin since Stalin.* Translated by E. Wiskemann and M. Jackson. New York: Praeger, 1962.

MILLS, C. WRIGHT. *The Power Elite.* New York: Oxford University Press, 1956.

NOVE, ALEC. *An Economic History of the U.S.S.R.* Harmondsworth: Penguin Books, 1972.

PACKARD, VANCE. *The Hidden Persuaders.* Baltimore: Penguin Books, 1962.

SAMPSON, ANTHONY. *Anatomy of Europe.* New York: Harper & Row, 1968.

SHONFIELD, ANDREW. *Modern Capitalism: The Changing Balance of Public and Private Power.* Corrected ed. New York: Oxford University Press, 1969.

WILLIAMS, PHILIP M. *French Politicians and Elections, 1951–1969.* London: Cambridge University Press, 1970.

Revolt Against Colonialism

ALBERTINI, RUDOLF VON, *Decolonization: The Administration and Future of the Colonies, 1919–1960.* Translated by F. Garvie. Garden City, N.Y.: Doubleday & Co., 1971.

EMERSON, RUPERT. *From Empire to Nation: The Rise to Self-Assertion of Asian and African Peoples.* Cambridge, Mass.: Harvard University Press, 1960.

FANON, FRANTZ. *The Wretched of the Earth.* Translated by C. Farrington. New York: Grove Press, 1966.

HAMMER, ELLEN. *The Struggle for Indochina.* Stanford, Calif.: Stanford University Press, 1954.

ROTBERG, ROBERT I. *A Political History of Tropical Africa.* New York: Harcourt, Brace & World, 1965.

STRACHEY, JOHN. *The End of Empire.* New York: Random House, 1960.

Erosion of the Postwar Equilibrium

BARAN, PAUL A. and SWEEZY, PAUL M. *Monopoly Capitalism.* Baltimore: Penguin Books, 1968.

BOULDING, KENNETH E. *The Organizational Revolution: A Study in the Ethics of Economic Organization.* 2d ed. Chicago: Quadrangle Books, 1968.

BREZEZINSKI, ZBIGNIEW K. *The Soviet Bloc: Unity and Conflict.* Rev. ed. Cambridge, Mass.: Harvard University Press, 1967.

CLUBB, OLIVER E. *China and Russia: The Great Game.* New York: Columbia University Press, 1971.

GRAUBARD, STEPHEN, ed. *A New Europe?* Boston: Houghton Mifflin Co., 1964.

HOFFMANN, STANLEY. *Decline or Renewal? France since the 1930's.* New York: Viking Press, 1974.

LINDBERG, LEON N. and STUART A. SCHEINGOLD. *Europe's Would-Be Polity.* Englewood Cliffs, N.J.: Prentice-Hall, 1970.

TATU, MICHEL. *Power in the Kremlin: From Khrushchev to Kosygin.* Translated by H. Katel. New York: Viking Press, 1969.

Social Discontents of the Consumer Society

ARON, RAYMOND. *Progress and Disillusion: The Dialectics of Modern Society.* London: Pall Mall, 1968.

——. *The Elusive Revolution: Anatomy of a Student Revolt.* Translated by G. Clough. New York: Praeger, 1969.

AYA, RODERICK and MILLER, NORMAN, eds. *The New American Revolution.* New York: Free Press, 1971.

GILLIS, JOHN R. *Youth and History: Tradition and Changes in European Age Relations, 1770 to the Present.* New York: Academic Press, 1974.

GOODE, STEVEN. *Affluent Revolutionaries: A Portrait of the New Left.* New York: Watts, 1974.

GORZ, ANDRÉ. *Strategy for Labor: A Radical Proposal.* Translated by M. A. Nicolaus and V. Ortiz. Boston: Beacon Press, 1967.

LEFEBVRE, HENRI. *Everyday Life in the Modern World.* Translated by S. Rabinovitch. New York: Harper & Row, 1971.

———. *The Explosion: Marxism and the French Upheaval.* Translated by A. Ehrenfeld. New York: Modern Reader, 1969.

ROTHBERG, ABRAHAM. *The Heirs of Stalin: Dissidence and the Soviet Regime, 1953–1970.* Ithaca, N.Y.: Cornell University Press, 1972.

ROWBOTHAM, SHEILA. *Hidden from History: Rediscovering Women in History from the 17th Century to the Present.* New York: Pantheon Books, 1975.

Intellectual and Cultural Trends

BARZUN, JACQUES. *The House of Intellect.* New York: Harper, 1959.

FRYE, NORTHROP. *The Modern Century.* Toronto: Oxford University Press, 1967.

ORTEGA Y GASSET, JOSÉ. *The Modern Theme.* Translated by J. F. Mora. New York: Harper, 1961.

PLUMB, JOHN H., ed. *Crisis in the Humanities.* Baltimore: Penguin Books, 1964.

STROMBERG, ROLAND N. *After Everything: Western Intellectual History since 1945.* New York: St. Martin's Press, 1975.

Literature and the Arts

ALLSOP, KENNETH. *The Angry Decade: A Survey of the Cultural Revolt of the Fifties.* London: Owen, 1958.

BENTLEY, ERIC R. *The Theater of Commitment and Other Essays on Drama in our Society.* New York: Atheneum, 1967.

BERGONZI, BERNARD. *The Situation of the Novel.* London: Macmillan & Co., 1970.

BRUSTEIN, ROBERT. *The Theatre of Revolt.* Boston: Little, Brown & Co., 1964.

COHEN, JOHN M., ed. *Poetry of this Age.* London: Arrow, 1959.

DEMETZ, PETER. *Postwar German Literature.* New York: Pegasus, 1970.

EHRMANN, JACQUES, ed. *Literature and Revolt.* Boston: Beacon Press, 1970.

ELLMAN, RICHARD and FEIDELSON, CHARLES, eds. *The Modern Tradition: Backgrounds of Modern Literature.* New York: Oxford University Press, 1965.

HASSAN, IHAB. *Radical Innocence: Studies in the Contemporary American Novel.* Princeton, N.J.: Princeton University Press, 1961.

———. *The Dismemberment of Orpheus: Toward a Post-Modern Literature.* New York: Oxford University Press, 1971.

JAMESON, FREDRIC. *Marxism and Form.* Princeton, N.J.: Princeton University Press, 1971.

KAHLER, ERICH. *The Tower and the Abyss.* New York: Viking Press, 1957.

LUCIE-SMITH, EDWARD. *Movements in Art since 1945.* London: Thames and Hudson, 1969.

MALRAUX, ANDRÉ. *Museum without Walls.* Translated by S. Gilbert and F. Price. Garden City, N.Y.: Doubleday & Co., 1967.

MELLERS, WILFRID H. *Caliban Reborn: Renewal in Twentieth-Century Music.* New York: Harper & Row, 1967.

NADEAU, MAURICE. *The French Novel since the War.* Translated by A. M. Sheridan-Smith. London: Methuen, 1967.

READ, HERBERT. *Art and Alienation: The Role of the Artist in Society.* New York: Viking Press, 1969.

WILSON, COLIN. *The Outsider.* London: Gollancz, 1956.

WIND, EDGAR. *Art and Anarchy.* New York: Alfred A. Knopf, 1964.

Philosophy

BRÉE, GERMAINE. *Camus and Sartre: Crisis and Commitment.* New York: Delacorte Press, 1972.

BOCHENSKI, I. M. *Contemporary European Philosophy.* Translated by D. Nicholl and K. Aschenbrenner. Berkeley and Los Angeles: University of California Press, 1956.

CAPONIGRI, ALOYSIUS R. *A History of Western Philosophy.* Vol. 5. Notre Dame, Ind.: University of Notre Dame Press, 1971.

EHRMANN, JACQUES, ed. *Structuralism.* Garden City, N. Y.: Doubleday & Co., 1970.

HARNACK, JUSTUS. *Wittgenstein and Modern Philosophy.* Translated by M. Cranston. New York: New York University Press, 1965.

JAY, MARTIN. *The Dialectical Imagination.* Boston: Little, Brown & Co., 1973.

KLINE, GEORGE L., ed. *European Philosophy Today.* Chicago: Quadrangle Books, 1965.

KOCH, ADRIENNE, ed. *Philosophy for a Time of Crisis.* New York: E. P. Dutton & Co., 1959.

LEE, EDWARD N. and MANDELBAUM, MAURICE, eds. *Phenomenology and Existentialism.* Baltimore: Johns Hopkins Press, 1967.

MUNDLE, C. W. K. *A Critique of Linguistic Philosophy.* Oxford: Clarendon Press, 1970.

SCIACCA, MICHELE F. *Philosophical Trends in the Contemporary World.* Translated by A. Salerno. Notre Dame, Ind.: University of Notre Dame Press, 1964.

SMITH, COLIN. *Contemporary French Philosophy.* New York: Barnes & Noble, 1964.

WARNOCK, MARY. *Existentialism.* New York: Oxford University Press, 1970.

Religion and Theology

BRAATEN, CARL E. *History and Hermeneutics.* Philadelphia: Westminster Press, 1966.

FACKENHEIM, EMIL L. *Quest for Past and Future: Essays in Jewish Theology.* Boston: Beacon Press, 1968.

FALCONI, CARLO. *Pope John and his Council.* Translated by M. Grindrod. London: Weidenfeld & Nicholson, 1964.

GARAUDY, ROGER and LAUER, QUENTIN. *A Christian-Communist Dialogue.* Garden City, N.Y.: Doubleday & Co., 1968.

MACQUARRIE, JOHN. *Contemporary Religious Thinkers.* New York: Harper & Row, 1968.

MASCALL, ERIC L. *Christian Theology and Natural Science: Some Questions in their Relations.* Hamden, Conn.: Archon Books, 1965.

REINISCH, LEONHARD, ed. *Theologians of our Time.* Notre Dame, Ind: University of Notre Dame Press, 1964.

Science and Technology

COMMONER, BARRY. *Science and Survival.* New York: Viking Press, 1966.

DIZARD, WILSON P. *Television: A World Review.* Syracuse, N. Y.: Syracuse University Press, 1966.

ELLUL, JACQUES. *The Technological Society.* Translated by J. Wilkinson. New York: Alfred A. Knopf, 1967.

FULLER, WATSON, ed. *The Social Impact of Modern Biology.* London: Routledge & Kegan Paul, 1971.

GRODZINS, MORTON and RABINOWITCH, EUGENE, eds. *The Atomic Age.* New York: Simon & Schuster, 1965.

HANSON, NORWOOD. *Observation and Explanation: A Guide to Philosophy of Science.* New York: Harper & Row, 1971.

HUXLEY, JULIAN. *The Human Crisis.* Seattle: University of Washington Press, 1963.

KAHN, HERMAN and WIENER, ANTHONY. *The Year 2000.* New York: Macmillan Co., 1967.

KUHN, THOMAS H. *The Structure of Scientific Revolutions.* Chicago: University of Chicago Press, 1962.

KUHNS, WILLIAM. *The Post-Industrial Prophets: Interpretations of Technology.* New York: Harper & Row, 1971.

McLUHAN, MARSHAL. *Understanding Media.* New York: McGraw-Hill, 1964.

MULLER, HERBERT J. *The Children of Frankenstein: A Primer on Modern Technology and Human Values.* Bloomington, Ind.: Indiana University Press, 1970.

MUMFORD, LEWIS. *The Myth of the Machine.* New York: Harcourt, Brace & World, 1967-1970.

ORWELL, GEORGE. *1984.* London: Secker & Warburg, 1949.

POPPER, KARL. *The Logic of Scientific Discovery.* New York: Basic Books, 1959.

SKINNER, BURRHUS F. *Walden II.* New York: Macmillan Co., 1948.

SNOW, CHARLES P. *The Two Cultures and the Scientific Revolution.* Cambridge: University Press, 1959.

The Social Sciences and Psychology

ARON, RAYMOND. *Main Currents of Sociological Thought.* 2 vols. Translated by R. Howard and H. Weaver. Garden City, N.Y.: Doubleday & Co., 1969.

BOULDING, KENNETH E. *Beyond Economics: Essays on Society, Religion, and Ethics.* Ann Arbor: University of Michigan Press, 1968.

COHEN, PERCY S. *Modern Social Theory.* New York: Basic Books, 1968.

COLLINGWOOD, ROBIN G. *The Idea of History.* London: Oxford University Press, 1946.

DAHRENDORF, RALF. *Essays in the Theory of Society.* Stanford, Calif.: Stanford University Press, 1968.

FOUCAULT, MICHEL. *Mental Illness and Psychology.* Translated by A. Sheridan. New York: Harper & Row, 1976.

GERMINO, DANTE L. *Beyond Ideology: The Revival of Political Theory.* New York: Harper & Row, 1967.

LAING, RONALD D. *The Politics of Experience.* New York: Ballantine Books, 1968.

LAQUEUR, WALTER and MOSSE, GEORGE, eds. *The New History.* New York: Harper & Row, 1967.

LASSWELL, HAROLD D. *The Future of Political Science.* New York: Atherton Press, 1963.

MARSHALL, THOMAS H. *Sociology at the Crossroads.* London: Heinemann, 1963.

MATSON, FLOYD W. *The Broken Image: Man, Science, and Society.* New York: Braziller, 1964.

NAPOLEONI, CLAUDIO. *Economic Thought of the 20th Century.* London: M. Robertson and Co., 1972.

STORR, ANTHONY. *Human Aggression.* London: Allen Lane, 1968.

TRILLING, LIONEL. *Freud and the Crisis of our Culture.* Boston: Beacon Press, 1955.

WILSON, COLIN. *New Pathways in Psychology: Maslow and the Post-Freudian Revolution.* London: Gallancz, 1972.

WOLMAN, BENJAMIN B. *Contemporary Theories and Systems in Psychology.* New York: Harper & Row, 1960.

Political and Social Thought

AMERY, JEAN. *Preface to the Future: Culture in a Consumer Society.* Translated by P. Hilty. London: Constable, 1964.

ARENDT, HANNAH. *Between Past and Future: Six Exercises in Political Thought.* New York: Viking Press, 1961.

———. *On Violence.* New York: Harcourt, Brace & World, 1969.

ARON, RAYMOND. *Marxism and the Existentialists.* New York: Harper & Row, 1969.

CAUTE, DAVID. *Communism and the French Intellectuals, 1914–1960.* New York: Macmillan Co., 1964.

COOPER, DAVID, ed. *The Dialectics of Liberation.* Harmondsworth: Penguin Books, 1968.

DAHRENDORF, ROLF. *Class and Class Conflict in Industrial Society.* Stanford, Calif.: Stanford University Press, 1959.

DE GEORGE, RICHARD T. *The New Marxism: Soviet and East European Marxism since 1956.* New York: Pegasus, 1968.

HAMPDEN-TURNER, CHARLES. *Radical Man.* Garden City, N.Y.: Doubleday & Co., 1971.

KING, RICHARD. *The Party of Eros: Radical Social Thought and the Realm of Freedom.* Chapel Hill: University of North Carolina Press, 1972.

MARCUSE, HERBERT. *An Essay on Liberation.* Boston: Beacon Press, 1969.

MARTIN, DAVID, ed. *Anarchy and Culture: The Problem of the Contemporary University.* New York: Columbia University Press, 1969.

MERLEAU-PONTY, MAURICE. *Humanism and Terror.* Translated by J. O'Neill. Boston: Beacon Press, 1969.

PIERCE, ROY. *Contemporary French Political Thought.* New York: Oxford University Press, 1966.

SHKLAR, JUDITH N. *After Utopia: The Decline of Political Faith.* Princeton, N.J.: Princeton University Press, 1957.

SPENDER, STEVEN. *The Year of the Young Rebels.* New York: Random House, 1969.

STANKIEWICZ, W. J., ed. *Political Thought since World War II.* New York: Free Press, 1964.

INDEX

Sexual mores, 138, 144, 153–54, 195–97, 203–5, 217, 288
Shahn, Ben, 228, 295
Shaw, George Bernard, 105, 136, 148, 154
Sheeler, Charles, 228
Shelley, Percy Bysshe, 24–25
Shostakovitch, Dimitri, 226
Siberia, 182, 224–25, 280
Sicily, 238–40
Silesia, 22
Sinyavsky, Andrei, 280
Siqueiros, David Alfaro, 229
Skinner, B. F., 306
Slavic peoples, 51–53, 56–57, 86, 92, 134
Smiles, Samuel, 97
Smith, Adam, 20
Snow, Charles, 307
Social contract, theory of, 45
Social Darwinism, 104, 123, 129
Social Democratic parties, 132, 184, 210–13, 216, 251, 262, 281
Social revolution, 36, 95, 222, 284
Social sciences, 157–63, 205, 303–5, 308–11, 313
Socialism, 22, 35, 40, 45–53, 82, 87, 111, 115–16, 227–29, 257
    fear of, 38, 179
    Marx and, 93–96
    spread of, 111, 133
    State, 76
    Utopian, 65–66, 145
Socialist parties, 71–73, 132–33, 137–39, 183–84, 210–14, 218–21, 256, 261–63, 282–83, 289
Socialist realism, 226, 294
Solzhenitsyn, Alexandr, 225, 280
Sorel, Georges, 148, 151, 155–57, 212
South Africa, 113–14, 122, 222, 276–77
South America, 7, 51, 83, 116, 124–25, 128, 194, 273
Southey, Robert, 24
Soviet bloc, 251–58, 266–67, 270–75, 278–83, 304
Soviet Union, 185, 188–89, 207, 272, 275, 278–81, 289, 292–95, 307
    Cold War and, 250–55, 261, 265–67
    Popular Front and, 219, 221–23, 236–42
    Stalin era in, 209–10, 223–26, 231–33
Spaak, Paul-Henri, 264–65
Spain, 12–16, 50–51, 133, 232
    Franco and, 212, 264, 270, 285, 291–92
    revolution in, 36–37, 221–22
Spanish-American War, 114, 122
Spanish Civil War, 210, 218–23, 227–28, 231
Speke, John Hanning, 114
Spencer, Herbert, 107, 129, 155

Spender, Stephen, 228
Spengler, Oswald, 151, 165, 195, 205
Spinoza, Benedictus, 39
Stadler, Ernst, 198
Staël, Germaine de, 25, 30
Stalin, Joseph, 184, 192, 223, 261
    Five Year Plan of, 209
    foreign policy of, 222, 230–33, 250–52
    purges of, 224–26, 255, 292
    Second World War and, 236, 240–42
Stalinism, 266–68, 280–81, 294
Stein, Gertrude, 197
Stein, Karl von, 30
Steinbeck, John, 228
Stendhal (Marie-Henri Beyle), 27
Stephenson, George, 18
Stirner, Max, 30
Stolypin, Peter, 180
Strauss, Richard, 141
Stravinsky, Igor, 195, 198, 294
Streseman, Gustav, 190–92
Strindberg, August, 109, 144
Stroheim, Erich von, 229
Structuralism, 307–12
Students, 284, 286, 291
Sudentenland, 231, 257
Suez Canal, 76, 113–14, 276
Suffragette movement, 136, 289
Sukarno, 275
Surrealism, 195, 197, 227
Sweden, 233, 265, 280, 286, 289, 294
Switzerland, 2, 9, 58, 170, 181, 210, 265, 270, 294
Symbolism, 142, 145–46, 148
Syndicalism, 49, 133, 151, 196, 212–13

Taine, Hippolyte, 107
Talleyrand, Charles-Maurice, 36
Tate, Allen, 229
Taylor, Frederick Winslow, 127
"Technocratic social order," 107, 304, 313
Technology
    advances in, 126–28, 271, 287–89
    industry and, 67–69, 72–74, 258–59, 280
    transportation, and, 66–68, 192–94
    war and, 175, 179, 201, 235, 269
Tennyson, Alfred Lord, 97
Thackeray, William Makepeace, 99–100, 198
Thiers, Adolphe, 77
Third World, 285, 288
Thoreau, Henry David, 74
Tillich, Paul, 303
Tito, Josip Broz, 251, 256
Tocqueville, Alexis de, 42, 66, 72, 89–91, 111